W9-ALM-761

CUSTOMIZE THE RUGER 10/22

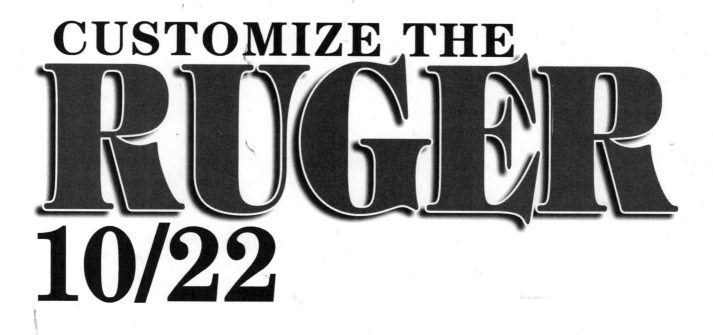

Comprehensive Do-It-Yourself Guide to Upgrading America's Favorite .22

**James E. House &
Kathleen A. House**

©2006 by
Gun Digest Books

Published by

Gun Digest Books
An imprint of F+W Publications
700 East State Street • Iola, WI 54990-0001
715-445-2214 • 888-457-2873
www.gunlistonline.com

Our toll-free number to place an order or obtain a free catalog is 800-258-0929.

All rights reserved.
No portion of this publication may be reproduced or transmitted in any form
or by any means, electronic or mechanical, including photocopy, recording, or any information
storage and retrieval system, without permission in writing from the publisher, except by a reviewer
who may quote brief passages in a critical article or review to be printed in a magazine or newspaper,
or electronically transmitted on radio, television, or the Internet.

CAUTION: Technical data presented here, particularly technical data on firearms
adjustment and alteration, inevitably reflects individual experience with particular equipment
and components under specific circumstances the reader cannot duplicate exactly. The addition
of aftermarket parts may void the warranty of your firearm. Such data presentations therefore
should be used for guidance only and with caution. Krause Publications, Inc., the authors and
distributors of this book accept no responsibility for results obtained using this data.

Ruger 10/22 is a registered trademark of Sturm, Ruger & Co., Inc. Southport, Conn. USA

Library of Congress Catalog Number: 2005935191
ISBN 13: 978-0-89689-323-8
ISBN 10: 0-89689-323-5

Designed by Patsy Howell
Edited by Kevin Michalowski

Printed in the United States of America

PREFACE

Stark County District Library
Main Library
715 Market Ave. N
Canton, OH 44702
330-452-0665   JUL   2007
www.starklibrary.org

A few firearms have special significance and broad recognition in the shooting sports. Several models would probably appear on almost everyone's list, and the Ruger 10/22 would be one of them. With production being almost 5 million since it was introduced in 1964, the sheer number of rifles would be enough to justify its inclusion. But a casual look at catalogs from suppliers of products for the shooting sports will show that the Ruger 10/22 provides employment and pays bills for a lot of people who do not work for Sturm, Ruger & Co., Inc.

With such a wealth of accessories produced for the Ruger 10/22, the shooter who wants to customize his or her rifle needs to obtain an overview of the types of products available. This book is intended to provide the owner or prospective owner of a Ruger 10/22 such a guide. Although we have endeavored to produce a book that deals with as much of the aftermarket industry as possible, there are undoubtedly some omissions for which we apologize.

In this book, we discuss the performance of factory Ruger 10/22s, ammunition choices, sights, and ballistics at an elementary level. Chapters are included on these topics as well as barrels, stocks, and components of the trigger group. Detailed instructions are presented on how to install many aftermarket parts.

This book is intended to be a comprehensive guide for the person who has never worked on a Ruger 10/22 rather than a shop manual for the expert. A serious hobbyist who has already spent a lot of time customizing Ruger 10/22s will almost certainly have progressed beyond the level of this book but may still find the chapters on performance of factory rifles, ammunition, and other topics useful. However, it is the amateur and learner that will benefit most from this book.

A book that deals with such an enormous range of products can not be written without the help and support of many individuals and businesses. It is a pleasure to acknowledge the help provided by the following companies.

Advanced Technology	Hornet Products	Richards Microfit Gunstocks
Battenfeld Technologies	Jard, Inc.	Revival Industries
Bell & Carlson	Jarvis, Inc.	Scheels All Sports
Boyds' Gunstock Industries	Kidd Innovative Design	Shilen, Inc.
Brownells	Leopold & Stevens, Inc.	Sightron, Inc.
Buffer Technologies	Lilja Precision Rifle Barrels, Inc.	Sturm, Ruger & Co.
Butler Creek	Magnum Research, Inc.	Tactical Solutions
Cabela's	Majestic Arms, Ltd.	Volquartsen Custom
Choate Machine & Tool, Inc.	McMillan Fiberglass Stocks, Inc.	Whistle Pig Gun Barrel Co.
E. R. Shaw, Inc.	Nostalgia Enterprises Co.	Williams Gunsight Co., Inc.
Graf & Sons, Inc.	(NECO)	XS Sight Systems
Green Mountain Rifle Barrels	Power Custom	
Hogue, Inc.	Ranch Products	

The authors would also acknowledge the help and guidance provided by Kevin Michalowski and Steve Smith of Krause Publications. They have helped to make this an enjoyable project.

CONTENTS

ABOUT THE AUTHORS

James E. House and Kathleen A. House are avid shooters who also enjoy travel and photography. Jim was a faculty member at Illinois State University for 32 years and is an emeritus professor of chemistry. In retirement Jim has become an active writer. He has authored *American Air Rifles* (Krause Publications, 2001), *CO₂ Pistols & Rifles* (Krause Publications, 2003), and *The Gun Digest Book of .22 Rimfire* (Gun Digest Books, 2005) in addition to books on chemical kinetics, quantum mechanics, and descriptive inorganic chemistry, a book he coauthored with Kathy. He holds B.S and M.A. degrees from Southern Illinois University and a Ph.D. from the University of Illinois.

In addition to doing a prodigious amount of shooting and photography while helping Jim with previous books, Kathy is an adjunct faculty member at Illinois Wesleyan University. She holds B.S. and M.S. degrees from Illinois State University and a Ph.D. from the University of Illinois.

Jim and Kathy are life members of the National Rifle Association and have coauthored articles for *Gun World* and *The Varmint Hunter*. Jim has also written many articles that have appeared in publications such as *The Backwoodsman, Small Caliber News, Predator Xtreme, The Illinois Shooter*, and *Gun List*.

ABOUT THE COVERS

BROWNELLS, A LONG TRADITION IN THE INDUSTRY

Bob Brownell was a "gun crank" in the 1920s and 1930s and did informal customizing and repair work for himself and friends while running a Shell gas station and Maid Rite restaurant. By 1938, he hung out his shingle as a part-time gunsmith and gun work began taking more of his time. Bob's search for tools in the 30s and 40s led him to realize that others might be having as hard a time as he was finding the right supplies to do their gunsmithing work. When he found those tools, chemicals and supplies, he began buying more than he needed and selling the rest to other gunsmiths. Today, the company carries more than 32,500 products for the gunsmith and hobbyist.

Bob was never afraid to share his knowledge with anyone that wanted to get into the trade. That helpful nature lives on today where virtually every one of thousands of Brownells products includes instructions for use. To further the spirit of customer service Bob started, the company now employs eight technicians to answer customer questions.

Early on Bob realized it might be tough to get people to send him money. He established a money-back guarantee that continues today; customers don't need special authorizations and there aren't any restocking fees, a customer simply sends the product back and receives a refund.

By 1951, Bob closed the gun shop and became a full-time supplier of tools and supplies to the industry. In 1959 he published *The Encyclopedia of Modern Firearms* a compilation of factory schematics, military instructions, parts lists, assembly/disassembly instructions and more, essentially a giant repair manual covering most of the U.S. firearms available at the time. Today, the Brownells web site, www.brownells.com, has hundreds of schematics of factory guns, with drawing numbers linked to ordering numbers to help folks get their guns repaired.

In 1964, Bob's son Frank, a University of Iowa graduate and a Lieutenant fresh out of the Navy, joined the company. Frank had grown up in the business, running the printing press, helping assemble catalogs, picking orders, packing them, packaging products, pushing a broom, and whatever else Bob assigned to him. One of his first projects was to put the information from Bob's famous newsletters into the first of a series of Gunsmith Kinks books. The "Kinks" were how-to tips customers had sent to Bob. They were published to help spread gunsmithing knowledge as far as possible. In the mid 1980s Frank became President and Bob became CEO. Frank led the company through the transition from Bob's administration to his own and grew the company tremendously in the process. Bob died in July of 1991. Frank's middle son, Pete, joined the company in 1998. Pete is also a University of Iowa grad. His first project was to insist on, then oversee the development of, the Brownells Web Site. In 2000, Pete was made Vice President.

While the company has grown, the principles Bob started with still guide his company today. They are: Selection. Service. Satisfaction.

CUSTOMIZE THE RUGER 10/22

Comprehensive Do-It-Yourself Guide to Upgrading America's Favorite .22

NO GUNSMITH REQUIRED

BROWNELLS

James E. House & Kathleen A. House

Chapter 1

HISTORY & CURRENT VERSIONS OF THE RUGER 10/22

Some products reflect an excellence of design that becomes synonymous with the company that produced them. Although Sturm, Ruger & Company is a relatively newcomer in the field of firearms manufacturing, it has established itself as a company that produces excellent firearms that are durable and represent good value. One of the products that has gone a long way toward establishing the reputation of Sturm, Ruger & Company is the .22 LR autoloader known as the Model 10/22©. Even though the 10/22 performs well, it is the fact that so much can be done to modify the 10/22 that has helped make it an American icon. It is truly a "tinker toy" rifle that can be configured to suit almost any taste or purpose. That this is so will be made clear in this book devoted to tinkering with the 10/22.

Sturm, Ruger & Company, Inc.

From a modest beginning about 60 years ago, Ruger has become the largest manufacturer of firearms in this country. The initial product, a .22 caliber semiautomatic pistol that sold for $37.50, was introduced

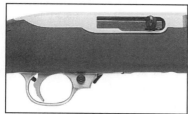

Left: The Ruger 10/22 Carbine has resulted in a huge aftermarket industry.

Right: One of the numerous variants of the Ruger 10/22 Carbine has a synthetic stock and a stainless steel barrel.

in 1949. Other manufacturers may produce handguns while others produce rifles and shotguns, but Ruger produces a comprehensive line of firearms that includes all of these types. Moreover, the handguns include numerous models of rimfire semiautomatics but also a wide variety of centerfire semiautos. The Ruger revolvers have from the beginning included both rimfire and centerfire single action models, and the current offerings of this type are numerous. Double action revolvers are also well represented by models that are suitable for sporting and law enforcement uses.

In recent years Ruger has also produced double barrel shotguns in both over and under and side-by-side models. Centerfire rifles are produced in a bewildering array of models that include the bolt action Model 77 Mark II, as well as the single shot No. 1, and several models of semiautomatics. There is even the lever action Model 96/44. Ruger also produces many rifles that are available in rimfire calibers. These include the bolt-action rifles in .22 LR, .22 WMR, .17 HMR, and .17 Mach 2 calibers and the lever action models in .22 WMR and .17 HMR calibers.

While these offerings include something for almost any shooter, it should be made clear that the first rimfire rifle offered by the Sturm, Ruger & Company was the .22 semiautomatic that has arguably become the most successful rimfire rifle of all time. That little rifle is known as the Model 10/22 Carbine, which was introduced in 1964. In the intervening 40 years, over 4 million 10/22s have been produced. Moreover, the 10/22 is produced in numerous versions that span the range from plinking rifles to target models to varmint rifles chambered for the 22 WMR caliber.

With a firearm as long-lived and successful as the Ruger 10/22, there are numerous dates that are significant with regard to the variants produced and when certain changes were made. The accompanying table summarizes some of the most important dates related to events in the life of the Ruger 10/22. In addition to the events listed, there are many others in which minor changes were made in sights, markings, etc., which are too numerous to list in detail in this book.

Year	Event
1964	Ruger 10/22 Carbine introduced
1966	Sporter version (noncheckered) introduced
1966	International version (noncheckered) introduced
1967	Canadian Expo version of the 10/22
1969	International version discontinued
1972	Deluxe Sporter introduced
1981	Hardwood stock replaced walnut
1986	Stainless steel/laminated stock version introduced
1994	International version reintroduced (checkered)
1996	Target model 10/22T introduced
1997	Stainless steel/composite all weather version
2000	Heavy barrel/thumbhole stock version
2004	Introduction of 10/22 Rifle version
2004	40th Anniversary edition of the 10/22
2005	Introduction of 10/22 Compact Rifle

Ruger 10/22 Versions

Although they are discussed in more detail later in this chapter, this section presents an overview of the several versions of the 10/22 that are available at the present time. The original Ruger 10/22, known as the Carbine, has distinctive styling. Being a true carbine and having a barrel that measures only 18.5 inches, it also sports a stock that has carbine styling. The butt plate is curved, and the forearm is circled with a barrel band. Loosely speaking, a 10/22 carbine bears some resemblance to the military M1 Carbine. However, in addition to the Carbine version of the 10/22, there are also variants known as the Rifle (introduced in 2004), which has a 20-inch barrel and the version with a heavy 20-inch barrel that is known as the 10/22 Target (introduced in 1996). In September 2005, Ruger announced the introduction of yet another version of the 10/22. This version, officially known as the 10/22 Compact Rifle, has a 16.5 inch barrel and a scaled down stock that gives a length of pull of only 12.5 inches. The 10/22 Compact Rifle has a stock that resembles that of the Rifle in that there is no barrel band and the butt plate is flat rather than curved like that on the Carbine.

Although current Ruger 10/22 products include the Carbine, Target, Rifle, and Compact Rifle models, there have been a very large number of small changes over the years. These include changes in sights, stocks, and other parts, but the basic design has remained the same. It is neither possible nor necessary to give a complete description of these variants although that information

Above Right: Ruger 10/22 fans will find the books by Workman and Wilson a source of a lot of information.

Left: The butt plate on the Ruger 10/22 has the unique carbine style.

At the forward end of the forearm, a barrel band circles the stock and barrel.

This version of the Ruger 10/22 is widely available through Wal-Mart stores. It has a 22-inch stainless steel barrel and a checkered hardwood stock.

The Current Ruger 10/22 Models[a]					
Designation	Model	Length, in.	Bbl. Length, in.	Weight, lb.	Stock
10/22RB	Carbine	37	18.5	5	Hardwood[b]
10/22DSP	Sporter	37	18.5	5.75	Walnut
10/22T	Target	38.5	20	7.5	Laminated
10/22RR	Rifle	38.5	20	5	Hardwood
10/22CRR	Compact	33.5	16.5	4.65	Hardwood
10/22RBM	Magnum	37.25	18.5	6.5	Hardwood

[a]The International model with full-length stock was discontinued in 2004.
[b]Some variants have been produced with composite and laminated stocks.

would certainly be of interest to the serious collector. The most complete catalog of Ruger 10/22 variants in the first 30 years of its production is the book by William E. Workman (1994), *The Ruger 10/22*, Krause Publications, Iola, WI 54990-0001. A wealth of information on the entire Ruger product line is also presented in R. L. Wilson's *Ruger and His Guns* (Simon & Schuster, 1996). These books are required reading for collectors and others who are serious about the Ruger 10/22.

There are also a number of variants that were prepared specifically for a particular distributor but were never Ruger catalog items. One of these has a 22-inch stainless steel barrel and checkered hardwood stock. Lipsey's, a large firearms distributor in Baton Rouge, Louisiana, marketed this variant through a large number of Wal-Mart stores, and on some internet chat rooms owners refer to it as the "Wal-Mart version" of the 10/22. As this is being written late in 2005, Lipsey's is marketing a version of the Ruger 10/22 that is finished completely in the camouflage pattern known as hardwoods. Over the years, there have been other short runs of 10/22s produced that had special characteristics. For example, the 40th Anniversary 10/22 that was produced in 2004 had a large medallion embedded in the right hand side of the buttstock to commemorate the event. A brother in law has a Ruger 10/22 with stainless steel barrel and laminated stock that was marketed with a 4X scope and sling with the Ruger logo. Apparently, this package was offered through a large chain of stores but never appeared as a catalog item.

The Carbine and Deluxe Sporter

The original Ruger 10/22, the Carbine, was offered with a walnut stock and 18.5 inch blue steel barrel. Over the many years of its production, it has been produced in many other forms that include some having stainless steel barrels and laminated, composite, or hardwood stocks. One of the most attractive versions is known as the 10/22 International, which has a full-length Mannlicher style stock. A personal

An adjustable folding rear sight is used on most versions of the Ruger 10/22 Carbine.

Left: One of the hallmarks of the Ruger 10/22 has always been the reliable 10-shot rotary magazine it uses. Shown here is recently introduced magazine made of clear plastic.

At one time, the Ruger 10/22 Carbine was available with a stainless steel barrel and a laminated stock.

With a scope of high magnification attached, the 10/22 Carbine is a versatile rimfire.

favorite of the authors is the version designated as the 10/22 DSP, which is known as the Deluxe Sporter version. It has the same length barrel as the Carbine, but it has a checkered walnut stock that has sling swivels installed. It is not surprising that over the 40 years since it was introduced, the 10/22 has undergone many changes most of which are minor.

Although the Ruger 10/22 broke with tradition in many areas, perhaps the most unique was the fact that it uses a 10-round rotary magazine that is completely enclosed in the action. This results in a clean profile with a magazine that does not protrude from the bottom of the action precisely where it is natural to hold the rifle while it is being carried in one hand. While this cartridge reservoir is novel, this is not sufficient to explain why the 10/22 is held in such high esteem. No, it is the fact that the Ruger rotary magazine enables it to rank among the most reliable .22 autoloaders that has endeared it to many shooters. The action of the 10/22 is

The rotary magazine does not protrude from the bottom of the action.

legendary for long life and reliability, and the 10/22 also has an excellent reputation for accuracy among rifles of this type. These attributes are responsible for many 10/22s being found in remote areas where the owners need a reliable rifle for pest control and small game hunting.

The Ruger 10/22 has always featured a receiver made of an aluminum alloy. While this is true of the 10/22 in .22 LR, those in .22 WMR and .17 HMR (if and when it becomes available) have steel receivers. If you fire both the .22 LR and the .22 WMR

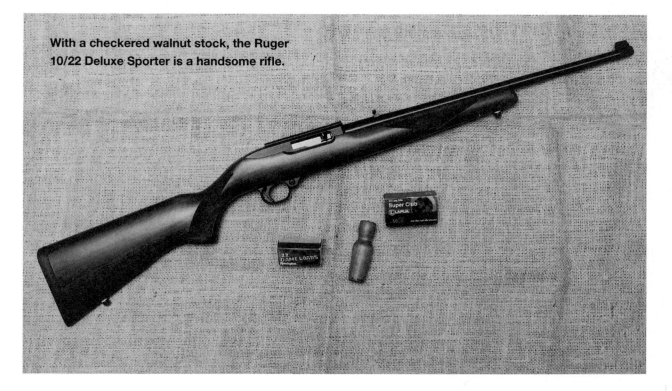

With a checkered walnut stock, the Ruger 10/22 Deluxe Sporter is a handsome rifle.

For many years, the Ruger scope base accommodated mounts that clamp in the grooves along the sides.

In the last few years, Ruger has supplied a scope base that not only has grooves along the edges but also transverse grooves that accept Weaver-type rings.

rifles, you will quickly see that they are in some respects different rifles. Because of this, they will be considered separately (the magnum will be discussed in Chapters 5 and 12).

Although the 10/22 comes with excellent open sights, the accuracy of any rifle is easier to demonstrate by adding a scope. However, because the receiver has a slightly rounded profile, it is not possible to have grooves milled in it to accommodate scope mounts. Instead, the top of the receiver has four dummy screws that fill the holes where the screws that attach a scope rail can be fastened. For many years, the standard scope rail had grooves

along the sides that resemble those milled into the receivers of most rimfire rifles. Beginning in 2004, all versions of the Ruger 10/22 were shipped with a scope rail that not only has grooves along the sides but also has transverse grooves that enable the enormously popular Weaver-type scope rings to be attached. The new scope rail thus increases the options that are available for the types of mounts that can be used to attach a scope to a 10/22. The steel receivers of the 10/22 in magnum calibers have raised sections that have milled into them the curved notches that are like those found on the centerfire Ruger rifles. Thus, mounting a scope on one of the 10/22 magnums is an entirely different situation.

The front sight on the Ruger 10/22 Carbine is a bead on a post that is held in a dovetail groove.

The Ruger 10/22 Magnum has scope bases that are part of the receiver to which Ruger rings can be clamped.

The 10/22 Rifle

Introduced in 2004, the Ruger 10/22 Rifle represents a sort of combination of the Deluxe Sporter and Carbine versions but with some unique features. First, the Rifle has a 20-inch barrel rather than the shorter 18.5-inch barrel used on the Carbine and Deluxe Sporter. Like the Carbine and Deluxe Sporter versions, the barrel of the Rifle is fitted with open sights. Second, the stock is slimmer than those used on either the Carbine or Sporter. One of the esthetic deficiencies of the 10/22 Carbine has always been that the stock is rather fat in cross section. The rotary magazine that is approximately twice as wide as a clip that holds stacked rimfire cartridges necessitates this. However, the stock of the Carbine is fairly thick throughout its entire length. On the Rifle version, the stock is slimmer and especially so in the areas of the grip and the forearm. With its longer barrel and slim stock, we developed a love at first sight relationship with the 10/22 Rifle. It would be some time before we owned one, but it was worth the wait. To date, the 10/22 Rifle is offered only with a hardwood stock and a blued steel barrel.

The Ruger 10/22 Rifle has a rounded end on the forearm without a barrel band.

The butt plate on the Ruger 10/22 Rifle is flat and checkered rather than curved and slick as on the Carbine.

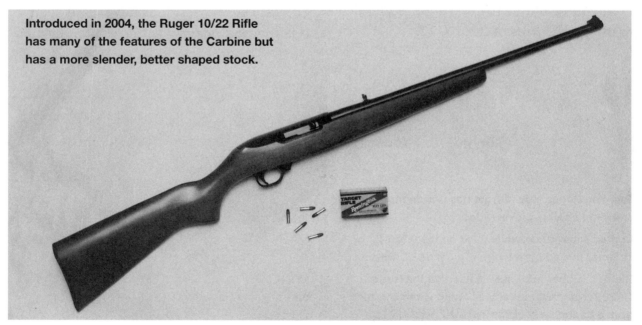

Introduced in 2004, the Ruger 10/22 Rifle has many of the features of the Carbine but has a more slender, better shaped stock.

The 10/22 Target

Rimfire shooting sports such as benchrest and silhouette competition demand a rifle that is much more accurate than the factory produced Ruger 10/22 Carbine. Although many shooters modify their carbines (the reason for this book), Ruger decided to offer a more capable rifle, and the 10/22 Target was the result. It features a 0.920-inch diameter hammer-forged barrel, a heavy target style stock, and an improved trigger. These attributes go a long way toward removing the necessity for adding aftermarket parts for many shooters.

While I never actually thought of the Ruger 10/22 Target as beautiful, it is impressive. With a 20-inch hammer forged barrel measuring almost an inch in diameter and an attractive brown laminated stock, the Target weighs 7.5 pounds. It comes with no sights attached because this rifle begs to have a scope attached and to be challenged. Target versions of the 10/22 are available with either blue or stainless steel barrels, and both come with target type crowns. Functioning of the 10/22 Target is identical to the other forms of the 10/22.

The Compact Rifle

The newest version of the Ruger 10/22 was announced in September 2005. Recognizing that in many situations a rifle of smaller dimensions is appropriate, Ruger produced a compact rifle by scaling down the Ruger 10/22. The resulting version, known as the 10/22 Compact Rifle, features a blued barrel measuring 16.5 inches and a shortened hardwood stock that gives a 12.5-inch length of pull. The stock has a regular flat butt plate, and gone is the barrel band. In many ways, the Compact resembles the Rifle version with a shorter stock and barrel.

Sights on the Compact consist of a front sight on a low ramp and a blade rear sight. Along the top of the front sight there is a fiber optic insert, and the rear sight has fiber optic inserts on either side of the notch. As with all current 10/22s, Ruger supplies a scope base with the Compact that can accommodate either tip-off or Weaver-type rings.

In 2004 Ruger produced the 10-shot magazines made of clear plastic for the 10/22. These magazines have a red rotor. It is the clear magazine that is standard on

Top: The Ruger 10/22 Target has a wide forearm, and sling swivels are provided.

Center: A target crown is used on the 0.920-inch hammer forged barrel of the Ruger 10/22 Target.

Right: A rubber butt plate is used on the Ruger 10/22 Target that prevents slipping when shooting from a bench.

Since it was introduced in 1996, the Ruger 10/22 Target has developed an excellent reputation as a highly accurate rimfire.

In late 2005, Ruger introduced the 10/22 Compact Rifle (right), which is a scaled down version of the 10/22 Rifle (left).

The 10/22 Compact Rifle utilizes a front sight that has a fiber optic insert along the top.

The rear sight on the 10/22 Compact Rifle has a fiber optic insert that gives a green dot on either side of the notch.

the Compact model. Altogether, the 10/22 Compact is a handy, sturdy autoloader that will travel well. It is convenient not only for shooters of small stature, but also anyone who wants a compact rimfire rifle, and that takes in a lot of territory.

Enhancing the 10/22

It is unlikely that there is any machine produced by a factory, even using modern manufacturing techniques, that could not be made better in some way. Manufacturers must make decisions based on availability of materials, cost-related issues, and marketability of the end product. A custom shop may not be forced to operate under all of these constraints, and the owner of a Ruger 10/22 certainly does not have to. Almost everything except the receiver housing is replaceable. Moreover, components are available that exceed the capabilities of the original factory components in many instances. The owner of a Ruger 10/22 can customize his or her rifle to almost any degree desired. As good as the Ruger 10/22 is in factory form, it can be made better. In the following chapters, we will describe many of the aftermarket products available

for the 10/22, and describe how you can turn your rifle into an elegant tack-driving machine.

The replacement of barrels and stocks on Ruger 10/22s is so common that several companies offer accessory kits that consist of a stock and barrel combination. Stocks range from elegant sporter type to tactical models with pistol grips, hand guards, and folding buttstocks. Laminated stocks are also available in various color combinations. One popular type of aftermarket stock is known as the thumbhole model, and several styles are produced. In general, stocks are produced with barrel channels that are cut to fit a factory barrel or to fit a heavy barrel having a diameter of 0.920 inch. Stock options for the builder of a custom Ruger 10/22 are discussed in Chapter 7.

When it comes to barrels for the Ruger 10/22, the term smorgasbord comes to mind. Some barrels have contours that match that of the factory Carbine barrel so they can be used with the factory stock. Probably the most popular style of aftermarket barrel is that which is not tapered but rather has a uniform diameter of 0.920 inch. Within this general type, the buyer can choose from those having a blue finish or those made of stainless steel. Another type of barrel has the same configuration as the factory barrel for most of its length but for the last four inches or so the diameter is increased to 0.920 inch. This allows the use of the factory stock or a stock that has a barrel channel of the same size. Finally, there are several barrels available that have an outside diameter of 0.920 inch, but which have an inner sleeve made of steel encased in a sleeve made of aluminum or a carbon fiber composite. These barrels are light in weight, but they can be used with a stock that is designed for use with a heavy barrel. General characteristics of barrels are presented in Chapter 8 while specific models and their performance are discussed in Chapter 11.

Because the array of items produced for the Ruger 10/22, not all of the aftermarket products available could be tested or even shown in this book. Those that are described are certainly representative of most of the accessories that are available, but it is not a complete list. Before you embark on customizing your 10/22, study the catalogs and web sites of the manufacturers listed in Chapter 13. You may find that there are many more options available than you ever imagined. It is a very large market indeed. After all, the Ruger 10/22 is that kind of machine, and it would be very difficult to out grow this little rifle. The remainder of this book is

With a concern for safety, Ruger supplies a lock with each of their rifles.

devoted to helping you make decisions on aftermarket items and getting the most out of your Ruger 10/22.

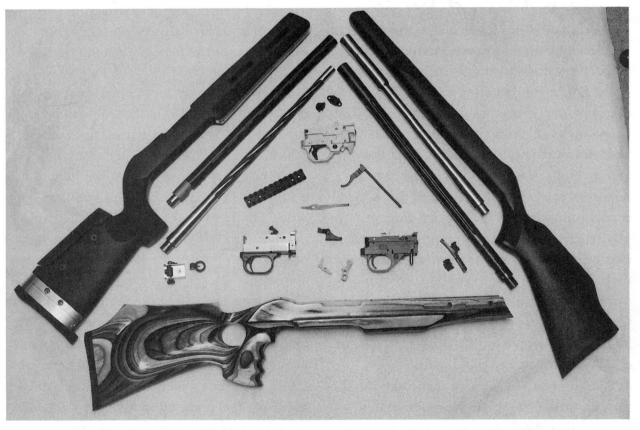

These are just a few of the aftermarket items that are available for the Ruger 10/22. This firearm is an industry in itself.

Chapter 2

DESIGN CHARACTERISTICS AND CONCERNS

Before setting out to create your ultimate 10/22, it is desirable to understand some of the basic aspects of firearm design. Some of these features and characteristics are related to the type of aftermarket items installed. For instance, replacing the factory firing pin by one made of titanium decreases the lock time. As a result replacing some parts may alter the design characteristics of the rifle, which may be desirable, or if not done properly, undesirable. Consequently, before discussing various aspects of customizing the 10/22, we will discuss some of the features of firearm design and function.

Please note that replacing almost any part on a Ruger 10/22 with an aftermarket part will invalidate the warranty! Please note also that returning a rifle that contains aftermarket parts to Ruger for service or repair will result in the aftermarket part being replaced by a factory part! The rifle will be restored to "original" condition whether you want it to be or not. For example, that special hammer and sear that you installed will be replaced by gritty, rough factory parts. Make sure that any rifle you return to the factory contains *only* factory parts, not your precious aftermarket goodies.

This .22 LR cartridge is resting on the face of a bolt from a Ruger 10/22. Note how the recess in the bolt face accommodates the cartridge rim.

Head Space

When a cartridge is placed in a chamber, there must be some clearance, not only along the chamber walls but also between the end of the barrel and the bolt. Rimfire rifles have a cut out area on the face of the bolt where the head of the cartridge rests.

When the bolt is fully closed, the cut out area has room for the cartridge head in addition to a small amount of clearance. On semiautomatic rifles, the bolt goes forward until it makes contact with the rear end of the barrel, and the head of

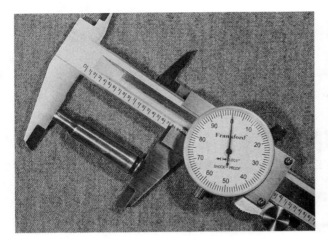

The dial on this caliper has been set to read zero when an empty .222 Remington case is placed between the jaws.

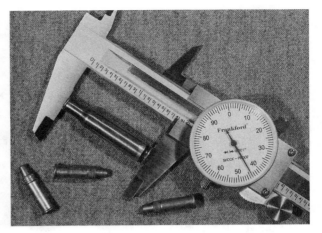

With a .22 LR cartridge inserted in the mouth of the .222 Remington case, the dial reads 0.044 inch, the thickness of the .22 LR rim.

the cartridge rests in the cut out area in the face of the bolt. In a rimfire rifle, the distance between the back of the recess in the bolt face and the rear end of the barrel is referred to as the headspace.

Cartridges in .22 LR caliber normally have rims that are about 0.037-0.042" in thickness. Since the bolt face in this rifle rests against the rear end of the barrel, the recess in the bolt face must allow for rims that are at least 0.042" with a couple of thousandths of clearance. In most .22 LR rimfire rifles, the headspace is about 0.043-0.045". If the headspace is too small, closing the bolt causes some deformation of the case head, which could cause the cartridge to fire if the bolt action is vigorous as it is in the case of an autoloading rifle. If the headspace

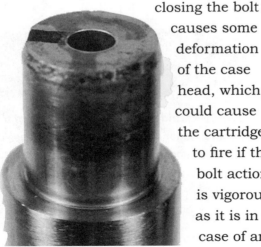

The barrel tenon or shank shows the effect of being struck by the bolt during firing.

is slightly too large, firing the cartridge can cause the case head to expand to fill up the empty space. In such cases, the head of the fired case can show noticeable rounding or ballooning. If the headspace measures about 0.003-0.004" too large, the firing pin can move the cartridge forward in the chamber, which will result in a dent that is too shallow in the case rim. Misfires can result in such instances.

Most aftermarket barrels for the Ruger 10/22 are produced so that when they are placed correctly in the receiver the bolt simply butts against the rear of the barrel extension. When a barrel is removed from a Ruger 10/22 it is easy to see the slight discoloration or roughness where the bolt has struck the barrel. The depth of the recess in the bolt face controls headspace so there is little likelihood that it will be incorrect. This is not the case when the barrel is changed with a bolt-action rifle such as the Ruger 77/22. In the case of a bolt-action rifle, the bolt locks in place against the receiver in a specific location regardless of where the end of the barrel is located. Therefore, it is essential that the headspace be controlled by how far the barrel extends back into the action. Rifle

This fine Green Mountain barrel has a shank that determines how far the barrel protrudes into the receiver.

barrels have a step where the barrel shank has been turned to smaller diameter, and this step fits against the face of the receiver. If the barrel shank protrudes too far into the action, the bolt may not close. This condition can be corrected by placing thin spacers around the barrel shank so that it will not extend too far back in the receiver.

If the barrel does not protrude far enough into the action, headspace will be too large and the cartridge may not fire because the rim is not crushed sufficiently. It is also possible that the case head could rupture on firing. This condition can be corrected, but it requires some machine work that is beyond the scope of the projects described in this book. Although headspace is generally not a problem with replacement barrels for the 10/22, if you have any question about the headspace in any rifle, have the rifle examined by a qualified gunsmith.

Chambers

The chamber is the rear part of the bore in which the cartridge is held. The cartridge could remain in the chamber indefinitely, but it is during the firing process that concerns us. In front of the chamber is the area known as the throat, which leads to the rifling at the rear of the barrel. It is tempting to regard the portion of the barrel where the cartridge is held as being less important than the rifled portion, but that is not always true. It is the chamber area that holds the cartridge in correct alignment with the bore.

Chambers of rimfire rifles tend to have rather wide variations in dimensions. In front of the chamber is a throat that in some cases has no rifling for a short distance, which allows the bullet to jump slightly to engage the rifling. A chamber that has minimal dimensions is known as a Match Chamber. Such a chamber normally has little if any free bore, and in this case the rifling extends back far enough that the bullet engages the rifling as the cartridge is chambered. Withdrawing a cartridge from the chamber will show the grooves engraved on the bullet by the rifling as the cartridge was seated in the chamber. Although a cartridge is usually driven forward with enough force to push it fully into the chamber, pulling the bolt back may not withdraw the cartridge. The reason is that the rifling is gripping the bullet sufficiently to cause the extractor to slide over the rim of the case. Several aftermarket barrels are inscribed with the

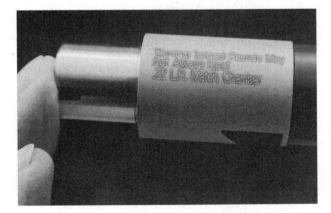

As on many barrels that have match chambers, this barrel carries the warning that the unfired cartridges may not eject because of the bullet being held by the rifling.

warning that unfired cartridges may not eject when the bolt is pulled back. This situation can occur with ammunition that has bullets having diameters slightly larger than normal.

With different objectives in mind, chambers for the .22 LR are produced having different dimensions. Rifles that are intended for ordinary sporting use (including the Ruger 10/22) have chambers that are cut to certain dimensions that define the Sporting Chamber. These dimensions are nominally 0.7751 inch in length, 0.2307 inch in mouth diameter, and 0.2270-inch in throat diameter. On the other hand, a Match Chamber for bolt-action rifles is 0.6876 inch in length, 0.2267 inch in mouth diameter, and 0.2248 inch in throat diameter. Note that the diameter in each region of a Match Chamber is smaller than in the case of the Sporting Chamber.

A third type of chamber is known as the Bentz chamber, which is the type of match chamber normally found in target autoloaders. The dimensions for the Bentz Chamber are 0.6900 inch in length, 0.2270 inch in diameter at the mouth, and 0.2255 inch in diameter at the throat. There is also a 1.5° taper at the throat. Note that the Bentz Chamber, while tighter than the Sporting Chamber, is slightly larger than a true Match Chamber. Such dimensions are consistent with the ideas already discussed about how .22 LR cartridges fit in the chamber.

Chambering a cartridge in a bolt-action rifle is somewhat different than in an autoloader because turning the bolt during closing results in a cam action that forces the cartridge into the chamber with enough force to engrave the bullet. In the case of autoloaders, the bolt is forced forward by the recoil spring, but this does not apply nearly as much force on the cartridge as is normally the case with a bolt action. Therefore, bolt-action rifles can have a true "match" chambers with tighter dimensions. Even within those match chambers that have no free bore, there are some differences. For example, some barrels have rifling that begins abruptly while others have rifling that is tapered to its full depth.

When the bullet starts out in contact with the rifling, accuracy in usually enhanced, which is why target rifles have match chambers and no free bore. However, there is another advantage to the match chamber. It has been shown that rimfire cartridges have a certain amount of runout which a way of expressing the fact that the axis of the bullet and the axis of the case are not in perfect alignment. In other words, there is a lack of concentricity between the case and the bullet (see Chapter 3). When a cartridge has some lack of concentricity, the tight chamber and the bullet engaging the

Figure 2.1 A Cartridge showing lack of concentricity.

rifling can help "straighten" the cartridge by bringing the bullet more nearly into alignment with the case. In other words, the degree of concentricity of the cartridge is improved. Therefore, when ammunition that is not particularly uniform is fired from a match chamber, accuracy is likely to be better than when the same ammunition is fired from a chamber with larger dimensional tolerances. The absence of free bore and the tighter fit of the cartridge in the match chamber are both beneficial to accuracy.

Autoloaders (other than target models) frequently have chambers that are not as tight as those on match rifles. This is necessitated by the fact that the "slam bang" mechanism must allow a wide variety of types of ammunition to feed reliably. Therefore, the chambers of such rifles must easily admit cartridges of different types. As a result, the chambers are often looser and there is a certain amount of free bore so that the cartridge can enter the chamber fully. With larger chamber dimensions and some free bore, the chamber of most autoloaders will not correct for the lack of concentricity in the cartridges to the extent that the chamber in a bolt-action rifle might. Autoloaders typically do not deliver accuracy equal to that of bolt-action rifles which is in part a result of the differences in chambers.

Let there be no mistake. Some autoloaders are extremely accurate, but it is typically because of the design characteristics that include a match type chamber and a high quality barrel that is not free bored. Rifles are individuals. It is possible to find some autoloaders that will equal the accuracy of some bolt actions, but in the majority of cases they do not. If you are reading this book with the goal of

developing a super accurate Ruger 10/22 autoloader, keep in mind the differences between some of the aftermarket barrels. Also, keep in mind the differences between the factory barrel and some of the elegant barrels that are available in several configurations. Gilt-edge accuracy is usually the result of doing several things right, but the barrel is certainly a major component. The chamber is a significant factor in determining the accuracy that a barrel produces.

Free bore

When a rifle barrel is chambered, the region at the rear end of the barrel is enlarged to accommodate a cartridge. Depending on the intended use of the barrel and the manufacturer's tolerances, the fit of the cartridge may be rather tight or somewhat loose as was described above. If the barrel is rifled so that the bullet engages the rifling, there is no free bore (which refers to the amount of space between the front of the chamber and the rearmost section of the rifling). Some of the barrels described in this book are of that type. However, in some barrels, particularly inexpensive factory barrels, the rifling does not extend back far enough for the bullet to engage the rifling as a cartridge is chambered. In other words, there is some "free bore" in the barrel, which the bullet must "jump" to engage the rifling as the cartridge is fired.

Target rifles usually have match type chambers in which there is almost no free bore. It is generally believed that the bullet "jumping" to engage the rifling allows it to become slightly tipped which does not result in best accuracy. This is one reason why .22 Short cartridges fired in .22 LR chambers are not particularly accurate, but the rate of twist (one turn in 21 inches for the Short and one in 16 for the LR) is another.

Some high power centerfire rifles are free bored which allows the use of larger powder charges. This practice is followed so that higher velocity can result. On the other hand, in rimfire rifles match chambers with no free bore can result in slightly higher velocities. The rifling helps to hold the bullet in the case until a higher pressure builds up, and this higher pressure before initial bullet movement can lead to slightly higher velocities. It is not uncommon to measure velocities given by a target type barrel that are slightly higher than one of the same length that has some free bore.

Rifling

The bore inside the barrel on a rifle has two diameters. This results from the fact that the distance between rifling "ridges" (known as the lands) gives a smaller diameter than the distance between the grooves. The lands are frequently about 0.002-0.005" in height depending on the caliber. For example, in .30-caliber rifles like the .308 Winchester, the bore is 0.308" in diameter and the distance between the lands is 0.300". The bore diameter is known as the distance between the grooves so bullets of .308" diameter are used in the .308 Winchester. In the .270 Winchester

By looking at the muzzle, it is easy to see the lands and grooves in a rifle barrel.

(named for the distance between the lands) the bore diameter is 0.277" so bullets having this diameter are used. With centerfire rifles such as these, jacketed bullets are employed and pressures are high so it is important that bullets of the correct diameter be used. In some cases, centerfire calibers are given names that do not correspond to either the bore or groove diameter. Examples of this type are the .260 Remington (bullet diameter 0.264") and the .17 HMR (bullet diameter 0.172").

Bullets used in .22 LR cartridges are made of lead and are quite soft so they can easily be squeezed a small amount if the bore is undersize. The nominal bore diameter for the .22 LR is 0.223" and the bullets should be of this diameter. However, bullets in .22 LR cartridges are frequently oversize which can make them difficult to chamber in rifles that have minimum chamber dimensions. We measured the bullet diameter to be 0.225" in some instances, and feeding problems occurred in some barrels with this ammunition (see Chapter 11).

A projectile moving through air needs to be spinning to stabilize it. The rate of spin imparted by a rifled barrel is expressed

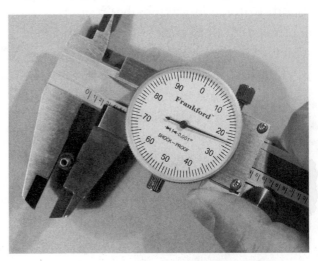

Bullets used in .22 LR ammunition measure about 0.223 inches in diameter as shown by this photo.

in terms the number of inches of travel required to cause one revolution of the bullet. For example, it may be one turn in 16 inches (1 in 16), one turn in 14 inches (specified as 1 in 14 or 1:14), etc. The vast majority of barrels for the .22 LR have twists of 1 in 16, but some barrels have slightly different twists.

The rate of spin necessary to stabilize a bullet depends on the weight and diameter of the bullet and the velocity at which it is traveling. It requires a relatively slow rate of rotation to stabilize a thrown Frisbee, but it would require a rapid rate of rotation to stabilize a pencil spinning on its point. A long, heavy bullet must rotate faster to be stabilized than does a short, stubby one. For example, the 40-grain bullet used in .22 LR cartridges is optimally stabilized by a 1 in 16 twist, but the 29-grain bullet used in .22 Short ammunition is stabilized by a twist of about 1 in 21. Best accuracy is achieved when the bullets are not greatly over stabilized. It is very unlikely that a .22 LR barrel with a 1 in 8 twist would deliver outstanding accuracy.

Considering two centerfire cartridges, the .243 Winchester and the .244 Remington, provides a practical example illustrating these principles. Both use bullets of 0.243" diameter, but the .243 Winchester was introduced with a twist of 1 in 10 while the .244 Remington had a twist of 1 in 12. The result was that the .243 would stabilize bullets as heavy as 100 grains, but the .244 Remington was limited to bullets of about 90 grains or less. This meant that the .243 Winchester was suitable for use on larger game such as deer while the .244 Remington was primarily intended as a varmint rifle using light bullets. Remington realized their mistake in giving the .244 a slower twist and changed it to 1 in 10 while giving the cartridge the name of 6mm Remington. The .244 Remington and the 6mm Remington *cartridges* are identical, but the rifles were produced with different twists.

It has been found that at long ranges where the velocity has decreased significantly, a bullet that is not rotating at the correct rate becomes unstable and accuracy suffers. In order to make the .223 Remington more accurate at long range, a relatively heavy bullet is used and a twist of 1 in 9 required to stabilize this bullet.

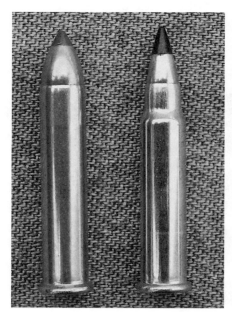

Left: The bullets used in .17 HMR caliber cartridges (right) require 1:9 twist to stabilize them while those in .22 WMR cartridges are stabilized by a 1:16 twist.

Right: Optimum rate of twist for the .22 Short (left) is 1:21 while that for the .22 LR (right) is about 1:16.

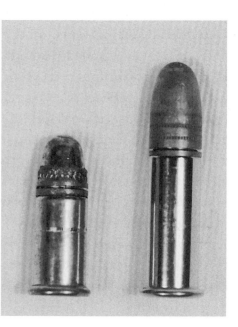

While the above illustrations are useful for heuristic purposes, the user of a .22 rimfire is more than likely going to be using a barrel having a 1 in 16 twist. However, not all rifling is the same. There are four processes that can be used to produce a rifled barrel. The first, known as broach rifling, is produced by pulling a cutting tool known as the broach through the bore while it is rotated to give the correct pitch to the rifling. The broach is a tapered tool that has teeth with spaces between them. The teeth are cut on the broach in such a way that those on the leading edge are shorter so they remove very little metal. The next set of teeth is slightly higher, the next row slightly higher still, and so on. The result is that as the broach is pulled through the bore the grooves are made slightly deeper as each set of teeth on the broach removes some metal. This technique is not commonly used in producing barrels for rimfire rifles.

Drawing a cutting tool through the barrel while the tool is rotated to give grooves with the proper twist produces cut rifling. The tool cuts out one groove slightly as it makes a pass through the bore. Then, the cutting tool is rotated one-sixth of a revolution (if the barrel is to have six lands and grooves) and pulled through the barrel again. This is continued until six grooves have been inscribed in the barrel. However, only a small part of the depth of the groove is produced in each pass because the cutting tool removes only a very slight amount of metal on each pass. Producing a barrel having cut rifling is a slow (which translates into expensive) process. Therefore, although when properly done this rifling process works extremely well, it is not commonly used to produce barrels for rimfire rifles.

Most barrels used on rimfire rifles have the rifling produced by the procedure known as button rifling. A hard cutting tool known as a button is drawn through the bore as it is also rotated to produce the desired twist. The button has grooves and ridges along its edges and these are impressed on the walls of the bore as the button passes through. In order compensate for the metal being forced out of the path of the ridges on the button, some expansion occurs. This may or may not be exactly uniform in different directions due to differences in hardness or barrel diameter. If shaping of the barrel is carried out after it is rifled, there can be a small amount of expansion in regions where the barrel is thinnest. These factors can adversely affect accuracy in extreme cases, but button rifling is by far the most commonly found type in rimfire calibers. The reason is that button rifling is a quick, efficient process because all of the grooves and lands are cut in one pass of the button through the bore.

Hammer forging is a process in which a mandrel having the impression of the grooves and lands is placed in the bore, and the exterior of the barrel is struck repeatedly with hammers which forms the

The barrel on the Ruger 10/22 Target is rifled by hammer forging.

inside of the barrel to the configuration of the mandrel. Although this process is not commonly used to make barrels for rimfire rifles, it is the process used to produce the barrels found on the Ruger 10/22 Target rifles.

Unless the rimfire shooter is seeking something extraordinary for his or her rifle, there is no reason to worry much about how the rifling was produced. Aftermarket barrels are of high quality and are capable of delivering fine accuracy. An advanced shooter seeking the absolute epitome of accuracy might want to investigate barrels produced in different ways, but such experimentation is beyond the scope of this book.

Crowns

The term crown is used to denote the front end of the barrel around the bore. Many shooters do not fully appreciate the importance that this area has in relation to accuracy. If a bullet exits from a barrel that has been damaged (or poorly constructed) at the muzzle, there is a good chance that the flight of the bullet will be affected. For example, if the muzzle is cut at a slight angle to the bore rather than perpendicular to it, the bullet is supported farther on one side than it is on the other. This can cause the bullet to be tipped slightly as it leaves the barrel, which has a detrimental effect on accuracy. If the end of the bore is rough or if the rifling is damaged, a similar effect can result.

It is very easy to bump a rifle against a hard object that can result in damage to the critical muzzle area. It is also possible to damage the muzzle by cleaning from that end of the barrel. Some experts simply refuse to clean a rifle barrel from the muzzle for fear that some damage may

The crown on this barrel from Magnum Research is has an 11-degree bevel for protection of the muzzle.

occur which will cause a deterioration in accuracy. Whether it is that crucial or not is open to some debate, but it is certainly true that cleaning from the muzzle end of the barrel must be done very carefully. The bolts can be removed from bolt-action rifles and cleaning done from the breech, but shooters who clean many types of semiautos, lever actions, or pumps must do so from the muzzle. This topic will be discussed in greater detail later.

Several types of crowns are employed by barrel makers in an effort to reduce the likelihood of damage to the muzzle. In one type of crown, the barrel is simply beveled inward so that the outside edge of the barrel extends farther than the muzzle

The crown on this Green Mountain barrel has a recessed muzzle.

A countersunk recess in the crown of this heavy Butler Creek barrel helps protect the muzzle.

area. As a result, bumping the barrel against something causes the outside edge to make contact, which protects the muzzle from damage.

Another type of crown has the bore countersunk below the outside edge of the barrel. This creates a rim on the barrel that will make contact if the barrel is bumped and protects the sensitive area around the muzzle. As shown in the photos, barrels with this type of protective area are made in several configurations. Some barrels are made so that the crown is rounded, and this leaves the rifled region at the muzzle farther back than the highest point of the crown. Whatever the technique used, the vast majority of aftermarket barrels for the Ruger 10/22 have some sort of provision for protecting the muzzle and the rifling in that critical region.

Barrel Lapping

Although there are probably some exceptions, rifles that have rough bores generally do not give outstanding accuracy. As the bullet travels along a rough bore, there is some damage to the external surface of the bullet, which can affect its flight characteristics as it passes through air. The most accurate rifles generally have bores that are extremely smooth.

Some of the outstanding barrels described in this book have bores that are almost mirror smooth. In order to keep prices reasonable, factories simply cannot expend the time and effort to produce such barrels on mass-produced rifles. The region of the barrel just in front of the chamber is known as the leade. This area and the muzzle are the most sensitive regions of the barrel as far as accuracy is concerned. However, when a tight cleaning patch is pushed through a barrel, it may be noted that there are places where more force is required to move the patch. In other words, there are rough places in the bore. Roughness in the leade area can be the result of the chambering operation leaving tool marks and sharp edges in that region.

If a barrel has a rough bore, it is possible to smooth it. The process is known as lapping the bore. There are two processes by which this is done. In the classic manner, lapping is done by casting a lead slug the size of the bore and applying an abrasive powder. Working the lead slug back and forth in the barrel causes polishing of the bore. The process is referred to as hand lapping, and some manufacturers of aftermarket barrels use it. Although this procedure works, it is not the most commonly used lapping process today.

Someone came up with the idea that firing a bullet coated with abrasive through the barrel would polish the bore with a lot less work. Therefore, in the second type of barrel lapping, the process involves embedding abrasive in the lubricant that normally coats the bullets in .22 LR cartridges. Firing the cartridges laps the bore. Accordingly, the process is referred to as fire lapping (also sometimes called pressure lapping) the bore.

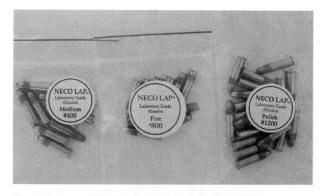

The kit from NECO for fire lapping a .22 LR bore contains cartridges that have abrasive grit on them.

The abrasive is a special type of silicon carbide that has a narrow range of particle size that depends on the grit designation. Grits designated as 220 (coarse), 400, 800, and 1200 (fine) are available. Generally, the coarser material is used first and the lapping is concluded with the finest grade. Some knowledgeable workers recommend only the two or three finest granulations be used in lapping barrels for .22 rimfires, and this is probably a good idea. Two sources of lapping materials are NECO and Superior Shooting Systems (Final Finish). You can buy the abrasive paste and prepare the cartridges yourself, or you can buy cartridges that have already had abrasive applied. In either case, it is essential that the directions provided by the manufacturer be followed carefully.

As part of the evaluation of the factory stainless steel barrel on one version of the

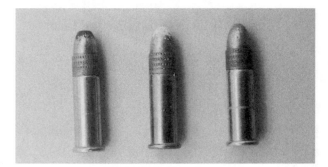

The color on the tip identifies these cartridges as having (left to right) medium, fine, and polish (very fine) grit for fire lapping the bore.

Ruger 10/22, we performed the fire lapping procedure using cartridges supplied by NECO. In this case, the cartridges have a color code on the tip of the bullet. The red tip signifies that the bullet is coated with 400 grit abrasive, the white tip indicates 800 grit abrasive, and the blue tip indicates 1200 grit abrasive. The numbers of rounds utilized were 10, 10, and 20, respectively, with thorough cleaning after each five rounds. There was no doubt that the cleaning patches went through the bore more easily as the lapping process was underway. The results of test firing this lapped barrel will be discussed more fully in Chapter 4.

In some cases, lapping a barrel can improve accuracy considerably and make the barrel much easier to clean. It is a technique to consider if you have a rough factory barrel that does not shoot with acceptable accuracy but you do not want to replace the barrel before exhausting every avenue to make it shoot.

Barrel Vibrations

In the simplest, classic terms, a rifle consists of lock, stock, and barrel. This is a naïve view of a rifle that does not address the importance of many aspects of the basic components. Few would deny that a beautiful stock enhances the appearance of a fine rifle, but many may not fully appreciate how important the stock is to accuracy. In spite of the metal-to-metal nature of the fit of the barrel and action, it is the stock that holds the metal parts in their proper locations shot after shot.

When a rifle is fired, the motion of the bullet that results from gases at high pressure causes the barrel to vibrate. While the vibration of a rifle barrel does not resemble that of a plucked guitar

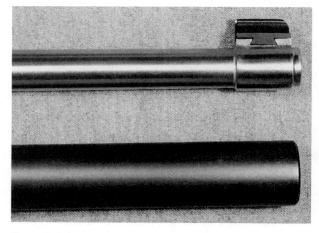

One of the reasons that barrels differ in accuracy is because a heavy barrel (bottom) helps control vibrations that may impair accuracy from a light barrel (top).

Flutes cut along the barrel may help control vibrations as well as reduce the weight.

string, it is significant and knowledgeable shooters refer to these vibrations as barrel harmonics. Reproducible vibrations allow bullets to exit from the muzzle at the same point in the barrel vibrations. This is one factor that determines the intrinsic accuracy of a barrel.

The problem facing barrel makers is how to control barrel vibrations or to minimize them so that bullets can leave the muzzle in the same manner shot after shot. One technique that is used to help control barrel vibration is to make the barrel very heavy. A stiff, heavy barrel is subject to smaller vibrations than is a slender one. As a general rule, barrels having a diameter of 0.920" are likely to be more accurate than those having the configuration of the factory barrel. Of course the other characteristics of the barrel (chamber dimensions, smoothness, amount of free bore, crown condition, etc.) can make a particular lightweight barrel more accurate than a heavier one. Accuracy is determined by many factors, not just barrel weight.

Another attempt to control barrel vibrations is made by cutting grooves in the external surface of the barrel. These grooves can be straight following the lines of the barrel (a fluted barrel) or some other pattern. The so-called "serpentine" barrels make use of curved channels cut in the barrel surface. Some believe that these grooves of either type help to control vibrations.

Contact between the barreled action and the stock is generally referred to as bedding. Classically, the recess where the action resides was made to fit the action precisely, and the barrel was allowed to touch the barrel channel in the stock. Ideally, the stock supplied slight, constant

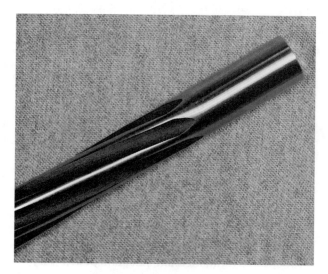

Spiral flutes are used in this barrel from E. R. Shaw.

Sliding a dollar bill between the barrel and the stock shows clearly that this barrel is free floating.

Sleeved barrels have a slender steel barrel that is encased in a larger tube. In this case, the outer tube is made of a carbon fiber composite.

upward pressure on the barrel, especially in the last few inches of the forearm. Getting precise bedding of the action and barrel was a time consuming process that required considerable skill. In recent years, there has been a general shift to allowing the barrel to be free floating and to make no contact with the forearm except perhaps just in front of the action. It is generally believed that free floated barrels vibrate in the same way for each shot, and that superior accuracy results. However, the way in which the barrel is attached to the receiver of the 10/22 makes free floating problematic. The barrel is attached only to

the aluminum extension on the bottom of the receiver into which two large screws are threaded. This extension is not sufficiently rigid to support the barrel for its entire length, especially if the barrel is of the very heavy target variety. It is the opinion of some (including the authors) that the

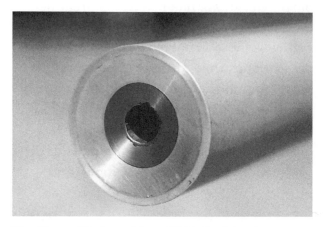

The Aluma-Lite barrel from Majestic Arms has a barrel made by Lothar Walther that is encased in an aluminum sleeve.

Ruger's unique barrel attachment involves two screws pulling backward on a block that locks into a recess in the bottom of the barrel.

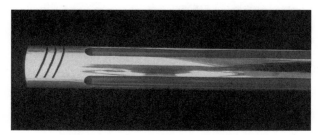

This unusual barrel made by Whistle Pig has a highly polished aluminum sleeve that has flutes that have been enameled bright red.

barrel needs to be supported by the stock. Whether this should be for the entire length of the forearm or only the last two or three inches is open to some debate.

Aftermarket barrels for the Ruger 10/22 are produced in many styles. One type has a slender steel barrel that is surrounded by a sleeve made of some other material to produce a barrel having a diameter of 0.920 inch. Some manufacturers utilize sleeves made of carbon fibers while others make the sleeves of aluminum. Barrels of the former type are produced by Butler Creek, Magnum Research, and Volquartsen while Majestic Arms produces barrels with sleeves made of made of aluminum. It is believed that in addition to giving a barrel having 0.920-inch diameter, the sleeves help control vibrations.

Because it is so important, control of barrel vibrations has received a great deal of attention. Sims Vibration Laboratory makes a slip-on rubber device, a barrel deresonator, that can be moved along the barrel to find the spot where best accuracy results. The rubber collar dampens vibrations, and at some point along the barrel the effect is greatest. By placing the rubber collar at different positions and

One of the easiest ways to improve the trigger on a Ruger 10/22 is to simply install an aftermarket unit like this fine trigger from Kidd Innovative Designs.

firing groups to determine accuracy, the shooter can obtain the maximum benefit of controlling vibrations by dampening.

Volquartsen Custom Ltd. produces a device known as a stabilization module, which clamps to the barrel at the muzzle. While not designed to control vibration, it is intended to control gas emission at the muzzle so that the bullet is stabilized by equalizing gas flow around the bullet to impart some stability. The stabilization module is made of aluminum and fits on .920-inch barrels.

Lock Time

As we have already mentioned, the three basic components of a rifle are the lock, stock, and barrel. Although dealing with these components represent the content of later chapters in this book, it is appropriate here to describe the characteristic known as the lock time. This represents the length of time that elapses between the release of the sear and the firing pin striking the rim of the cartridge. When trying to achieve the ultimate in accuracy, it is important to have the lock time as short as possible. In this way, the effect of the slight motion of the rifle during firing is minimized.

There are several factors that determine the lock time. After the sear is released, the hammer begins its motion toward the rear end of the firing pin. How long it takes for the hammer to make contact with the firing pin is determined by the tension of the hammer spring and the weight of the hammer (which is initially at rest). The stronger the spring, the faster it accelerates the hammer. However, the heavier the hammer, the slower it moves when pushed by a particular spring. As a result of these issues, a shorter lock time results when the

This custom Ruger 10/22 has an Aluma-Lite barrel from Majestic Arms and a Bell & Carlson Odyssey target stock. This rimfire provides outstanding performance.

Some shooters of Ruger 10/22s prefer a bolt handle with a shape that is different from that of the factory part. This titanium Power Custom bolt handle is a popular choice.

hammer spring is strong and the hammer is light in weight.

Unless the precisely correct contact between the hammer and sear is used, a strong hammer spring can result in a heavy pull required to release the sear from its engaging notch on the hammer. If the hammer is too light in weight, it does not deliver a heavy enough blow to the firing pin which can result in misfires or at least in ignition that is not uniform from shot to shot. All of these factors must be considered by engineers when designing the lock (trigger mechanism).

Many of the aftermarket parts for the Ruger 10/22 are designed to overcome some of the problems associated with what happens between the release of the sear and the ignition of the primer. Special sears, hammers, firing pins, etc. are available from many suppliers of parts for the Ruger 10/22. In some cases, these parts are made to closer

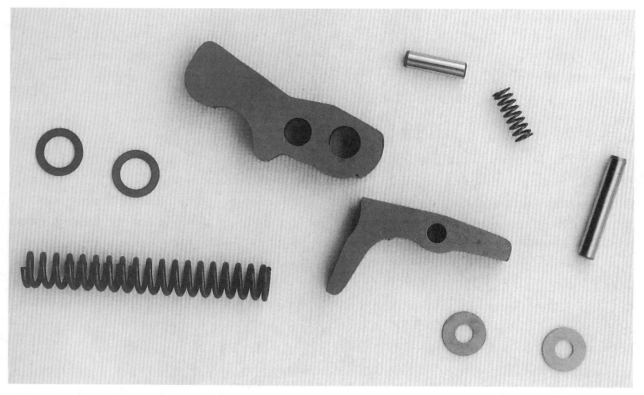

Installing a trigger kit consisting of a hammer, sear, and shims will provide good trigger action.

This fine Ruger 10/22 is the Target which wears a Smart Stock® from Boyds' Gunstock Industries.

tolerances than the equivalent factory items, and they may be more highly finished. The firing pin may move more freely with less friction because of the absence of burrs or rough places. Hammers and firing pins made of titanium are quite common. Titanium is a strong, hard metal that has a lower density than steel so parts made of titanium have less weight than the same parts made of steel. Using titanium parts results in a shorter lock time and increased durability.

All these little things have an effect on accuracy. The effect of each one may be small, but they work symbiotically. Replacing the barrel on a Ruger 10/22 will likely result in a more accurate rifle. Replacing the stock may also produce some improvement in accuracy as a result of the barrel and action being supported better. Finally, reworking the lock (or replacing the entire trigger assembly) will give additional improvement in accuracy and make the rifle more pleasant to shoot. How far the owner of 10/22 will go in the quest for accuracy depends on motivation and money. One nice thing about modifying a 10/22 is that it doesn't have to all be done at one time. You may start by replacing the factory barrel and stock. After gaining experience with the rifle, you may decide to replace the lock work. Such experimentation is endless, but it is generally advisable to buy high quality items so you do not end up replacing one aftermarket item with another.

Chapter 3

AMMUNITION

A metallic cartridge consists of the projectile, the propellant, the primer, and the case that holds everything together. Although black powder was the propellant used in small arms for many years, it was replaced by smokeless powder a little more than a century ago. Smokeless powder is essentially nitrocellulose with several minor constituents included, and when it burns very little smoke is produced. The primer used in most small arms ammunition is lead styphnate, an explosive that is sensitive to shock.

Today, there are two basic types of cartridges that differ in the placement of the primer. In a centerfire cartridge, the primer is contained in a cup that is placed in a recess in the center of the cartridge head. The firing pin strikes the primer in the center of the cartridge. In a rimfire cartridge, the primer is contained in the rim of the folded cartridge case. When the firing pin strikes the cartridge rim, the primer is crushed as the rim collapses under the blow causing it to explode which in turns ignites the propellant. The general design of a rimfire cartridge has remained essentially the same for over 140 years. That is not to say that rimfire cartridges are archaic. There have been enormous improvements in rimfire ammunition over the years, and the cartridges produced today are technically advanced, highly uniform products. In this chapter, we will describe some of the characteristics of rimfire ammunition that are important to shooters of both factory and tricked out 10/22s. This is entirely appropriate because the objective when modifying a 10/22 is improved accuracy, and the ammunition used is of equal importance to the alterations made on the rifle.

General Comments

Ammunition in .22 LR caliber is produced in a bewildering array of types and price ranges. Available products range from the promotional types that sell for about one dollar per box of 50 rounds to the highest quality ammunition that sells for well over $10 per box. Although there are general specifications for dimensions of the .22 LR cartridge, considerable variation exists especially in bullet diameters. The nominal bullet diameter for the .22 LR is 0.223 inches, but we found some bullets that were as large as 0.225 inches in diameter.

Rimfire cartridges are fired by a blow to the rim (left) while centerfire cartridges have the primer located centrally (right).

Chambers in the barrels of rifles that fire the .22 LR cartridge are cut to certain dimensions. As we have noted elsewhere, match chambers are normally smaller than those on most so-called sporting rifles. If the chamber tends toward to the maximum

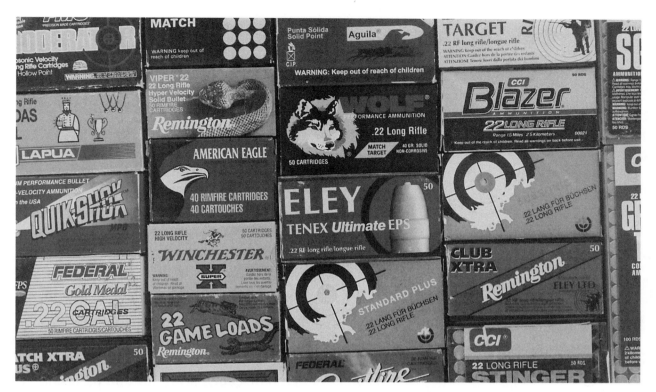

The rimfire shooter today has an enormous range of ammunition from which to choose.

dimensions, cartridges enter easily but fit somewhat loosely. If the chamber tends toward the minimum in size and cartridges having bullets that are somewhat large are loaded, the cartridge may stick in the chamber before it is fully inserted. Failure to feed occurs which usually involves the bolt not being returned to battery.

The makers of .22 autoloaders generally market their products with chambers that will readily accept almost any .22 LR cartridge. If they didn't, the rifle would jam frequently when certain types of ammunition were used. However, this is not particularly conducive to fine accuracy. Later in this book we will describe some of the numerous aftermarket barrels that are available for the Ruger 10/22. The majority of these barrels are manufactured with so-called match chambers, which have minimum dimensions. When these barrels are called on to fire cartridges that contain bullets that tend toward maximum

diameter, feeding problems arise. One example, but by no means the only one, will serve to illustrate the situation. We have found that bullets in the Remington Target load measure around 0.224-0.225 inches. These cartridges that feed reliably in factory 10/22 barrels regularly failed to feed when some of the aftermarket barrels

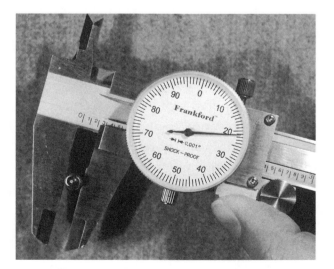

The bullet in this rimfire cartridge measure 0.221 inch in diameter, which is slightly smaller than most.

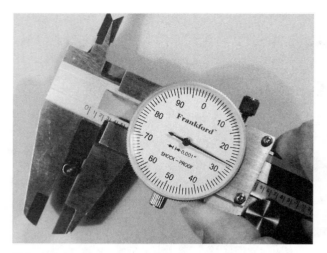

This bullet measures 0.226 inch in diameter, which means it may not chamber easily in a match chamber.

were used. This is a manifestation of the conditions just described. However, if you have a rifle that has a chamber that tends toward the maximum in size (as many inexpensive .22s do), the Remington Target load might be just the ticket for your rifle.

It is absolutely essential that the rimfire shooter seeking fine accuracy must do some serious testing. No problem of feeding certain types of ammunition (among them Standard Plus, Wolf Match Target, Eley Match, and Lapua Super Club) was ever encountered. These are target loads, and they work flawlessly in target chambers.

Accuracy and Precision

One of the noted writers of yesteryear, Colonel Townsend Whelen, is quoted as saying, "Only accurate rifles are interesting." This may not be universally true, but it is frustrating to shoot at a target after taking careful aim and following all of the rules for good marksmanship only to find that the bullet hit somewhere else. The object, whether the target is a circle only 0.10 inches in diameter or a squirrel,

is to place the bullet in exactly the desired location. In the best-case scenario, this can be done shot after shot. It is certainly true that most of the work done on the Ruger 10/22 and the aftermarket items sold are directed toward improving accuracy.

Shooting a group of shots at the same target is a common practice among rifle shooters. The object is to produce a cluster of shots (usually five or 10) that is as small as possible. A "one-hole" group is highly desired! The group may not be centered around the exact aiming point, but that is a secondary concern because the sights can be adjusted to move the group to a different location.

Although they are frequently used interchangeably, accuracy and precision are two different things. Suppose an archer

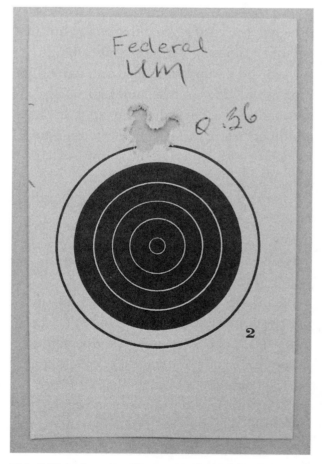

This 0.36-inch group shows good precision but poor accuracy since it is not at the point of aim.

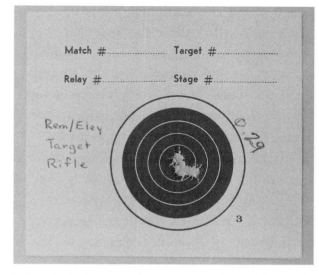

This 0.29-inch group shows excellent precision and accuracy.

launches an arrow at the target and it hits exactly one foot below the center of the target face. Suppose that a second arrow launched at the target hits 11 inches below the center of the target face. After a series of six arrows have been shot, there might be a small cluster of arrows about a foot below the intended point of impact. The archer has shown good precision because

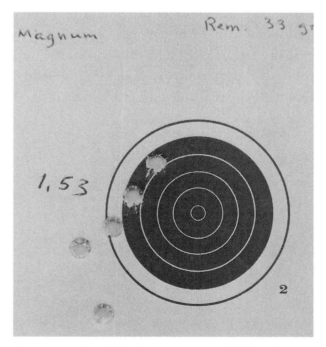

A group such as this shows poor precision and poor accuracy.

the group is small, but the accuracy is poor because the shots have not struck near the point of aim.

When groups are fired using a rifle, it is precision that is being determined rather than accuracy. If the groups measure 0.5 inch at 50 yards (measured as the distance between the centers of the two widest spaced shots), the rifle shows good precision. If the group is located two inches above and an inch to the right of the exact aiming point, the shooter can adjust the sights to bring the group to the point of aim. Then, the rifle will exhibit good accuracy as well as precision.

Precision of a series of shots is not of much importance to a squirrel hunter because it is the first shot that will bag the game. However, unless the rifle being used is capable of placing shots within a very small area, the hunter will have little confidence in where that first shot will land. Therefore, rifle shooters need a piece that is capable of good precision and sighted so that the shots are placed accurately.

Ammunition Selection

The shooter of a rimfire firearm has a wide selection of ammunition from which to choose. Cartridges are available in standard velocity, high velocity, hyper velocity, match, and other types. The ammunition selected should be based on the type of shooting which is anticipated. One would not normally go out to compete in a benchrest match using high velocity ammunition with hollow pointed bullets. Nor would one normally try to dispatch called in predators using standard velocity loads. Generally, the high velocity loads are considered to be applicable to hunting small game and pests while the match,

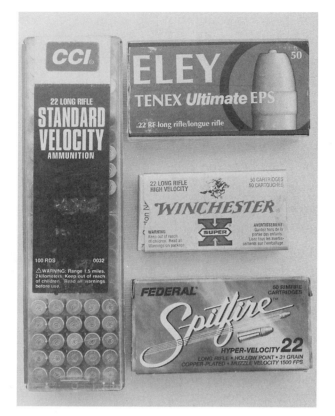

Ammunition in .22 LR caliber includes standard velocity, high velocity, hypervelocity, and target types.

target, and standard velocity loads are considered appropriate for target shooting.

Regardless of whether the target is a fox or a piece of paper, accuracy is the most important consideration. Since this book is concerned with the Ruger 10/22 in factory and modified configurations, reliable feeding of the autoloader action is important. Although we have found that factory barrels will readily accept virtually any type of ammunition, some of the aftermarket barrels do not. Because some of the barrels have tight match chambers, cartridges that have bullets of larger diameter will not chamber fully. For example, with the Lilja and Jarvis barrels (see Chapter 11), Remington/Eley Club Xtra, Remington Target, CCI Blazer, and Winchester Power Point cartridges often failed to go into battery as the action

cycled. This does not indicate anything wrong with either these fine barrels or these types of ammunition! Some loads simply have bullets that have a maximum diameter while some barrels have very tight chambers. If you install a fine aftermarket barrel on your 10/22, be prepared for this to happen and try several types of ammunition. It is extremely unlikely that there is anything wrong with the barrel.

Although this point will be made several times in this book, many rifles are highly individualistic in their accuracy. As you will see when looking at the tables shown in Chapters 4 and 11, accuracy varies significantly if cartridges of different types are fired in the same rifle. There may easily be a factor of two difference in the average group size just by changing type of ammunition. As you study the tables shown in Chapters 4 and 11, certain types of ammunition seem to give outstanding accuracy in almost any barrel. Among them are SK Jagd Standard Plus, Lapua Super Club, Wolf Match Target, Eley Match, and Remington/Eley Target Rifle. On the other hand, one would not normally expect a type of ammunition that sells for $0.99 per box to perform as well as a match load that sells for ten times as much. To some

All of these target loads are capable of delivering fine accuracy.

Two of the most popular types of hypervelocity .22 LR cartridges are the CCI Stinger and CCI Quick-Shok.

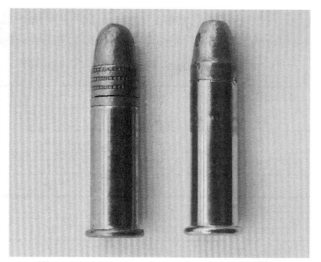

The CCI Stinger and Quik-Shok (right) utilize a case that is longer than that of the standard .22 LR (left).

extent, you get what you pay for. On the other hand, accuracy is not particularly critical when plinking cans at 25 yards. If you plan to snipe small varmints or get small groups on a paper target, be prepared to do some testing to find the ammunition that performs best in your rifle. Hyper velocity loads feature lightweight (29-34 grain) bullets at high velocity. This is not a combination that produces highest accuracy in most rifles, but if they are sufficiently accurate in your rifle, by all means use them when appropriate. Both CCI Stinger and Quik-Shok cartridges utilize a case that is approximately 0.1 inch longer than that of the conventional .22 LR. Consequently, they should not be used in match type chambers because the case will engage the rifling and could damage the rifling at the mouth of the chamber.

The accompanying table is included in order to provide the reader with an overview of the types of ammunition that are available. Keep in mind that at the present time the calibers used in 10/22 factory and customized rifles include .22 LR, .22 WMR, .17 HMR, and .17 Mach 2. Accordingly, the table includes those calibers but omits the .22 Short, .22 Long, .22 WRF, and .22 CB rounds. Volquartsen produces a conversion kit that allows the owner of a Ruger 10/22 to configure the rifle to fire .22 Short ammunition, but it

is a specialized unit that applies to only a few converted rifles. However, some barrels are chambered for the .17 Aguila (or PMC) so data for that cartridge is included in the table. Most manufacturers produce a .22 LR with a 40-grain solid bullet with a muzzle velocity of about 1080-1100 ft/sec. If one company lists a velocity of 1080 ft/sec for its load and another lists a similar load at 1100 ft/sec, these are combined as a single entry in the table.

From the table, it is apparent that the shooter of a 10/22 in a particular caliber has a lot of options when it comes to selecting ammunition. Even if you do not plan to do target shooting in competition,

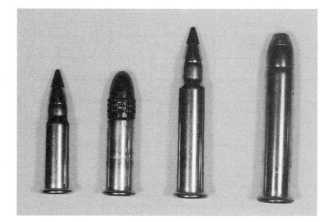

The popular rimfire calibers are (left to right) the .17 Mach 2, .22 LR, .17 HMR, and .22 WMR.

A Summary of Rimfire Ammuntion Types*

Cartridge	Bullet Type	Wt. Gr.	Vel., ft/sec Muz./100 yd.	E., ft. lb. Muz./100 yd.	Notes
17 Aguila/PMC	JHP	20	1850/1353	152/81	A, PMC
17 Mach 2	JPT	17	2100/1510	166/88	H, CCI, E
17 HMR	JPT	17	2550/1900	245/135	E, H, F, R, CCI
17 HMR	JHP	17	2550/1900	255/135	CCI
17 HMR	JHP	20	2375/1775	250/140	H, CCI
22 Long Rifle	HP	38	1000/854	84/62	PMC Mod.
22 Long Rifle	HP	38	1050/901	93/69	R, E Sub.S.
22 Long Rifle	SRN	40	1050/—	98/—	Wolf MT
22 Long Rifle	SRN	40	1033/—	95/—	Wolf ME
22 Long Rifle	SRN	40	1080/930	105/75	Most Mfrs.
22 Long Rifle	SRN	40	1150/976	117/85	W T22
22 Long Rifle	HP	38	1280/1020	140/90	Most Mfrs.
22 Long Rifle	SRN	40	1255/1020	140/93	Most Mfrs.
22 Long Rifle	SRN	40	1312/1100	154/107	E
22 Long Rifle	HP	37.5	1312/1100	143/100	E
22 Long Rifle	HP	40	1280/1001	146/89	W P.P.
22 Long Rifle	STC	36	1410/1056	159/89	R Viper
22 Long Rifle	HPTC	33	1500/1075	165/85	R Yel.Jkt.
22 Long Rifle	HP	32	1640/1124	191/90	CCI Stgr.
22 Long Rifle	HP	40	1435/1112	183/110	CCI Vctr.
22 Long Rifle	SFP	40	1235/1015	135/91	CCI SGB
22 Long Rifle	HP	30	1750/1191	204/95	A
22 Long Rifle	SRN	30	1750/1191	204/95	A
22 Long Rifle	SRN	48	1040/920	117/90	L Scoremax
22 Long Rifle	SRN	60	950/802	120/86	A SSS
22 WMR	JHP	30	2200/1419	325/120	CCI, F
22 WMR	PT	33	2000/1495	293/164	R Premier
22 WMR	JHP	34	2120/1435	338/155	W Supreme
22 WMR	JHP	40	1910/1326	324/156	W, R, PMC, F
22 WMR	JHP	40	1875/1375	312/168	CCI
22 WMR	FMJ	40	1875/1375	312/168	CCI
22 WMR	FMJ	40	1910/1326	324/156	W, R, PMC, F
22 WMR	JHP	50	1650/1280	300/180	F

*In some cases such as that of the 40-grain round nose 22 LR, the high velocity load is listed as 1235, 1250, 1255, or 1260 depending on the manufacturer. These are not considered as constituting different loadings. Velocities for the standard velocity 22 LR are given as 1050, 1070, 1080, or 1085 depending on the manufacturer.

Abbreviations: SRN=solid round nose; SFP=solid flat point; HP=hollow point; STC=solid truncated cone; HPTC=hollow point truncated cone; JPT=jacketed polymer tip; JHP=jacketed hollow point; JSP=jacketed soft point; FMJ=full metal jacket; TGT=target; SSS=Sniper SubSonic.

Notes: Most Mfr. indicates that they offer this load or one very similar to it. A=Aguila; CCI=CCI; E=Eley, F=Federal; H=Hornady; L=Lapua R=Remington; W=Winchester; PMC=PMC; Vctr.=Velocitor; Stgr.=Stinger; SGB=small game bullet; P.P.=power point; Mod=Moderator; ME=Match Extra; MT=Match Target; Sub. S.= Subsonic.

Bullets used in .22 LR cartridges have (left to right) round nose, flat point, hollow pointed truncated cone, and hollow point styles.

you should try several brands and types of ammunition in your rifle. Measure the groups and enter the data in a notebook. If you do, you will not find yourself wondering what it was that gave those small groups last year when you want to use the same load on some pests. We have accumulated an enormous amount of data of this type and find occasion to refer to it frequently. The next section will present a discussion of some of the factors that you should consider as you carry out your experiments in accuracy.

Testing

At the end of a season, be it football or baseball, there is invariably a comparison of statistics for different teams. In many cases, the comparisons are made of the statistics for individual players. Data constitute the basis for comparisons of all types. It is no different in the case of firearms. However, there many variables involved in collecting data for rifles. The

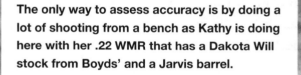

The only way to assess accuracy is by doing a lot of shooting from a bench as Kathy is doing here with her .22 WMR that has a Dakota Will stock from Boyds' and a Jarvis barrel.

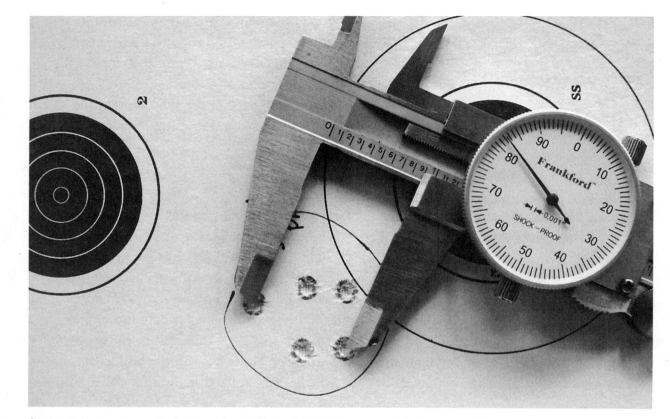

Accurate measurement of group sizes is important. Keep a record of your results.

first is that of the type of ammunition selected. It is well known that the performance of rifles depends to a great extent on the ammunition being fired. It is not uncommon for the average group size to vary by a factor of two when the only thing being varied is the type of cartridges used.

It is also not uncommon for two rifles that are nominally identical to exhibit a considerable difference in accuracy. Each rifle is an entity unto itself. Whether it is the result of slight differences in dimensions, bore smoothness, or other factors, the differences are there. When testing rifle accuracy, the object is to try to control or eliminate as many variables as possible. First, the rifle is fired from a steady rest, usually a shooting bench with the rifle supported on sandbags. Second, sighting equipment is used which allows the aiming point to be determined

as accurately as possible. Generally, this means a scope, preferably one with considerable magnification. Studies have shown however that the aiming error at 50 yards when using a scope of even four power is only a tiny fraction of an inch.

When testing accuracy, the shooter tries to hold the rifle in the same way for each shot, tries to align the sights the same way, and tries to squeeze the trigger in the same way. Shooters differ in these abilities. Shooting from a steady bench with the rifle supported on sandbags minimizes procedural differences, but some shooters can shoot smaller groups than others. Differences in eyesight, manual dexterity, and experience come into play when shooting groups. Even as simple a factor as how the butt plate fits the shoulder can make a difference in group size. We have found that the very slick plastic butt plate used on the Ruger Carbine makes it

Using a scope of high magnification like this 3-12X AO rimfire model from Scheels All Sports that has a sunshade attached minimizes sighting error.

difficult to hold the stock securely enough to prevent slight movement as the trigger breaks. With all of these things considered, one should take the accuracy data reported to be *indicative* of the accuracy potential of a specific combination on a particular day by a particular shooter. On top of that, all shooting was conducted outdoors under real world conditions over a period of months.

Our standard routine consisted firing five 5-shot groups at a distance of 50 yards. Group size was determined by measuring the distance between the two widest holes. The problem associated with this procedure is that it is possible to have four shots in one hole and if the fifth shot is an inch away from that cluster, the group is a one-inch group. The accuracy of the rifle is clearly much better than one inch at 50 yards, but the group size is determined by the one stray shot. A better procedure is to measure what is known as the mean dispersion for the group. This is done by determining the geometrical center of the group and then determining the distance between that point and the center of each hole. The average of these distances is then taken as the group size. The effect of one stray shot is averaged with all of the other shots so that it constitutes only one point in the data. Although this is a more correct way to interpret group sizes, it is rarely done. The group sizes reported here were determined in the conventional way.

No two rifles shoot exactly the same with all types of ammunition, but this should come as no surprise. A rifle is made from many parts, and two rifles may be constructed from the same number and type of parts but still not be identical. Even two aftermarket barrels produced by the same manufacturer may not be equally accurate (it may take extensive and exacting testing to show the difference). For a given rifle, even small factors like changing the tension on the stock screw or switching stocks can affect accuracy.

Testing ammunition generally refers to determining precision with regard to placing bullets on the target. In order to determine precision, it is necessary to control variables to the greatest extent possible. A rock-steady rest helps control movement of the rifle, and a light, crisp trigger also reduces this tendency. A scope of high magnification makes it possible to align the crosshair on the target in the same way for each shot. Because the vast majority of rifle ranges are outdoors, there is a possibility for the wind to cause the bullets to deviate from the chosen path. Do not shoot groups outdoors with a gusty cross wind and expect the data to indicate much about the accuracy of your rifle.

Superimposed on all of the factors given above is the fact that any rifle will perform differently when different types of ammunition are used. Generally, the target loads that have moderate velocity perform best although there are exceptions. Even after you have selected a type of cartridge for testing, you must remember that a

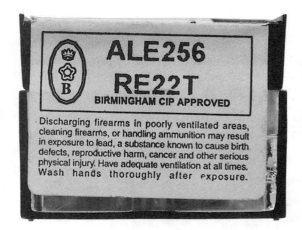

The lot number for this box of ammunition is printed on the end.

Even cartridges of the same type from different lots may show differences in accuracy. This box flap has the lot number printed inside.

different manufacturing lot will probably not perform exactly the same. In other words, if you fire five 5-shot groups with Speedy Special out of Lot No. XXX1, you may find that cartridges from Lot No. XX22 made a couple of months later do not perform as well or may perform better. Automated loading machines dispense powder, and even the humidity can affect the way the powder flows. The general rule is that if you find a lot of a particular type of ammunition that gives outstanding accuracy, buy as much of that lot as you can. Manufacturing lot numbers are generally stamped on the outside of the box or on the inside of the end flap.

We will revisit this topic later in this chapter and in Chapters 4 and 11, but it must be stressed that our testing was conducted outdoors under a range of temperatures, elevations, and wind conditions. It was simply the best we could do under the circumstances, but this is not the ideal way to test accuracy. Moreover, in some cases the ammunition tested was limited to a single lot. Other lots may perform either better or worse, but it is not practical when testing two or three dozen types to buy from multiple lots. For a thorough test of one rifle (not dozens of combinations of barrels, stocks, triggers, and sights as in this work), you would probably test only a few types of ammunition. After firing a couple of groups, you would discontinue testing of a type that did not indicate that good accuracy might be achieved. In a work of this magnitude, we did not have this luxury.

Internal Ballistics

The science of ballistics is concerned with launching and the flight of projectiles. There are two branches of the science. Interior ballistics is concerned with the forces on and motion of the projectile during its launching. Exterior ballistics is concerned with the flight of the projectile after it leaves the launching machine. Incidentally, it is correct to use the singular verb "is" after the word ballistics. Ballistics is not the plural of ballistic so the word represents a singular area of study. It is unfortunate that we recently read about a situation that will exist until "the physics are worked out" as if physics were the plural of physic rather than a branch of science.

An extensive discussion of ballistics is beyond the scope of this book. The interested reader may want to consult a book such as J. E. House, *The Gun Digest® Book of the .22 Rimfire* (Gun Digest Books, 2005) for a more complete discussion of the topic. References for further study are provided in that book.

The factors that come into effect when a .22 rimfire cartridge is fired are largely beyond the control of the shooter. As a result, there is little that can be done to change internal ballistics. When centerfire cartridges are loaded, there is a wide range of powders from which to choose as well as brands and types of primers. These can be loaded with many types of bullets. In other words, the cartridge can be constructed to achieve desired ballistic characteristics. Rimfire cartridges are already assembled using the primer and powder chosen by the manufacturer. Even the bullet is of a specific type with few if any choices as to type. For example, Federal Ultra Match ammunition is loaded with only one type of bullet, a 40-grain solid with a round nose. However, this does not mean that the rimfire shooter should not have some appreciation of the internal and external ballistics that govern his or her type of shooting.

A firearm is engineered is such a way that pulling the trigger releases the sear and the hammer moves forward to strike the firing pin which then strikes the cartridge. The user of a Ruger 10/22 has many options to alter the machinery so that it performs in a way that is somewhat different from the way a factory rifle does. The internal ballistics associated with firing a cartridge begins when the firing pin strikes the cartridge. This action causes the case rim to be dented, which crushes the priming mixture, which, in turn, causes it to explode. The priming mixture consists of several components, but the most important component is a compound known as lead styphnate. This compound is sensitive to shock so crushing it causes the primer to explode, which in turn causes the powder to ignite. Propellant powders are mixtures, the chief component of which is nitrocellulose. Propellants do not explode but rather they burn rapidly. As they burn, they produce gases that expand rapidly to generate a high pressure within the cartridge case held in the chamber. These gases push on the base of the projectile forcing it out of the case into the bore.

Bullets are crimped securely in the cases of rimfire cartridges. It takes a certain amount of "pull" to cause the bullet to move out of the case into the bore. Also, if the cartridge is held in a match type chamber, the bullet may already be in contact with the rifling before the cartridge is fired. The result is that the chamber pressure must be substantial before the bullet starts moving. If the bullet is not in contact with the rifling before firing (as is the case with most inexpensive .22s), the bullet can start to move as soon as the pressure is sufficient to overcome the crimp. Therefore, it takes more pressure to start the bullet moving in a match type chamber than in an ordinary chamber. This higher initial pressure is the reason that match chambers frequently result in slightly higher velocity than that given when the same cartridge is fired in a chamber having more generous dimensions and normal rifling.

As the bullet starts to move, additional powder burns generating more gas, which increases the pressure. Because the powder charge used in a .22 LR case is so small and is of a fast burning type, the powder is consumed before the bullet has traveled more than a few inches. This is the reason why a .22

Cartridges in .22 LR caliber have the bullet crimped in place. Note how the case is turned inward where it meets the bullet.

semiautomatic pistol with a 4.5-inch barrel gives a velocity that is as much as 85% of the velocity produced in a 20-inch rifle barrel. The powder charge is burned completely in the 4.5-inch barrel, and the peak pressure is achieved in the first couple of inches of bullet travel. It is also true that a .22 LR barrel that is 24-26 inches in length often gives a velocity that is lower than one that measures 16-18 inches in length.

Firing a cartridge in a firearm generates the same pressure in all directions. The pressure backward on the case head is the same as the pressure outward and on the base of the bullet. In a semiautomatic firearm like the Ruger 10/22, this generates an impulse on the face of the bolt as the cartridge case pushes backward on it. However, the bolt is held in its forward position by the recoil spring, and the bolt weighs a lot more than the bullet. Therefore, the bolt moves backward very slowly compared to the bullet, but the same gas pressure that moves the bullet moves the bolt.

In semiautomatic firearms, the basic problem is how to design the piece so that the bolt moves in such a way that it can withdraw the empty case and move to the rear without moving too vigorously and causing damage to the firearm when the bolt hits the back of the receiver. Actually, in the Ruger 10/22 the bolt moves backward until it makes contact with the recoil buffer. If the motion of the bolt is too slow and does not compress the recoil spring sufficiently, it will return to its forward position without ejecting the empty case or picking up a loaded round from the magazine or both. If bolt flies to the rear with too much velocity, damage to the firearm will result. In conjunction with

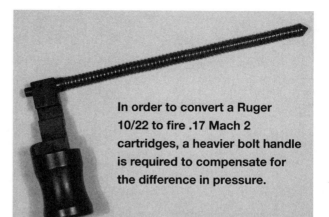

In order to convert a Ruger 10/22 to fire .17 Mach 2 cartridges, a heavier bolt handle is required to compensate for the difference in pressure.

these problems is the fact that the pressure within the chamber must have dropped to some low level before the bolt opens in order to avoid sending gas at high pressure and unburned powder grains out of the action.

It is these considerations that makes it impractical to simply change the barrel on a Ruger 10/22 chambered for the .22 LR to convert it into a .17 Mach 2. The smaller bore of the .17 caliber does not allow the gas to expand as rapidly so the pressure remains higher until the bullet is considerably farther down the bore. Also, the larger charge of slower burning powder that results in a longer push on the bullet and gives high velocity causes the pressure to remain high longer than it does with a .22 LR cartridge. To correct for these forces, the bolt should be heavier (which is usually accomplished by utilizing a heavier bolt handle) and the recoil spring stronger than those used in the 10/22 chambered for .22 LR. The suppliers of aftermarket barrels in .17 Mach 2 caliber for the Ruger 10/22 also include a heavier bolt (larger bolt handle) and a recoil spring as part of the kit. DO NOT CHANGE THE BARREL ON A RUGER 10/22 FOR ONE IN .17 MACH 2 WITHOUT ALSO MAKING THE OTHER CHANGES!

Figure 3.1 The qualitative relationship between the pressure and the distance the bullet has traveled in a 20-inch barrel.

As a result of the design requirements for semiautomatic firearms, care must be taken to match components correctly. If the bolt is too light or the recoil spring too weak, the bolt cycles with a velocity that causes damage. It is recommended that when a Ruger 10/22 is converted to .17 Mach 2, a steel recoil buffer should be used. Although the polymer types are popular and cushion the blow of the bolt when shooting .22 LR, they are not recommended when shooting the .17 Mach 2 cartridges. Also, replacement bolt buffers made for .22 WMR and .17 HMR should not be made of polymer alone.

We have already described how pressure within a rifle varies as the bullet moves down the barrel. The relationship can be illustrated as shown in the accompanying figure (Figure 3.1). Before the bullet leaves the mouth of the case, there must be enough pressure to overcome the crimp that holds the bullet in the case. The pressure rises rapidly to a maximum and then decreases as the powder charge (which is very small in a .22 LR cartridge) is consumed.

A firearm is a very inefficient machine. If one determines the heat content stored in the propellant and compares that to the kinetic energy of the bullet, it will be seen that only relatively small percent of the potential energy of the powder gets transferred to the bullet. Much of it is lost as heat transferred to the firearm, heat transferred to the bullet, kinetic energy of the gaseous decomposition products, and energy used to overcome friction as the bullet passes through the barrel.

The amount of work done by a force applied to an object is expressed as the magnitude of the force multiplied by the distance that force operates. For example, if a 200 lb object is raised to a height of 2 feet, the work done in lifting the object is

$$\text{Work} = \text{Force} \times \text{Distance}$$
$$\text{Work} = 2 \text{ ft} \times 200 \text{ lb} = 400 \text{ ft lb}$$

If a .22 LR cartridge generates 140 ft lbs of kinetic energy at the muzzle of a barrel that is 24 inches (2 feet) in length, the work done on the bullet (which is the amount of kinetic energy the bullet has) must equal 140 ft lbs. Since we know the amount of work and the distance that the force operates, we can calculate the average net force on the bullet. In this case, two of the three quantities in the equation are known so we can calculate the third.

$$\text{Work} = \text{Force} \times \text{Distance}$$
$$140 \text{ ft lbs} = \text{Force} \times 2 \text{ feet}$$

Therefore, solving for the force we find that

$$\text{Force} = \frac{140 \text{ ft lbs}}{2 \text{ feet}} = 70 \text{ lb}$$

In other words, the bullet exits the muzzle with an energy that is equivalent to a force of only 70 lbs being applied to the base of the bullet over a distance of 2 feet.

Pressure is defined as the force per unit

area and is expressed as pounds (force) per square inch (area). This can be expressed in the form of the equation

$$\text{Pressure} = \frac{\text{Force (lbs)}}{\text{Area (in}^2)}$$

Pressure is represented as lb/in² or psi. Since we know that the area of a circle is given as Area = πr^2 (where π=3.1416 and r is the radius), we can determine the area of the base of the bullet. A .22 LR bullet has a nominal diameter of about 0.224 inch so the radius is one half that value or 0.112 inch. Therefore, the area of the base (A) is given by

$$A = \pi r^2 = 3.1416 \times (0.112 \text{ in})^2 = 0.0394 \text{ in}^2$$

Earlier, we calculated the *average* net force on the bullet to be 70 lbs. Since pressure is related to area by means of the equation given above,

$$\text{Pressure} = \frac{70 \text{ lb}}{0.0394 \text{ in}^2} = 1,777 \text{ lb/in}^2$$

Therefore, even though the maximum pressure may be as high as 22,000 lb/in2 for a .22 LR, the average net pressure is much lower. The reason for this huge difference is that the maximum pressure is maintained only for an instant and both before and after that the pressure is much lower. By the time the bullet reaches the muzzle, the pressure has dropped so low that it probably does not even supply enough force to equal that caused by friction on the bullet. In fact, after a .22 LR bullet has traveled about 16 inches down the barrel, the maximum velocity has been reached. It is not uncommon to find, all other things being equal, that a longer barrel actually gives a slightly lower velocity than one that is shorter. Dimensions of the chamber and bore as well as smoothness of the bore have some bearing on this situation.

External Ballistics

Having discussed some of the principles involved in getting the bullet to the muzzle, we now turn our attention to the flight of the bullet. The basic principles are not difficult to understand, but expressing these factors in precise mathematical terms is a very complex problem indeed. Consequently, we will be satisfied with presenting the principles in a general way rather than mathematically.

After leaving the muzzle, a bullet has its velocity reduced by the resistance caused by its passing through air. The ability of bullets to pass through air is expressed by a number known as the ballistic coefficient. The higher the ballistic coefficient, the less the loss of velocity. Bullets differ significantly in the value of their ballistic coefficients. For example, a sharp pointed bullet (a spitzer) like those used in centerfire rifles might have a ballistic coefficient of 0.300-0.500, but the rather blunt projectiles used in .22 LR cartridges have ballistic coefficients in the 0.120-0.150 range. The short, stubby bullets used in the .22 Short have ballistic

Even though they are both rimfire cartridges, the ballistic coefficient of the bullet in the .22 Short (left) is considerably lower than that used in the .22 LR (right).

Both the .17 Mach 2 (left) and .17 HMR (right) use polymer tipped bullets having the same ballistic coefficient.

coefficients of approximately 0.100-0.105. The 17-grain polymer tipped bullets used in the .17 HMR and .17 Mach 2 have a ballistic coefficient of 0.125.

If two bullets exit from the muzzle of a rifle at the same velocity, the one with the higher ballistic coefficient will be traveling faster after both have traveled a specific distance. Consider two .22 LR bullets that have ballistic coefficients of 0.110 and 0.130 that both have a muzzle velocity of 1200 ft/sec. By the time the bullets have traveled 100 yards, the remaining velocities will be 957 and 982 ft/sec, respectively. This is not a great difference, but it does illustrate the importance of the ballistic coefficient being as high as possible. If we consider two .30 caliber 150 grain bullets having ballistic coefficients of 0.250 and 0.350 with both having a muzzle velocity of 2500 ft/sec, after the bullets have traveled 100 yards, their velocities will be 2,166 and 2,259 ft/sec, respectively. In this case, the difference is substantial, and if the range were 200 yards, the velocities would be 1,859 and 2,031 ft/sec. We see that the ballistic coefficient has a greater effect the longer the range. Consequently, for shooting at

long ranges, bullets having high ballistic coefficients will retain more of the energy that they have initially.

Because rimfire rifles are normally used at comparatively short ranges, a small difference in ballistic coefficient will have little effect on the remaining velocity and energy. Rimfire shooters can simply pick the bullet style they want to use and not worry much about whether it has a ballistic coefficient that is as high as some other type of bullet. However, the hyper velocity loads have lightweight bullets that have low ballistic coefficients. As a result, they lose their velocity more rapidly than do those of normal weight. A bullet from a hyper velocity cartridge may produce as much as 25-30% more energy than a typical high velocity .22 LR round at the muzzle. However, at 100 yards, the two bullets will have approximately the same remaining energy. This is the result of the stubby, lightweight bullet used in hyper velocity loads having a significantly lower ballistic coefficient.

The ballistic coefficient of a bullet depends on its diameter, weight, and shape. Bullets with flat noses are less

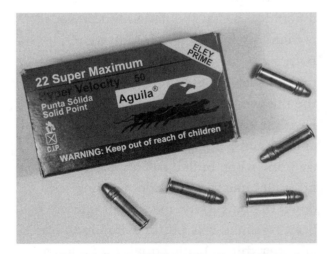

The Aguila .22 Super Maximum has an advertised muzzle velocity of 1750 ft/sec, but the short, lightweight bullets lose velocity quickly.

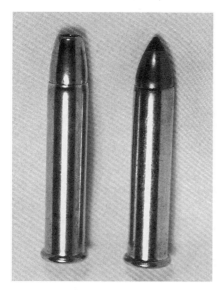

The bullets loaded in these .22 WMR cartridges do not differ much in weight, but the one on the right has a much higher ballistic coefficient.

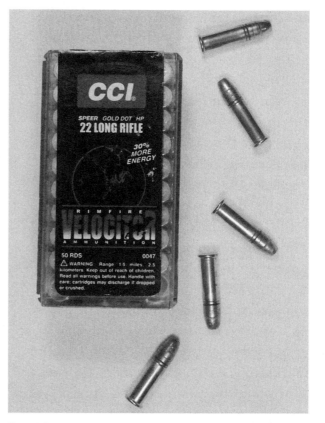

The CCI Velocitor utilizes a 40-grain hollow point bullet that holds its velocity well at longer ranges.

efficient at penetrating air than are those with round points that are in turn less efficient than those with sharp points (known as spitzers). However, as long as the velocity is comparatively low (as is the case with the .22 LR), the difference is not great. However, the .17 HMR has a muzzle velocity of 2550 ft/sec with a 17-grain bullet. With the velocity being this high, there would be a considerable difference in ability to penetrate air if the bullet had a round nose. That is one reason why the .17 HMR uses the polymer tipped bullets that have very sharp points.

Because the .22 LR has a muzzle velocity of only about 1100-1200 ft/sec with most bullets, the trajectory is quite curved. This essentially makes these cartridges suitable for use at relatively short ranges. However, the knowledgeable rimfire shooter sights in his or her rifle to make best use of the load. Since rimfire rifles are normally used on small targets, the shooter does not want to have much more than about an inch or so difference between the path of the bullet and the line of sight. A .22 LR can be sighted in at 100 yards (as in the case of outdoor competitive shooting), but the bullet will rise about four inches above the

line of sight at 50 yards. This would be unacceptable to the small game hunter.

The accompanying figure (Figure 3.2) shows the trajectory of bullets from a standard velocity .22 LR (muzzle velocity of 1100 ft/sec) and a CCI Velocitor (muzzle velocity of 1435 ft/sec) in relationship to

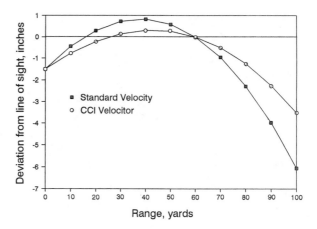

Figure 3.2 Trajectories of Standard Velocity and CCI Velocitor .22 LR sighted in at 60 Yards

the line of sight. In each case, the rifle is assumed to have a line of sight that is 1.5 inches above the bore and the rifle is sighted in at 60 yards.

From the figure, it can be seen that the trajectory of the Velocitor has less curvature than the standard velocity bullet, not because of having a higher ballistic coefficient but because of having higher velocity. Note also that in order to sight in a rifle firing standard velocity cartridges at 60 yards, the path of the bullet is almost an inch above the line of sight at 40 yards. This is not enough difference to cause misses on small game or pests so it represents a very practical sight adjustment for the .22 LR when shooting standard velocity ammunition. Note also that when the rifle is sighted in at 60 yards with Velocitors, the path of the bullet is less than one-half inch high at 40 yards.

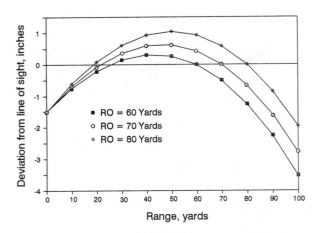

Figure 3.3 Trajectories of CCI Velocitors sighted in at 60, 70 and 80 Yards

The trajectory of the Velocitor is flat enough that it can be sighted in at a longer range and still not have the path of the bullet deviate more than one inch from the line of sight.

The accompanying figure (Figure 3.3) shows the trajectory of the Velocitor when it is sighted in at 60, 70, and 80 yards.

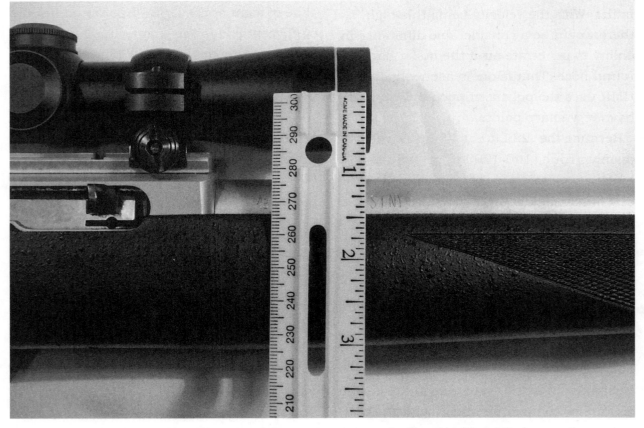

Most rifles with scopes have about a 1.5-inch difference between the line of sight and the bore.

In this figure, the vertical axis has an expanded scale so that the distance of the bullet path from the line of sight can be determined more accurately. Note that the path of the bullet is never more than about 0.3 inch above the line of sight when the rifle is sighted in at 60 yards and only about one inch above the line of sight when it is sighted in at 80 yards. When sighted in at 80 yards, the bullet will strike about two inches low at a range of 100 yards. This makes a .22 LR a reasonably effective pest rifle out to about 100 yards when Velocitors are used. Moreover, the remaining energy is about 110 ft lbs at that distance which is about 20% higher than that of other .22 LR loads. Even though some of the hyper velocity loads have greater energy at the muzzle, the lightweight bullets lose velocity more rapidly. As a result, the hyper velocity loads have lower energy than the Velocitors at longer ranges. An additional advantage is that unlike CCI Stingers, the Velocitor uses a standard length case and can therefore be used in match-type chambers.

From the discussion given above, it is clear that the small game and varmint hunter who uses a .22 LR should determine the accuracy of CCI Velocitor loads in his or her rifle. This is the most effective .22 LR load available if they are accurate enough. We have found that they give good accuracy in some rifles, but it seems that almost no rimfire rifle gives outstanding accuracy with all types of ammunition.

If the rimfire shooter is using a .22 WMR, the trajectory will be much flatter than it is for a .22 LR. A 40-grain bullet used in a .22 LR cartridge has about the same ballistic coefficient as a 40-grain bullet used in a .22 WMR. The difference is that a bullet fired from the .22 WMR has a velocity that is about 50% higher than a high velocity .22 LR bullet. Therefore, it is possible to sight in a rifle firing the .22 WMR at a distance of 100 yards and still have the path of the bullet no more than an inch or so above the line of sight at any intermediate distance. With the .17 Mach 2, the trajectory is similar to that of the .22 WMR. Because of its high velocity, a .17 HMR can be sighted in at 125 yards or perhaps slightly farther and still have the bullet path no more than an inch above the line of sight.

The rimfire shooter who wants to use his or her rifle to best advantage will spend some time determining the accuracy of several types of ammunition. Having done that, the rifle will then be sighted to take the best advantage of the trajectory of the load. One does not have to study a lot of mathematics to use a rimfire effectively, but understanding trajectory is essential.

Concentricity

When a bullet is inserted in a cartridge case, it is possible for the bullet to be held in such a way that the axis of the bullet is in line with the axis of the case. If the axes coincide, the bullet and case are said to be concentric. However, it may

Note how much the bullet is tipped in this .22 WMR cartridge that was removed from the box in this condition.

happen that the axis of the bullet is tipped slightly with respect to the axis of the case. If this condition exists, the cartridge has some lack of concentricity. The amount by which the bullet is tipped is called the run out, and it is measured in thousandths of an inch. A special gauge is used to determine the amount of run out. Typical values range from 0.000 inches for a cartridge with concentricity to as much as 0.005 inches or 0.006 inches.

Studies have shown that when the run out is measured for a large number of cartridges there is a correlation between accuracy and the amount of run out. For example, when a group of cartridges having no run out are fired, the group is smaller than when cartridges having a run out of 0.005 inches (a relatively large amount) are fired. In one interesting study using Eley Tenex ammunition, Frank Tirrell grouped cartridges having run out values of 0.000, 0.001, 0.002, 0.003, 0.004, and 0.005 inches then fired 25 rounds of ammunition having each degree of run out (*Small Caliber News*, Vol. 8, No. 2, Summer 2005, pp. 51-53). The group sizes given by the 25 cartridges in each category increased regularly as the amount of run out increased.

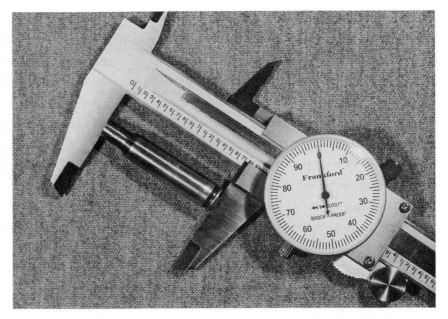

Rim thickness can be determined by first measuring the length of a cartridge case that will accommodate a .22 LR cartridge in the mouth and setting the dial to read zero can measure rim thickness.

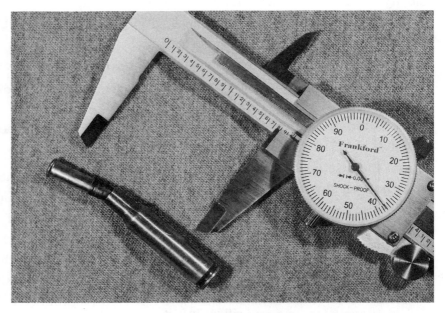

After inserting the .22 LR cartridge in the empty case, measuring the length again gives the thickness of the rim.

When a .22 LR rimfire cartridge is placed in a chamber, the bullet generally remains pointed out of the case in the same way it was before being chambered. This would certainly be the case if the rifle is one in which the chamber tends toward having maximum dimensions. If the bullet is tipped slightly when it is fired, it enters the bore slightly tipped and may move down the barrel without the axis of the bullet being perfectly aligned with the bore. This can happen because the bullets used in .22 LR cartridges are soft and are easily deformed to fit in the bore.

If the rifle has a match type chamber, which has relatively small dimensions, the bullet may become straightened slightly in the case thus reducing the amount of run out. This may certainly be the case if the rifling extends back to the mouth of the chamber. If this should occur, a series of cartridges may exhibit better accuracy than they would when fired in a chamber of somewhat more generous dimensions. Holding the cartridges in a chamber of smaller dimensions generally improves accuracy. This is one reason why many high quality barrels give good accuracy even with inexpensive ammunition that is made to rather loose tolerances. Most of the barrels tested in this project (see Chapter 11) are of this type.

While most rimfire shooters will not buy an expensive gauge to measure the run out of their ammunition, shooters who compete in matches where 0.01 inch in group size makes a difference might. The average shooter who is serious about the sport should at least be aware that concentricity in ammunition is an important consideration.

Although we are unaware of studies conducted in which the accuracy of .22 WMR, .17 HMR, .17 Aguila, and .17 Mach 2 ammunition has been determined as a function of run out, there is no question that concentricity is important. In fact, concentricity is routinely measured by benchrest shooters who compete using centerfire rifles.

Rim Thickness

In Chapter 2, we discussed headspace in regard to rimfire cartridges. The bolt face of a rimfire firearm has a recess in which the head of the cartridge resides. The clearance between the face of the recess and the rear end of the chamber is the headspace in the rifle. This distance must be adequate to allow the rim of the cartridge to be in contact with the rear end of the chamber and yet not be pressed too tightly against the back face of the recess. For the .22 LR, the correct headspace is approximately

Two budget priced types of ammunition used in studying the effect of rim thickness are the American Eagle and Remington Thunderbolt.

0.043-0.046 inches because the rim thickness of most .22 LR cartridges varies from about 0.038 inches to 0.042 inches.

As part of a testing program carried out to determine the uniformity of many types of ammunition, we measured the rim thickness of the first 20 cartridges out of the boxes. The results of those measurements are shown in the accompanying table.

Rim Thickness for 24 Types of 22 LR Ammunition. Entries Indicate the Number of Cartridges Having That Thickness Out of a Sample of 20 Cartridges of Each Type.						
Ammunition type	Rim thickness, inches					
	0.037	0.038	0.039	0.040	0.041	0.042
CCI Blazer	0	0	0	0	13	7
CCI Green Tag	0	0	0	1	19	0
CCI Mini Mag	0	0	0	3	17	0
CCI SGB	0	0	0	0	1	19
CCI Standard Velocity	0	0	0	14	6	0
CCI Velocitor	0	0	0	6	14	0
Eley Match	0	0	0	0	14	6
Eley Silhouex	4	9	7	0	0	0
Eley Tenex	0	0	11	9	0	0
Federal Champion	0	0	2	8	10	0
Federal Gold Medal Target	0	0	0	2	18	0
Federal Ultra Match	0	0	0	0	0	20
Lapua Scoremax	0	0	0	17	3	0
Lapua Super Club	0	0	0	9	11	0
PMC Scoremaster	0	0	0	12	7	1
Remington Cyclone	3	8	9	0	0	0
Remington Golden Bullet	0	1	7	9	3	0
Remington Match Xtra Plus	0	0	11	9	0	0
Remington Thunderbolt	0	4	9	7	0	0
Remington Target	4	5	8	3	0	0
Remington/Eley Club Xtra	0	16	4	0	0	0
Remington/Eley Target	0	11	9	0	0	0
RWS Target Rifle	0	0	4	15	1	0
SK Jagd Standard Plus	0	0	0	5	15	0
Winchester Power Point	5	10	4	1	0	0
Winchester Supreme	0	0	0	3	17	0
Winchester T22	5	15	0	0	0	0
Wolf Match Target	0	10	7	3	0	0

In order to determine the effect of rim thickness, the superbly accurate CZ 452 (left) and Ruger 10/22 Target (right) were used.

Several factors are immediately obvious. First, the 20 cartridges of Federal Ultra Match all had a rim thickness of 0.042 inches. Ammunition cannot get any more uniform than this, and there is a reason why this superb product has a reputation for outstanding accuracy. Second, there are several types of ammunition (e.g. CCI Green Tag, CCI SGB, Lapua Scoremax, Lapua Super Club, Remington Match Xtra Plus, Winchester Supreme, etc.) for which all 20 of the cartridges in the sample differed by no more than 0.001 inch in thickness. Eley Tenex, Remington/Eley Target, SK Jagd Standard Plus, and Eley Match cartridges also had rims that were this uniform in thickness. As will be seen later, these are types that are noted for delivering excellent accuracy. On the other hand, several types of cartridges had rim thickness that varied by 0.002-0.003 inch. These include Federal Champion, Remington Cyclone, and Remington Thunderbolt, types that are known as promotional or "price leader" ammunition. Obviously, one cannot expect ammunition that sells for $1 per box to be as well made as that which sells for about $12 per box.

Does rim thickness matter? When you consider that the headspace in most .22 LR rifles is about 0.043-0.046 inch, it stands to reason that a cartridge that has a rim thickness of 0.037 inch has a considerable amount of free space in which to move. This can result in ignition that is not optimal or as uniform as if the cartridge had a rim thickness of 0.042 inch, which more closely matches the headspace. There is no question that rim thickness is important, but it may be that uniformity in rim thickness is more important than whether the thickness closely matches the headspace, particularly

in the case of autoloading rifles like the Ruger 10/22.

In order to assess the effect of rim thickness on accuracy, we performed the following experiment. Bricks of 500 Remington Thunderbolt and Federal American Eagle cartridges were obtained and the rim thickness was measured for all of the 500 rounds of each type. The results of those measurements were as follows:

Rim Thickness, inches	Number of Cartridges	
	Remington Thunderbolt	Federal American Eagle
0.038	55	0
0.039	159	0
0.040	169	25
0.041	90	219
0.042	27	223
0.043	0	33
	Total 500	Total 500

After segregating the cartridges according to rim thickness, they were fired in two rifles of known accuracy. These were a CZ 452 American bolt action and a Ruger 10/22 Target. Both of these rifles have given average group sizes as small as one-half inch or smaller with target ammunition. Five 5-shot groups were fired using cartridges having the same rim thickness and also with cartridges having random rim thickness. However, because the rims of the American Eagle cartridges were fairly uniform, there were only two thicknesses that could be tested, 0.041 and 0.042 inches. With there being only 25 cartridges having a rim thickness of 0.040 inches and some of them being required to make up the sample of cartridges having random rim thickness, we were able to obtain only four groups using only one rifle.

When fired in the CZ 452, Remington Thunderbolts gave average group sizes that varied with rim thickness as follows (rim thickness/average group size): 0.038 inch/0.84 inch; 0.039 inch/0.83 inch; 0.040 inch/0.67 inch; 0.041 inch/0.68 inch; 0.042 inch/1.04 inch. The unsorted cartridges gave an average group size of 1.76 inches. It is clear that when the rim thickness is uniform, accuracy improves. It is also clear that the best accuracy was obtained not only when the rim thickness was uniform, but also when it measures 0.040 inch. The CZ 452 definitely seems to prefer cartridges (at least the Remington Thunderbolt) that are sorted, and we could say that it appears that a rim thickness of 0.040 inch is the optimum value. Note that an average group size of only 0.67 inch comes close to what this rifle gives with some types of target ammunition. Incidentally, the Ruger 10/22 Target also gave its smallest average group size with the cartridges having a rim thickness of 0.040 inch, and the improvement was about 0.27 inch, which is about the same as with the CZ 452.

Results obtained with the Federal American Eagle are less conclusive. First, there were not enough cartridges for a complete set of groups to be fired except with those having rims measuring 0.041 inch and 0.042 inch. With these cartridges fired in the CZ 452, average group sizes obtained were as follows (rim thickness/ average group size): 0.040 inch/0.58 inch; 0.041 inch/0.79 inch; 0.042 inch/0.81 inch. However, the unsorted cartridges gave an average group size of only 0.76 inch so it is not clear that much improvement in accuracy results from

sorting. One of the reasons is that the American Eagle cartridges showed much less variation in rim thickness compared to the Remington Thunderbolt. This was also observed with the Ruger 10/22 Target, which gave group sizes that varied from 0.65 inch for cartridges having a rim thickness of 0.042 inch to 0.87 inch for the unsorted cartridges.

Is sorting cartridges by rim thickness worth the effort? If you are using a high quality target load, the answer is clearly that it is not worth it. Cartridges of most of those types of ammunition have rim thicknesses that are uniform enough that sorting will accomplish nothing. However, if you are using an inexpensive load, you may see some improvement in accuracy by using cartridges that have been sorted. Out results indicate this is the case with Remington Thunderbolt (the cartridges of which have considerable variation in rim thickness) but not necessarily so with Federal American Eagle. It depends on which inexpensive ammunition you are using. When trying to get the best accuracy with a particular promotional type of ammunition, it may be worth measuring the rim thickness for a sample of cartridges to see how uniform they are. If they show considerable variation, you may get better accuracy if you sort the cartridges and fire those having the same rim thickness together. Keep in mind that the experiment described above involved only two rifles and two types of ammunition. Only by testing will you know how your rifle will respond to cartridges sorted by rim thickness.

Matching Ammunition to the Rifle

Most shooters who customize a Ruger 10/22 will likely make selections of aftermarket items based on anticipated improvements in performance. Certainly in almost all cases there will be such improvements. Suppose you have already decided that your 10/22 must wear a barrel made by Acme Barrel Company, a stock produced by Apex Stock Makers, and a trigger from Terrific Trigger Specialties (all fictional names of course). Now comes a most important part of your experimentation.

Suppose you take your 10/22 with its premium parts and a box of Super Pest Poppers and head for the range. After getting the scope regulated so that the shots hit near the point of aim, you begin to shoot five shot groups at 50 yards. Lo and behold your first group measures 1.25 inches, which is very little better than the factory rifle produced! You repeat the process and get a group that

measures 1.06 inches. The third measures 1.32 inches. Needless to say, you are discouraged! Has building a tricked out 10/22 been a waste of time and money?

Before you go any farther, check to see that all screws are tight and that nothing obvious is wrong. Assuming that this check of the equipment reveals no abnormalities, try a different type of ammunition. If you look at the accuracy results shown in Chapter 11, you will see that some barrels, even very fine ones, give greatly different accuracy with different types of ammunition. What you need to do is to determine to what extent the group sizes you found are dependent on the type of ammunition. The first thing to do is to obtain a few boxes of ammunition of the types that are known for delivering fine accuracy. We have found that Wolf Match Target, SK Jagd Standard Plus,

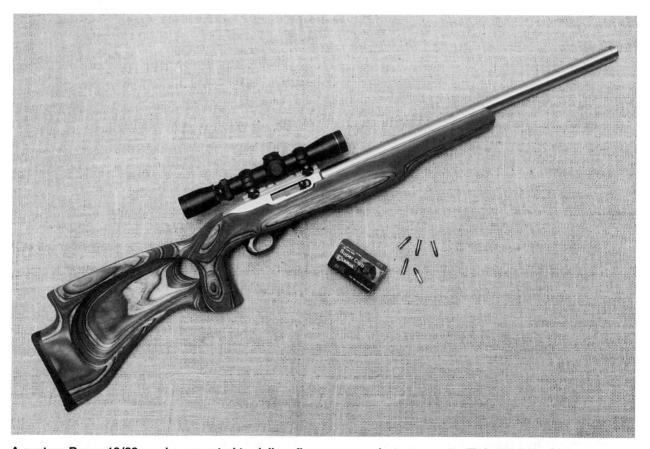

A custom Ruger 10/22 can be expected to deliver fine accuracy, but you must still determine which ammunition to use.

Eley Match, Remington/Eley Target, and Lapua Super Club (among others) generally perform well. In some barrels, CCI Standard Velocity, CCI Green Tag, Winchester T22, and Remington Game Loads give good accuracy.

Suppose you have several types of ammunition to test. First, fire a couple of five-shot groups with one of the types being careful with the rest, sight picture, breathing, and trigger squeeze. Measure the groups and record the sizes for future reference. Almost always, any of the types of ammunition mentioned performs better than Super Pest Poppers, at least they do in all of the rifles we have tested. Now carefully run a patch through the bore and try another type of ammunition using the same procedure. How do the groups compare in size to those obtained with the other type of ammunition.? Perform this preliminary set of tests with the other types. Now, take an objective look at the results. You should find that two or three types (let us suppose there are three) of ammunition performed significantly better than the others and much better than the Super Pest Poppers. Be careful to note things like groups that are strung out horizontally or vertically as well as groups that consist of four shots that are very close together with the fifth being rather far away. These types of signs can yield information about sources of problems.

With this preliminary work done, you are now ready to determine the accuracy

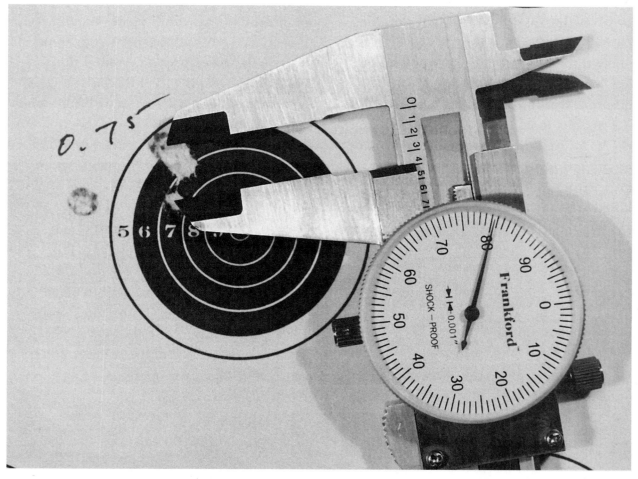

In this group, four shots form a cluster that measures 0.38 inch, but the fifth enlarged the group to 0.75 inch. Do not count one shot too heavily when determining accuracy.

of your rifle. With a clean barrel, fire a couple of fouling shots into the backstop. Now, fire five 5-shot groups with one of the types of ammunition being tested using your best technique. Make a note of any time you jerked a shot, let the forearm slip, etc. which can result in an errant shot. Carefully label the groups. Repeat the process with the other two types of ammunition being tested. Measure the groups carefully and record the data. Now, you have collected sufficient data to get some insight as to how your rifle is really performing.

Determine the average size for each set of five groups obtained with each type of cartridge, and rank them in smallest to largest order. Unless you rifle is a rare one, all of the average group sizes will be much better than those initially obtained using Super Pest Poppers. However, it is likely that one or two of the types tested will have performed better than the other(s). Before you leave this phase of the testing, look at the measurements for the individual groups. In some cases, one large group causes the average size to be larger than that obtained with another kind of ammunition. Therefore, throw out the largest group in each set and compare the results. When ranked as before, is the ranking the same? If not, take the two better performing types of ammunition and repeat the process of firing five 5-shot groups. Now compare the results from these two types while taking note as to whether one large group is skewing the

results. If you have five groups of 0.54, 0.59, 0.67, 1.08, and 0.62 inches (average 0.70 inch), the group measuring 1.08 inch is not typical of the performance of this cartridge in your rifle. Another type might give groups of 0.74, 0.66, 0.81, 0.60, and 0.70 inch (average 0.70 inch), but is only one group (the one measuring 1.08 inch) that makes the first load look worse than the second. If a type of ammunition has the potential to produce four groups that average only 0.61 inch, a fifth group that measures 1.08 inches is not the norm.

Two other factors are worth mentioning here. First, we have observed that the first group or two are frequently larger than subsequent groups with the same type of ammunition. There is a seasoning of the bore to the particular lubricants of the ammunition that takes place. Second, we have observed that accuracy from some barrels improves over a period of time as a result of a breaking in of the barrel. Best accuracy is not always obtained from a new barrel.

By the time, you have tested several types of ammunition, you will probably have found that your rifle performs very well. If you plan to use the rifle for hunting small game and pests, repeat the tests using several types of high velocity cartridges. You should find one or two types that give the excellent accuracy needed to place the shot on the target. If not, stick with the type of ammunition that gives best accuracy regardless of the velocity and place your shots with surgical precision.

Chapter 4

PERFORMANCE OF FACTORY RIFLES

Although this book is primarily concerned with techniques to improve the accuracy and performance of a Ruger 10/22, we should first consider what it is we are trying to improve. In other words, what can one expect from a factory version of the Ruger 10/22? In order to provide a backdrop against which to judge the performance of a customized 10/22, we have conducted accuracy tests with the factory versions that are currently available. In this chapter we present the results of those experiments.

The manufacturer of any product must face several constraints. First, the product should

Three of the versions of the Ruger 10/22 are the (top to bottom) 10/22 Rifle, Target, and Carbine.

perform reliably the functions for which it is designed. Second, the product should give a reasonable length of service. Third, the product must be capable of being produced at a cost that makes it attractive to the consumer. Let us take a can opener as an example. If turning the handle does not open the can, the can opener will be replaced with a different model in short order. If opening two or three cans wears out the device, some other product will occupy the drawer very soon. Finally, if the can opener is made of tungsten with platinum handles (platinum is selling for over $900 per ounce as this is written), sales will be sluggish because the can opener will cost a few thousand dollars.

For making a can opener, stainless steel would be a wonderful material. It gives long life and such a device could be sold at a reasonable price. In general, Ruger 10/22s are made of metal and wood. The receiver is an aluminum alloy, and the butt plate is made of plastic. The barrel is made of steel. In general, the parts are durable and constitute a rifle that performs satisfactorily. Although much of this book is concerned with making modifications on the Ruger 10/22 to enhance operation and performance, it should be pointed out that a Ruger 10/22 is capable of fine performance even in its factory configurations. There are always ways to improve a factory product, and the Ruger 10/22 is no exception.

To improve a factory 10/22, one might begin by replacing the stock with one of better design. Because of safety concerns, the triggers on many factory rifles are heavy and rough of pull, and the aftermarket industry in triggers is alive and well as a result of this situation. Therefore, the second item that the owner of a Ruger

10/22 might replace is part or all of the trigger assembly.

Because of cost limitations, the bores of the barrels of factory rifles are often not as smooth as desired. Removing tool marks and making sure that dimensions are controlled to within small tolerance are costly operations. Certainly the rifle maker could alleviate these conditions, but the cost of the rifle would be higher. Therefore, the owner of a Ruger 10/22 who wants top performance will probably replace the factory barrel. As will be shown throughout this book, the choice of aftermarket goods in these areas is very large.

Although this book is concerned primarily with alterations that can be made to a Ruger 10/22, a basis for comparison must be provided to assess how performance of the factory product has been affected. Therefore, in this chapter we will present the results of our testing with six versions (five in .22 LR and one .22 WMR) of the factory Ruger 10/22. We measured trigger pulls of the factory rifles using a Lyman Digital Trigger pull gauge.

Rifle shooting is about accuracy. The late Colonel Townsend Whelen has been quoted as saying, "Only accurate rifles are interesting." Although other aspects of performance are important, it is with the goal of improving accuracy that alterations to the Ruger 10/22 are most often made. The aftermarket industry has little application to reliability because that has always been one of the hallmarks of Ruger 10/22 performance. Our accuracy testing of the factory versions of the 10/22 involved firing five 5-shot groups at 50 yards from sandbags on a bench using several types of ammunition. Group size was measured as the distance between the centers of the two widest shots.

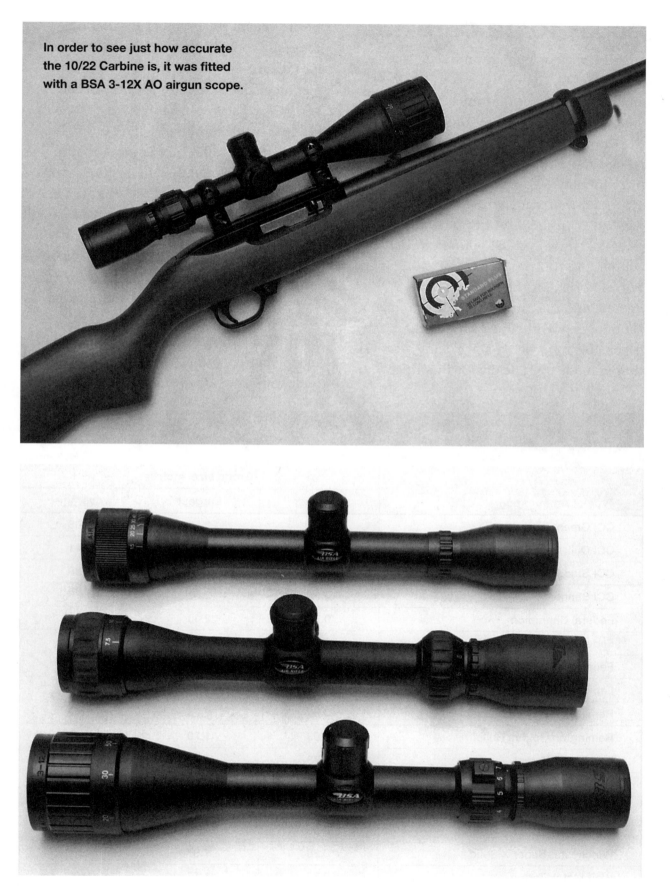

In order to see just how accurate the 10/22 Carbine is, it was fitted with a BSA 3-12X AO airgun scope.

BSA air rifle scopes work well on rimfire rifles. These AO models are (top to bottom) the 4X, 2.5-7X, and 3-12X.

Ruger 10/22 Carbine

Of the various configurations of the Ruger 10/22, the Carbine is by far the most common. With its thick, chunky stock, curved butt plate, and barrel band, the Carbine has become one of the most recognizable of American firearms. From its introduction, feeding of cartridges from its 10-round rotary magazine has been almost flawless. Our factory Carbine had a trigger pull of slightly over six pounds, which is common in this day of excessive litigation. Barrel length for the Carbine is 18.5 inches, and the barrel is fitted with a good set of open sights. The barrel band makes it possible to attach a sling using a swivel that is made specifically for this rifle.

With regard to accuracy, the 10/22 is generally considered to be above average for inexpensive .22 LR autoloaders. Our testing involved mounting a BSA 3-12X AO Air Rifle scope and firing five 5-shot groups with several types of ammunition. The results obtained are summarized in the accompanying table. Incidentally, the BSA Air Rifle scopes perform very well on rimfire rifles. To be able to withstand the jolt produced by a break action air rifle, they are built rugged, and tests such as shooting the square (see Chapter 10) show that adjustments are precise and repeatable. We have made considerable use of this scope in testing ammunition because of its magnification, but other models from BSA include the 4X AO and 2.5-7X AO models.

Accuracy of the Ruger 10/22 Carbine With BSA 3-12X AO Air Rifle Scope

Type of Ammunition	Group size, inches		
	Smallest	Largest	Average
CCI Green Tag	0.69	1.53	1.08
CCI Quik Shok	1.80	3.00	2.41
CCI Standard Velocity	0.65	1.10	0.88
CCI Stinger	0.94	2.59	1.96
Federal Champion	0.73	2.00	1.45
Federal High Velocity HP	0.95	1.94	1.31
Federal Target 711 B	0.95	2.00	1.47
Lapua Super Club	0.84	1.39	1.09
Remington Game Loads	0.92	2.06	1.42
Remington Golden Bullet	0.99	1.79	1.39
Remington Target	0.73	1.42	1.11
SK Jagd Standard Plus	0.53	0.94	0.78
Winchester Power Point	0.91	1.54	1.24
Winchester Super X HP	0.68	1.88	1.31
Winchester Super X Solid	0.90	1.67	1.18
Wolf Match Target	0.77	1.17	0.95
		Overall average	1.31

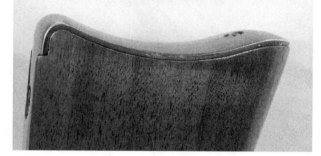

When firing the Ruger 10/22 Carbine, it sometimes difficult to prevent the slick butt plate from slipping.

The Ruger 10/22 Carbine has long been characterized as a dependable, accurate rimfire. Although an overall average group size of 1.31 inches is not stellar, it is certainly adequate for many purposes. A look at the data shows that this particular Carbine does not like CCI Quik Shok or Stinger. By a fair margin, these are the two worst performing loads of the 14 types tested. When the average group sizes for only those two types are deleted, the composite group size decreases to 1.19 inches. While one could hope for better accuracy, there are few situations in field use where an average that is one or two tenths of an inch less would make any perceptible difference. The data show that three types of standard velocity ammunition gave average group sizes of less than one inch. When highest accuracy is needed from the Ruger 10/22 Carbine, try CCI Standard Velocity, SK Jagd Standard Plus, or Wolf Match Target. You may be surprised just how well they perform in your rifle.

The slick plastic butt plate made it difficult to hold the Carbine securely against the shoulder during firing. We have solved that problem by spraying

Accuracy of the Ruger 10/22 Rifle With Simmons 3-9X AO Rimfire Scope

Type of Ammunition	Group size, inches		
	Smallest	Largest	Average
CCI Blazer	0.49	2.76	1.79
CCI Green Tag	0.49	1.00	0.83
CCI Standard Velocity	0.55	1.48	0.99
Eley Match	0.75	0.89	0.83
Federal High Velocity HP	0.81	1.51	1.11
Federal Target 711 B	0.76	1.17	0.91
Lapua Super Club	0.62	0.83	0.76
Remington/Eley Target	0.54	0.86	0.68
Remington Game Loads	0.55	1.30	1.00
Remington Target	0.89	1.90	1.37
SK Jagd Standard Plus	0.67	0.90	0.75
Winchester Power Point	1.04	1.91	1.40
Wolf Match Target	0.78	1.26	0.99
		Overall average	1.03

The Ruger 10/22 Rifle is a handsome rimfire and with the Simmons 3-9X AO scope attached it performed very well.

the butt plate with a special paint that is used around pools and hot tubs to reduce slipping. Another way to make the butt plate have better traction is to cover it with a plastic liner that is used to attach cell phones to dashboards on vehicles. These modifications are discussed in Chapter 7. Although the forearm is round, it is slick enough that it makes rock-steady holding somewhat difficult. The Ruger 10/22 was never designed with benchrest shooting as the primary activity.

Ruger 10/22 Rifle

It is not likely that a purist would consider the chunky Ruger 10/22 Carbine with its 18.5-inch barrel to be a sleek firearm. Although mechanical attributes remained unchanged, the issue of looks was addressed in 2004 with the introduction of the 10/22 Rifle. With its 20-inch barrel and slender stock without a barrel band, the Ruger 10/22 Rifle is indeed a handsome sporting rifle. Our 10/22 Rifle has a trigger let off at approximately 5.7 pounds.

Accuracy of the 10/22 Rifle was assessed with a Simmons Model 1022T 3-9X AO scope mounted. Simmons has recently made some changes in the .22 Mag scope series, but the 1022T is an outstanding optic that is described in detail in Chapter 10. The results obtained from accuracy testing are shown in the accompanying table.

In this particular 10/22 Rifle, Remington/Eley Target, Lapua Super Club, and SK Jagd Standard Plus performed extremely well with the average group sizes being only 0.76, 0.68, and 0.75 inch, respectively. When the eight types of target and standard velocity ammunition are considered, the average group size is only 0.84 inch! Accuracy at this level is comparable to some highly respected rimfire rifles that cost considerably more.

An average group size of only 1.03 inches for 13 types of ammunition is quite good for a five-pound inexpensive sporter like the 10/22 Rifle. Particularly noteworthy is the fact that eight of the 13 types of ammunition gave average group sizes that were less than one inch. Based on the performance of this 10/22 Rifle, the shooter should have no trouble selecting several types of ammunition that will deliver outstanding accuracy. The data show that this particular specimen does not like CCI Blazer, Winchester Power Point, or Remington Target loads which all give group sizes in the range 1.37-1.79 inches. In fact, the next worst performance was by the Federal High Velocity hollow points, which gave an average group size of 1.11 inches. Therefore, 10 of the 13 types of cartridges gave group sizes in the range

This outstanding scope is the Simmons 1022T 3-9X AO model for rimfire rifles.

0.68-1.11 inches, and that is outstanding. Of course, the accuracy results shown are based on testing only one 10/22 Rifle, but if this is indicative of how others perform, this version of the 10/22 in its factory configuration may perform well enough to satisfy many shooters.

Ruger 10/22 Target

The aftermarket industry associated with the Ruger 10/22 began to develop soon after the carbine version was introduced in 1964. With the stock, barrel, and trigger unit being the most often modified components, Ruger eventually decided to offer the 10/22 in a configuration that represents what many users were producing with aftermarket items. Thus, in 1996 the 10/22 Target version was introduced.

The 10/22 Target provides a factory rifle that has a heavy, hammer forged barrel, a robust semi-target style stock, and a trigger that is more user friendly than that of the Carbine. The trigger of the 10/22 Target is advertised as a "target" trigger, and while it is much better than those on the other factory versions of the 10/22, it is not a true target trigger as are some of those described in Chapter 9. Some of us could live with the trigger of the 10/22 Target very well. Although the target version sells for approximately twice the price of the Carbine, it is still lower in price than the total of a Carbine, a barrel, a stock, and a trigger. In short, the 10/22 Target goes a long way toward removing the perceived deficiencies of the 10/22 Carbine without having to interchange parts. Our factory 10/22 Target had a trigger pull of approximately 4.6 pounds with a crisp let off.

The statements above do not mean that if you buy a Ruger 10/22 Target no

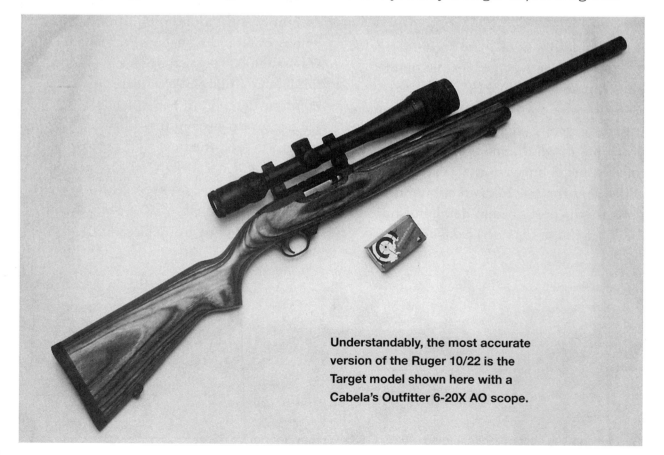

Understandably, the most accurate version of the Ruger 10/22 is the Target model shown here with a Cabela's Outfitter 6-20X AO scope.

Ruger 10/22 Target
With Cabela's 6-20X AO Outfitter Scope

Type of Ammunition	Group size, inches		
	Smallest	Largest	Average
Standard Velocity and Target Types			
CCI Green Tag	0.54	1.14	0.93
CCI Standard Velocity	0.29	0.96	0.68
DN/RWS Rifle Match	0.55	1.15	0.85
Eley Match	0.50	0.73	0.63
Federal Target (711 B)	0.77	0.92	0.84
Lapua Super Club	0.52	0.82	0.66
Remington/Eley Club Extra	0.68	0.92	0.82
Winchester Power Point	0.64	0.93	0.75
Winchester T22	0.57	1.08	0.82
Wolf Match Target	0.31	0.82	0.60
		Overall average	0.76
High and Hyper Velocity Types			
*Aguila Super Maximum HP	0.88	2.84	1.91
*Aguila Super Maximum Solid	1.34	1.89	1.64
CCI Blazer	0.70	1.23	0.93
CCI Velocitor	0.55	1.46	1.10
Federal American Eagle	0.50	1.13	0.87
Federal Champion	0.51	0.87	0.72
Federal High Velocity HP	0.69	1.32	1.13
*Federal Spitfire	1.30	2.12	1.82
Peters	0.68	0.93	0.84
Remington Game Loads	0.78	0.93	0.84
Remington Golden Bullet HP	0.56	0.98	0.74
Remington Target	0.74	1.44	1.05
Remington Thunderbolt	0.97	1.37	1.21
*Remington Viper	1.10	1.60	1.33
*Remington Yellow Jacket	2.34	3.14	2.68
Winchester Dynapoint	0.62	1.14	0.86
*Winchester Super Speed	1.17	2.05	1.56
Winchester Xpert	0.89	1.06	0.97
		Overall average	1.04

*Hyper velocity cartridges.

further improvement is possible. Later chapters of this book will show that this isn't the case. However, the 10/22 Target provides considerably better accuracy than does the Carbine. In order to determine the accuracy potential of the 10/22 Target, our testing involved firing five 5-shot groups at 50 yards with a Cabela's Outfitter 6-20X AO scope in place. Almost 16 inches long with the detachable sunshade, the Outfitter scope is an impressive sighting device. The Cabela's Outfitter series has been renamed as the Alaskan Guide Premium series and currently appear that way in Cabela's catalog. The results of that testing are shown in the accompanying table.

Although the Ruger 10/22 Target was tested with a large number of types of ammunition, it is actually a target rifle.

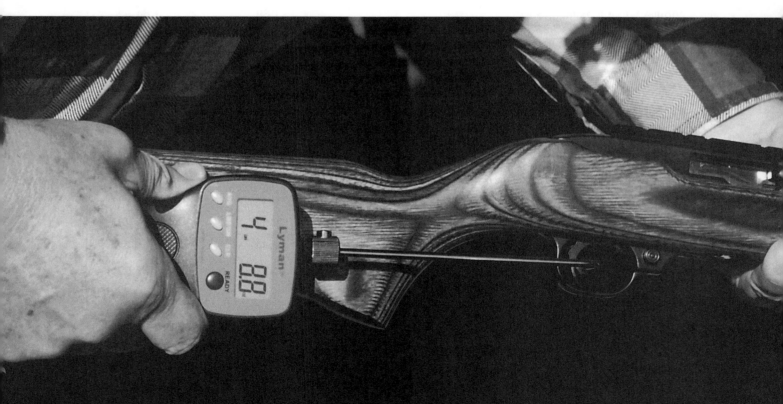

For serious accuracy testing, the Cabela's Outfitter 6-20X AO is a superb choice.

Accordingly, the accuracy given with 10 types of standard velocity and target loads was considered first. With these types, the average group size was only 0.76 inch, which compares quite favorably with the accuracy delivered by some of the fine aftermarket barrels. The outstanding performer in this rifle was SK Jagd Standard Plus, which gave an average group size of only 0.45 inch. Wolf Match Target, Eley Match, and Lapua Super Club performed extremely well.

In general, high velocity hunting loads gave group sizes of approximately an inch, but Winchester Power Point gave an

The Lyman trigger pull gauge shows that the 10/22 Target requires a pull of 4.5 pounds to fire.

average of only 0.75 inch. Both Remington Game Load and Golden Bullet hollow point also performed about this well. For a pest shooter who wants to use a Ruger 10/22 Target for this work, which requires good accuracy, there are several high velocity hollow point loads from which to choose.

We often see reviews of rimfire rifles published in various magazines. Some of the rifles are inexpensive autoloaders and some are more expensive bolt-action sporters. Very frequently, the overall group size reported for these rifles is around one inch. It is interesting that the Ruger 10/22 Target produced an overall group size that is 1.04 inch, but that is grossly misleading. As expected, the six types of ammunition that performed worst were the hyper velocity loads from Aguila, Federal, Remington, and Winchester. Although the cartridges function reliably and might be useful for some purposes, they are not known for giving outstanding accuracy, and we have not found them to give particularly good accuracy in many rifles that we have tested. If we delete data for only the hyper velocity loads from consideration, the overall group size shrinks to 0.84 inch with 18 of the remaining 22 types giving an average group size of less than one inch.

While not on a par with an expensive, highly tuned target rifle, the Ruger 10/22 is capable of giving excellent accuracy. Keep in mind that the retail price of the 10/22 Target with blue barrel is normally about $325 so it is not an expensive model. As a result, the Ruger 10/22 Target represents a high level of performance for the money. Most people who buy a 10/22 to serve as a starting point for building a custom rifle choose the Carbine, which is the least expensive 10/22. However, with judicious selection of ammunition,

the performance of the 10/22 Target in factory configuration may be adequate. In any event, starting with the Target version gives the shooter a nice laminated stock that can be used with any barrel of 0.920" diameter. During the test firing, it became apparent that the generous stock of the 10/22 Target fits sandbags very well. It is possible to achieve a very steady hold with this rifle.

The stock of the 10/22 Target is designed with a slightly raised section in the barrel channel that extends back a couple of inches from the front end. It is this section that is supposed to support the barrel. During the course of the testing of this rifle, the stock was removed. It was observed that the screw holding the front sling swivel in place had penetrated the forearm sufficiently to split the surface in the barrel channel. Even though the screw is positioned behind the raised section of the barrel channel, the bump was high enough that it was the only point making contact with the barrel. Although this did not appear to have any adverse effect on accuracy, it shows that things like this do make it out of the assembly room.

When the stock was removed, it was found that the screw that holds the front swivel had cracked the bottom of the barrel channel. The barrel was resting only on the high point.

10/22 Compact Rifle

Compact rifles are very much in vogue, and most manufacturers produce firearms of this type. Rifles (both rimfire and centerfire) are available in scaled down configurations as are shotguns. Part of the motivation for offering such products is the realization that youthful shooters and women often find some firearms unwieldy and tiring. Ruger's response to the demand for a scaled down rimfire rifle came in the form of the 10/22 Compact Rifle version. This makes sense because the Ruger 10/22 has been the most popular autoloading .22 for some years. Announced in a press release in September 2005, the 10/22 Compact version began arriving in gun shops in October of that year. The newest 10/22 is designated as the 10/22CRR.

There is no need to review the operation of the 10/22 Compact because all of the controls are identical to those of other versions of the 10/22.

There are some unique features of the Compact Rifle perhaps the most striking of which are the sights. The front sight has a red fiber optic insert running along the top of the post. It is the rear sight that is unique. Made by Williams, the sight has a "U" shaped fiber optic insert that is green. With the insert having the ends projecting on either side of the rear notch, the rear sight appears as a notch with green dots on either side. These can be aligned with the red dot provided by the insert in the front sight to achieve a good sight picture. The rear sight is fully adjustable by means of two screws. The first projects through the

The newest version of the Ruger 10/22 is the Compact Rifle, which is shown here with the outstanding Weaver 2.5-7X rimfire scope attached.

A fiber optic insert rests along the top of the front sight on the Ruger 10/22 Compact Rifle.

sight support blade, and turning it raises or lowers the rear sight to adjust elevation. Windage is adjusted by loosening a screw that locks the sight in a dovetail notch and moving the entire sight laterally. While some fiber optic sights are not particularly appealing, those on the Ruger 10/22 Compact are better than most. The 10/22 Compact Rifle that we tested had a trigger pull of approximately six pounds.

The stock of the 10/22 Compact Rifle bears a strong resemblance to that of the 10/22 Rifle except for being shorter. It is nicely shaped, and does not have a barrel band around the forward end. The butt plate is flat and checkered rather than being curved and slick like that used on the Carbine.

The old cliché that you can't tell a book by its cover applies to the 10/22 Compact Rifle. It should be remembered that accuracy is not necessarily correlated with barrel length or overall length of the gun. The Compact was evaluated just like any other rifle by mounting a scope and firing five 5-shot groups with several types of ammunition. In keeping with the size of the rifle, we mounted a compact Simmons 1022T 3-9X AO rimfire scope for testing. This outstanding scope is perfectly mated to the 10/22 Compact Rifle. The accompanying table shows the results obtained during the accuracy testing.

The Ruger 10/22 has an excellent reputation for accuracy and dependability, and the Compact Rifle exhibited these traits. During the firing that produced all of the groups, only two misfires resulted. In each case, the cartridge head was dented

Ruger 10/22 Compact Rifle With Simmons 3-9X AO Rimfire Scope

Type of Ammunition	Group size, inches		
	Smallest	**Largest**	**Average**
Eley Match	0.65	0.88	0.81
Lapua Super Club	0.99	1.31	1.12
Remington/Eley Target	0.67	1.05	0.82
Remington Game Loads	0.56	1.43	1.02
SK Jagd Standard Plus	0.71	1.17	0.84
Winchester Power Point	1.54	2.02	1.67*
Wolf Match Target	0.64	0.94	0.82
		Overall average	0.91

*This average is large because two groups that measured 1.90 and 1.41 inches had four shots in 0.84 and 0.69 inches, repectively. This value not included in computing overall average.

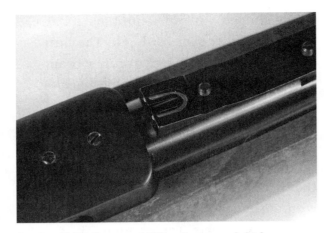

On the 10/22 Compact Rifle, the rear sight has a fiber optic insert that gives green dots on either side of the notch.

deeply, but the cartridge did not fire. This was absolutely no fault of the rifle, and functioning was perfect.

Knowing that best accuracy results when standard velocity and target rounds are used, the Ruger 10/22 Compact Rifle was tested using primarily these types. As a result, the accuracy exhibited was excellent. One surprise was the group size obtained with Lapua Super Club, which is among the most accurate in several of our

rifles. The average group size measured 1.12 inches, which was the second worst of all the types tested.

Many rimfires are expected to produce groups at 50 yards that average about 1.0-1.5 inches. We have tested some rimfires that will not deliver even that level of accuracy. The data presented in the table show clearly that our Ruger 10/22 Compact Rifle can easily give groups that average less than an inch when suitable ammunition is used. In this case, that means target type ammunition such as Eley Match, SK Jagd Standard Plus, Wolf Match Target, and Remington/Eley Target. Accuracy shown by the Compact Rifle with these cartridges is superb for this type of rifle. Even the very inexpensive high velocity Remington Game Load hollow points averaged slightly over one inch. Although the 10/22 Compact is not going to win benchrest competition, it is certainly accurate enough for informal target shooting as well as small game and pest hunting. Because bullets can

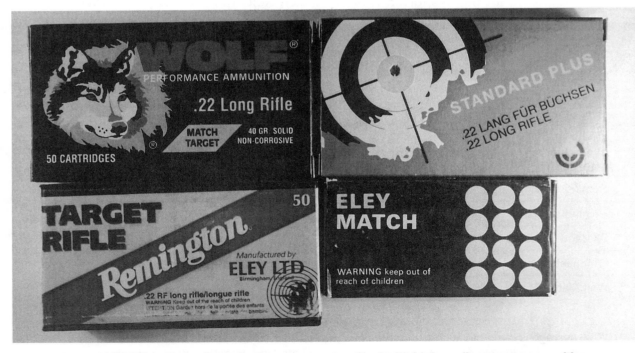

Factory Ruger 10/22 rifles showed excellent accuracy when fired with high quality target ammunition.

be placed more accurately with the target loads, there seems to be little justification for using high-velocity hollow points, which are less accurate. Bullet placement is more important than is a hundred feet per second higher velocity.

Another reason that the Ruger 10/22 Compact Rifle would be a good choice for a young shooter is that the entire range of aftermarket products can allow the rifle to grow as the shooter grows (both in stature and skill). After all, it *is* a Ruger 10/22! If a 10/22 Compact Rifle is chosen, it should be fitted with a rimfire scope of high quality. This rifle is capable of outstanding performance that can be achieved with a good scope. So equipped, the Ruger 10/22 Compact Rifle should meet any need for a rifle of this type.

Wal-Mart or Lipsey

One version of the Ruger 10/22 is described in discussion in chat rooms on the internet as the "Wal-Mart" version. Ruger produces this rifle for Lipsey, a large firearms distributor in Baton Rouge, Louisiana. Production of special runs of firearms having somewhat different characteristics is a common occurrence. For example, Smith & Wesson has produced several special runs of particular handguns for a well-known distributor. We will refer to this 10/22 as the "Wal-Mart Version" because it has no other official name.

In some ways, the Wal-Mart version of the 10/22 is a very attractive rifle. With its slender 22-inch stainless steel barrel and checkered hardwood stock with a rubber butt plate, this version appears downright sleek compared to the chunky little Carbine. To some extent, it resembles a stainless steel version of the 10/22 Deluxe

The "Wal-Mart" version of the Ruger 10/22 has a nicely shaped, functional rubber butt plate.

Sporter but with a hardwood stock and longer barrel. Our 10/22 rifle from Wal-Mart had a trigger pull of approximately 5.5 pounds with almost no creep. Sights on this version are identical to those found on the 10/22 Carbine.

The Wal-Mart rifle was put through a series of accuracy tests using 13 types of ammunition. The accompanying table shows the results when a Scheels 4-12X AO rimfire scope was mounted on the rifle. This scope provides outstanding performance on rimfire rifles, and a more complete discussion of the scope appears in Chapter 10.

The data show that the Wal-Mart version gave an overall average with all of the types of ammunition tested of 1.36

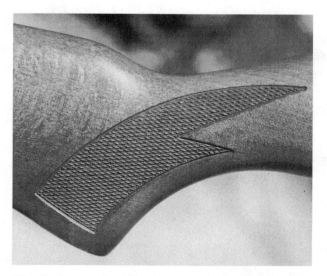

Checkering on the "Wal-Mart" version of the Ruger 10/22 is both attractive and functional.

This version of the Ruger 10/22 is not a catalog item, but it has been produced for a major distributor and is most often seen in Wal-Mart stores.

Ruger 10/22 Wal-Mart Version With Scheels 4-12X AO Rimfire Scope

Type of Ammunition	Group size, inches		
	Smallest	Largest	Average
CCI Blazer	0.72	2.19	1.41
CCI Green Tag	0.70	1.15	0.87
CCI Standard Velocity	1.05	1.69	1.45
CCI Velocitor	1.46	2.63	1.77
Federal High Velocity HP	0.59	1.86	1.24
Federal Target 711 B	1.69	3.11	2.34
Lapua Super Club	0.92	1.38	1.16
Remington Game Loads	0.96	1.41	1.06
Remington Target	0.94	1.32	1.09
SK Jagd Standard Plus	0.80	1.69	1.16
Winchester Power Point	0.92	2.57	1.65
Winchester T22	1.07	1.97	1.49
Wolf Match Target	0.58	1.19	1.00
		Overall average	1.36

inches making it the least accurate of the factory production rifles tested. This rifle particularly disliked the Federal Target 711B load that gives good accuracy in many rifles. The high velocity CCI Velocitor and Winchester Power Point loads did not fare well either. On the other hand, an average group size of 0.87 inches with CCI Green Tag is quite respectable. Whether the accuracy exhibited by our particular

A fine scope for use on a rimfire such as the Ruger 10/22 is this 4-12X AO model available from Scheels All Sports stores.

One of the elegant scopes intended for use on rimfires is this 2-7X model from Leupold, and it is unbelievably bright and sharp.

rifle is typical of this model is unknown. It would be nice to try a different specimen to determine whether this situation is characteristic of the type.

Although we did not have a second rifle of this style for testing, we performed fire lapping on this one. The special cartridges prepared by NECO were utilized. These cartridges consist of three groups that have the bullet lubricant impregnated with abrasive of three granulations (400, 800, and 1200 grit). The procedure consists of firing 10 cartridges that contain 400 and 800 grit and 20 cartridges that contain 1200 grit with thorough cleaning of the bore after each five shots. After the lapping was complete, we conducted limited accuracy tests by firing 5-shot groups as before. However, in these tests, the rifle was fitted with the superb Leupold 2.5-7X rimfire scope.

To determine whether lapping the barrel improved the accuracy, we selected a few types of ammunition that performed badly in the factory barrel. When using Federal High Velocity hollow points, the average group size was 1.13 inches, which is smaller than the average of 1.24 obtained initially. After lapping the barrel, Federal Target 711B gave groups that averaged 1.70 inches. In both cases, the groups were smaller after the barrel was fire lapped, but this particular barrel simply isn't very accurate. However, there is a noticeable difference in smoothness when cleaning the lapped barrel.

Ruger 10/22 Magnum

The Ruger 10/22M chambered for the .22 WMR is often chosen by shooters who want to hunt larger varmints with a rimfire rifle. Because of the greater stresses produced by the larger magnum cartridge, the receiver of the 10/22M is made of steel. Even with this difference, the pressure curve that results from firing the .17 HMR can lead to problems. The pressure remains higher for a longer period of time, which causes the bolt to open while the pressure is still high. Because of the difficulties that this can cause (see Chapter 12), the autoloader advertised as the 10/17 has not been marketed in spite of it appearing in both the 2004 and 2005 catalogs but not in the 2006 catalog. Therefore, the only factory produced magnum caliber available for testing is the .22 WMR.

Sightron is well known for producing high quality rifle scopes, and this 3-9X .40 model worked extremely well on the Ruger 10/22M.

Our 10/22M came with a trigger pull estimated to be about 12 pounds. Let off was crisp, but only after applying finger-breaking pressure. A few groups were fired using the CCI Maxi Mag TMJ load. The average size was in the 0.7-inch range, which is not bad considering the trigger. After gaining some experience with the rifle, the trigger was sent to Mr. Herman Tom of Hornet Products (contact information is given in Chapter 13). He performed his outstanding service at a reasonable price and reduced the trigger pull to about

four pounds with a crisp let off. With this improved trigger, testing of the Ruger 10/22M was carried out. A Sightron SII 3-9x36 AO scope was attached and sighted in. The Sightron scope is a beautiful optic that is discussed more fully in Chapter 10. It should be mentioned that the rifle used was purchased new and was tested with no break in period or tuning of any kind other than the trigger work. Groups were fired at 50 yards using several types of ammunition yielding the data shown in the accompanying table.

Ruger 10/22 Magnum With Sightron 3-9x36 AO Rimfire Scope

Type of Ammunition	Group size, inches		
	Smallest	Largest	Average
CCI Maxi Mag 40 gr. JHP	0.49	0.76	0.69
CCI Maxi Mag 40 gr. TMJ	0.48	1.04	0.73
Federal 50 gr. HP	0.61	1.01	0.89
Remington Premier 33 gr. V-max	0.69	1.53	1.08
Remington 40 gr. PSP	0.50	1.02	0.88
Winchester 40 gr. JHP	0.47	1.16	0.84
Win. Supreme 34 gr. JHP	0.93	1.35	1.14
		Overall average	0.89

The autoloading magnum rimfire offering from Ruger is the Ruger 10/22M chambered for the .22 WMR.

Although other authors have reported rather undistinguished accuracy with factory 10/22M rifles, our data show that with most of the types of ammunition tested groups of about three-quarters of an inch are the norm. Under optimum conditions with a rifle that has had a little tuning, many groups are going to be in the 0.5-0.6 inch range. It is also clear from the data shown in the table that this particular rifle does not seem to do well with cartridges that have bullets of lighter weight. Such bullets are rather short for their diameter, so they do not represent the optimum in terms of rotation with a 1:16 rate of twist. The results with the Remington Premier that uses the 33 grain V-Max bullet were somewhat surprising because that load has given very good accuracy in other .22 WMR rifles that we have tested. With any of the five best performing loads (which give an average group size of 0.81 inch), the Ruger 10/22M is going to be a very satisfactory varmint rifle when used within its range limitations.

With the Sightron 3-9X AO scope aboard, Kathy tested the Ruger 10/22M with several types of ammunition. It proved to be an excellent combination.

Chapter 5

HOW THE RUGER 10/22 WORKS

Unlike some firearms, the Ruger 10/22 is engineered in such a way that the "hobby gunsmith" can do a great of deal alteration easily. That is, in fact, the basis of the statement on the cover of this book, "no gunsmith required." Having said that, it must be emphasized that certain operations are best left to a qualified gunsmith. We do not recommend that anyone except a qualified gunsmith perform any work on the contact surfaces of the hammer and/or sear. For someone else to do so is to run the risk that the trigger could become unreliable, and that the hammer could be released inadvertently causing the rifle to fire. In this chapter, we will describe the operation and disassembly of the Ruger 10/22, and in the following chapter, we will describe some of the basic techniques that are employed when working on firearms. If you are not absolutely sure of what you are doing, don't do it!

The Ruger 10/22 is a classic in firearm design that supports a huge aftermarket industry.

Although some aftermarket trigger units having a trigger pull measured in ounces are available for the Ruger 10/22, we believe that these are specialized products that should be used only on rifles that are to be fired from a bench by experienced shooters. A trigger pull of six pounds may be excessive, but a trigger pull of eight ounces can be downright unsafe. It is simply far too easy to touch the trigger inadvertently with clothing or a twig and cause the rifle to fire if the safety is off. For general use, a trigger pull of around three or four pounds is perfectly acceptable. Do not attempt to obtain a trigger pull that is much lighter than this on any rifle that is going to be carried. For the trigger assemblies used in the testing program for this book, we obtained no trigger with a pull lighter than two pounds even knowing that the rifles would be used only in target shooting.

The Autoloading Action

Semiautomatic rifles chambered for centerfire calibers have the bolt locked in place at the time of firing. After firing takes place, the bolt is unlocked (usually by gas pressure that is allowed to drive a piston to the rear), and the action cycles. The locked breech is required because of the high pressures these firearms generate. In rimfire calibers, the action is of the "blowback" type. In this type of action, the bolt is not locked in place, and it is free to move backward as a result of pressure generated by the cartridge case on the bolt face. How rapidly the bolt moves back is controlled by the force on the bolt face, weight of the bolt, and the stiffness of the recoil spring. This type of action is satisfactory for rimfire calibers as a result of their operating at pressures that are

Cartridges feed reliably from the 10-shot rotary magazine used in the Ruger 10/22.

much lower than in the case of centerfire rifles.

The action of the Ruger 10/22 has much in common with other .22 autoloaders, but it also has some significant differences. The basic operation of any rimfire autoloader involves firing a cartridge, increased pressure causing the bolt to move at the appropriate time, and the bolt moving backward against the force supplied by the recoil spring. As the bolt moves to the rear,

As the bolt moves forward, it strips the top cartridge from the magazine.

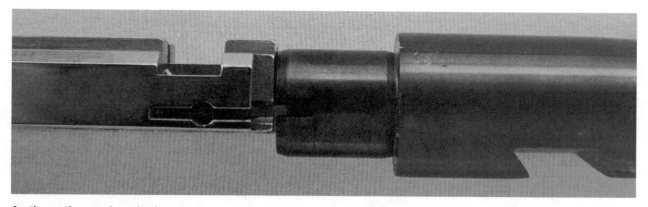

As the action cycles, the bolt face impacts on the rear end of the barrel. Note how the extractor fits in a groove in the barrel tenon.

it moves the hammer backward so that it is cocked in the process. As the bolt moves forward, a notch, step, or other retaining surface on the hammer engages the sear. A ridge along the bottom surface of the bolt is shaped so that it makes contact with the top cartridge in the magazine and pushes it forward. Therefore, as the bolt moves forward, it removes a cartridge from the magazine and pushes it into battery. All of these actions result from pulling the trigger to fire a shot. All that is required to fire subsequent shots is to pull the trigger because the rifle is "self loading."

In some rimfire autoloaders (including the Ruger 10/22) the bolt goes forward until the bolt face makes contact with the rear end of the barrel. Unless the end of the barrel is hardened, it can eventually

be damaged because the recoil spring forces the bolt forward with considerable momentum. One aspect of the 10/22 that is different from other .22 autoloaders is that the magazine holds the cartridges around a centrally located spindle. Most .22 autoloaders utilize magazines that hold cartridges in either a vertical clip that resides below the bolt or a tube that is held below the barrel.

Ruger has done an outstanding job in making numerous parts interchangeable between several models of firearms. For example, the magazines can be interchanged between the bolt action Model 77/22 and the semiauto 10/22 although the bottom surfaces have slightly different shapes (autoloaders have magazines with rounded bottom surfaces and bolt action

The magazine used in the Ruger 77/22 bolt-action has a flat bottom while that used in the 10/22 autoloader has a slightly rounded bottom.

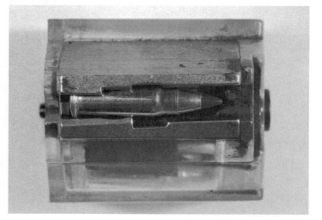

The same magazine can be used to hold .22 LR and .17 Mach 2 cartridges.

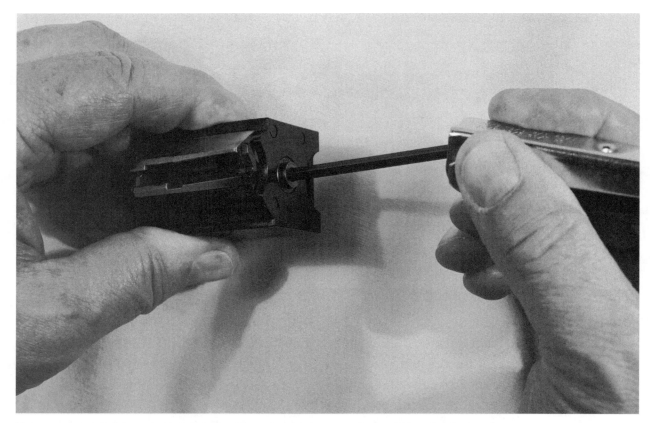

If the rotor is sticking, try inserting an Allen wrench in the spindle and loosening it slightly.

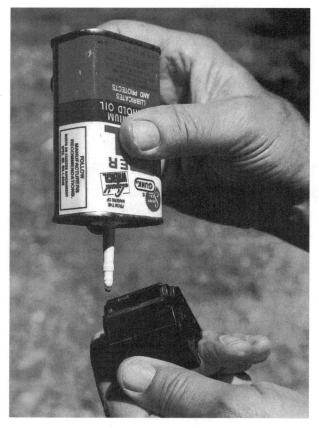

A drop of oil on the pivot points of the magazine rotor helps keep it feeding reliably.

rifles have magazines with flat bottom surfaces). The correct magazine for the 10/22 is designated as BX-1 while that for the 77/22 is designated as JX-1, but either magazine can be used in either rifle. Cartridges in .17 Mach 2 feed correctly from the .22 LR magazines. Even the lever action Model 96 in .22 WMR (the .22 LR version was discontinued in 2004) can be used with the same magazine as the 10/22M autoloader and 77/22M bolt action. The magazines utilized in .22 WMR rifles will also feed .17 HMR cartridges. Moreover, the barrels of all these models are attached to the receiver by two screws that pass through a block that fits in a mating groove that runs across the bottom of the barrel. However, the barrels are NOT directly interchangeable among all of the autoloaders, lever actions, and bolt actions because the barrel shanks or tenons are not of identical lengths.

Magazines for the Ruger rimfire rifles *can* be disassembled, but it is not advisable to do so. Getting one back together is quite difficult. However, we have found that the rotors in some magazines are so tight that they do not rotate freely. One solution is to take an Allen wrench of appropriate size and loosen the spindle nut *slightly*. We have also found that a *small* amount of lubricant helps keep the rotor moving freely.

Although the Ruger 10/22 and 10/22M are greatly different in terms of their construction, many parts are interchangeable. If you look at the parts list for these models in a catalog such as that from Brownells, you will see a table labeled as "10/22 Common Parts" which lists the parts that are used in all versions of the 10/22. Following that are a series of tables showing parts that are unique to each specific 10/22 version (the Deluxe Sporter, Carbine in its various configurations, etc.)

●●●●●●	10/22 - Common Parts			●●●●●●
#780-000-001	OB8001	Barrel, Blue	.22	8G29C54 $ 36.93
#780-000-338	K0B8001	Barrel, SS	.22	8G60H00 $ 75.00
#780-010-040	B67	Barrel Retainer Screw, Blue	.22	8G01D19 $ 1.49
#780-010-039	B66	Barrel Retainer V-Block, Blue	.22	8G03Z25 $ 4.06
#780-000-093	B10	Bolt, Blue, Stripped	.22	8G18A77 $ 23.46
#780-010-028	B42	Bolt Lock Spring, Blue	.22	8G01Y19 $ 1.49
#780-010-032	B46	Bolt Stop Pin, Blue	.22	8G01T19 $ 1.49
#780-010-041	B48A	Cocking Handle, Guide Rod & Recoil Spring Assembly	.22	8G06X69 $ 8.36
#780-010-017	B25	Disconnector	.22	8G03H56 $ 4.45
#780-012-010	KE02800	Disconnector & Trigger Pivot Pin	.22	8G01D47 $ 1.84
#780-010-016	B24	Disconnector/Sear Spring	.22	8G01Z19 $ 1.49
#780-010-044	B8	Ejector	.22	8G01A19 $ 1.49
#780-010-034	B51	Escutcheon	.22	8G01Y19 $ 1.49
#780-010-005	B14	Extractor	.22	8G01T19 $ 1.49
#780-010-007	B16	Extractor Plunger	.22	8G01P19 $ 1.49
#780-010-006	B15	Extractor Spring	.22	8G01U19 $ 1.49
#780-010-002	B11	Firing Pin	.22	8G03A11 $ 3.89
#780-000-058	A20000	Firing Pin Rebound Spring	All	4C01V19 $ 1.49
#780-000-096	B22	Firing Pin Rebound Spring Stop	.22	8G01B19 $ 1.49
#780-010-004	B13	Firing Pin Stop Pin	.22	8G01X19 $ 1.49
#780-010-029	B43	Hammer Bushing, 2 Req'd	.22	8G01C19 $ 1.49
#780-010-010	B19	Hammer Pivot Pin	.22	8G01H19 $ 1.49
#780-010-030	B44	Hammer Spring	.22	8G01D19 $ 1.49
#780-010-009	B18	Hammer Strut	.22	8G01Z46 $ 1.83
#780-010-031	B45	Hammer Strut Washer	.22	8G01A19 $ 1.49
#780-001-236	90222	Magazine, 10-Round, BX-1-40, Clear, Red Rotor	.22	8G12Y89 $ 16.11
#780-000-107	90041	Magazine, Model BX,15, 5-Round	.22	8G10T85 $ 13.56
#780-002-122	90005	Magazine, Model BX 1, 10-Round	.22	8G10P85 $ 13.56

Because of the design, many parts are interchangeable on various models of the Ruger 10/22. This is a partial list from Brownells catalog.

including the 10/22 RBM, which is the .22 WMR version. In that table of "Common Parts" there are listed the firing pin, bolt stop, hammer, barrel retaining screw, extractor, and the various springs and pins. In fact, it is surprising how many parts are interchangeable among the various 10/22 versions, including the magnum. This ability to interchange parts is, in fact, a Ruger characteristic.

Cautions

Although the Ruger 10/22 is a fine rifle, it is important to remember that the receiver is made of an aluminum alloy. Anything that fastens to the receiver by screws must not be tightened too much. This especially includes scope bases that attach by means of four rather small screws. It would not be difficult to strip the threads in the top of the receiver by applying too much torque when attaching the screws. Tighten these screws until they are snug then give them one rather short, quick turn and stop. If they work loose (we have not had any problem in this regard), coat the threads with a locking compound such as Loctite®. This material comes in various forms that provide different degrees of "sticking", and they are available from suppliers such as Brownells.

The barrel is held to the receiver by means of a steel wedge that fits in a matching groove in the bottom of the barrel. However, the wedge is drawn back to pull the barrel into the receiver by two large screws that require a 5/32 inch Allen wrench to tighten and loosen them. Although the screws and locking block are made of steel, the screws thread into the lower front section of the aluminum receiver. Consequently, these screws should be tightened *carefully* to prevent

On the Ruger 10/22, the barrel is held in place by a wedge that pulls backward as the two retaining screws are tightened.

damage to the holes in the receiver. A drop of oil on each screw before inserting it helps prevent some of the galling that sometimes occurs when steel screws are threaded into a piece of aluminum. The screws should be started carefully by turning them with the fingers to prevent cross threading which will damage the receiver. If barrels are removed and replaced carefully, no damage will occur to the receiver, but do not plan to replace barrels too often because the steel bolts do cause some wear on the threads in the aluminum receiver.

Although there is not much concern with the Ruger 10/22, some firearms have strong springs that are under a great deal of compression. For example, the strong firing pin spring of a centerfire rifle or pistol is under enough compression to launch the firing pin with enough force to cause injury. Be especially careful when disassembling and assembling a firearm in which a spring is being compressed or stretched. If the restraining force is suddenly released, something is likely to leave the work area with considerable velocity. The springs themselves are likely to become projectiles. Always wear safety glasses when performing work of this type.

Tools

Only a few simple tools are required to perform most modifications on the Ruger 10/22 when making use of aftermarket products. No specialized wrenches or other items are needed. This is partially the result of the 10/22 being held together by means of pins and screws. In contrast, one .22 autoloader of our acquaintance has the barrel attached to the receiver by a rotating collar that pulls on a threaded flange located around the barrel extension as the flange is screwed into the receiver. The flange has two slots on its face that lie on opposite sides of the barrel. A special "U"-shaped wrench having tabs on the ends is required to fit around the barrel while engaging the slots in the flange. The Ruger 10/22 has no such idiosyncrasies, and only ordinary tools are required.

To remove the barrel band, butt plate, and takedown screw, only blade or Phillips screwdrivers of appropriate sizes are required. Removal of the trigger assembly from the action requires that two pins be pushed out of their retaining holes, but this is rarely a problem since many of them fit so loosely that they often fall out when the barrel and action are removed from the stock. A 5/32-inch Allen wrench is the only tool required to remove the barrel from the

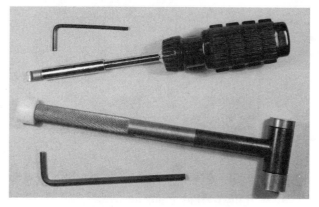

Only a few simple tools are required to do a lot of work on the Ruger 10/22.

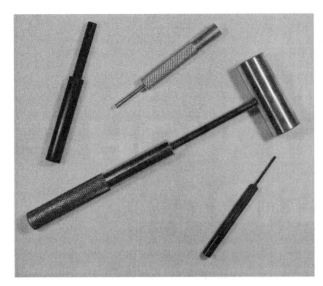

A hammer and punch set will find a lot of use in disassembling the Ruger 10/22.

action. A small gunsmiths hammer and a brass punch or two will easily remove the pins that must be taken out during disassembly of the trigger unit. Other types of work may need to be performed, and in Chapter 6 more details are presented about some of the operations that are helpful when working on firearms.

With a few simple tools, the Ruger 10/22 can be separated into its major components. However, if one wants to completely disassemble the trigger assembly, the process is somewhat more complicated owing to the necessity for keeping several parts in place at one time as a pin is inserted. Even though no special tools are required, some manual dexterity is needed.

Disassembly of Major Components

Reducing the Ruger 10/22 to its basic components of lock, stock, and barrel could hardly be simpler. That is one reason why the 10/22 is one of the most modified firearms in existence. Disassembly should always begin by making sure that the rifle is unloaded and that the magazine is removed. Assuming that you are starting with the Carbine version, the first step is removal of the barrel band. This requires

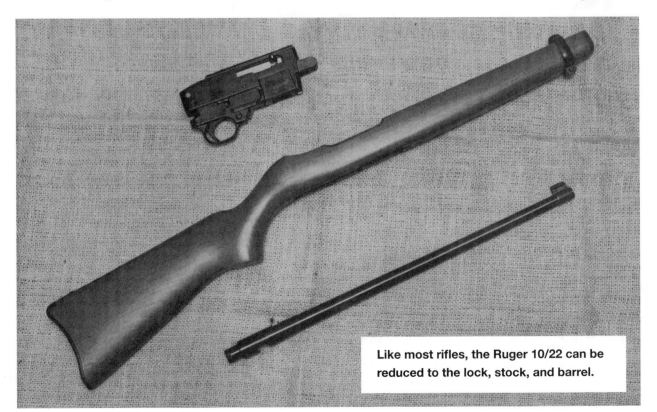

Like most rifles, the Ruger 10/22 can be reduced to the lock, stock, and barrel.

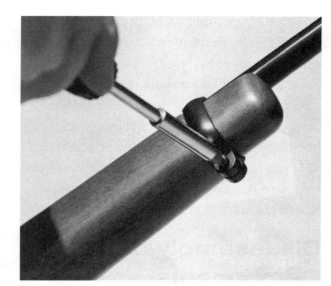

Removing the barrel band requires loosening a single screw.

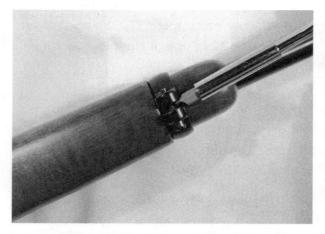

In most cases, the barrel band will not slide off easily unless it is forced open a small amount.

A single screw holds the stock to the barrel and action. Use a screwdriver that fits the slot correctly.

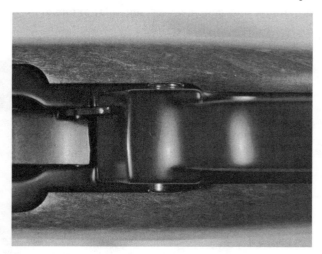

Before lifting the barrel and action out of the stock, make sure that the safety is half way between the "on" and "off" positions.

that the tensioning screw be loosened a few turns, but it is not necessary to remove it. Most of the barrel bands fit tight enough around the fore end that the band must be forced opened slightly in order for it to be slipped off the front end of the forearm. This can be done by inserting a wide blade screwdriver into the split section and turning it slightly to force the ends apart. Be careful not to scratch or mar the surfaces of the band. With the band expanded, it can be slid forward over the end of the forearm to remove it.

With the barrel band removed, only the single takedown screw located in front of the magazine well holds the stock to the barreled action. Note that the slot in the takedown screw is rather wide. Loosen this screw using a screwdriver blade that gives a good fit in the slot to avoid damaging the screw. As the screw is loosened, it becomes disengaged from the boss on the underside of the front of the action. Before removing the barrel and action from the stock, be sure that the safety is moved to the midpoint of its travel so that equal amounts protrude from each side of the trigger guard. If the safety is pushed fully to either side, it will hit the edge of the stock and cause some damage as the action is lifted out. At this point, the barrel and action can be lifted carefully from the stock. Be careful to keep the bolt stop pin and the two pins that hold the trigger assembly in place from dropping out and being lost. The takedown screw will remain in the stock because the screw is also threaded through the escutcheon bushing. If there is some reason to do so, the butt plate can be removed from the stock by using a screwdriver with a Phillips tip that matches the width of the screws.

On the Ruger 10/22, the barrel is held to the action by two screws that pull backward on a block that fits in a groove in the underside of the barrel. The screws pass through the steel block and thread into mating holes on the front edge of the action. A 5/32-inch Allen wrench is required to fit the screw heads. Although removal of the barrel from the action is a simple process, some care should be exercised because the action is made of an aluminum alloy. The screws should be loosened carefully, and great care should be exercised when replacing the barrel to make sure that the threads in the aluminum receiver are not damaged. With the two retaining screws removed, the block can be removed from the bottom of the barrel, and the barrel can

be withdrawn from the action. Although some aftermarket barrels may need some polishing to enable them to be inserted into the receiver, we have not found any factory barrel that required much force to remove it from the action. Usually the barrel does not fit tightly enough to require it to be pulled out of the receiver.

On the Ruger 10/22M, the receiver is made of steel so there is less likelihood of it being damaged by removing or tightening the barrel locking screws. Although this will be stated several times in this book, do not apply undue force when tightening the screws that hold the barrel in place on a Ruger 10/22! In the several instances in which we have removed the factory barrel for the first time, the screws have never required much torque to loosen them. The authors do not know the exact torque specification, but it certainly is not very high. After these simple steps, the Ruger 10/22 has been separated into the basic components of lock, stock, and barrel.

With the barreled action removed, the entire trigger assembly can be separated from the receiver by removing the two pins that hold it in place. In most of the Ruger

When the two retaining screws are removed, the block that locks the barrel in place can be removed and the barrel pulled out of the receiver.

The large pin indicated by the numeral 3 is the bolt stop. Pins 1 and 2 in this photo hold the trigger unit in place.

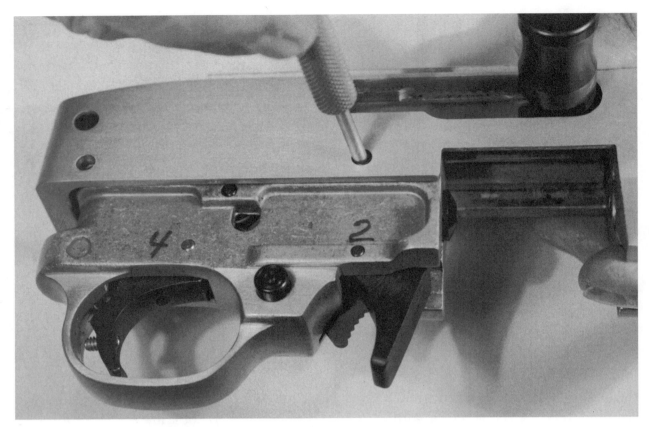

The two pins that hold the trigger unit in place can be pushed out from either side.

10/22s that we have worked on, these pins fit so loosely that they sometimes drop out simply by turning the action on its side. If they do not, take a small brass punch and apply slight pressure to move the pin out of its retaining hole. With both pins removed, the trigger assembly is free from the action. Although the retaining pins holding the trigger assembly in place may fit loosely, the action fits in the stock in such a way that the pins can not slide out because they are held in place by the inside walls of the stock.

Bolt Removal and Disassembly

The bolt assembly (consisting of the bolt, firing pin, extractor, and retaining pins and springs) of the Ruger 10/22 would ordinarily not be removed except to replace the firing pin or extractor.

However, in keeping with the purpose of this book, we present here a description of the disassembly process. It is necessary to remove the bolt stop before the bolt can be moved fully to the rear prior to lifting it out of the receiver. The bolt stop is the large pin that passes through the receiver at the upper rear area, and it can be pushed out of the receiver to either side. The bolt stop pin can be easily removed (on a couple of our rifles they fall out when the rifle is turned on its side) by pressing on one end of it with a punch.

The bolt, firing pin, and extractor are removed as a unit.

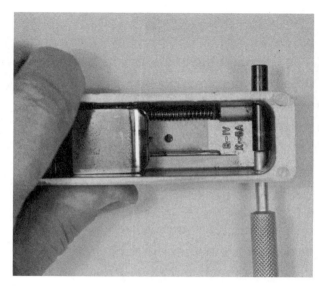

With the bolt stop removed, the bolt can be moved fully to the rear of the receiver.

Turning the rifle bottom side up with the trigger assembly removed as described above effects removal of the bolt. As you look into the inverted receiver, you will see that a rail along the side of the receiver keeps the bolt supported as it moves forward and backward during cycling of the action. In order to clear the rail, the bolt must be slid backward far enough that it can be lifted out. Pull the bolt back to the rearmost position inside the receiver. With the bolt fully to the rear, lift up (toward the bottom of the action since it is inverted) on the front end of the bolt which will disengage it from the bolt handle. With the bolt handle disengaged, the bolt can be lifted out of the receiver. The bolt handle, guide rod and recoil spring can be removed as a unit.

Under normal use, the owner of a Ruger 10/22 will have no reason to remove the firing pin and extractor from the bolt. Of course they must be removed if you wish to install an aftermarket firing pin or extractor as described in Chapter 9. The firing pin assembly consists of the pin itself, the retaining pin that holds it in place in the

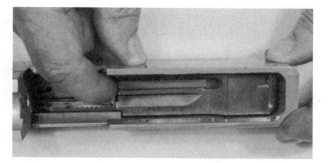

Note the rail that runs part way along the bottom in the forward part of the receiver. To remove the bolt, it must be pushed backward far enough to clear this rail.

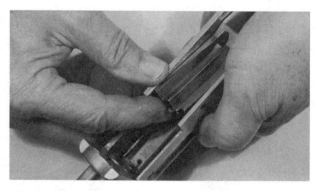

Lifting upward on the front end of the bolt frees it from the bolt handle and allows it to be lifted out of the receiver.

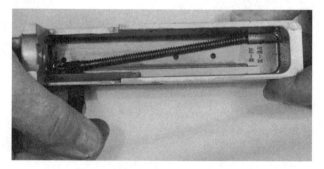

The bolt handle, guide rod, and recoil spring are removed as a unit.

Removing the firing pin requires the retaining pin to be driven out with a punch.

bolt, and the small spring (known as the firing pin rebound spring) that causes the firing pin to be moved to the rear during cycling of the action. Removal of the firing pin requires the firing pin stop pin to be pushed out of the bolt to either side, which allows the firing pin and the rebound spring to be removed. On our rifle, the pin holding the firing pin in place was the part that was most difficult to remove from the entire action. The pin is a roll pin that is press fitted into the hole in the bolt. To drive it out, you must use a sturdy punch while the bolt is supported on its side. We removed the firing pin stop pin by using a machine screw of slightly smaller diameter than the pin as a punch with the bolt

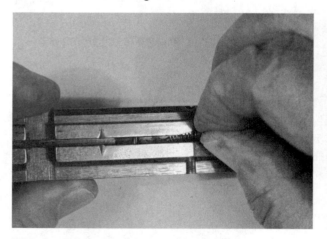

With the retaining pin removed, lift the firing pin out of the bolt while moving it backward.

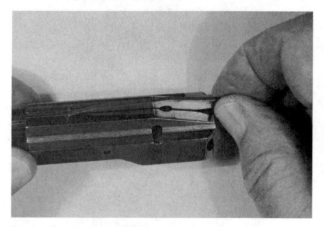

With the firing pin removed, the rebound spring can be lifted out. Note the transverse pin that holds the rebound spring in place.

resting on a barbell plate which allows the pin to fall free as it is punched out.

As the retaining pin is driven out and the firing pin removed, take special care not to lose the small rebound spring that is contained within the bolt below the firing pin! The firing pin rebound spring pushes backward on the firing pin to keep it pushed to the rear until the hammer strikes it. The spring is mounted in a recess in the bolt so that one end pushes backward against a ridge on one edge of the firing pin while the other rests against a permanently mounted pin that passes only part way through the bolt.

On the Ruger 10/22, the firing pin has an oval-shaped hole in it through which passes the firing pin retaining pin. This allows the firing pin to move backward and forward a short distance, but not far enough forward to strike the rear end of the barrel when the there is no cartridge in the chamber. In other words, it is a limited travel firing pin. The rebound spring keeps the firing pin in its rear position away from the cartridge head until the hammer moves forward. When putting the firing pin back in place, insert the rebound spring against the small pin that holds it in place, insert

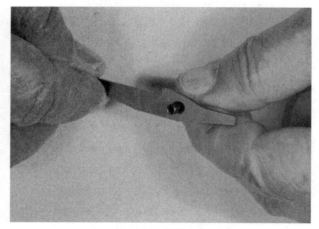

The oval hole in the firing pin allows it to move forward and backward while being held in place by the retaining pin.

the firing pin in the groove where it slides in the bolt, and insert the pin in the bolt so that it passes through the oval hole in the firing pin. Keep the firing pin pushed into the slot in the bolt so that the oval hole in the firing pin lines up with those in the bolt where the firing pin stop pin passes through.

The extractor of the Ruger 10/22 is a movable lever that has a hook that passes over the cartridge rim as the bolt closes. In order to be able to move the hook outward over the cartridge rim as the bolt moves forward, the extractor is pivoted. A spring-loaded plunger resting against a notch in the outside edge of the extractor keeps the extractor hook pushed inward over the bolt face so it rests over the rim of the cartridge head. Removing the extractor requires the spring-loaded plunger to be pushed to the rear to take pressure off the extractor and allow it to be lifted out of the retaining hole.

If you examine the plunger and its location, you will see that a small, sharp pointed tool must be used to fit in the small groove that gives access to the

The forward end of the extractor is a hook that fits over the cartridge rim.

With the plunger held back, the front end of the extractor can be swung outward away from the bolt face.

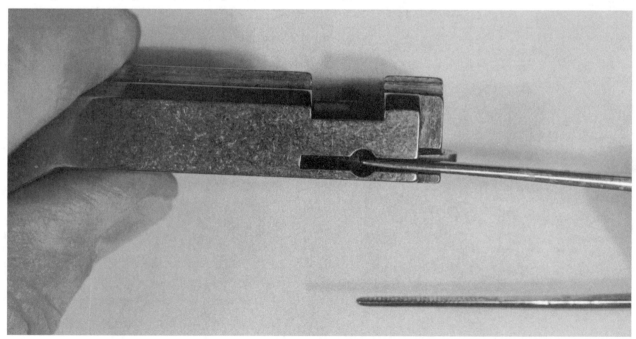

Removing the extractor requires the spring-loaded plunger to be moved to the rear.

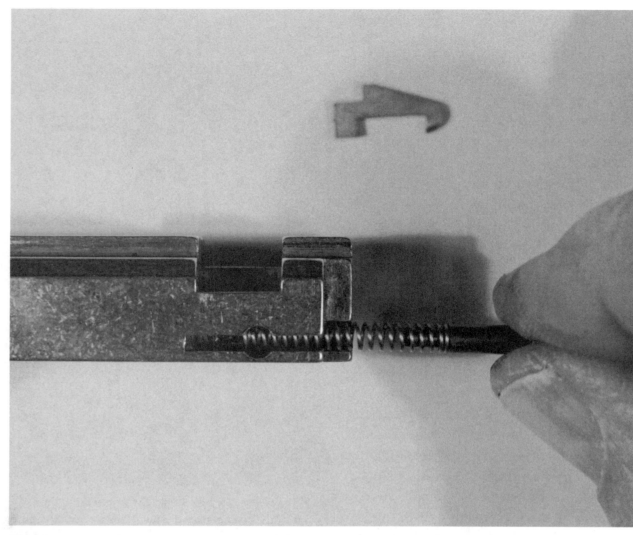

After the extractor is removed, the plunger and spring can be lifted out of the recess in the bolt.

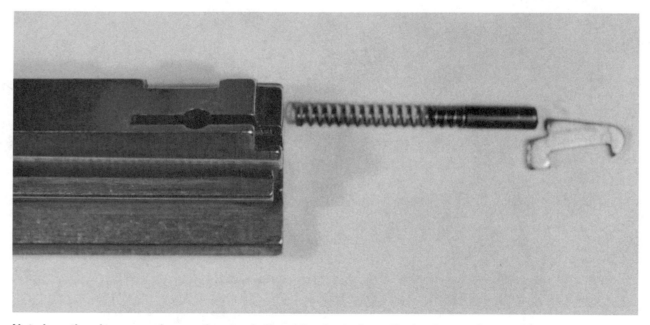

Note how the plunger pushes on the step in the extractor to force the hook over the cartridge rim.

plunger. One such tool that we have found to work well is a very small Allen wrench. The Allen wrench is bent so that the short end can be used as the probe or hook to push back on the plunger while the longer end serves as a handle. A large, bent paper clip would also work. With the plunger pushed backward against the spring and held there, the extractor can be removed from its retaining slot. Slowly allowing the plunger to move forward will allow you to remove both it and the extractor spring. When installed normally in the bolt, the extractor itself holds the plunger and extractor spring in position within the bolt.

Disassembly of the Trigger Unit

The only reason to disassemble the trigger unit of a Ruger 10/22 would be to replace a broken part or to install an aftermarket part. *In no case do we recommend that the owner of a Ruger 10/22 disassemble the trigger unit in order to make modifications of the factory parts.* While others may do so when trying to improve the pull of the factory trigger, this is work that requires the services of a professional gunsmith. The safety issues are such that an amateur with a file or stone is treading on thin ice, possibly even in a legal sense. Do not take that chance. There are many professionals who perform this type of work very well for a nominal fee.

Assuming that the owner of a Ruger 10/22 wants to install one or more of the fine aftermarket parts that are available, the trigger unit can be disassembled without too much difficulty. Keep in mind that any mechanical system that is composed of numerous small parts is

rather complex and that it is easy for some small part to be lost. Consequently, work on the trigger unit should be undertaken on a clean surface that is covered with a large piece of plastic or cloth. It is difficult to locate tiny springs, pins, or other parts that have embedded themselves in carpet or have completely left the work area when set free.

Leave the safety button alone. Do not remove it. The factory safety works very well, and you are not going to replace it with an aftermarket item. Complete aftermarket trigger assemblies come with all parts, including the safety, in place.

The trigger unit consists of an aluminum casting that houses the hammer, sear, springs, bolt release, magazine release and pins that make up the entire trigger assembly. We recommend that as you remove parts of the trigger assembly (as

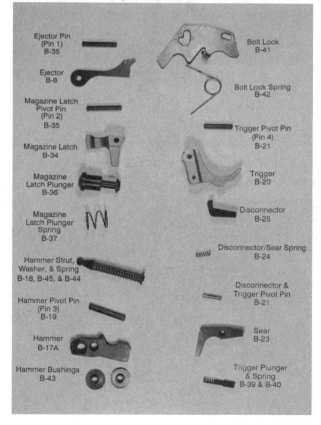

In addition to the trigger housing, these are the parts that make up the trigger assembly.

for example the hammer with its bushings and the bolt latch spring) try putting them back in place immediately. In that way, you will not only see how the parts are removed but also how they must be oriented to be reassembled.

The aluminum housing that contains the trigger assembly and magazine release does not come apart, but all of the other items are held in place within the housing by means of four pins. This means that each pin has multiple functions with regard to holding parts in place. During disassembly these pins must be forced out of the housing, but this must be done carefully. On the factory trigger being used as a model for this discussion, the pins can all be moved by pushing very lightly on them with almost any object of suitable diameter. Our "punch" is simply an aluminum nail that has had the pointed end cut off and filed to give a smooth, blunt end. In no case was any tapping on the punch required to remove the pins. Other trigger assemblies may have pins that fit more tightly so more pressure may be required. For clarity, the four retaining pins are labeled on the accompanying photo as Pins 1, 2, 3, and 4.

First, cock the hammer by pulling it back until it locks in place and make sure that the safety is "on" so the hammer will not be released by accidentally hitting the trigger. Carefully remove Pin 1 from the trigger housing. This will release the

Four pins hold all of the parts in the trigger assembly in place.

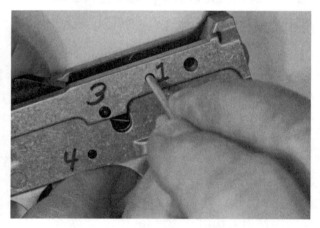

The first step in disassembling the trigger is to push out Pin 1.

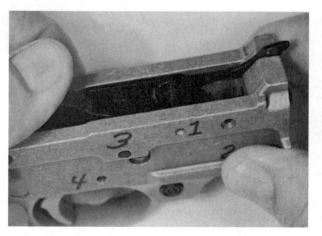

Disassembly of the trigger unit begins with the hammer cocked and the safety on.

With Pin 1 removed, the ejector can be lifted out. Note the end of the bolt lock spring that points upward after it is freed from below Pin 1.

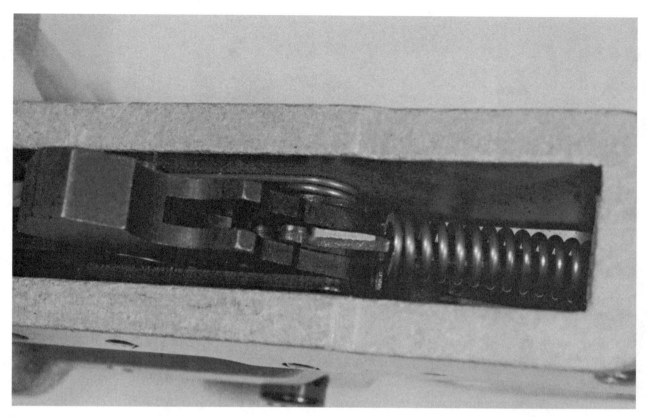

The bolt lock spring is the coil that is located on the right hand side of the hammer while the hammer spring is the coil spring behind the hammer.

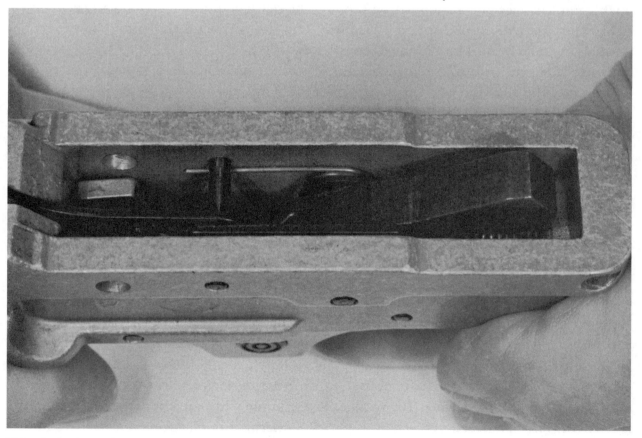

This photo shows how one end of the bolt lock spring is placed below Pin 1.

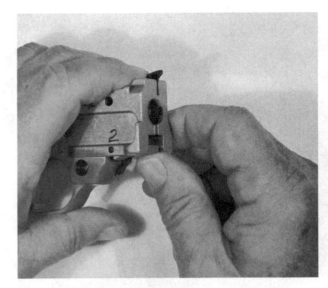

The magazine latch or release is located on the bottom of the trigger unit.

Pressing upward on the front edge of the magazine release moves the latch plunger backward into the trigger unit.

ejector, which pivots on that pin. Note that the bolt lock and release (which protrudes from the bottom of the trigger assembly just in front of the trigger guard) has a hole that also fits over Pin 1. The bolt lock is activated by a spring that fits around the bushing at the base of the hammer on the right hand side. Part of this spring is visible through the hole below Pin 3 in the trigger housing. This spring (it looks like a coil of wire around the large pin that the hammer rotates on) has one end that hooks over a tab that projects from the bolt release plate. The other end is held in place under Pin 1. Therefore, removing Pin 1 will not only free the ejector and the upper end of the bolt release but also free one end of the bolt lock spring.

The magazine release on the Ruger 10/22 works by pressing upward on the front end of the pivoted bar (the magazine latch). It is "L"-shaped so when the bottom of the "L" is pressed upward, the vertical part acts as a lever which draws back the magazine latch plunger against the pressure of the magazine latch plunger spring. The plunger is normally forced forward by the coil spring, and the front end of the plunger

has a recess that fits over a mating pin that is located on the rear of the magazine. Pushing the plunger to the rear allows the magazine to drop down out of the rifle. Before removing the magazine release, look inside the trigger assembly while operating the release. In this way you can easily see how the parts fit together and how they function.

The magazine release is held in place by Pin 2 (see the accompanying photo bottom of next page). When that pin is removed, the magazine release and the plunger are freed from the trigger housing. Note that the plunger is under some spring pressure, and when it is released it will be expelled out of the trigger housing. Hold your thumb over the plunger when Pin 2 is removed so that the plunger and its spring stay in the work area! After Pin 2 is removed, carefully take the magazine latch plunger and the spring that surrounds it out of the trigger housing.

Many users of Ruger 10/22s object to the flat magazine release of factory design. Certainly there are enough different types of aftermarket magazine releases available to suit the taste of almost anyone. If the

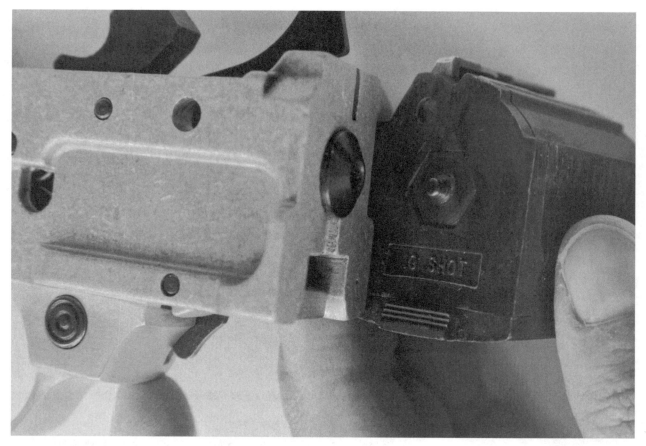

Note how the spindle on the magazine fits in the recess on the magazine latch plunger.

objective is to simply install a different type of magazine release, it is necessary to remove only Pin 2. The magazine latch, plunger, and spring can then be removed so that the aftermarket magazine release can be installed. This is done by placing the plunger spring around the plunger and inserting it into the hole at the front of the trigger housing. After pressing the plunger and spring fully into the trigger housing, insert the magazine release in the bottom of the trigger housing so that the lever that

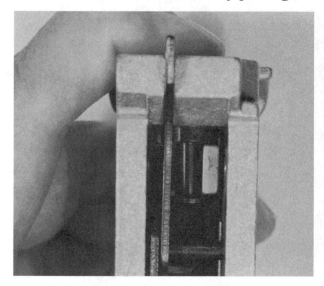

In this photo, the light colored magazine release can be seen along the side and locked by the plunger.

The next step in disassembly of the trigger unit is to press out Pin 2. As you do this, hold your finger over the magazine release plunger.

105

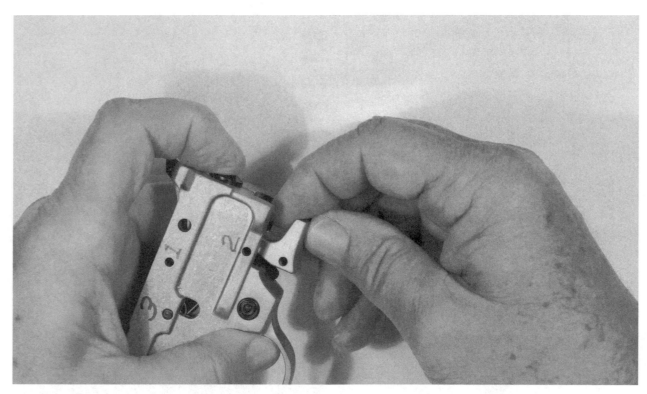

While holding the magazine release plunger in place, lift the magazine release out of the bottom of the trigger housing.

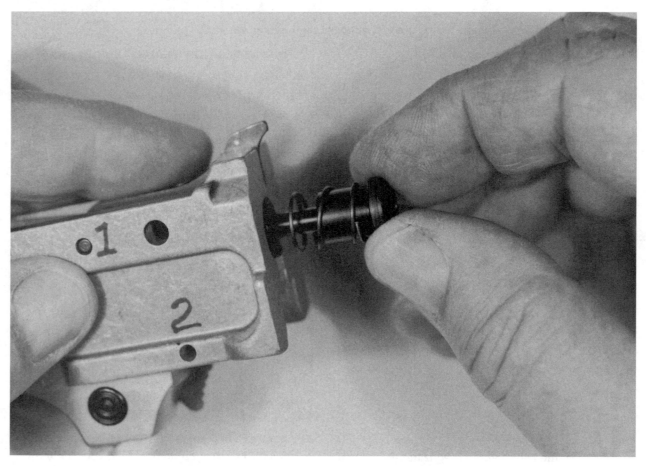

The magazine release plunger and spring can be lifted out of the trigger housing.

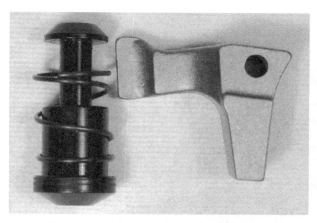

These parts are the magazine release, the plunger, and the plunger spring. Note how the curved end of the magazine release fits along side the cut out section of the plunger.

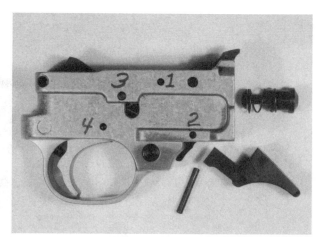

This photo shows an aftermarket magazine release, the magazine latch plunger, and the plunger spring about to be installed.

moves the plunger is resting in the notch on the plunger. While holding the plunger, spring, and magazine release in place, insert Pin 2 in the appropriate hole in the trigger housing. Since the bolt lock also pivots on Pin 2, make sure that the pin passes through the hole in the bolt lock plate when replacing the pin.

When the 10/22 is fired, the hammer is driven forward by force supplied by a strong coil spring located around the hammer strut, which is anchored in a

Insert the magazine latch plunger and spring into the trigger housing.

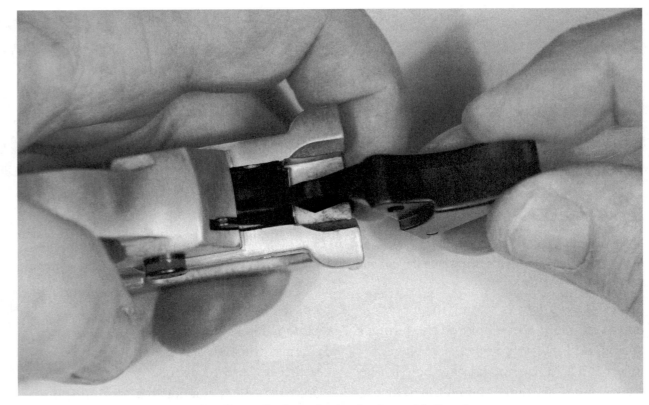

Insert the magazine release so that the vertical member rests along side the plunger.

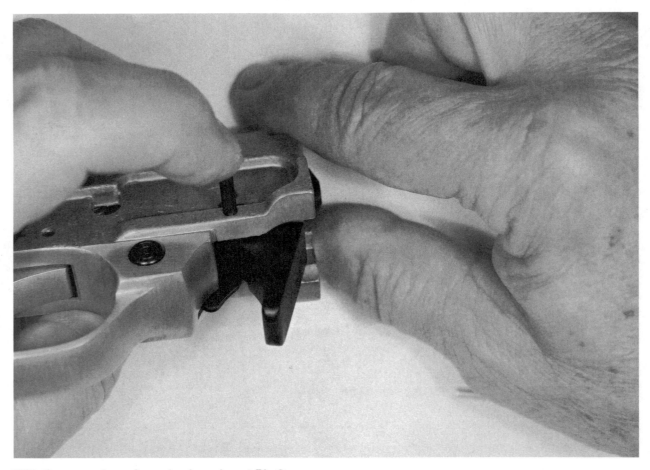

With the magazine release in place, insert Pin 2.

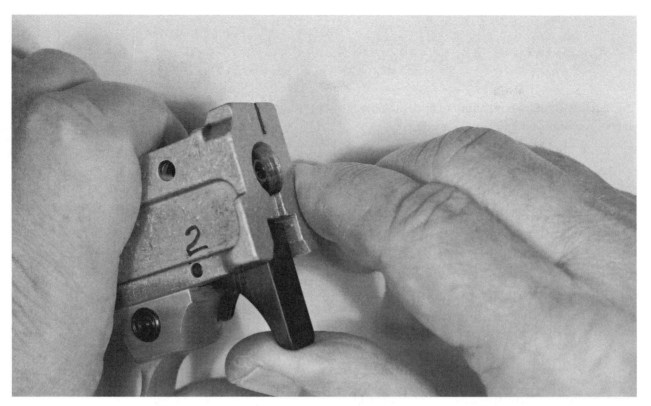

Push the lever of the magazine release forward to make sure it pulls the plunger back into the trigger housing.

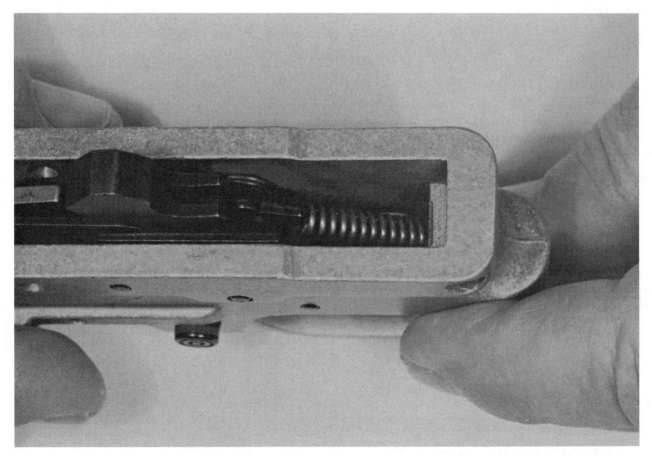

The hammer spring is a coil that fits around the hammer strut and pushes on the back face of the hammer.

The hammer strut, hammer spring, and retaining washer are removed and kept as a unit.

recess in the trigger housing. The forward end of the hammer strut rests in a slot on the backside of the hammer. Cocking the hammer compresses the hammer spring. Fortunately, the spring has a washer on one end that locks in notches in the strut that keeps the spring and strut together so that they can be removed and inserted as a unit. The washer is slotted so that it can be slid off the strut after compressing the spring. Although this allows the hammer spring to be removed, this should NOT be done! Compressing the spring and sliding the washer over the slot in the hammer strut cannot be done by hand because this spring is very strong.

Note the slot in the washer that allows it to be slid off the strut after the spring has been compressed.

Removing the hammer strut and spring as a unit is very easy. Simply lower the

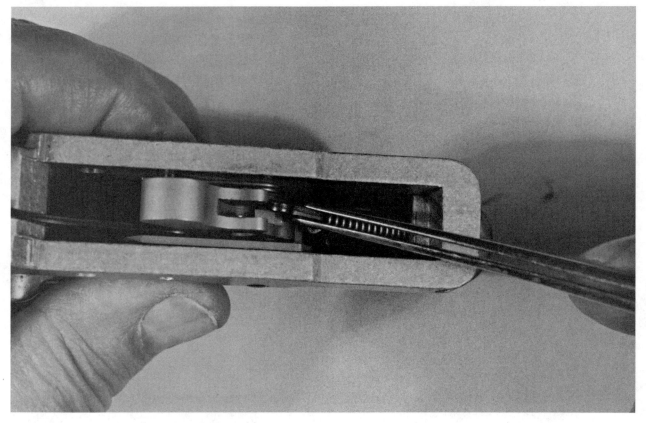

A pair of forceps can be used to easily remove the hammer strut and spring.

hammer slowly after taking pressure off the spring by pulling the trigger while holding the hammer with your thumb. With the pressure off the hammer strut and spring, the hammer spring assembly (strut, spring, and retaining washer) can be lifted out with tweezers or by simply inverting the trigger housing and shaking it out. In some cases, the spring assembly tends to stick in the recess at the rear of the trigger housing. If it does, a tool such as a punch or Allen wrench can be inserted in the hole at the back of the trigger housing to push the strut out of the hole in which it is anchored. On our specimen, the hammer strut and spring fall out when the housing is inverted.

The hammer and several other parts are removed by pushing out Pin 3. Other parts include the bushings on either side of the hammer and the bolt lock spring that is

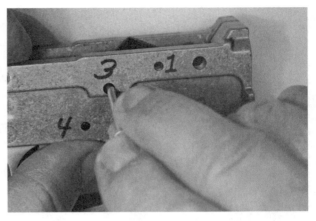

To remove the hammer, push out Pin 3.

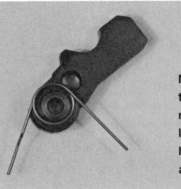

Note that as the hammer is removed the bolt lock spring and hammer bushings are also removed.

With the hammer removed, the bolt lock can be lifted out of the trigger housing.

The trigger, sear, and disconnector are removed by pushing out Pin 4.

wrapped around the hammer bushing. On our trigger, the bushings are metal. Note that the bolt lock spring is wound around the *right* hand side of the hammer (when the trigger housing is pointing away from you as it is when installed in a rifle). Note also that the bolt lock spring has one end (which is straight) that fits under Pin 1 and the other which has a bend or "step"

in it. The *bent* end of the bolt lock spring fits in a notch on the bolt lock when it is in its normal position inside the trigger housing, and the *straight* end fits under Pin 1. Remove Pin 3 and carefully lift out the hammer and other parts. If Pin 2 has already been removed, the bolt lock can also be lifted out of the trigger housing.

The trigger and related parts (sear, sear spring, and disconnector) are removed by pushing out Pin 4. When pushing out this pin, leave the punch (or whatever was used to move the pin) in place until you can turn the trigger housing upside down over your hand. This is done so that the small sear spring does not exit the scene. Now slowly remove the punch and allow the trigger parts to fall into your hand. Although the sear and trigger are held together by the trigger pivot pin (Pin 4), the trigger and disconnector are held together by a separate short pin, and

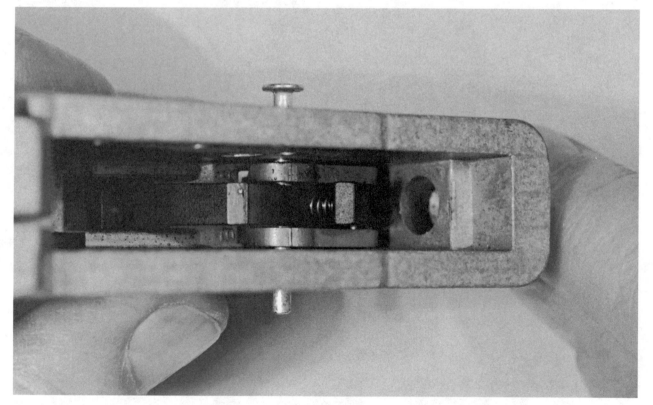

This photo shows the trigger, sear, and disconnector still in place inside the trigger housing. Turn the housing over and remove the nail.

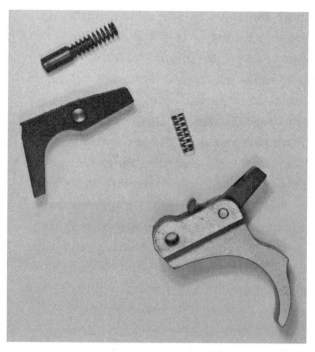

This photo shows the trigger (with the disconnector still in place), the sear, the sear/disconnector spring, and the trigger plunger and spring.

they are removed as a unit. A small coil spring rests in recesses in the sear and the disconnector. Note that the trigger moves backward against a spring-loaded plunger (the trigger plunger). With the trigger removed, the trigger plunger and trigger return spring can be removed.

To separate the trigger and disconnector, push out the short pin that holds the disconnector in place. At this point, disassembly of the trigger unit is as complete as it ever needs to be.

Assembling the trigger unit, whether with factory or aftermarket parts, is essentially the reverse of the processes described above. There are a few small nuances but they are minor. Insert the trigger plunger and its spring into the recess at the back of the trigger guard.

The trigger plunger and spring fit in a recess at the back of the trigger guard.

When assembling the trigger, disconnector, sear, and disconnector spring, place one end of the spring in the hole in the sear. That hole is deep enough for the spring to remain in place while the other parts are being assembled. First attach the disconnector and trigger by inserting the short pin that holds

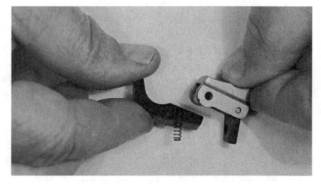

This photo shows the trigger, sear, and disconnector in their proper orientation.

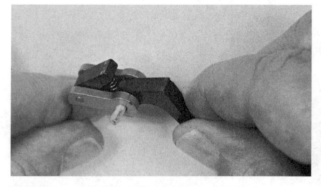

The trigger, sear, and disconnector can be assembled using a short section of a matchstick so they can be replaced in the trigger housing as a unit.

Pressing Pin 4 in place pushes out the matchstick and locks the trigger components in place.

them together. To assemble the trigger and disconnector to the sear, make a short temporary pin of a piece of dowel or matchstick. This enables you to insert the assembly consisting of the trigger, disconnector, sear, and the disconnector/sear spring as a unit into the trigger housing. Make sure that the disconnector/sear spring is located correctly with its ends in the recesses in the sear and disconnector. When the assembly is in place inside the trigger housing, inserting Pin 4 will push the matchstick (temporary pin) out as Pin 4 is inserted with the assembly being held together in the process. It would be very difficult try to hold the sear and trigger in place inside the trigger housing while trying to insert Pin 4 through the separate parts.

Assemble the hammer, bushings, and bolt lock spring. While holding them together, insert the lower end of the

The hammer, bushings, and bolt lock spring are inserted in the trigger housing as a unit. Make sure that the bent end of the bolt lock spring points inward within the trigger housing.

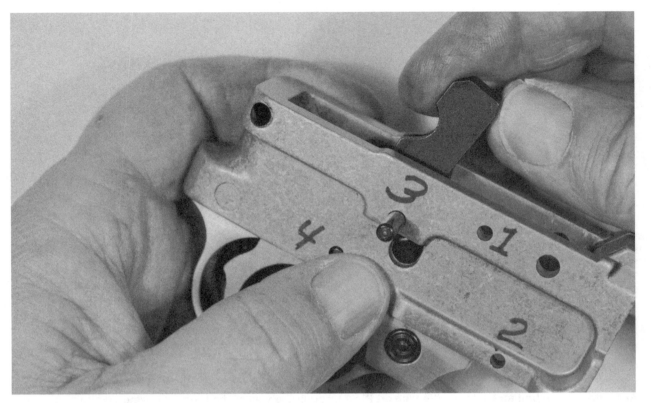

Pushing Pin 3 in place fixes the hammer within the trigger housing.

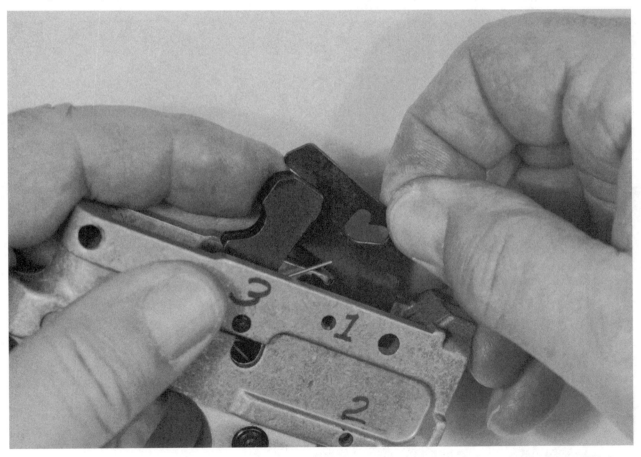

After the trigger and hammer groups are in place, the bolt lock can be inserted in the trigger housing. Make sure that the bent end of the bolt lock spring is under the tab on the bolt lock.

After moving the bolt lock into position, insert Pin 1 through the wall of the trigger housing and bolt latch and slide the end of the ejector over the pin.

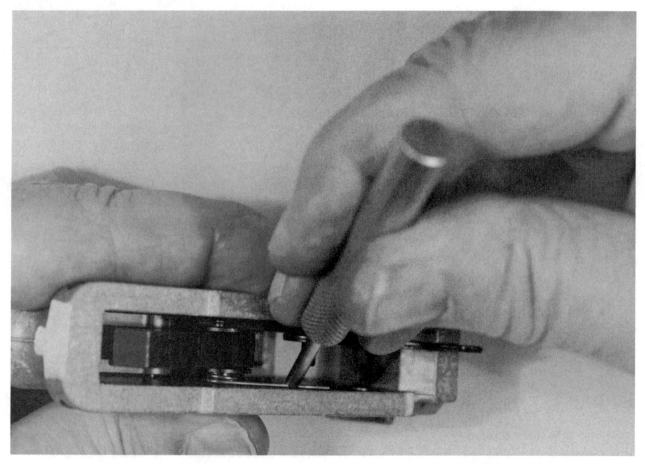

With a punch, press downward on the straight end of the bolt lock spring so Pin 1 can be inserted over it.

assembly into the trigger housing and insert Pin 3 making sure that it passes through the hole in the hammer. With the hammer in place, insert the bolt lock while making sure that the bent end of the bolt lock spring rests in the notch in the tab that sticks out on the bolt latch. Now partially insert Pin 1 from the left hand side of the trigger housing so that it passes through the bolt lock and ejector. The straight end of the bolt lock spring must rest under Pin 1 so push downward on the spring to compress it slightly. We used the head end of the nail used as a punch to do this. With the spring pushed downward enough so that Pin 1 will pass over the straight end, fully insert Pin 1. The hammer strut and spring are inserted last.

Although most of the process of reassembly of the trigger unit is simply the reverse of the disassembly procedure, additional details will be revisited in Chapter 9. In that chapter, we will deal with installation of aftermarket parts for the firing mechanism and magazine release.

Removal of Factory Sights

Removal of the open sights from Ruger 10/22 barrels is a straightforward process. A brass punch and a small hammer can be used to drift the rear sight out of the dovetail groove. The front sight is also held in a dovetail groove and can be removed in

When inserting a barreled action into a stock, put the safety in the middle of its travel, insert the back of the action first while making sure that it fits properly on the ledge that supports the action.

Removing the rear sight requires it to be drifted out of the retaining slot with a suitable punch and hammer.

The front sight on the Ruger 10/22 is also mounted in a dovetail notch and can be driven out.

a similar way. When tapping on the sight bases to slide the sights out of the grooves, support the rifle carefully to prevent marring of the stock or barrel surfaces. When one is available, a commercial sight pusher is a better way to move sights from dovetail grooves.

The Ruger 10/22 is convenient to work on, and only a few simple tools are required for disassembly and assembly. If you are doing the work yourself, work slowly. Inspect the parts carefully to see how things fit together and how they move. Be extremely careful not to lose small parts. It is both beneficial to the rifle and rewarding to the shooter to make some changes in the Ruger 10/22. Fortunately, the aftermarket parts are available to let you change anything you want to.

Chapter 6

SOME BASIC OPERATIONS, TOOLS, AND TECHNIQUES

Shooters who own and use several firearms often reach a point where something about a firearm needs to be altered or replaced. In many instances, it is not practical or even necessary to haul the piece to a professional gunsmith if the owner has some inclination

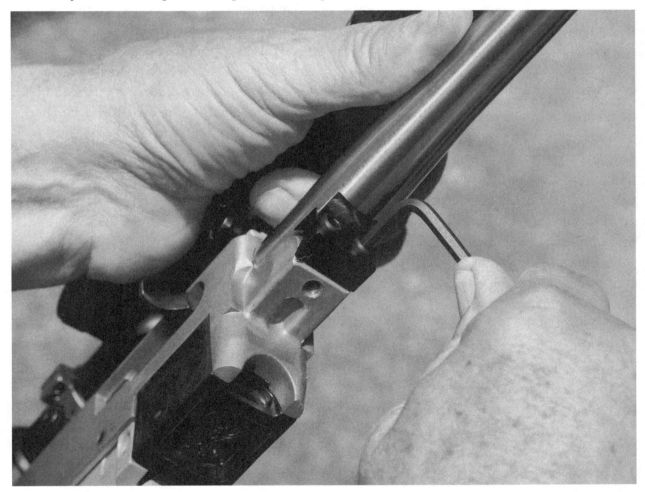

The Ruger 10/22 is one of the most user-friendly firearms ever made. Even removal of the barrel requires only an Allen wrench.

to work on his or her rifle. That is the basic premise related to this book. The owner of a Ruger 10/22 can perform most work on the rifle if due care is exercised. In this chapter, we will describe some of the basic procedures and the tools necessary to perform the work. This chapter is for the beginner, not the professional. In many instances, a professional or even a serious amateur will have progressed well beyond the level presented in this chapter because this book is not written for the specialist. But for the shooter who has had a Ruger 10/22 for some time and has reached the point where he or she wants to make some changes, this chapter should prove helpful.

If you are a rank beginner, study the diagrams in the owner's manual that show the parts of the firearm. Try to understand how the parts function together to allow the firearm to operate. When you begin to work on the firearm, work slowly. Trying to hurry an operation can lead to mistakes, damage, or a result that does not achieve the desired goal. It could even result in the firearm being unsafe. The legal aspects of making modifications are why the factory tells you in no uncertain terms that making modifications on a firearm will void the warranty. If you are unsure about some aspect of the job, take time to learn before acting. The result will be a job that is performed correctly. In this chapter, we will give a brief overview of some types of shop operations and the tools that will be useful when working in firearms.

If you lack the necessary tools and supplies to carry out the work on your firearm, collect these items before you get to a point where you need something you don't have. One of the premier sources of items for gunsmiths is Brownell's of Montezuma, Iowa. If it isn't in Brownell's

enormous catalog, you probably do not need it. Other major suppliers of tools and materials are Midway USA of Columbia, Missouri, Numrich Gun Parts Corporation of West Hurley, New York, Graf & Sons of Mexico, Missouri, and Sinclair International of Fort Wayne, Indiana. Chapter 13 lists these and many other sources of products and services for the Ruger 10/22 shooter.

What To Use To Do What

This may sound very simplistic, but you should not try to drive a nail with a screwdriver or to remove a screw with a hammer. Of course there are no nails to drive when working on firearms, but there are some small parts to be manipulated. Probably the most frequently removed parts are screws. Using the wrong screwdriver will almost certainly damage the heads of screws by marring the area along the slot, which is detrimental to the appearance of the firearm. To circumvent this, screws having Allen (hex), Phillips, or torx recesses to accept the appropriate driving tools have come into use on firearms and scopes mounting systems in recent years. Regardless of the type of head, using a

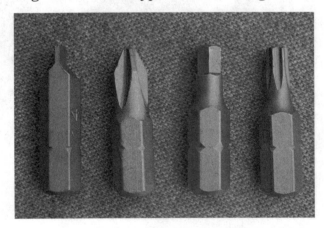

Screw removal may require the use of (left to right) blade, Phillips, hex, or torx tips.

Blades on screwdrivers may have tapered (left) or parallel (right) points. Those with parallel sides are appropriate for working on firearms to prevent damage to the screws.

screwdriver of the correct type and size is essential to prevent damage to screws.

Blade screwdrivers for use on firearms have the surfaces ground so that the faces are parallel near the tip of the blade. In that way, the blade makes flush contact with the sides of the slot in the screw head.

An ordinary screwdriver blade gets thicker the farther away from the edge. As a result, only the thickest part of the blade that fits within the slot makes contact so that damage to the extreme edges of the slot can result.

For moving slotted screws, always use a blade that fits tightly in the slot and which has a width that matches the width of the slot. Using a screwdriver with a blade that is much too thin or of insufficient width will damage the screw head. For both torx and Allen headed screws, there is only one size that correctly fits the drive slot. Always use the correct size. Remember that Allen headed screws may have either English or metric sizes so you will need two sets of Allen wrenches to work effectively, particularly on scope mounts which may be of foreign manufacture. Phillips screw drivers come in several sizes so be sure

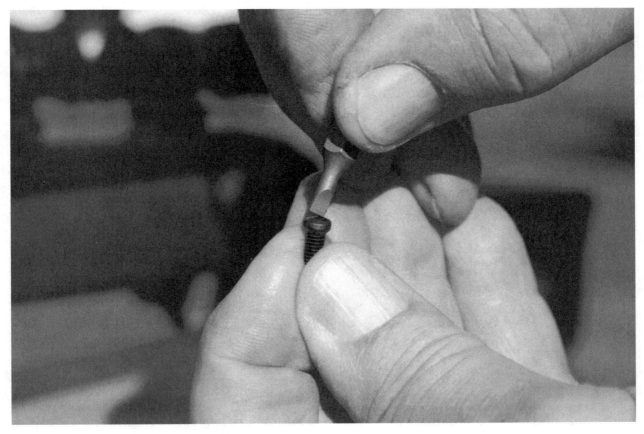

For slotted head screws, use a blade that fits tightly in the slot.

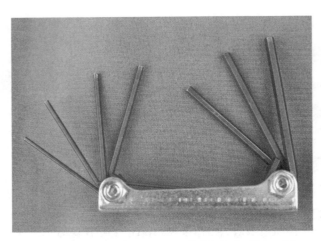

Sets of Allen wrenches are available in both metric and SAE sizes.

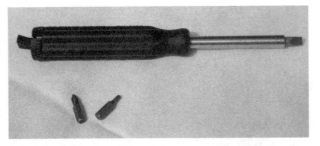

Hoppe's markets a convenient screwdriver set that contains the tips in the handle.

to use one that has a point that closely matches the size of the recess in the screw head.

One of the most useful items in the gun hobbyist's kit is a gunsmith's screwdriver set. These sets contain the most useful sizes and types of blades that have a hexagonal shank that matches the recess in the handle. Therefore, one handle can be used with a large number of blades of different types. Generally, the whole set is contained in one box that has slots for

holding each component. One such set that we use an unbelievable amount is the Pachmayr screwdriver set which contains blade, Phillips, hex, and torx tips in sizes that are useful for working on firearms. The handle and removable drive heads are stored in a convenient plastic box. Hoppes produce another handy set for the kit bag or toolbox, and it has hollow tubes in the handle where the blades can be stored. This highly portable and practical set contains fewer tips than the Pachmayr set, but it is more readily portable. In addition to these kits, other suppliers market screwdriver sets for the gunsmith.

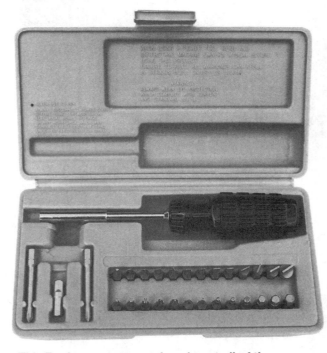

This Pachmayr set contains almost all of the screwdrivers you will need.

A solvent such as Liquid Wrench® is helpful when removing stubborn screws.

After the tip of the screwdriver is inserted in the recess, try turning the screw in the direction that moves the screw the way you want it to move. If you are trying to loosen the screw and it doesn't budge, do not simply keep increasing the torque on the screwdriver because the tip may slip out of the recess and damage the screw. Apply a solvent that can help free stuck parts. One such solvent is Liquid Wrench®, but there are several others. After letting the solvent work for a while, try again to move the screw by turning in *slightly* in alternating directions. This allows the solvent to enter the threads and continue its work. Apply another drop of solvent and try turning the screw back and forth again. After each solvent application, try to turn the screw a little farther than you could the time before. It is roughly equivalent to trying to move an auto that is stuck in snow by rocking it (which is usually more effective than simply putting it in drive and pushing on the accelerator). We have on several occasions used this technique to remove stubborn screws without damaging the heads.

Pinning is a convenient and inexpensive way to hold parts in a particular orientation within the firearm. The hobbyist who works on his or her firearms will eventually have to remove pins of various types and sizes. In some cases the pins fit tightly and must be driven out, but in others they fit so loosely that they will fall out if the part is turned so the pin is vertical. The two pins holding the trigger assembly to the receiver in most of the Ruger 10/22s we have worked on belong in the latter category. In fact, it is not uncommon to have both of the pins drop out when the barreled action is removed from the stock. When the action

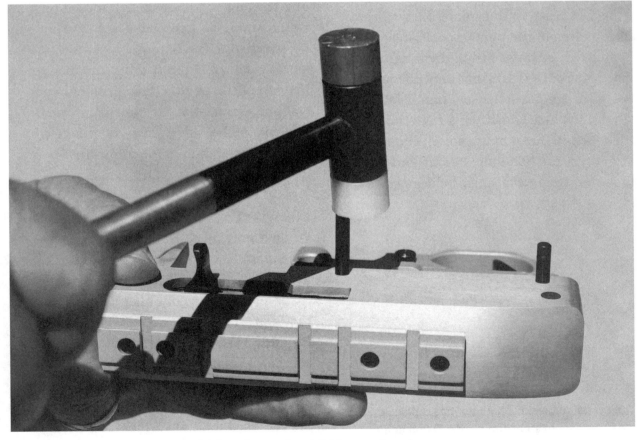

A small hammer such as the model from Lyman is useful for moving pins.

Graf & Sons markets this set that contains brass, steel, and plastic punches and a hammer in this handy kit.

is held in place in the stock, the walls of the stock hold the pins in position so there is no need for press fitting them tightly in place. On our 10/22 Magnum, the factory bolt stop pin fits so loosely that it falls out when the barreled action is removed from the stock. While making some changes at the range, the bolt stop fell out, but it was found on the next visit to the range. Now

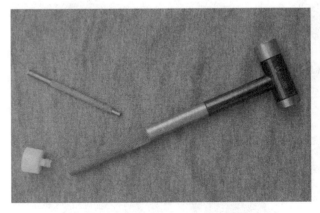

The Lyman gunsmith's hammer has replaceable striking faces of steel, brass, and Teflon and a hollow handle for storing a punch.

it has a piece of tape on both sides of the receiver to prevent it from falling out.

When pins fit tightly, they must be removed by force. Generally, that force is supplied by tapping on a punch of correct diameter (which is just slightly smaller than that of the pin to be driven out). Use a brass punch to avoid damaging the pin and work slowly. Brass is softer than steel so even if some color is imparted to the end of the pin the steel will not be deformed. Incidentally, brass punches of various diameter can be made easily from brass rod that is available at most large hardware stores or hobby stores. The hammer used should be a small one, and the Lyman Gunsmith's hammer is one example of this type. This hammer has three striking surfaces (steel, brass, and nylon), and the hollow handle contains a brass punch the ends of which are of different diameter. The striking surfaces are cylindrical in shape and have a threaded section that can be attached to the hammer head (one on either side) while the third is attached to the end of the handle. This little hammer will provide most of the blows that the hobbyist will require. There is little need for a ball peen hammer with a three-pound head when working on firearms.

Another operation that is often required when working on firearms is measurement. While it may be satisfactory to measure the length of a barrel using a yardstick, measuring dimensions of small parts or the sizes of groups of bullet holes in targets requires a more accurate measuring device. In times past, a micrometer was the most commonly used device used by gunsmiths, but in recent years the use of calipers has become much more common. Gone are the hard to read vernier calipers of a couple of generations ago. Calipers today

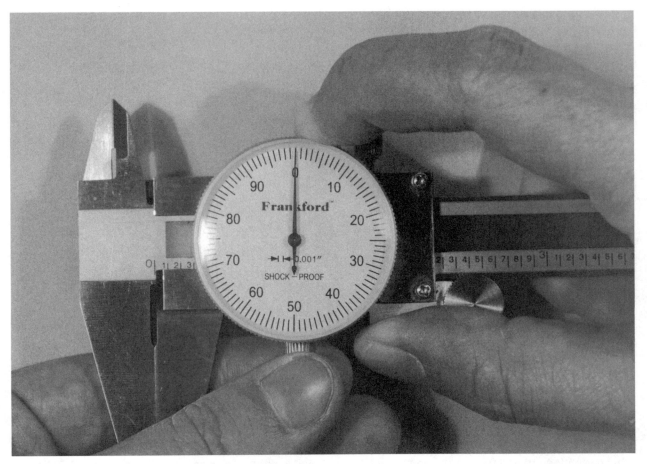

A dial caliper is a useful measuring device. It is set to zero by closing the jaws, loosening the screw at the bottom of the dial, and turning the dial until the pointer is opposite zero.

are of two basic types, dial and digital. The most commonly encountered types allow measurements in the range of zero to six inches to the nearest thousandth of an inch.

Dial calipers have a circular dial with a pointer that moves as the jaws are opened or closed. One revolution of the pointer amounts to 0.1 inch, and the position of the pointer can be read using divisions that are equivalent to 0.001 inch. Inches and tenths of an inch are engraved on a scale on the steel frame. With the jaws closed, the pointer can be set to read 0.000 by loosening a setscrew and rotating the dial until the pointer is exactly at zero. When the object being measured is placed between the jaws, the dimension can be determined by noting the position of the

movable jaw on the engraved scale to read inches and tenths. The dial has index marks at 10, 20, ..., and 90, which are actually those numbers of thousandths of an inch. Thus, 10 on the dial mean 10/1000 or 0.01 inch and 20 means

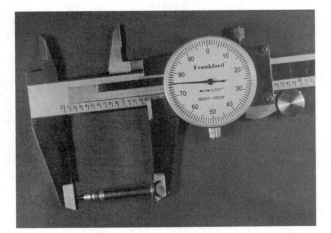

This .17 HMR cartridge measures 1.375 inches in length.

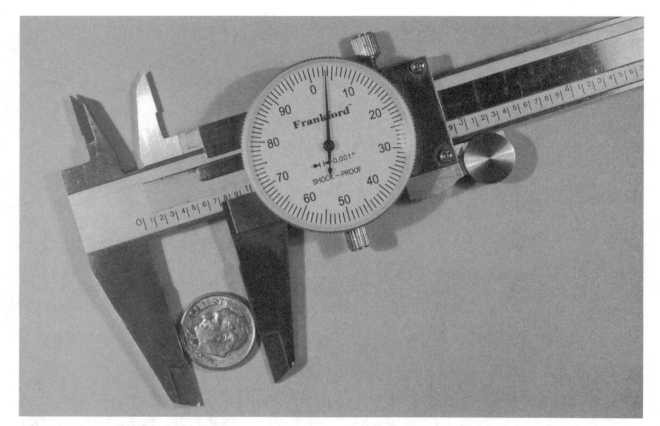

The diameter of the dime is just over 0.7 inch. The first digit is 7 as indicated by the position of the right hand jaw along the frame. The second digit is 0 because the indicator is between 0 and 1. Because the pointer is between the third and four marks on the dial, the last digit is either 3 or 4 so the dime measures 0.703 or 0.704 inch.

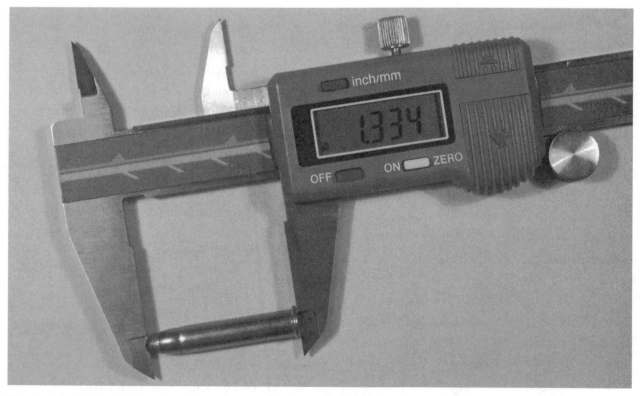

The length of this .22 WMR cartridge can be read directly as 1.334 inches by using a digital caliper.

20/1000 or 0.02 inch. Between the 10 and 20 markings there are 10 divisions each of which represents 1/1000 or 0.001 inch. The photos show illustrations of reading specific measurements.

In recent years, the digital caliper has become much more common. This device is similar to the dial caliper except for that the dimension is shown on a LCD display. Resetting to a zero reading is as simple as moving the jaws together and pressing a button. When the object being measured has the jaws tightened against it, pressing a button shows the dimension on the display. Moreover, pressing another button allows measurements to be given in millimeters or inches. Dial calipers are generally less expensive than the digital types, but the digital calipers are easier to read.

Measurements such as rim thickness (see Chapter 3), cartridge length, bullet diameter, group size, etc. require an accurate measuring device. A dial or digital caliper will allow you to determine such distances accurately.

Smoothing and Polishing of Metal

As a young man, I had a shooting buddy who was a veteran of World War II and who was without doubt one of the most skilled craftsmen of my acquaintance before or since. He had a real insight as to how a firearm worked. He knew what moved what, what rubbed where, and how to improve things. Two of his firearms that I had numerous occasions to examine and shoot were a Ruger Blackhawk .357 Magnum single action and an M1 .30-06 Springfield. Both of these firearms had been taken apart (numerous times) and all

metal surfaces that rubbed together had been highly polished. The result of this handwork was two firearms whose actions were unbelievably slick. Drawing back the hammer on the Ruger Blackhawk was a smooth operation that was accompanied by no grinding or rasping. The trigger let off was without noticeable motion before the sear released, and the cylinder rotated with absolutely no hint of abrasion or friction. Moving the bolt on the M1 backward was also without any discernable friction.

How did these two mechanical objects get so that the mechanisms operated with fluid smoothness? The answer is by smoothing and polishing metal surfaces. Machined metal surfaces have minute striations, burrs, ridges, and pits. When two such metal surfaces rub together, there is some resistance and friction as these rough sections move in contact with each other. If the surfaces are rough enough, there may be some grinding or rasping that accompanies the movement. With most firearms, metal surfaces are reasonably smooth, but doing a lot of hand fitting is expensive and results in a very high price tag. As a result, some parts are left with a finish that is less than perfect. What my shooting buddy had done was to painstakingly polish all the metal surfaces to a glass smooth condition. With a light film of lubricant coating them, they moved over each other with almost no friction. It is possible to make the action of a Ruger 10/22 operate in a similar manner.

Manufacturers of moderately priced firearms cannot afford to spend the time necessary to polish every metal surface to a mirror finish. Consequently, almost any firearm can be made to operate more smoothly by doing some polishing and smoothing. However, the intent is

Many polishing operations can be accomplished using simple materials such as crocus cloth, steel wool, and sandpaper.

consists of a heavy cloth backing with an iron oxide (or other abrasive) facing. Because the abrasive is so fine, almost no metal is removed. It is possible to obtain a mirror finish on steel by polishing it with crocus cloth.

For some operations, it may be desirable to use extra fine sandpaper or steel wool, at least for preliminary polishing. These abrasives remove more metal than does crocus cloth so they should be used sparingly, and the final polishing should be done with a finer abrasive.

The bores of many inexpensive .22s are not given a mirror finish. One specialized type of polishing is known as lapping the bore. This process was described in Chapter 2. In the process of fire lapping, the coarsest abrasive is used first and the finest granulation is used last.

One of the handiest tools for the hobbyist who works on guns is the Dremel® tool. This device is like a drill in that it can

not to remove metal beyond that which is required to give a smooth surface. Therefore, in most cases, filing or grinding is out of the question. How can a smooth surface on metals be produced? Some of the time-honored techniques involve manually working on the surface with an extremely fine abrasive. One such abrasive is known as crocus cloth. This material

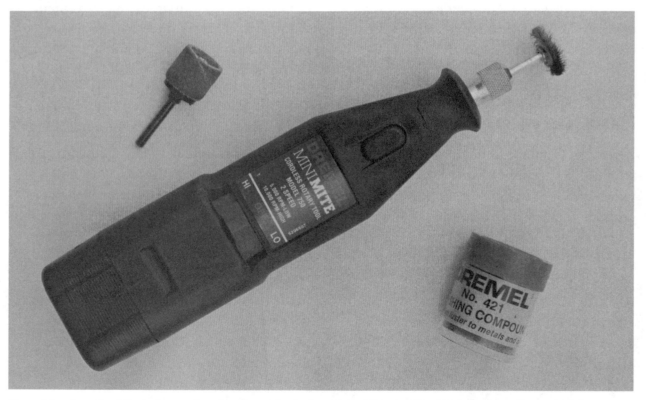

One of the handiest tools for performing many tasks is a Dremel® tool like this small cordless model.

accept a wide range of tools by locking them in a chuck. However, the Dremel tool is intended for work on a very small scale so the accessories are tiny. The rotational velocity produced by the Dremel may be up to 20,000 rpm. Accessories include drill bits, grinding wheels, router heads, polishing wheels, etc. By mounting a felt wheel on a mandrel and coating it with abrasive paste, the Dremel tool becomes one of the most effective devices available for polish operations. Moreover, it is possible to work in small spaces and on objects having irregular shapes. A flexible shaft is also available for the Dremel tool, which allows the operator to hold the actual power head like a pencil. There is also a drill stand available. Moreover, several models of the Dremel tool are available that include variable speed versions as well as cordless, rechargeable types. The range of attachments available

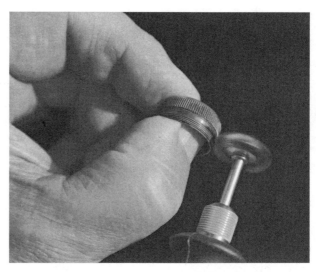

Using a wire wheel in the Dremel tool, it is easy to clean threads like those on this scope cap.

for Dremel tools is truly enormous. Such a tool is useful for much more than just polishing, but that is the type of operation that is being addressed here. A cordless Dremel tool accompanies us on our travels, and it finds numerous applications to craft and hobby projects when we are camping.

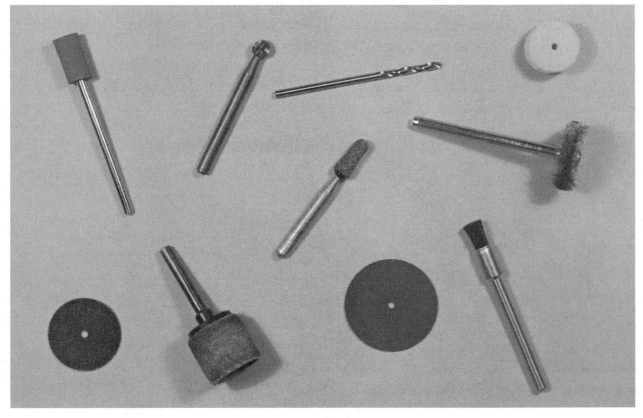

A wide assortment of attachments makes the Dremel tool extremely versatile.

Regardless of the polishing procedure being employed, the best advice is to hasten slowly. The idea is not to remove a significant amount of metal but rather to produce smooth surfaces. Try mating the parts being polished together frequently so you can ascertain the progress being made. Be careful not to round any edges that are supposed to be sharp. Removing too much metal may make tolerances sloppy so that parts do not fit together correctly. Polish the part but do not change it dimensionally.

One area in which polishing may be required is in fitting an aftermarket barrel to the receiver of a Ruger 10/22. Most of the barrels we have tested slipped easily into the receiver, but some did not. If the barrel does not enter the receiver easily, it is necessary to polish the barrel shank sufficiently to reduce the diameter slightly. The instruction sheets supplied with some of the barrels describe how to polish the barrel shank. The best way is to hold the barrel securely in a vice equipped with rubber jaws to prevent marring the surface of the barrel. Then, take a long strip of emery cloth or very fine sandpaper that

It is necessary to polish the tenons on some aftermarket barrels to permit them to be inserted into some receivers.

has a width that matches the length of the barrel shank. Wrap the strip around the barrel shank and pull it back and forth by the ends. After working in one direction (which allows the abrasive to contact about half the circumference of the barrel shank) pull the abrasive strip from the opposite direction to polish the other half. Rotate the barrel a quarter turn in the vice and polish from two directions again. After the entire circumference of the barrel shank has been polished, try to insert the barrel into the receiver. If minor polishing of the barrel shank does not allow it to enter the receiver, you should contact the manufacturer of the barrel to discuss how to proceed.

As we progress through the various chapters in this book, some of the areas of the Ruger 10/22 action that can benefit from polishing will be pointed out. Obviously, not everything needs to be polished because nothing is to be gained by polishing some areas that do not make contact with other parts. It is by polishing the areas where metal slides on metal that the operation of the action of a firearm can be improved.

Bluing Steel

Although the receiver of the Ruger 10/22 is made of an aluminum alloy that has a black coating, the barrel is made of steel that is blued (except for those made of stainless steel). Therefore, a few words about bluing are in order because touching up may be required. The topic of metal polishing is also appropriate to consider because before bluing is carried out the surface must be prepared. The surface to be blued should be absolutely smooth and free of oil so that the bluing solution can be applied to bare metal. Although the project

This old Weaver K6 scope clearly showed the effects of years of neglect and was bought as a "project" scope.

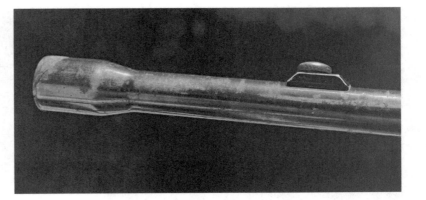

does not involve bluing a Ruger 10/22 barrel, the restoration of a scope will be described in order to illustrate what can be done using only simple techniques.

Many years ago, the metal tubes used in fabricating scopes were made of steel that usually had a blue finish. Today, virtually all new scope tubes are made of some type of aluminum alloy that is given a durable black finish. As a result, scopes of recent manufacture are lighter in weight and not subject to rusting. When we were in a pawn shop in Gillette, Wyoming we saw an old scope lying on the counter. It looked as if the scope had spent the last decade in a barn somewhere. The bluing was worn off in many places, and there were areas that showed heavy rusting. It was mentioned to the shop owner that the scope was in rather bad condition, and he was asked if it were for sale. His response

was, "How much is it worth to you?" If this comment has been heard once, it has been a hundred times. With a use in mind for the old scope, the decision had been made to buy it if the price was right so the answer was, "Five dollars." The owner responded immediately, "Its yours!" Never make an offer on anything unless you are ready to buy it. There is no doubt the owner had obtained the old scope in a box of junk as part of an estate sale and that any amount he received for it was all profit.

What had just been bought was an old Weaver K6 scope with a steel tube that was made in El Paso, Texas before Weaver became part of Meade Optical Company.

No part of the steel scope and caps were spared from the ravages of rust.

The forward bell was in such bad condition that it was unclear that the scope could be salvaged.

With a wire wheel on the Dremel tool, removing the rust on the forward bell was a simple task.

Optically, the scope seemed to be useable if the external appearance could be improved enough to make it acceptable.

The worst area of rust was on the forward bell. Because the area was just over the edge from the objective lens, I cut a cardboard disk the size of the lens and taped it in place so the lens would be protected during polishing to remove the rust. If there are sensitive regions near the areas that are to be polished, protect them first. It is better to prevent the polishing operation from spilling over to sensitive areas than to try to remedy the situation later.

Unlike many old scopes that have seen hard use, the tube of the $5 scope had no dents. The old steel scopes are extremely

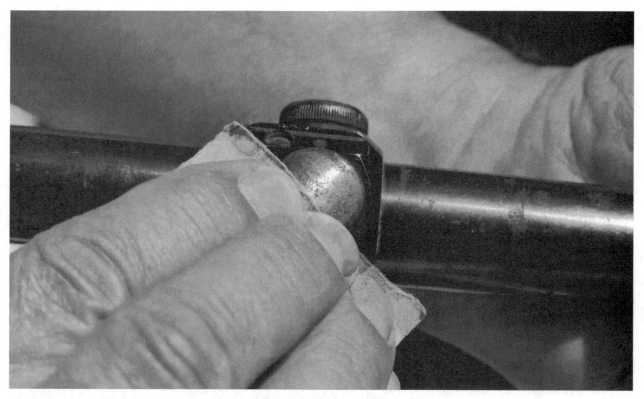

Rust was removed from the caps by sanding lightly with fine sandpaper.

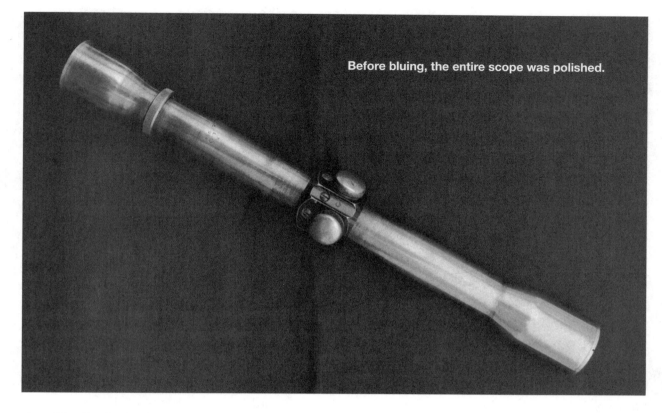

Before bluing, the entire scope was polished.

durable. With the lens protected, a wire wheel on a Dremel tool was used to remove the most of the loose rust from the worst areas. Next, extra fine steel wool (the grade known as 0000) was used to rub the entire scope. Although the original finish was still in reasonably good condition in some areas, I made no attempt to protect them. In order to get a uniform blue surface, the entire scope was polished. The brass rings around the ends on the scope were polished with the idea of leaving them that way, but they could have been blackened by painting them or they could have been made black by application of Birchwood Casey Brass Black solution.

After the surface was suitably prepared, it was wiped with a cloth wet with Coleman fuel to remove any residual oil. Birchwood Casey Perma Blue® was applied liberally with a piece of cloth, and the scope was allowed to stand for a few minutes. After wiping the surface with a damp paper towel, a second application of the bluing solution was applied. After rinsing the surface with water and drying it, the metal was buffed lightly with 0000 steel wool. These steps were repeated until six or seven coats of bluing had been applied. After the last application of bluing, the surface was rinsed, dried, and coated with Birchwood Casey Sheath® which protects the surface from rusting. After all, the

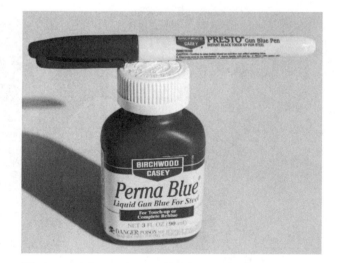

Birchwood Casey Perma Blue® is available in both liquid form and in a convenient felt tipped pen.

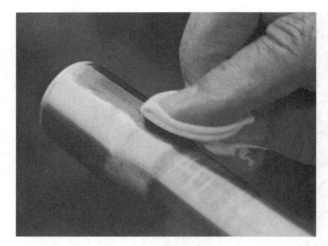

Birchwood Casey Perma Blue® was applied to the scope tube using a soft cloth.

The scope caps were blued, and the black turret base was touched up with black paint.

scope still has a steel tube that we want to protect from ever getting to the state where it was when we found it. When working with bluing solutions, follow the directions on the bottle, including cautions. Bluing solutions are toxic and should not be left in contact with the skin.

For many years, there was a reluctance on our part to try to repair blued surfaces or to completely reblue some part of a firearm. Now, we have no reservation about doing so, but probably would leave such work on an expensive firearm to a professional. The process is relatively simple and the results are generally good. Home blued steel certainly looks a lot better than rusted steel. Although the work described here involved a scope (partially so we could obtain photos of the work), the same procedures are applicable to other firearm-related projects. A young man that we visited with while camping in the mountains came over one day with his Ruger 10/22 that had no blue left on

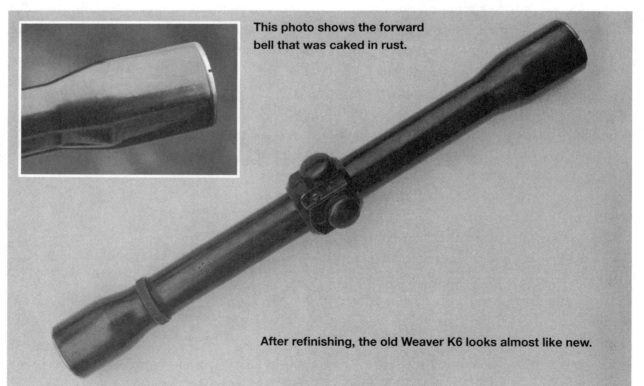

This photo shows the forward bell that was caked in rust.

After refinishing, the old Weaver K6 looks almost like new.

a section of the barrel because of the way in which he carried the rifle. The salts in perspiration had removed the bluing on steel. The procedures described above quickly made his rifle look much better.

Finishing Nonferrous Metals

Although the classic material for making parts for firearms is steel, many parts are made of aluminum, brass, or composite plastic materials. The reason for this is that aluminum and brass are easier to shape than steel, and composite materials can be molded to shape. Generally, composites have a color that is uniform throughout the piece. Changing the finish is not really feasible although some shooters paint composite stocks to give them a camouflaged appearance. Finishing aluminum or brass is often necessary because these metals are frequently given

a black finish to rather closely match the blued surface of steel, but some of the black coatings rub off rather easily.

There is an increasing use of aluminum alloy in the manufacture of firearms. The receiver of the Ruger 10/22 is made of such an alloy although that of the 10/22M is steel. Generally, the surfaces of aluminum parts are coated with a black enamel. Along edges, normal abrasion will often cause the black coating to be worn or flaked off. This is also true of the edges

Birchwood Casey offers felt tipped pens that contain flat or gloss black paint.

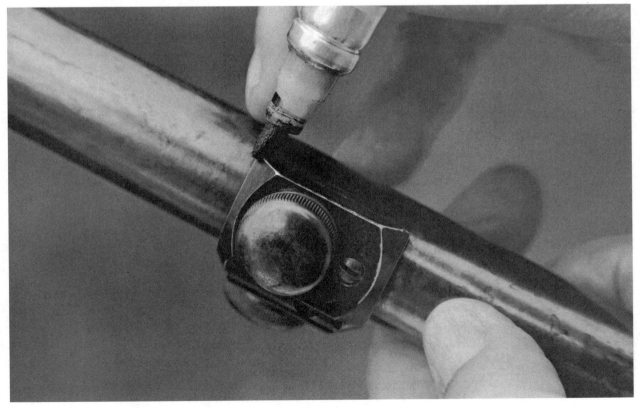

A paint pen is convenient for touching up areas where the paint has been rubbed off.

of scope rails and mounts that are made of aluminum alloy. While a spray can of enamel would certainly perform a touch up job, it is difficult to keep the sprayed enamel going exactly where you want it. A convenient item to have in the cleaning and maintenance kit is a black paint pen of the type marketed by Birchwood Casey. These paint pens have a felt chisel point and come in both flat and gloss black types. We have used these paint pens to touch up a wide range of aluminum parts on scopes and firearms.

Other commercial products for blackening aluminum and brass are available. Birchwood Casey markets products that are known as Aluminum Black and Brass Black. These solutions can be applied (always follow the directions on the bottles) to touch up the finish on a part or to completely coat one that has no finish. Although not applicable to the Ruger 10/22, many antique firearms

Using Brass Black from Birchwood Casey can restore brass objects that have lost their black coating.

had browned steel surfaces. Birchwood Casey markets a product known as Plum Brown® for restoring the surfaces on such firearms.

Finishing Wood

The basic processes involved in finishing wood have been well described in many publications. We will have a great deal more to say about finishing a stock in Chapter 7 where we discuss this topic in conjunction with restyling and refinishing a take off Ruger 10/22 factory stock. The essence of wood finishing is to prepare

Preparing the surface of a stock for finishing requires that it be made smooth with sandpaper.

All of the materials needed to finish a stock are contained in this kit from Outers®.

For cleaning old stocks or polishing new ones, Birchwood Casey Stock Sheen & Conditioner is an excellent product.

the surface by shaping and sanding, and then to apply the actual finish (oil, varnish, polyurethane, etc.). If the wood has open pores (as does walnut), the wood is generally treated with a sealer before applying the finish. Stain may be applied to give the wood the desired hue.

Several companies market complete stock finishing kits for the do it yourself hobbyist. These kits contain sandpaper, steel wool, stain, and finish with an applicator for applying the solutions. We have used the kits from Birchwood Casey and Outers with complete satisfaction. Prepare the surface meticulously and follow the directions on the kit. If you do, the result is likely going to be a stock that looks very good.

Although the details of the process used to finish a stock will be described and illustrated in Chapter 7, we should point out that it is often possible to make an old stock to look better simply by giving it a good cleaning. A product such as Birchwood Casey's Stock Sheen and Conditioner® contains a very small amount of fine abrasive in addition to the polish. When rubbed vigorously with a cloth containing the solution, the stock has the oxidized surface removed. The result is a brighter, more attractive stock. We have been amazed to see the difference between "before and after" treating some old stocks.

Cleaning

It has been stated that more rifle barrels are ruined by cleaning than by firing bullets through them. This may or may not be true, but there is no question that proper cleaning and maintenance are important to longevity and proper functioning of a firearm. Autoloaders get a lot of residue spewed into the action as the bolt opens which draws combustion products from the barrel into the action. Some autoloaders do not function well when dirty, but the Ruger 10/22 is among the most reliable. There is no need to completely disassemble a Ruger 10/22 to clean it. However, the more parts that are removed, the easier it is to clean them and the nooks and crannies where debris collects.

Cleaning a rifle that has the receiver and barrel permanently attached can be a problem. If the rifle is a bolt action, simply remove the bolt and clean the barrel from the breech. However, if the rifle is an autoloader, it is not advised to remove the barrel just so it can be cleaned from the breech. Cleaning can be done from the muzzle as long as it is done *carefully*. Fortunately, rimfire rifles do not present difficult cleaning situations because

One of the oldest cleaning solvents is Hoppe's No. 9. After all these years, it is still effective.

leading is minimal and there is no coating of jacket material the way there is in the bores of centerfire rifles. In most instances, only a gentle swabbing of the bore with a patch that has been wet with a solvent is necessary. However, we have

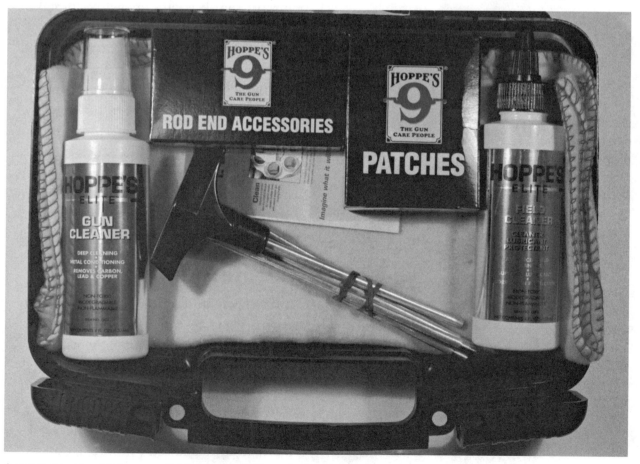

A good cleaning kit is essential for maintaining a rimfire rifle.

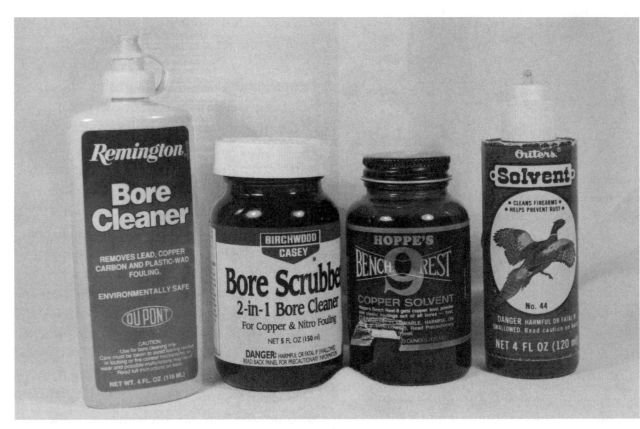

There are many excellent products available for cleaning firearms.

found that some rifles in .17 HMR caliber require much more frequent cleaning than do those in .22 LR. If the bores are not kept clean, the groups tend to increase in size as the firing continues.

The choice of solvent is somewhat arbitrary since many of them work well. One of the authors has been using Hoppe's No. 9 for about 60 years so a good supply is always on hand. Hoppe's also markets the No. 9 Benchrest Copper Solvent, which works well. Birchwood Casey Bore Scrubber is described as a "2-in-1 bore cleaner" that removes copper and fouling from nitrocellulose powders. Remington Bore Cleaner is described as removing lead, copper, carbon, and plastic-wad fouling. Outers offers a solvent for cleaning rifle bores that has been produced for many years. In addition to those listed, all of which we have used, there are many more available. A look at a catalog from one

of the large suppliers such as Sinclair International, Graf & Sons, Brownell's, or Midway USA will show that the choice of cleaning products is enormous. The point is, you do not have to settle for the first product you see. While most shooters probably have a favorite product, the truth is that all of them work satisfactorily for cleaning a rimfire rifle.

The most important aspect of cleaning the rifle bore is to prevent damage to the crown. In Chapter 2, we described how important this area of the barrel is to accuracy. If you must clean the bore from the muzzle, be extremely careful. We use two different procedures depending on the circumstances. First, use a bore guide that fits over the muzzle and directs the cleaning rod straight into the bore. Bore guides are available that fit over the muzzles of standard and heavy weight (0.920") barrels. Second, when cleaning the

A bore guide slipped over the muzzle of a Ruger 10/22 allows a cleaning rod to be inserted correctly.

bore, we always use a loosely fitting patch wet with solvent so little force is required. We also use a one-piece cleaning rod that is small enough in diameter to work with .17 calibers, and it has a polymer coating that prevents scratching the muzzle or bore. Under some conditions, we have used a 1/8-inch dowel rod. This small diameter rod made of wood cannot damage the barrel, but it is sufficiently strong to push a wet patch through the bore. After using a wet patch or two, let the rifle stand for a few minutes so the solvent can do its work.

Then, run a dry patch or two through the bore to remove the solvent and debris. If the rifle is not going to be used for a period of time, run a patch through the bore that has been wet with a drop or two of oil or Birchwood Casey Sheath® to prevent rusting.

An alternative to using a cleaning rod is to use a flexible cleaner. One type is the Hoppe's BoreSnake, which is available in numerous sizes to clean bores of different diameter. The BoreSnake has a brass weight on a pull cord, which is attached to the cleaning sections. Dropping the brass weight through the bore allows the user to pull on the cord to make the cleaning sections pass through the bore. A short section of the fabric has brass bristles embedded in it so pulling the BoreSnake through the bore not only gives the effect of using a brass brush, but also the effect of using several patches. The BoreSnake can also be used to apply cleaning solvent or oil to the bore.

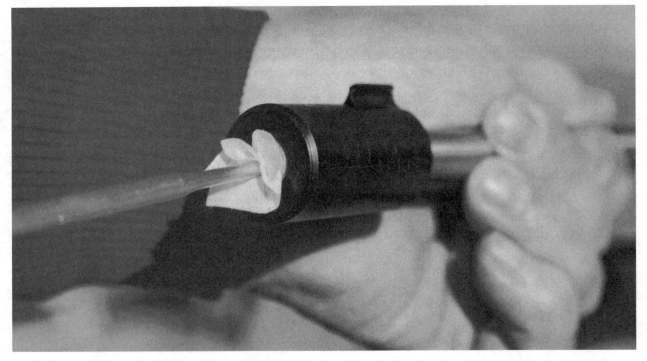

With the bore guide in place, push the patch in carefully while keeping the cleaning rod aligned with the barrel.

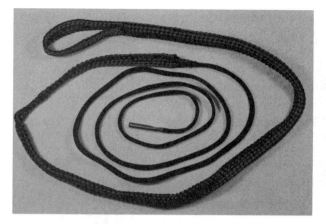

The BoreSnake® from Hoppe's can be used to clean the bore without the use of a cleaning rod.

A bore light is a useful device for inspecting the bore before and after cleaning.

In the case of a .22 autoloader, cleaning the action is probably more important than cleaning the bore. With the Ruger 10/22, cleaning the action is somewhat easier than it is for some other models. For a "light" cleaning, just pull the bolt back and lock it back. Remove the magazine and you will be able to access much of the action. First wipe out the accumulated solid debris with a cloth or paper towel. After the larger deposits have been removed, use a cloth wet with a cleaning solvent to wipe out as much of the remaining dirt as possible. At this point, a spray solvent is handy. We spray a solvent or even Birchwood Casey Sheath® into the open action and then wipe as much of out as possible. Use a small probe such as a toothpick or match stick to scrape the debris out of nooks and crannies. With as much of the debris removed as possible, apply a drop of oil to the extractor, the firing pin, bolt guide rod, and the upper part of the action. Cycling the action a few times will spread the oil to surfaces that need to be lubricated.

For a more thorough cleaning of the 10/22 action, remove the barreled action from the stock and press out the two pins that hold the trigger assembly to the receiver. You now have access to the area behind the bolt and the trigger

mechanism. It is now possible to remove more completely the debris using the same techniques described above. Before replacing the trigger mechanism, apply a drop of oil at the contact points in the trigger mechanism (hammer pivot pin, trigger pivot pin, hammer strut, etc.). Attach the trigger mechanism to the receiver using

Although there are many lubricants available, reading the labels shows that these two are drastically different.

the two pins and wipe the metal surfaces that will be hidden by the stock with a cloth on which has been placed a few drops of oil. Make sure that the bolt stop pin is in place because some fall out easily. Attach the barreled action to the stock and wipe the external metal surfaces with an cloth that has had oil or a protecting product such as Birchwood Casey Sheath® applied. Scope mount screws and the screw that holds the stock to the barreled action do work loose so before storing the rifle, check to see that all screws are tight using an appropriate screw driver.

Even if you do not perform a complete cleaning, wipe the external surfaces of your rifle before putting it away. Dirt, moisture, and perspiration can take a toll on the finish of barrel, action, and stock. Keep scope lenses clean by using a suitable lens cleaner.

After the rifle has been cleaned and lubricated, rub the external surfaces with a cloth containing a protector such as Birchwood Casey Sheath® to prevent rust.

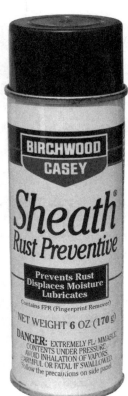

Rimfire rifles do not require an inordinate amount of maintenance, and a complete disassembly is seldom required. When you clean your rifle, be especially careful with the muzzle area. Given the fine gun care products available today, it is not difficult to keep firearms looking good and functioning well.

You may find it convenient to remove grime and oil from a magazine by using a solvent such as Coleman fuel.

GRANDMASTERS, L.L.C. Formerly Known As Power Custom, Inc.
is the world's foremost suppliers of Ruger 10-22® Internal Accessories.

10/22® MATCHED HAMMER & SEAR PACK

Mfg. by E.D.M. process, carbon steel 56-58RC, precision ground w/honed engagement surfaces. E.P. hammer & disc./sear spg., 2 trigger shims, 2 hammer shims. Repl. trigger ret. spg. Allows for 2-1/2 lb. pull.
DROP-IN PARTS, possible minor fitting
10/22® HS PAC.
   Works in **10/22®** Magnum.
10/22® Pretravel Adj. Sear and Hammer
   (eliminate most of your pretravel for a crisper Trigger pull)

10/22® Hammer & Sear Pack

10/22® TITANIUM ACCESSORIES

TFP TBHA TT TMR

Mfg. by E.D.M. process produces improved geometrical designed corrosion resistance parts that have a higher tensile strength and are 40% lighter than steel. Shorter, faster lock/cycle time, more positive feeding with less chance of misfires.

DROP-IN PARTS

10/22® Firing pin-TFP
10/22® Ext. Operating Bolt Handle Assy-TBHA
10/22® Trigger w/overtravel Adj. Stop-TT
10/22® Extended Mag. Release-TMR
ORDER ALL OF THE ABOVE AS A KIT AND SAVE 17%-10/22® **GMAK**
10/22® Titanium Sharp Claw Extractor

ACCESSORIES

CST Auto Bolt Stop Kit, .22 LR includes 1 new 10 rd. magazine for standard Ruger Trigger Assemblies
CST Auto Bolt Stop Kit, .22 Mag, with 1 new 10 rd. magazine for standard Ruger Trigger Assemblies
CST 10 round Modified Magazine for CST Auto Bolt Stop
CST 9 round Modified Magazine for CST Auto Bolt Stop
10/22® COMPETITION HAMMER Decrease lock time-w/E.P. Hammer Spg., Replacement Trig. Spg., 2-.004 Shims.- **10/22® HO**
10/22® COMPETITION SEAR Compatible w/Factory & DROP-IN Hammers-w/E.P. Sear/Disc. Spg., Assy. Pin, 2-.004 Shims- **10/22® SO**
10/22® COMPETITION SPRING GUIDE STAINLESS STEEL- Compatible w/Factory or Power Custom E.P. Operating Spg.- **10/22® SG**
10/22® EXTRA POWER OPERATING SPRING-10/22® EPS
HAMMER & TRIGGER SHIMS- 302 Stainless, .004 thick, 10 of one size per pkg.
HAMMER SHIMS-10/22® HS
TRIGGER SHIMS-10/22® TS
10/22® CUSTOM SPRING KIT (All springs in GMAK)-**10/22® SK**
10/22® ACTION SCOPE BASE (Black Hard Coat Alum.)-D&T Bbl.- **10/22® ABB**
10/22® ACTION SCOPE BASE (Silver Anodized Alum.)-D&T Bbl.- **10/22® ABS**
10/22® MAG. Titanium Firing Pin
10/22® DOUBLE BIGHEAD SAFETY Blue. Works with **10/22®** Mag.
10/22® DOUBLE BIGHEAD SAFETY Stainless. Works with **10/22®** Mag. (Double Bighead Safety is protected under design patent #D458,333)
10/22® Hogue Bull Barrel Stock
10/22® Mag. Hogue Bull Barrel Stock
10-22® Buffer Technologies Bolt Buffer
10-22® Titanium Ext. Auto Bolt Release
10-22® Mag. Titanium Ext. Auto Bolt Release
10-22® A-2 Tool Steel Firing Pin
10-22® Mag. A-2 Tool Steel Firing Pin
10-22® Comp. Hammer w/Auto Bolt Release
10-22® Power Grade Competition Trigger Kit (Includes Trigger, Hammer, & Sear Pack, Buffer Technologies Buffer, Ext. Mag. Release, and Titanium Ext. Auto Bolt Release)
10-22® Factory 10-rd. magazine
10-22® LR Aluma-lite Target/Varmint Barrel
10-22® Mag. Aluma-lite Target/Varmint Barrel
20" Stainless Steel Kidd Bull Barrel (.920")
Kidd Trigger Guard super match (6-14 oz. Trigger pull)
Kidd Trigger Guard match (14-28 oz. Trigger pull)

Kidd Trigger Guard sportsman (1-1/4 - 2-1/2 lbs Trigger pull)
10-22® Competition Trigger Kit (Includes Trigger, Hammer, & Sear Pack & Buffer tech buffer)
10-22® Assembly/Disassembly Video
10-22® Fiber Force Stock
10-22® Feather weight Bipod Swivel Model
10-22® Feather Weight Bipod Non Swivel Model
10-22® Extra Power Hammer Spring
10-22® Extra Power Extractor Spring
10-22® Extra Power Disconnector Spring
10-22® Replacement Trigger Return Spring
10-22® Kidd Receiver Pin Kit (Includes Counter Sink)
10-22® Kidd Receiver Pins only
10-22® LR Whistle Pig Barrel Mat. Alum. 16"
10-22® LR Whistle Pig Barrel Mat. Alum. 17"
10-22® LR Whistle Pig Barrel Mat. Alum. 18"
10-22® LR Whistle Pig Barrel Mat. Alum. 20"
10-22® LR Whistle Pig Barrel Polished Alum. 16"
10-22® LR Whistle Pig Barrel Polished Alum. 17"
10-22® LR Whistle Pig Barrel Polished Alum. 18"
10-22® LR Whistle Pig Barrel Polished Alum. 20"
10-22® LR Whistle Pig Barrel Gloss Black 16'
10-22® LR Whistle Pig Barrel Gloss Black 17'
10-22® LR Whistle Pig Barrel Gloss Black 18'
10-22® LR Whistle Pig Barrel Gloss Black 20'
10-22® Innovations Buffer
10-22® Kidd Buffer
10-22® Modified Blot with the correct .044" Headspaceing
10-22® Stainless Steel Ext. Blot Handle
10-22® A-2 Tool Steel Extractor
10-22® Titanium Sharp Claw Extractor
10-22® Competition Sear
10-22® Competition Trigger Kit
10-22® Pretravel Adj. Sear & Hammer Pack
10-22® Grandmaster Action Kit w/ A-2 Tool Steel Firing Pin
10-22® Grandmaster Action Kit w/ pretravel Adj. Sear & Hammer
10-22® Grandmaster Action Kit w/ pretravel Adj. Sear & Hammer w/ A-2 Tool Steel Firing Pin
10-22® Pretravel Adj. Sear & Hammer Pack
10-22® Kidd Trigger 6-14 oz. w/ Mod. Bolt w/ Ext. Bolt Handle & TFP & TE
10-22® Kidd Trigger 14-28 oz w/ Mod. Bolt w/ Ext. Bolt Handle & TFP & TE
10-22® Kidd Trigger 1-1/4 to 2-1/2 lbs. W/ Mod. Bolt w/ Ext. Bolt Handle &TFP &TE
10-22® Kidd Trigger 6-14 oz. w/ Mod. Bolt only
10-22® Kidd Trigger 14-28 oz. w/ Mod. Bolt only
10-22® Kidd Trigger 1-1/4 - 2-1/2 lbs. W/ Mod. Bolt only .22 LR
10-22® Kidd Trigger 6-14 oz. w/ Aluma-Lite Barrel .22 LR
10-22® Kidd Trigger 14-28 oz. w/ Aluma Lite Barrel .22 LR
10-22® Kidd Trigger 1-1/4- 2-1/2 lbs. w/ Aluma Lite Barrel .22 LR
10-22® Action Kit w/ A-2 Tool Steel Firing Pin
10-22® Pretravel Adj. Sear
10-22® Disconnector Shims
10-22® Christies Recoil Buffer
10-22® Auto Bolt Release
10-22® Polymer Mounting Base
10-22® Polymer Ext. Mag. Release
10-22® Jumbo Cocking Handle
10-22® E-Z Loader
10-22® Polymer Flash Hider
10-22® Magazine Caps
10-22® Christie's Mag. Caddy

22® RECEIVER ACCESSORIES

10/22® Weaver Style Receiver Mount Black Hardcoat
10/22® Weaver Style Receiver Mount Silver Anodized

10/22® Receiver Mount

GUNSMITHING SERVICES

NEW! For those of you who are not confident in your ability to install Power Custom parts in your Ruger 10-22®, we now offer gunsmithing services for professional installation of our parts in your 10-22®. **Trigger Group Installation** (not including parts), if you already have our Ruger 10-22® parts and need them installed? Please send us your Ruger 10-22® Trigger Guard/Action (with all internal parts) and we will install your Power Custom parts.
Trigger Group Installation (including Hammer & Sear pack), if you would like your trigger pull reduced to around 2-3/4 lbs and need our Ruger 10-22® Hammer & Sear-this service includes our Ruger 10-22® Hammer & Sear pack plus installation and shipping.

Trigger Group Installation (including Competition Trigger kit), this service includes: shipping, installation and the Competition Trigger kit
Trigger Group Installation Grandmaster Action kit, this service includes: shipping, installation and the Grandmaster Action kit

POWER CUSTOM QUALITY RUGER 10-22® CNC MACHINED WEAVER STYLE SCOPE BASE

- Attaches to your receiver without drilling and tapping.
- Includes 6 cross slots to allow for some scope ring adjustments.
- Includes 4 screws and an Allen wrench.
- Choose Black Hardcoat or Silver Anodized.
- Is .437" high.

10-22® Bolt Buffer
10-22® Hammer & Sear Pack (reduce trigger pull to 2-3/4 lbs)
10-22® Titanium Ext. Bolt Handle
10-22® Titanium Firing Pin
10-22® Titanium Sharp Claw Extractor
10-22® Majestic Arms Barrel (.22LR)
Ruger 10/22® is a registered trademark of Sturm, Ruger & Co., Inc.

10-22® COMPETITION TRIGGER KIT

Includes all the parts in the 10-22® Hammer & Sear Pack along with the Titanium Trigger w/overtravel adj. screw and a Buffer Technologies Bolt Buffer.

10-22® Titanium Trigger Only
10-22® Titanium Firing Pin Only
10-22® Competition Hammer Only
10-22® Competition Sear Only
10-22® Titanium Extractor
10-22® Buffer Technologies Bolt Buffer

CHRISTIE'S 10-22® PRODUCTS

Christie's Recoil Buffer Pin for Ruger 10/22®

10-22® Recoil Buffer
10-22® Auto Bolt Release
10-22® Polymer Accessory Mounting Base
10-22® Polymer Ext. Mag. Release
10-22® Jumbo Cocking Handle
10-22® E-Z Loader
10-22® Polymer Flash Hider
10-22® Magazine Caps
10-22® Christie's Mag. Caddy

GRANDMASTERS, L.L.C.
F.K.A.: POWER CUSTOM, INC.

Detailed instructions: **DEALERS INQUIRE** - Manufacturer of Tools, Fixtures and Accessories of ADVANCED DESIGN for the PROFESSIONAL GUNSMITH & SERIOUS COMPETITOR.

MasterCard VISA   **MC - VISA - DISCOVER - AMEX**   DISCOVER   AMEX
29739 Hwy. J, Dept. SGN • GRAVOIS MILLS, MO 65037
Ph. (573) 372-5684 • Fax. (573) 372-5799
Ruger 10/22® is a registered trademark of Sturm, Ruger & Co., Inc.
www.powercustom.com

"Hobbyists, and professional gunsmiths rely on our gunsmithing tools to perform their gunsmithing projects."

All prices are subject to change. Store hours 9:30 a.m. to 4:00 p.m. CST. Superior Service and Quality Guaranteed.

Check out our Web site at www.powercustom.com current prices.
Grandmaster is a registered trademark of Grandmasters, L.L.C. Registered #1179035

Customize your 10/22 Today!

Pistol & Rifle Barrels/Stocks
Triggers, Custom Kits, Scopes
Magazines, Shooting accessories,
& Much More!

Hornet Products
P. O. Box 1664
Sarasota, FL 34230-1664

Call (941)359-1319

Visit Us Online!
www.hornetproducts.com

RUGER 10/22 SUPERSTORE

MUST-HAVE REFERENCES FOR ACTIVE SHOOTERS

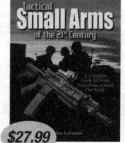

Gun Digest 2007 — $29.99

CARTRIDGES OF THE WORLD 11th Edition — $29.99

The 1911 — $27.95

The 1911 Volume 2 — $27.99

These books and other Gun Digest® Books are available from booksellers and other retailers nationwide or directly from Gun Digest® Books by calling 800-258-0929 Offer GNB6 or online at www.gundigestbooks.com.

RIMFIRE RIFLES Assembly/Disassembly — $27.99

Tactical Small Arms of the 21st Century — $27.99

THE ABC'S OF RELOADING 7th Edition — $21.99

THE AR-15 — $27.99

Gun Digest® Books
An imprint of F+W Publications
700 E. State St. • Iola, WI 54990-0001

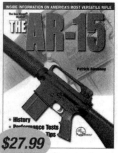

Introducing the New Ruger 10/22® Compact Rifle

NEW RUGER
10/22 COMPACT RIFLE

Fiber optic front sight with contrasting color for quick target acquisition

Shorter (16 1/8") barrel

Correctly proportioned tapered forend with no barrel band

Ruger 10/22 Rifle
10/22RR • .22 LR
Overall length - 38 1/2"
Weight - 5 lbs.
Suggested retail price of $275.00

New Ruger 10/22 Compact Rifle
10/22CRR • .22 LR
Overall length - 33 1/4"
Weight - 4.5 lbs.
Suggested retail price of $275.00

The first Ruger 10/22 was introduced in 1964. Over 5 million have been sold – making the legendary 10/22 the most successful rimfire carbine ever produced. With great features like its patented detachable rotary magazine that mounts flush with the stock and combination tip-off and Weaver-style scope adapter, the 10/22 is the top choice among rimfire shooters.

In 2004, the 10/22 Rifle was introduced, with a slim new rifle-style stock, fiber optic sights, and a 20-inch tapered barrel. In response to the overwhelming demand, Sturm, Ruger now introduces the New 10/22 Compact Rifle – the perfect lightweight companion. With its 16 1/8-inch barrel, compact rifle-style stock with a short forend and length-of-pull, and fiber-optic front and rear sights, the New 10/22 Compact Rifle is a lightweight, fast-handling rifle worthy of the 10/22 legacy.

Flat buttplate

Slim, rifle-style hardwood stock with shorter (12 3/4") length-of-pull

Rifle-style fiber optic rear sight gathers maximum light and provides easy sight alignment

www.ruger.com

MADE IN USA

RUGER®

ARMS MAKERS FOR RESPONSIBLE CITIZENS®

Sturm, Ruger & Company, Inc.
Southport, CT 06890 U.S.A.

FREE Instruction Manuals are available online at www.ruger.com

The Green Mountain "Aero Series" of competition and sport barrels.

Green Mountain Rifle Barrel Company is pleased to offer its most technologically advanced barrels for the Ruger 10-22 rimfire rifles.

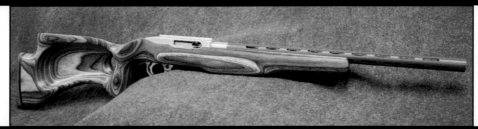

The Aero Series combines a precisely machined barrel made of extremely rigid and durable 410 stainless steel surrounded by a shroud of 6061T6 seamless aerospace tubing. The shroud is double o-ring dampened at the chamber end to ensure consistent alignment and vibration abatement. The 16" barrel is free floated from 1" in front of the chamber to the 11-degree muzzle crown. The stainless steel barrel is stress relieved after all machining to ensure stability and accuracy. The semi-auto match chamber is of the Bentz type and mated to a faster 1:15 rifling twist for better performance with competition ammunition and great performance even with the least expensive bulk ammunition available. The barrel shroud is .92" in diameter allowing use in all readily available stock made for traditional "bull" type barrels. The Competition Model has an adjustable barrel weight integral to the shroud and never touches the inner barrel. The Sporting Model utilizes the same chamber and rifling as the competition models but features an ultra-light, machined tube with a tough anodize surface finish in five color choices. The Sporting Model shrouds are interchangeable with the Competition Model's barrel weight version allowing for a great deal of flexibility. At a weight of about one pound these barrels bring a degree of flexibility, style and performance rarely achieved in ultra-light rifle design.

The Sporting Model barrels are also available for the 10-22 .22 Magnum in a 19" version with all the same features.

Tapered octagon in .17 HMR

GM has available a wide variety of barrels to personalize the performance and style of your Ruger rimfire rifle.

16" fluted stainless with William's Fire Sights

Accessory Full Float Tubes Are Available.

Green Mountain Rifle Barrel Co. Inc.

PO Box 2670 • Conway, NH 03815 • 603-447-1095
www.gmriflebarrel.com

Classic to Fantastic

Green Mountain barrels has the key to make your custom Ruger rimfire rifle unique in style and unmatched in performance.

www.gmriflebarrel.com

GreenMountain
Rifle Barrel Co. Inc.

P.O. Box 2670 • Conway, NH 03815 • 603.447.1095

CUSTOM SUPPRESSORS

WE SPECIALIZE IN INTEGRALLY SUPPRESSED 10/22 RIFLES!

OUR INTEGRALLY SUPPRESSED RIFLES ARE AMONG THE QUIETEST AND MOST ACCURATE IN THE INDUSTRY. WE DESIGN OUR GUNS TO HAVE THE APPEARANCE OF A FACTORY BARREL, AND WE TUNE AND CHRONY EVERY BARREL ASSEMBLY SO THE BULLET WILL REMAIN SUBSONIC WITH A WIDE VARIETY OF STANDARD AMMO.

10/22 available stainless or black. Also, MKII Pistols!

MORE AFFORDABLE than you think!

FG Frank's Gun

1315 W. Zora
Joplin, MO 64801
(417) 850-1649
www.atfmachinegun.com

BUY THE BEST!

ROSS

SS EVOLUTION

BLASTER

DAKOTA WILL

THE WORLD'S FOREMOST SUPPLIER OF HARDWOOD GUNSTOCKS

UNLEASH YOUR 10/22!

4 STOCK STYLES & 15 LAMINATE COLORS plus Accessories!

See BOYDS' website for

on-line purchasing of Thousands o

Makes and Models of Gunstocks,

Accessories and Gunsmithing Tool

www.boydsgunstocks.com

(605)996-5011

BOYDS'

GUNSTOCK INDUSTRIES, INC.
In the WOODS for 25 Years!

Your Source for 10/22 Parts

Numrich Gun Parts Corporation is the world's largest supplier of original and reproduction firearm parts and accessories. — We carry over 650 million obsolete, antique and current parts, as well as military surplus and parts for foreign guns. —

RUGER 10/22 MAGNUM 20" .17 HMR BULL BARREL

Machined from .920" OD 4140 bar stock. Features a blued finish, 6-groove rifling and a 1/9 twist.
ITEM#RU881640 $146.95

RUGER 10/22 20" 17 MACH 2 BULL BARREL CONVERSION KIT

Our drop-in blued-steel barrel features a .920"OD, 6-groove rifling and 1/9 twist. The oversized steel bolt handle and recoil spring unit allows the factory bolt to open slower providing safe and reliable cycling of this high-speed ammunition.
ITEM#RU931930 $159.95

RUGER 10/22 AUTO BOLT RELEASE

Made in the U.S.A. from hardened blued-steel. Eliminates the two-handed procedure needed to release the factory bolt. Closes bolt with just a slight pull of the handle. Installs easily with no modifications. Instructions and diagram included.
ITEM#RU955720 $8.95

RUGER 10/22 LAMINATED BARRACUDA STOCKS

Features a radical, ergonomic design for maximum shooting accuracy. The custom cut-away portion of the stock, combined with a hand conforming thumbhole, tear-drop pistol grip, wide-tapered forend and black rubber rifle pad, provide the perfect weight and balance for target acquisitions. The free-float barrel channel accepts .920" OD target barrels.
Brown Barracuda Stock, .22 LR/.17 Mach 2. . . . . **ITEM#RU851030 $157.45**
Black Barracuda Stock, .22 LR/.17 Mach 20. . . . . **ITEM#RU851040 $157.45**
Brown Barracuda Stock, .22 Magnum/.17 HMR. . . . . **ITEM#RU884740 $157.45**
Black Barracuda Stock, .22 Magnum/.17 HMR . . . . . **ITEM#RU884750 $157.45**

RUGER 10/22 MUZZELITE BULLPUP STOCK CONVERSION KIT

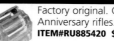

Drop-in stock features glass-filled nylon construction. Rifle measures just 26 1/2" when assembled. Includes a windage adjustable rear sight, elevation adjustable front sight, weaver-style scope mount and 1" black nylon sling. Hardware, tools and instructions included. Note: Sling swivel, scope, scope rings and 10/22 barreled action are not included. Note: Fits standard .22 LR models only.
ITEM#RU885410 $104.95

RUGER 10/22 10 ROUND .22 LR SEE-THRU MAGAZINE

Factory original. Clear plastic. Fits standard and 40th Anniversary rifles.
ITEM#RU885420 $17.80

RUGER 10/22 / MG42 DRESS-UP KIT

Converts a standard 10/22 .22 LR into a 2/3 scale WWII German MG42 M.G. replica with no modifications required. Kit includes a two-piece black composite stock, vented barrel shroud, windage adjustable front sight, elevation adjustable rear sight and a flashhider. Hardware and instructions included. For an even more authentic look or display, press a length of blank, linked .223 ammo into the left receiver port. Clamp-on style black nylon bipod is also available, ITEM#296870.
ITEM#RU717900 $157.45

CAN'T FIND THE PART YOU NEED? WE'VE GOT OVER 180,000
MORE ON-LINE AT:
e-GunParts.com

NUMRICH
CORPORATION
GUN PARTS
Established 1950

Shipping and handling costs for parts orders additional. Call for details.

Mail: 226 Williams Lane, P.O. Box 299, West Hurley, NY 12491 • Order Toll-Free: 866-686-7424 • Toll-Free Fax: 877- GUNPART • Web: e-GunParts.com

STOCKS FOR THE RUGER 10/22

Far from being just a handle on a rifle, the stock is the platform on which the other components rest. It provides the interface between the shooter and the mechanism that launches the bullet. The stock is a vital component in determining how accurately a rifle can be fired, and it can also be the most attractive part of the rifle. The owner of a Ruger 10/22 does not have to be stuck with the carbine stock that came on it. Aftermarket stocks for the 10/22 are available in almost any configuration imaginable. One thing to keep in mind is that some manufacturers offer a particular style of stock in several combinations of materials and colors. For example, laminated stocks can be produced with layers in almost any color combination. The result is that the 10/22 owner has available a huge assortment of stocks from which to make a selection. We have not had the opportunity (or time) to test, evaluate, and photograph all of the optional stocks. Consequently, the discussion in this chapter is meant to survey the general types of stocks that are available, but certainly not every variation offered.

Firing a rifle from a bench is easier if the stock is properly shaped. The Boyds' Smart Stock that Jim is using is such a stock.

Stocks of all types are available for customizing a Ruger 10/22.

Stock Styles

The stock on a rifle (since this book is concerned with a specific rifle, we will omit shotguns) serves more than one function. Of course, it is what the shooter holds when firing the rifle, but looks play a role in stock design. Like any other object that is created to appeal to the esthetic senses, rifle stocks often reflect the artistic tastes of the makers. Stocks produced for use on inexpensive rifles are often designed with ease of manufacturing as a design goal. As a result of these factors, there are many individual aspects that appear on stocks from one manufacturer that are different from those from another. For example, the stock on the 10/22 Carbine is quite different from those on most other .22 rifles.

Over a period of many years, certain stock designs have become recognizable. For example, Roy Weatherby of South Gate, California designed a series of centerfire rifles known as the Weatherby Magnums that offered higher velocities than those produced by standard calibers of that time. The rifles that chambered those cartridges were initially offered with a stocks having a rakish style that has become known as the California style. It features a high rollover cheek piece, a grip with a pronounced hook that actually curves forward at the bottom, and lavish inlays and fore end tips.

Another style of rifle stock is essentially recognizable as that which appears on such rifles as the Ruger Model 77 Mark II, Remington Model 700, and the Winchester Model 70 centerfire. Such stocks are also

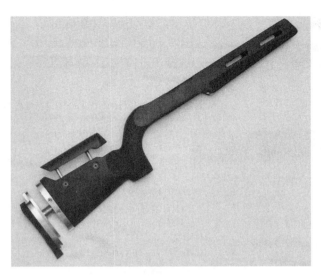

The ultimate in versatility is exhibited in the Odyssey from Bell & Carlson.

exaggerated curves at the grip. This is generally known as the classic sporting rifle stock.

The stocks on rifles intended for formal competitive shooting represent another stock form. Target stocks are generally somewhat blocky in shape with large fore ends and squarish combs and grip areas. It is readily apparent that this type of stock is intended for precise, secure holding of the rifle rather than to appeal to a sense of artistic beauty. In the best target stocks, the fore end may have a metal rail inletted into the bottom where a hand stop and sling can be attached. Target stocks are highly functional, utilitarian pieces that perform extremely well their intended uses.

As you work through the remainder of this chapter, you will see that another type of stock has appeared in modern times, and it is frequently found on 10/22s. It

found on the Ruger 77/22 series. Although made of uncheckered hardwood, the stock of the Ruger 10/22 Rifle has a similar overall configuration. These stocks are generally unadorned with regard to inlays, fore end tips of a different material, and

The factory stock on the Ruger 10/22 Rifle has the lines of the classic sporter style.

These Choate stocks represent the tactical look. A folding model is shown at top.

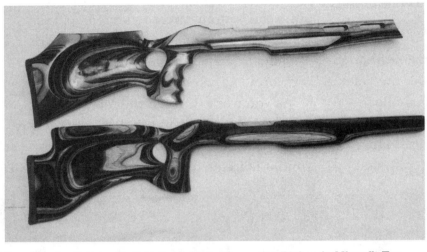

Two stocks that typify the dramatic look are the Richards Microfit Tac-Driver Silhouette (top) and the Revival Industries Yukon (bottom).

the high cheek pieces and broad forearms that characterize target stocks, these stocks are quite different. They have a large area scalloped out on one side of the buttstock, a thumbhole grip area, and some rather bizarre shape to the forearm. They are almost always made of laminated wood, and many are highly colored. We choose to call this type of stock a fantasy model. In form it is certainly not a California, classic, target, or tactical stock. Many such stocks are available for the Ruger 10/22, and as we move through this chapter some of the more common styles will be seen. Although we have for sake of convenience referred to them as fantasy stocks, they are nonetheless quite functional, beautiful, and sturdy. Keep in mind that a stock with a large raised cheek piece interferes with the earmuff type of hearing protectors.

Although stocks are produced in a bewildering array of styles, there are three basic materials most often used in their construction. Solid wood, laminated wood, and composite (a term that applies to a combination of plastics, resins, fiberglass, carbon fibers, etc.). These materials will be used as the basis for separating the discussion of stocks into three categories. In order to provide reference data on the stocks that were evaluated while preparing this book, the following table is included.

is an outgrowth of what we might call the "tactical" movement. A tactical style stock is virtually always made of a black composite material. It may have a skeleton style buttstock (such as the Dragunov style), a pistol grip, and even a hand guard to cover the barrel along the middle region. Tactical style rifles have become quite popular in recent years, and the number of available models has increased. This trend has even carried over in to the airgun market.

Even with the broad categories described above, there are still many stocks produced for the Ruger 10/22 that do not fit in any of the categories. Although some have

Characteristics of the Stocks Evaluated for the Ruger 10/22 and 10/22M

Stock	Weight (oz.)	Length (in.)	Approximate Length of Pull (in.)	Approx. Price
.22 LR Standard Barrel Channel				
Advanced Technology Fiberforce	22.5	29.00	13.50	$59.99
Choate Folding Pistol Grip	34.7	19.25/28.25[a]	13.25	$98.75
Choate Pistol Grip	21.3	29.00	13.50	$69.99
Factory Carbine Hardwood	29.2	29.50	13.25	NA
Factory Carbine Walnut	28.6	29.25	13.25	NA
Factory Compact	24.1	27.50	12.63	NA
Factory Rifle	24.8	29.75	13.5	NA
Factory Wal-Mart Hardwood	37.8	29.50	13.63	NA
Factory Deluxe Sporter Walnut	30.3	29.25	13.75	NA
Factory Target	38.6	29.50	13.75	NA
Hogue Nylon OverMolded	39.7	29.25	13.75	$79.95
Hogue Rubber OverMolded	31.7	29.25	13.88	$79.95
.22 LR 0.920" Barrel Channel				
Bell & Carlson Anschutz	40.8	29.63	13.25	$160.10
Bell & Carlson Odyssey 2-Way	57.8	27.88[b]	12.75[b]	$245.61
Boyds' Smart Stock	42.9	28.38	13.63	$152.40[c]
Butler Creek	36.1	29.13	13.50	$55.00
Cabela's Thumbhole Sporter	45.4	29.25	13.88	$159.99
CoreLite	32.3	29.25	13.88	$69.99
Fajen Thumbhole	41.9	29.13	13.50	$199.99
Hogue OverMolded Rubber	31.6	29.25	13.75	$84.95
McMillan Custom Sporter	24.3	29.00	13.38	$225.00
Revival Industries	42.7	29.25	13.63	$129.99
Revival Industries	46.4	29.63	13.63	$129.99
Richard's Microfit[d]	46.6	28.50	13.88	$177.00
.22 WMR/.17 HMR Standard Barrel Channel				
Factory Carbine Hardwood	31.8	29.38	13.38	NA
Boyds' Dakota Will	44.4	29.00	13.88	$87.94[d]
.22 WMR/.17HMR 0.920" Barrel Channel				
Butler Creek	33.9	29.13	—	
Hogue Rubber OverMolded	30.3	29.25	—	$99.95

[a] 19.25" when folded / 28.25" when opened.
[b] With stock fully collapsed. It can be lengthened.
[c] Also available unfinished for $99.99.
[d] Unfinished.

Wood Stocks

The classical stock maker generally selected some type of wood as the material of choice for making rifle stocks. High quality firearms have most often had stocks made of some variety of walnut, but several other types of wood have been used. Walnut typically has attractive grain, and it is a durable wood that can be beautifully finished. Being an open grain wood, a filler is usually applied before the finish is applied. Staining can easily be done to give walnut a wide range of appearances. Walnut can be finished to produce an exquisite stock.

Because of the cost and limited availability of fine walnut, inexpensive firearms often have stocks made of some type of hardwood such as birch, aspen, beech, maple, or other types of wood. In general, these types of wood do not have the attractive grain of walnut and when

finished they sometimes appear of almost uniform (often described as "muddy") color. Nevertheless, such stocks are functional and durable.

Stocks made of wood have been used on the Ruger 10/22 since its introduction. Early production carbines had stocks made of walnut, but around 1981 hardwood became the material of choice. Hardwoods most often used to produce stocks for low cost rifles include birch and maple. The version of the 10/22 known as the Deluxe Sporter has a stock made of walnut that is checkered at the grip and forearm. Except for the undercut shape of the fore end, it is a well-shaped stock. The discontinued Ruger 10/22 International, which has a full-length stock, was initially produced with a checkered walnut stock, but those produced later have a checkered hardwood stock. A version of the Ruger 10/22 referred to as the "Wal-Mart model" has a

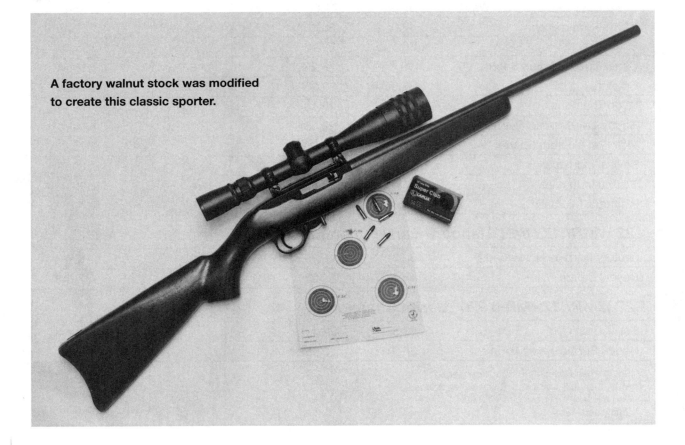

A factory walnut stock was modified to create this classic sporter.

checkered hardwood stock, and it features a 22-inch stainless steel barrel. It is know as the "Wal-Mart model" because this variant is produced for a large distributor, Lipsey's of Baton Rouge, LA, who markets them primarily through Wal-Mart stores.

Aftermarket stocks made of solid wood are not commonly available except for those produced by custom stock makers. Because they are essentially hand made, custom stocks tend to be very elegant and very expensive. However, the vast majority of shooters who modify a Ruger 10/22 will opt for a readymade aftermarket stock, and those are almost always laminates or composites. One exception that we know about is the Dakota Will style stock from

Boyds' Gunstock Industries for the Ruger 10/22 with a 0.920-inch barrel channel. This stock is available both finished and unfinished.

Laminated Stocks

With high quality woods such as walnut becoming more scarce and costly, many items are being fabricated from thin sheets of wood glued together. Objects made from laminated wood sheets actually have several advantages over those made from a single piece of wood. One advantage is that of directional stability. The sheets can be arranged so that the grain does not all run in one direction. When a single piece of wood becomes moist (and wood can absorb

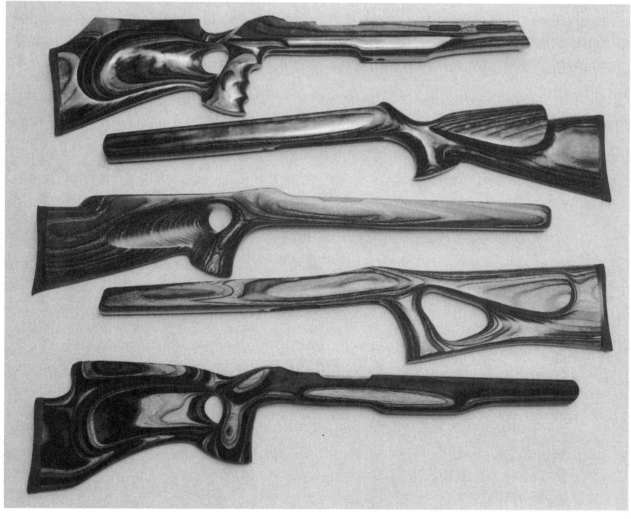

Laminated stocks are available in a wide variety of styles and colors.

moisture), it may change shape slightly either by becoming moist or when drying out. The layers of wood in a laminated stock tend to average out these effects so that such stocks are less sensitive to moisture and drying.

Another advantage of laminated stocks is that they can be produced in a virtual rainbow of colors. The sheets of wood can be dyed different colors so the stock has a striped look when viewed along the edges, but have swirls of different color when viewed toward a curved surface. Some stocks present dramatic color combinations such as blue and gold, red and black, blue and gray, etc. The visual effect can be most pleasing to the eye. Moreover, laminated stocks are produced in several configurations that include sporter, target, thumbhole, and other types. Objects made of laminated wood tend to be heavier than

the same objects made of a single piece of wood. That is probably one reason why so many of the laminated stocks have large cut out areas around the grip (thumbhole models), scalloped out regions along the butt stock, or slots along the forearm.

A unique laminated stock for a heavy barreled Ruger 10/22 in .22 LR caliber is produced by Boyds' Gunstock Industries. Known as the Smart Stock®, this thumbhole model is shaped in the grip and comb areas so that it can be used by both left handed and right handed shooters. Even the cheek piece is a large, raised section that flows over the stock to provide an identical raised area on each side of the stock. The Smart Stock has a wide, flat forearm with finger grooves along the sides and bedding that utilizes two contact points. It is available as a finished stock in a wide variety of color combinations.

This fine stock is the Smart Stock from Boyds' Gunstock Industries.

The Boyds' Smart Stock is an ambidextrous model that has identical cheek pieces on both sides of the buttstock.

It is also available as an unfinished stock in three color schemes. Boyds' offers several stocks in multicolor combinations known as nutmeg and pepper. The nutmeg is a combination of light and dark brown layers while the pepper combination is gray and black. Our stock has the color combination known as Forest Camo, which is a combination of olive, black, and brown.

Boyds' also produces a laminated stock known as the Dakota Will that has a broad, heavy forearm and is generously proportioned. It is produced for the 10/22 Magnum only with a barrel channel that matches the factory barrel contour in nutmeg and pepper color schemes. However, the Dakota Will for use on the 10/22 LR is available in a wide range of color combinations (finished and unfinished), but it is produced only with a barrel channel to accommodate a 0.920-inch barrel. Boyds' also produces stocks known as the Blaster® and Ross® which are thumbhole styles.

The Dakota Will is available as an unfinished VIP (Virtual Inlet Part), which has the port for the action and the barrel

Another fine laminated stock is the Dakota Will from Boyds' Gunstock Industries.

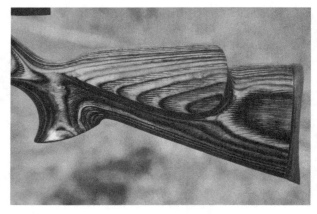

With its hooked grip and massive cheek piece, the Dakota Will is an elegant stock.

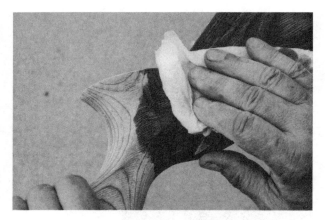

To raise the grain, the stock was rubbed with a wet paper towel prior to final sanding.

channel already cut. Minor shaping, sanding, and finishing of the external surfaces are required. For this project, we selected a VIP Dakota Will in nutmeg color for the 10/22 Magnum. The surface was sanded with fine (150 grit) sandpaper and that was followed sanding with 220 and 320 grit papers. Birchwood Casey Tru-Oil® was used as the finish. The stock was

buffed lightly with steel wool (extra fine 0000) between coats, and after about six coats the stock was pronounced finished. After the stock was attached to the barreled action (we had installed the Jarvis standard weight barrel), we found that the barrel channel gave more pressure on one side of the barrel than the other. To relieve this pressure, fine sandpaper was wrapped

Available as an unfinished stock, the Dakota Will was first sanded and prepared for finishing.

Several coats of Birchwood Casey Tru-Oil® were applied to give a fine finish.

Another laminated stock that we used in testing was the thumbhole sporter model that is available from Cabela's. This stock is featured in the Cabela's catalog both alone and with a heavy barrel from Green Mountain. It is a well-constructed and finished stock although like some of the other larger laminated stocks, it is rather heavy (45.4 ounces). This stock has a forearm with a flat bottom, a small raised cheek piece, and it is available in colors known as coffee (brown) and midnight (gray). Cabela's also offers a target-style stock in the same colors.

Richard's Microfit produces an extensive line of unfinished laminated stocks. We worked with a Tac-Driver Silhouette style thumbhole stock that was obtained in a color combination known as Apache Gold (yellow, purple, orange, and brown). This stock is sure to turn heads! Our stock was finished with Birchwood Casey Tru-Oil®

around a plastic plug that matched closely the width of the barrel channel. After sanding for a few minutes (with several trials of putting the barrel and action back on the stock as the work progressed) we found that we had achieved a better fit. This is the type of situation that can occur when the stock is not mated to a particular barrel and action.

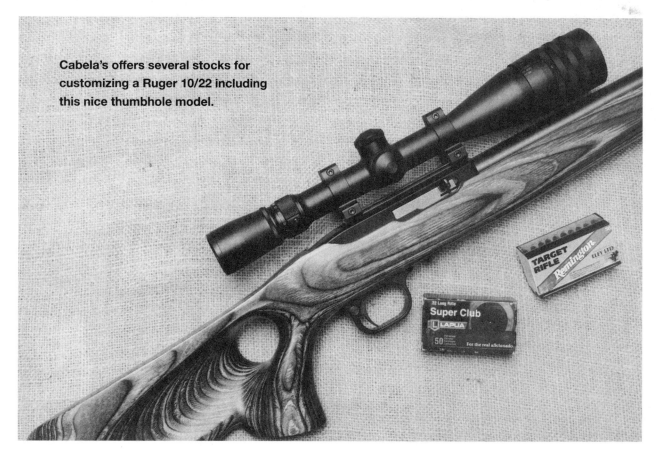

Cabela's offers several stocks for customizing a Ruger 10/22 including this nice thumbhole model.

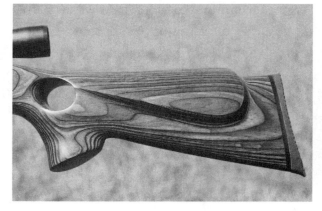

Elegant styling is evident in the Cabela's thumbhole stock.

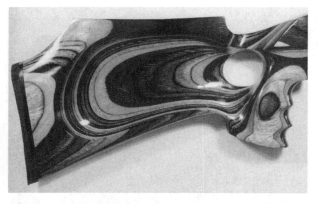

With its scalloped butt, thumbhole, and finger grooves, the Richards Microfit Tac-Driver Silhouette is a distinctive stock that is available unfinished in several color combinations.

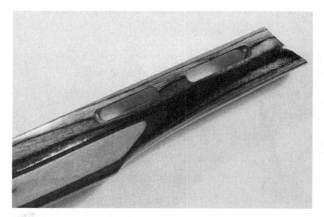

The Richards Microfit Tac-Driver Silhouette stock has cut outs along the forearm.

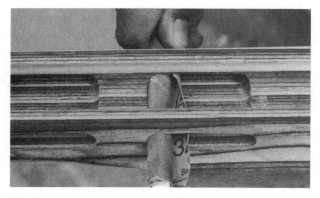

The insides of the cut out sections were also prepared for finishing.

as described above. This stock has a large raised cheek piece and a larger scooped area in the right hand side of the buttstock. It also has a slotted forearm and finger grooves in the grip area.

Revival Industries produces thumbhole laminated stocks for the Ruger 10/22 in several styles including the Tundra and Yukon. We worked with the Yukon, which is available in a variety of colors

The Tundra from Revival Industries is an elegant thumbhole model with a high comb.

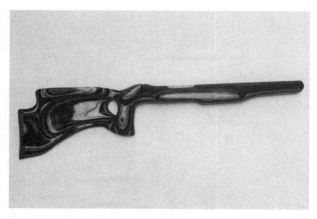

In a combination of red, black, and gray, the Revival Industries Yukon is a colorful and functional stock.

Fajen produces a very
attractive version of
the thumbhole stock.

The butt plate on the Fajen thumbhole stock provides for a secure fit against the shoulder.

including the red and black combination that we tested. The Yukon has a large cheek piece, a scooped out buttstock, and stepped forearm. We also worked with the buckskin brown version of the Tundra, which is available in several other colors. The Tundra has a flat-bottomed forearm and a smaller cheek piece than the Yukon. These stocks retail for approximately $130 and are offered with barrel channels to fit standard or heavy weight barrels in both .22 LR and .22 WMR.

The Fajen name has long been associated with aftermarket gunstocks. A target style thumbhole stock bearing the Fajen name is currently available from Battenfeld Technologies to fit the Ruger 10/22. This fine stock is produced in brown and gray colors with a barrel channel to fit heavy barrels. With a broad, flat forearm and a small roll over cheek piece, this stock works well for firing from a bench.

Composite Stocks

Two aspects of rifle construction that have undergone enormous change in recent years lie in the use of stainless steel and the use of synthetic materials.

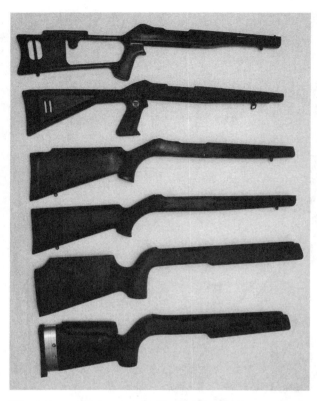

When it comes to composite stocks, the range is from the tactical (top two) to the sporter (middle two) to the target (bottom two).

Although not exclusively so, the major use of synthetic materials in the manufacture of firearms is in the production of stocks. These materials consist of some sort of plastic that is generally reinforced with fibers of fiberglass, carbon, or some other material. In the low priced models, the plastic material is injection molded to produce a one-piece stock. Some of these

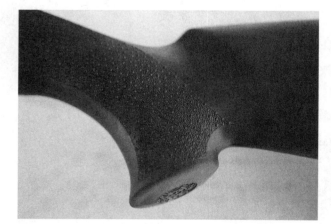

Hogue OverMolded stocks feature pebbled rubber surfaces on the grip and forearm.

stocks tend to flex slightly when subjected to stress (such as when using a tight sling), which can change the pressure on the barrel. This can result in a change in point of impact compared to where it is when the stock is "at rest" on a bench. The more elegant (and expensive) composite stocks have some type of support molded inside the synthetic material. Aluminum, graphite fibers, and fiberglass have been used to provide a sturdy frame for composite stocks. Ruger has marketed the 10/22 with a composite stock with a stainless steel barrel.

Composite stocks can be molded to high dimensional accuracy and in various colors. It is also a relatively simple matter to produce such a stock with an attractive and functional checkering pattern. In some cases, the stock may have the areas where it is gripped covered with a different material that will give a comfortable, secure grip. The Hogue OverMolded stock has rubber overlays with a pebbled surface in the grip and forearm areas.

Initially, the vast majority of composite stocks were black in color. However, it is

no more difficult to mold a plastic having some other color, and they can be painted. Consequently, composite stocks are now available in olive drab and camouflage pattern. For example, McMillan offers black, brown, gray, and olive stocks in addition to the black versions. A swirled marble pattern is available in a wide range of colors for the shooter who wants something other than a solid color. Bell & Carlson produce composite stocks with a variety of camo patterns and with a pattern know as Spiderweb, which has a marbleized look.

Since the stock is produced in a molding operation, it is possible to mold the stock in almost any configuration. Stocks having sporter, tactical, and target configurations are available for the Ruger 10/22. The tactical style stocks have features such as folding butt sections (which may not be legal in all jurisdictions), pistol grips, barrel bands, and molded hand guards. In this category are the stocks produced by Choate Machine & Tool and Advanced Technology. Choate produces a black composite stock that is rigid as well as one

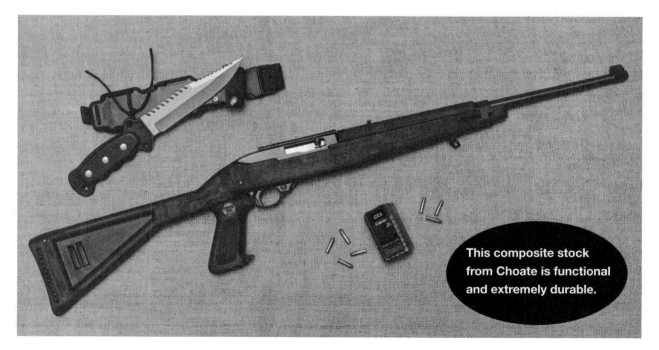

This composite stock from Choate is functional and extremely durable.

A customized Ruger 10/22 can be fitted with a folding stock like this Choate model where it is legal to do so.

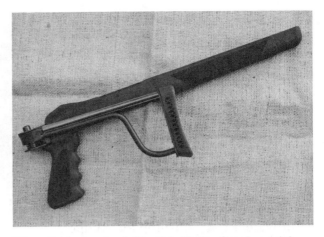

When folded a stock like this Butler Creek model makes a compact rifle that is easy to transport.

that has a folding butt, both of which have a matching hand guard that snaps over the barrel. These utilize metal clips that snap over the barrel, and they may scratch the barrel when installed or removed. A folding stock is also available from Butler Creek. Stocks of these types turn a Ruger 10/22 into something resembling a tactical model. Advanced Technology produces a black stock that is of the Dragunov style. These stocks have pistol grips and accommodate barrels of standard weight.

Composite stocks having shapes that are essentially sporter styles are available from Butler Creek, CoreLite, and Hogue. These models are typically in the $60-100 range. The Butler Creek and CoreLite stocks are also offered as combinations with a replacement barrel at attractive prices. Generally found with retail prices of about $60, the rubber OverMolded stocks from Hogue are extremely popular replacement options. These stocks have rubber coverings with a pebble surface in the grip and forearm areas. These stocks provide a very secure grip under almost all conditions. The nylon OverMolded stocks from Hogue are made of a harder plastic

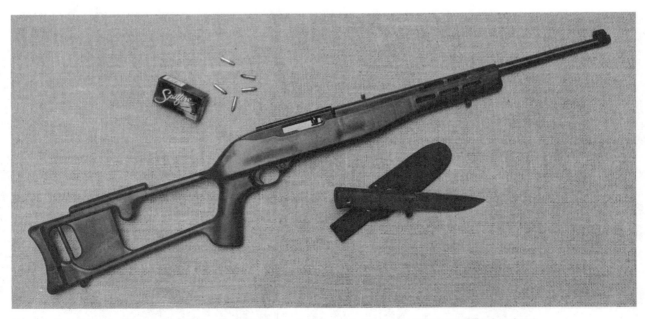

For the fancier of a Dragunov style stock, this model is available from Advanced Technology.

The Hogue OverMolded stock is a good choice for a rifle that may be exposed to all types of weather.

but are shaped in the same way. The Butler Creek and CoreLite stocks made of a hard plastic with checkered areas in the grip and along the forearm. We have used all of these stocks and found them quite satisfactory.

One of the most elegant (and expensive) composite stocks is the Odyssey from Bell & Carlson. This target stock has a 0.920-inch barrel channel, and it is available in a 2-way or 3-way adjustable butt model. The adjustments are continuous which provides for minute changes in dimensions. For example, the cheek piece can be set at any reasonable height by loosening two Allen headed screws, changing the height by sliding the cheek piece, and tightening the screws. The butt plate is

mounted on a large aluminum rod that is locked in place by large locking screws with heads that accepts an Allen wrench. The length of pull can be adjusted within wide limits by loosening two Allen headed bolts and placing the butt plate at the

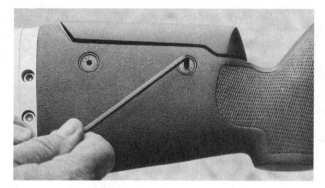

On the Bell & Carlson Odyssey, the height of the comb can be adjusted after using an Allen wrench to loosen the two screws that hold it in place.

This fine, durable composite stock is available from Butler Creek.

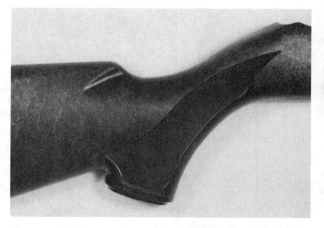

Elegant classic touches are evident in the detailing shown in this CoreLite stock.

Two bolts lock the butt plate in place after it is placed at the desired length.

Because it can be adjusted, the Bell & Carlson Odyssey is extremely versatile.

desired location. If the shooter prefers to have the butt plate canted while the rest of the rifle is vertical, the Odyssey will permit the butt plate to be so arranged.

With the length of pull and height of the comb adjusted, it is also possible to cant the butt plate on this stock.

The rail on the underside of the forearm of the Odyssey can be used for mounting a hand stop and sling.

The 3-way adjustable model allows the butt plate to be adjusted vertically. Finally, there is an aluminum rail that is inset along the bottom of the forearm where a stop can be attached. While the Odyssey is intended to be used as the stock on a target rifle, it is light enough to be used on a rifle that is customized for hunting small game and varmints. With a list price of over $300, this stock will not be found on many 10/22s used for plinking tin cans or hunting small game, but it is a superb choice for the connoisseur who is interested in competition, either position shooting or bench rest.

Another fine target style stock produced by Bell & Carlson is known as the Anschutz target style. Having a barrel channel that fits a 0.920-inch barrel, it has a broad, straight forearm, a high cheek piece, and a deep pistol grip. Retail price of the Anschutz-style stock is approximately $170. For the shooter who wants a high quality target stock of this style, it is a good choice. In addition to the Anschutz style and the Odyssey, stocks in several other styles are available from Bell & Carlson for the Ruger 10/22. They also offer kits consisting of a stock, match barrel, extended magazine release, barrel

The shape of the cheek piece on the Bell & Carlson stock is unlike those on most sporter styles.

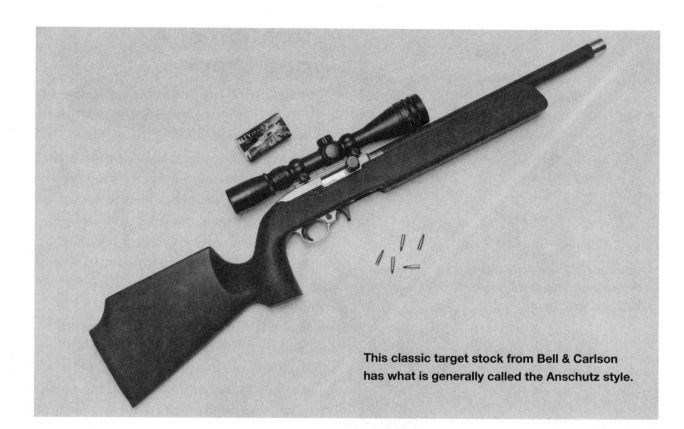

This classic target stock from Bell & Carlson has what is generally called the Anschutz style.

change tool, and an instructional video on installing the parts. The synthetic stocks from Bell & Carlson are claimed to have stability at temperatures from -50° F to +150°F.

The McMillan name is well known to shooters who are seeking aftermarket stocks. Composite stocks produced by McMillan are manufactured by making use of multi-layers of 8-ounce woven fiberglass cloth that are bound together

This photo shows how the barrel is bedded in front of the receiver and at the tip of the forearm, but it is free floated throughout most of its length.

by epoxy resin. The material is then cured at high temperature and pressure to produce a strong, rigid stock. In the area of the receiver, the stock is filled with solid fiberglass. The stock is inletted to fit the receiver by a milling machine rather than simply molding it to the desired shape. The buttstock is filled with a urethane foam rather than being left hollow. All of these operations take time, which means that the McMillan stocks are not the lowest priced composite stocks available.

In addition to models for centerfire rifles, McMillan also produces models for the Ruger 10/22. The stock we tested when compiling information for this book is the black 10/22 Sporter, which is available with a barrel channel to accept a free floated barrel of 0.920-inch diameter. The Sporter is also available for the 10/22 Magnum. Someone who is customizing a Ruger 10/22 and wants to install a composite stock of sporter style should

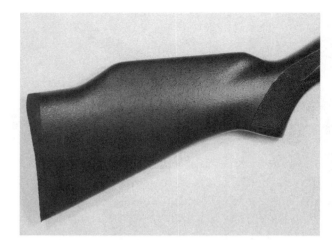

Composite stocks are available in classic sporter configurations. This elegant stock is a custom model from McMillan.

Note how the McMillan stock has a shape that matches that of the action.

certainly examine this stock before making a decision.

In addition to the Sporter, McMillan also produces two other stocks for the Ruger 10/22. One of these is the STC (Sportsman Team Challenge) model, which is a highly modified version of the Anschutz target style stock. The second is known as the STC Intimidator, which was produce for the competition known as the Chevy Truck Challenge. This stock has a comb that can be adjusted for height and a butt plate that can be moved to adjust the length of pull and to adjust the height of the butt plate relative to the bore. It is truly a high tech masterpiece.

Alteration of A Wood Stock

The beauty of any firearm is in the eye of the observer. Rifles with classic lines have always had an artistic beauty. If there is one aspect of the Ruger 10/22 Carbine that does not represent art to many shooters it is the stock. To accommodate the rotary magazine, the stock must be rather large in cross section in the middle where the action is. This is especially true since the 10/22 Carbine uses a one-piece stock that completely encloses the magazine and bottom of the action. Moreover, the stepped fore end with the barrel band around it is hardly classic in appearance to some people. The rather square butt of the stock with its slick, curved butt plate is none too graceful. Of course, many people are perfectly happy with the appearance of an unaltered 10/22.

It is a simple matter to select an aftermarket stock having almost any desired configuration from those offered by the large number of suppliers. However, as the title of this book suggests, customizing a 10/22 may mean altering the one-piece, solid wood stock rather than installing a new one. Customizing the 10/22 with regard to the stock can be as simple as loosening one screw, setting the barrel and action on a new stock, and tightening one screw. We believe that some shooters who want to customize their 10/22s might want to get by with the factory stock but not in its original form. For those individuals, this section will provide the details of how we "customized" a 10/22 using a factory stock as the starting point.

With an eye to improving the appearance of the 10/22, Ruger introduced the 10/22 Rifle in 2004. With its slender stock, longer barrel, and butt plate of conventional style, the Rifle represents a substantial cosmetic improvement over the Carbine version. But suppose someone with a flair for woodwork decided to attack the Carbine stock with rasps and sandpaper. Could the stock be altered to produce one that more closely resembles those of sporters or the Rifle version? We decided to address that issue for the 10/22 shooter who wants something a little different from the factory stock without purchasing a ready-made model.

It was decided early on that the stock to be attacked would not be one that came on our rifles because we always wanted to be able to return them to the factory configuration if desired. Therefore, the first step in the stock alteration project was to obtain a stock. There are many factory stocks available for the 10/22 because replacement of the stock is one of the first steps taken during tricking out of a 10/22. Looking at eBay will show just how many factory stocks are out there at reasonable prices. However, we were fortunate to find a stock (without butt plate and barrel band) at a shop known as The Bullet Hole in Bozeman, Montana. Fortunately, it was an early model made of walnut rather than hardwood, as are the stocks of more recent manufacture. After a little discussion (make that bargaining) the stock was obtained for $20. Poking around in a bucket of parts, the shop owner produced a metal butt plate of the type used on the 10/22 for several years. Another $5.00 secured the butt plate.

Having the stock in hand, decisions as to how to shape it had to be made. In keeping with the spirit of this project, it was decided that the fore end would be reshaped in such a way that a barrel band

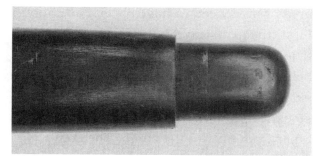

If a Ruger 10/22 Carbine stock is to be made into one having a sporter style, the step where the barrel band attaches must be removed.

would not be used. The part of the fore end that protrudes through the barrel band is quite thin so the stock would have to be reshaped to make the cut down area join smoothly with the rest of the forearm. This would necessitate that the forearm be made quite slender, but that was intended anyway. Originally, it was thought that the fore end should be shortened somewhat, but early Ruger 10/22 stocks were cut out below the barrel channel, and the barrel fit the channel only in the last couple of inches of the stock. Consequently, shortening the forearm by cutting off the end that normally protrudes through the barrel band would remove part of the supporting area. The stock would have to be left full length or very nearly so.

In order to make a stock of more sporting configuration, the entire stock would need to be made considerably slimmer. Two

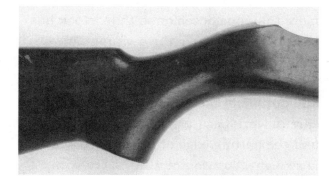

The grip area on the 10/22 Carbine stock is rather shapeless.

areas would need to have special attention. First, the grip would be shaped to give a true pistol grip by cutting away the area behind the grip as well as thinning the sides of the grip. Second, the top of the stock would need to be thinned with a taper from butt to the comb. The comb would need to be fluted to a modest degree as is done on the 10/22 Rifle. However, because of the way in which the butt plate is inletted at the top of the stock, it would be necessary to retain the carbine style type butt plate. It would be a difficult job to reconfigure the butt area to take a flat butt plate like that used on the Rifle and Target versions.

With the plan formulated (meaning we had some idea of what we wanted the stock to look like), the first step was to slim the forearm so that the step where the barrel band resides would be removed.

In order to modify the stock, a few simple items would be required. These include wood rasps and files, sandpaper, steel wool (grade 0000 which is very fine), etc. The entire project can be carried out (as we have done on several other occasions) by using only these simple items. However, a block plane comes in very handy in some types of wood removal, but it is not essential. Finishing materials will be described later.

A block plane is a wonderful device. On more than one occasion, a thick stock has been placed on the reducing program with that little plane. In this case, it was set to cut very little and moved along the sides and bottom of the fore end. This requires careful work because the stock is rounded and the cutting edge of the plane blade is straight. You do not want to cut with the edges of the blade, which will result in grooves. But with care, the removal of

wood is more uniform than is achieved with a wood rasp. Knowing that some serious sanding would occur later, the stock was left a little thicker than it was intended to be in the end.

The butt was left full width and height in order to use a factory butt plate. However, the stock was thinned somewhat along the top edge with the comb being considerably thinner than the butt. This was initiated with the block plane and finished by using medium sandpaper wrapped around a wood block. Avoid using coarse sandpaper if at all possible. It introduces scratches that require a lot of sanding with fine sandpaper to remove. Incidentally, a wood rasp also leaves scratches that have to be sanded out. We recommend that work with the rasps be terminated slightly before reaching the actual shape desired and then completing the wood removal with a fine file or sandpaper. The final shaping can be done while removing the marks left by the rasps.

Working around the grip and comb areas required the use of rasps. A round rasp works well when cutting in behind the grip and when cutting the flutes in the

Using a rasp, the end of the forearm was given a round shape.

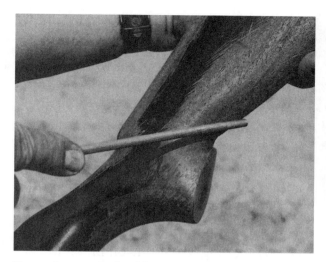

To produce a stock with more pleasing lines, the grip area was reshaped.

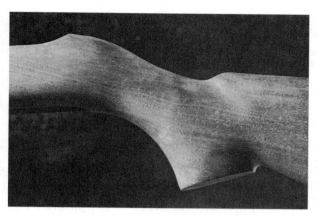

After reshaping, the walnut stock has a pistol grip and a fluted comb.

comb. Just work slowly and try to make everything blend together in a smooth way. When cutting the flutes in the comb, start cutting the flutes with a round file that does not remove much wood until the direction of the flutes is established. Ideally, the flutes should point toward the heel of the butt or nearly so. Look at photos of sporting rifles in catalogs to note the desired angle. The angle is not critical, but it is essential that the flutes on both sides be cut at the same angle. Inspect the work often to make sure that this is being done. Some change in direction is possible when the flutes are very shallow, but when they are fully cut, not much can be done to change the direction. When cutting the flutes, make sure that the top edge remains sharp and that the flutes open up gradually at the bottom to blend smoothly with the area of the stock behind the grip.

When working on the slender walnut factory stock in this project, we chose not to make deep flutes with sharp upper edges. Only shallow scalloped areas were rasped out to give a shape that is similar to that on the factory stock of the 10/22 Rifle. When reshaping the stock, just work slowly and inspect the area being modified

Prior to finishing, the surface was sanded to remove the rest of the old finish and give a smooth surface.

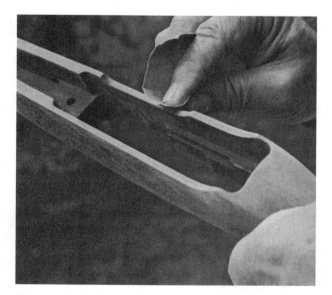

When sanding in areas with irregular shapes, be careful to preserve the original lines.

frequently. It is also a good idea to work in bright light. It is very easy to miss a small lump here or a small valley there if the light is dim. If the stock is held at the correct angle, even very small imperfections in the surface will be visible. By working carefully, it is not difficult to obtain a stock of a pleasing, symmetric shape. However, you will probably find that reshaping and refinishing a walnut stock is considerably easier than one made of hardwood. The final product will also be more elegant if the stock is walnut.

After the shaping process was essentially complete, the stock was sanded thoroughly with a medium grade (150 grit) sandpaper. This paper is coarse enough to remove marks left by files and rasps and to help with the final touches of shaping. When sanding, be careful not to round off edges and corners which could make the stock look as if the inletting were sloppy.

At this point, the stock was inspected critically by holding it so that a strong light could shine along the surfaces to make any uneven areas visible. With those areas having been given a final sanding with the medium paper, sanding was continued using fine (220 grit) sandpaper which was followed by extra fine (320 grit) paper. With the initial sanding completed, the stock was wiped with a wet paper towel to raise the grain. After drying, the stock was again sanded with 320 grit to remove the raised grain or whiskers. Repeating the process of raising the grain is a good idea. After again sanding carefully with extra fine sandpaper, the stock was rubbed briskly with 0000 (extra fine) steel wool.

Walnut is an open grain wood so before applying the actual finish a filler and sealer is normally applied in classical finishing techniques. To give a walnut stock a pleasing color a stain is often used. Times have changed and finishing materials have also changed. Products are now available to fill and seal the pores and stain the wood in one step. One of the classic stains used for gunstocks is known as French Red, and we have used it with beautiful results, but no stain was used on the walnut stock being finished.

Although stock finishing kits often come with a sealer, it is possible to seal the stock by making use of the oil finish itself. Sealing is accomplished by applying a coat of the finish then letting it dry thoroughly. Rubbing the stock with extra fine steel wool removes all of the finish except from the pores. Performing this process twice will seal the pores, which leaves the stock ready to finish.

Oil finishes are appropriate for gunstocks, and for many years we have used an oil type finish from Birchwood Casey known as Tru-Oil® although other types of oil finish are available. These are drying oils that can be rubbed on easily. Place the fingers over the mouth of an open bottle of Tru-Oil® and tip the bottle to get a few drops of the finish on

Birchwood Casey Tru-Oil was applied by hand to achieve a hand rubbed finish.

the fingers. Rub the oil on the stock and spread it out evenly. Repeat the procedure and make sure that the next area rubbed joins smoothly with the first. Keep doing this until the whole stock is covered with a smooth, thin coat of oil. Allow the stock to dry thoroughly.

The idea behind giving a stock a beautiful, durable oil finish is to build up the finish by applying several thin coats. After the stock is dry, rub it *lightly* with 0000 steel wool being careful not to apply pressure on edges. Next, apply another coat of oil in the same manner as the first. The application of oil and rubbing with steel wool should be repeated five or six times to build up the finish. Although this may sound very time consuming, it should be mentioned that Tru-Oil® dries

very quickly. We have been able to apply multiple coats on the same day without hurrying the process.

When the final coat of Tru-Oil® is dry, a decision must be made on the final appearance of the stock. Some people prefer the high gloss that will be present after the finish has been applied. If you are among those, just leave the stock as it is. On the other hand, some people prefer a satin surface. This can be obtained by *lightly* rubbing the surface with 0000 steel wool to remove the high gloss, but getting a uniform satin finish can be difficult. A better method is to use a product that is specially prepared for the task. Birchwood Casey Stock Sheen and Conditioner works well for this purpose. It contains just enough abrasive to remove the shine

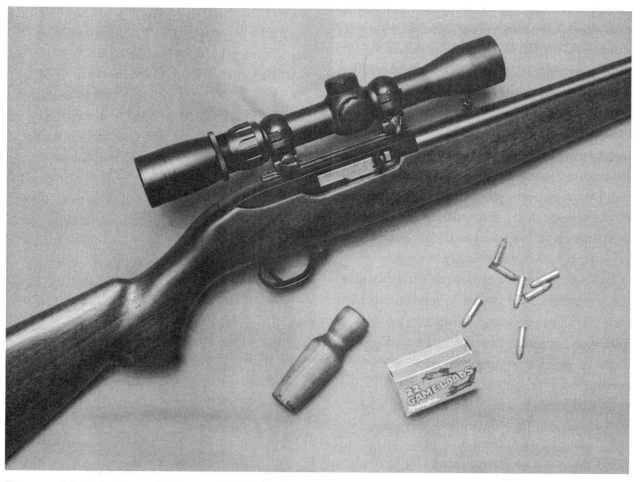

The completed stock now looks more like that of a sporting rifle than a carbine.

from the surface and give a satin surface. Incidentally, we have used this product to brighten and clean the finish on stocks on older guns. In one case, it was an old rifle that had hung in an antique store for a considerable period of time. Briskly rubbing the stock with the conditioner removed the collected grime and made the stock look almost new.

The steps described above need not be followed exactly, but they show the process that we followed to convert an old, dinged Ruger 10/22 stock into a pleasing stock. Prepare the surface carefully and follow the directions of the manufacturer of the finishing materials that you use. If you do, you will end up with a stock that shows more refinement and character than a factory can afford to put into a stock for an inexpensive rifle. Of course, the reshaping described here can be carried out on a hardwood stock, but the final result will not be as elegant as it is for a walnut stock.

A word of explanation is in order at this point. In the reference work on the versions of the Ruger 10/22 by W. E. Workman (*The Ruger 10/22*, Krause Publications, 1994), there is a discussion of the variations in stocks that appeared over the years. It turns out that the stock that we modified is a version known as the Type I walnut produced by Overton under an agreement with Ruger. Just as the stock modification was completed, an issue of a publication that lists firearms and related items for sale was received. It seems that two of the Type I stocks were listed for sale with the asking price of $250 each! Was the stock that was modified worth that much? No, not in its condition at the time of purchase. However, it most certainly was worth much more than the $20 that it cost. Would we have attacked the stock with a rasp and

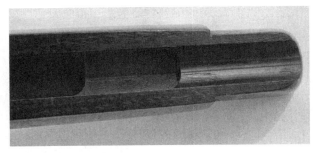

The early stocks produced by Overton have a stepped barrel channel. Only the forward end makes contact with the barrel.

a block plane had we known that it was something special? Probably not. It might have been carefully refinished to remove some of the dings, but it would likely have retained the carbine configuration. The moral of this story is that you should make sure of what you have before you work it over. You can bet that we will now keep a sharp lookout for any other Type I walnut stocks for the Ruger 10/22!

Stocks on Ruger 10/22 Carbines have slick butt plates made of plastic. It is very difficult to keep the butt from sliding during firing because there is almost no friction between the plastic and fabric. One solution to the problem is to give the butt plate a different surface. One way is to spray it with the type of coating that is used on floors around hot tubs and pools to give a nonskid surface. Such a product is Skid-Tex

A product such as Skid-Tex® can be applied to make the butt plate less slick.

Because it can be sprayed on, Skid-Tex® is easy to apply.

A Sticky Pad will adhere to the butt plate and make it less slick against the shoulder.

The coated butt plate gives a good grip on the shoulder.

from Bondex, which is available at building supply, lumber yards, and hardware stores. Brownells sells an epoxy paint product known as Spray Grit specifically for producing a nonskid surface. The coating is described as "clear", but it gives a light color to the butt plate.

To coat the plastic butt plate with Skid-Tex, it was held in place by a screw through one hole to attach it loosely to a board so it could be sprayed conveniently. Drying time was short, and the butt plate was given two coats of the spray. Although the finished butt plate does not have a black color, it could be painted black, and it certainly stays in place on the shoulder. Other Ruger rifles like the Model 96 lever action and the Mini 14 also have slick plastic butt plates that can profit from being sprayed with a non-slick coating.

Sticky pads made of a rubberized material are available for mounting cell phones to the dash of a vehicle. These pads are constructed to adhere to almost

any smooth surface. One of these pads was cut to the correct shape and attached to the butt plate. The result was a butt plate that stayed in

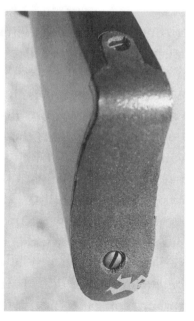

The tacky feel of the pad makes the butt plate feel more like rubber.

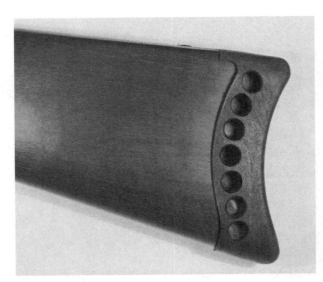

Choate produces a replacement rubber butt plate for the Ruger 10/22 that increases the length of pull and really stays in place against the shoulder.

Because slotted screws are easily marred, a hex headed screw like this Volquartsen product is a desirable alternative.

place on the shoulder regardless of the type of clothing worn.

Another solution to the slick butt plate problem is to install an aftermarket model. Choate produces a rubber butt plate that is about one inch in thickness that provides another way to remedy the problem of a slick butt plate.

Many of the aftermarket barrels available for the Ruger 10/22 have a diameter of 0.920". If an owner of a Ruger 10/22 wants to use such a barrel without buying a new stock, the factory stock must be modified to accept the diameter of larger diameter. This means that a substantial amount of wood must be removed from the barrel channel, which must be done carefully. The factory stock has enough wood to allow this to be done, but the walls of the barrel channel will be quite thin. Also, it is not possible to use the barrel band with the heavy barrel in place.

Because the Ruger 10/22 has an aluminum receiver (except for the .22 WMR version which has a steel receiver), the barrel should be supported by the stock rather than being free floating. Some of the

ultra lightweight barrels work well when free floated, and the suppliers recommend using them that way. However, for most barrels, it is essential that enough wood be left in the forward end of the barrel channel to support the barrel. In other words, remove *slightly* more wood from the barrel channel just in front of the receiver and in the midsection than from the forward end.

Although special tools are available for widening the barrel channel, the amateur will probably do the operation by using sandpaper wrapped around a section of dowel rod. This is a slow, tedious process. It is easier and more efficient to use pieces of dowel rod having successively larger diameter. In that way, as the channel is approaching the necessary width, the sandpaper will be supported and will remove wood uniformly from the sides and bottom of the barrel channel. Work with strokes that sand the entire length of the channel so that wide and narrow places do not result. As the barrel channel approaches the correct dimension, try placing the barrel in the channel frequently

A good case is a sound investment to protect your customized Ruger 10/22.

to make sure that you are achieving the desired result. Because the barrel is cylindrical, you can check progress by laying the barrel backward (with the action in front of the stock) so that you do not have to work the action down into the stock every time.

After the barrel channel is correctly shaped, the surface of the wood is completely bare. As a result, it is possible for the wood to absorb moisture, which can cause it to expand slightly resulting

an upward pressure on the barrel. It is a good idea to coat the barrel channel with a sealer to prevent moisture absorption. One easy way to do this is to apply a couple of coats of Birchwood Casey Tru-Oil®.

Although a factory stock can be modified to accept a heavy barrel, it requires some work, and many shooters will be happier with an aftermarket stock designed for the purpose. Many examples of such stocks are shown and described in this chapter and in other sections of this book.

Chapter 8

BARRELS FOR THE RUGER 10/22

A rifle is a platform for launching projectiles. In order to launch projectiles with a high degree of precision and accuracy, the lock, stock, and barrel must work together in a complementary way. Although these factors are being discussed separately in this book, they are in fact interrelated. A stock of mediocre design may work fairly well with a heavy target barrel, but may not work as well with a slender, mediocre barrel. In the first case, the target barrel is less sensitive to what is holding it, so the system is more forgiving of the inadequacies of the stock. In the second case, the slender barrel of mediocre quality needs to be supported exactly right for it to shoot with greatest accuracy. This is due to barrel vibrations, and the stock helps to control vibrations (which are more pronounced with lightweight barrels). Also, as a slender barrel heats up during repeated firing, it needs to be held in the most advantageous way. Even when the effects of barrel and stock are

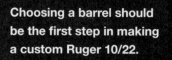

Choosing a barrel should be the first step in making a custom Ruger 10/22.

controlled, there is still the advantage of having a good trigger. If it requires excessive force to cause the trigger to release, movement of the rifle may negate some of the quality of the barrel and stock. Therefore, while this chapter will deal with barrels for the Ruger 10/22, the other components have a symbiotic effect on accuracy.

Many of the technical characteristics of barrels were discussed in Chapter 2. Therefore, this chapter will describe additional features of barrels and provide a survey of the types of barrels that are available to the shooter who is customizing a Ruger 10/22.

Factory Barrels

Factory barrels for the Ruger 10/22 are produced in several variants. By far the most common is the standard weight 18.5-inch blue version that has open sights on the barrel. A stainless steel barrel is also produced in the same configuration. The Ruger 10/22 Target model is produced with a barrel that is 20 inches long and 0.920-inch in diameter. This heavy, hammer-forged barrel is available in both blue and stainless steel. No sights are mounted on the target barrels in accord with their intended use. The Ruger 10/22 Rifle has a 20-inch barrel while the Compact Rifle has a barrel that is 16.5 inches long. One variant of the Ruger 10/22 has become known as the "Wal-Mart" rifle because they are most often found in the stores of this enormous merchandiser. Ruger produces the rifles to the specifications of Lipsey's, Inc. of Baton Rouge, LA who is one of the major suppliers of firearms to Wal-Mart. The stainless steel barrel of this rifle is 22 inches long, and it has a slender profile. Open sights are provided on this barrel.

Firearms manufacturers who produce millions of barrels for rimfire rifles selling at modest prices cannot afford to make a barrel that is of the highest quality. If they did, the price of the rifle would have to be twice as high, and sales would most certainly suffer. There must be a balance between quality and cost. Please do not misunderstand what this means. Factory barrels on rimfire rifles, including the Ruger 10/22, are perfectly adequate for most sporting uses of such firearms. However, they do not have the close tolerances and exquisite finish required to produce the highest possible accuracy. To underscore this, we have found that simply installing a good aftermarket barrel may cut the group size produced by a Ruger 10/22. However, for many shooters, the factory barrel is the only one they will ever use, and their 10/22s will perform all the tasks required of the rifles. An analogous situation exists in the area of photography. Many people who own cameras that will accept interchangeable lenses take all their photographs with the lens that came with the camera. Users of all sorts of equipment readily accept such limitations. However, many of the photographs in this book could not be taken without having more specialized equipment. Higher levels of performance and specialized applications require the use of special accessories in many fields of endeavor. Fortunately, the user of a Ruger 10/22 has an enormous range of products available to enhance the accuracy of the rifle.

Changing Barrels

If there is one user friendly aspect of the Ruger 10/22 compared to other rimfire semiautos it is the ease with which the barrel can be removed and another

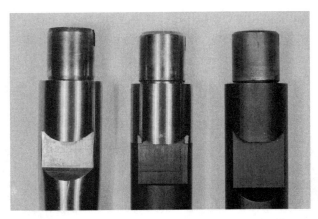

Aftermarket barrels attach to the receiver of a Ruger 10/22 in the same way as the factory barrel does, but they differ in the shape of the locking notch.

attached. On most rimfire rifles, the barrel is press-fitted in the receiver, and a retaining pin is placed laterally through the receiver and a notch in the barrel shank. Expensive rimfire rifles sometimes have the barrel threaded into the receiver, but this requires cutting the threads on the barrel tenon or shank and in the receiver, which is a slower, more expensive process. It is, however, the method that is generally acknowledged to be the best although some extremely accurate rimfire rifles do not have barrels attached in this way.

The barrel on a Ruger 10/22 is held in place by two large screws that require a 5/32- inch Allen wrench to turn. These screws pass through a V-shaped steel block that fits over an extension at the bottom of the receiver while a beveled surface on the block makes contact with the beveled surface of a notch that is cut transversely across the bottom of the barrel. When the screws are tightened, the block pulls the barrel back into the receiver holding it rigidly in place. The result is solid barrel attachment without having to cut threads on the barrel and inside the receiver.

There are several cautions that need to be made about changing barrels on Ruger 10/22 rifles. First, although the barrel,

the block that engages it, and the locking bolts are made of steel, the receiver is not. Receivers on Ruger 10/22 rifles are made of an aluminum alloy. It would be possible to apply torque to the retaining bolts to the point that the threads in the receiver are damaged or stripped. Do NOT try to tighten the locking bolts too tightly! Second, since the receiver is made of aluminum, repeated removal and attaching the barrel causes some wear on the threads in the softer receiver. Aluminum is not a metal that is very resistant to abrasion so the threads on the steel locking bolts abrade the aluminum somewhat each time they are removed and attached. Having changed barrels on two of our Ruger 10/22s a large number of times during the testing program carried out to produce this book, it is easy to see that the locking bolts now fit much looser in the receiver as they are inserted. Do not change the barrel on a Ruger 10/22 unless it is necessary to do so! The threads in the receiver may be worn excessively as a result of repeated barrel changing.

Installing Aftermarket Barrels

With the receiver of the Ruger 10/22 being made of cast aluminum, there is a considerable amount of variation in dimensions. As a result, the receiver of one of our rifles will accept barrels that will not even begin to enter the receiver of another. Some aftermarket barrels are produced with tenons (or shanks) having a diameter that tends toward the maximum allowed while some receivers may have openings with minimum dimensions. It is also possible that either the barrel extension or the hole in the receiver (or both) may not

Some polishing of the barrel tenon may be required to make the barrel fit in the receiver.

be perfectly round. As a result, it is not uncommon to find that a particular barrel does not slide easily into the receiver. We have found that this is by no means uncommon and does not indicate a defect in the barrel. In fact, some manufacturers deliberately make barrel tenons with maximum dimensions so that they will need to be polished and individually fitted to receivers. However, do NOT attempt to pull an oversize barrel into the receiver by means of excessive tightening of the locking bolts! If you do so, there is a very real probability that the screws will damage the threads in the receiver or strip them altogether. The locking screws provide a secure hold of the barrel to the receiver when they are fully engaged, but they should not be used as the means to pull a tight barrel into the receiver when they are only partially engaged.

If the barrel extension will not enter the receiver without undue force, you may have to polish it with emery cloth or sandpaper. If you do, make sure that you polish it uniformly around the barrel extension to keep it round. Be careful not to remove more metal around the extractor cut because there is less bearing surface

there as the emery cloth is pressed against the barrel. Aftermarket barrels from some sources are accompanied by instructions on how to polish the barrel tenon.

As you polish the barrel tenon (see Chapter 6), try frequently to fit it into the receiver. Although the cut for the locking block is across the bottom of the barrel, try inserting the barrel with the cut on top then rotating it in the receiver. In this way you can determine whether the barrel is equally tight all the way around or whether it is tight only in one orientation. If either the hole in the receiver or the barrel extension is not round, this will be revealed as you try to rotate the barrel while it is inserted into the receiver.

After you have nearly completed the polishing of the tenon of a blue barrel (you will know this by how tightly the barrel fits), you will need to blue the area that has been polished. Remove any oil from the surface by rubbing it with a small amount of alcohol or other solvent. Apply the bluing solution with a small piece of cloth while observing the cautions and directions given on the bottle. Bluing will require several applications of the solution. However, after the polished surface area is lightly blued by only one or two applications, insert it in the

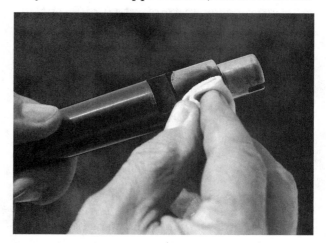

Blue the polished areas of the barrel and try inserting the barrel in the receiver.

Note the bright spots where blue has been removed. This indicates where additional polishing is needed.

receiver and rotate it. When you remove it, you will be able to see clearly where contact is excessive because the freshly applied blue will be rubbed off from those areas. You now know where to administer that final bit of polishing to achieve a perfect fit of the barrel to the receiver. When this is complete, finish the bluing process and rinse off any remaining solution and salts. Apply a light coat of oil or other protecting solvent and attach the barrel to the receiver.

Hopefully, the process described above does not sound complicated because it isn't. In fact, it may not be necessary at all. Of the many barrels that we have attached to our 10/22 receivers, only three or four have required any fitting. We have also noted that some barrels will slide easily into one receiver but not into a different one. The method of attaching the barrel to the receiver of a Ruger 10/22 allows the fit of the barrel in the receiver to be somewhat sloppy and the rifle to still function perfectly and give good accuracy. The beveled wedge and barrel recess still make for rigid attachment.

Accuracy

In Chapter 2, it was explained in detail how several factors come into play in determining how accurately a rifle barrel

shoots. Some of these factors will be reviewed briefly. One of the most important is the crown (the muzzle). The muzzle must be perpendicular to the axis of the bore for best accuracy. If it is not, the bullet will be in contact with the longer side of the barrel after it has cleared the shorter side. This results in tipping of the bullet, which has an adverse effect on accuracy.

Another factor that determines the accuracy produced by a rifle barrel is related to the chamber. In order to allow almost any cartridge to be chambered, factory barrels are produced with chambers that are somewhat larger in dimensions than those that would give best accuracy. When a cartridge is placed in a tight chamber, it is held more closely aligned with the bore than when it is in a chamber in which it fits loosely. A bullet that starts out tipped in the bore will be deformed (more than simply the engraving by the rifling) so accuracy suffers. Many custom rifles that are built specifically for benchrest competition have particularly tight chambers. However, a chamber that is tight enough to prevent entry of some cartridges would not be a good choice for a hunting rifle. As will be discussed in Chapter 11, we found that it was very difficult to chamber certain types of cartridges in some of the match grade

Barrels with match chambers may grip the bullet tight enough to make unfired cartridges difficult to remove.

barrels. As a result, barrels having match chambers may fail to feed some types of ammunition. If this occurs, try other types of ammunition.

Many of the fine aftermarket barrels have a statement on them to the effect that unfired cartridges may not eject from the barrel. The reason for this is that the rifling extends back to the mouth of the chamber and bullet engages the rifling. As a result, there may be enough traction on the bullet so that as the bolt moves back the extractor slides over the rim of the cartridge rather than pulling the cartridge out of the chamber.

The breech face of a rifle barrel should be perpendicular to the bore. If the rim of a cartridge fits against the rear edge of the chamber, it will be tipped if that edge is not perpendicular to the bore. When the cartridge is fired, the bullet will leave the chamber somewhat tipped in comparison to the axis of the bore. Because crushing the priming mixture held in the rim fires a rimfire cartridge, the rim must fit against the rear edge of the chamber in a fixed, reproducible way. Therefore, the rear edge of the chamber must not only be perpendicular to the bore, but also it must be smooth.

Having addressed some of the issues related to crowns and chambers, it should also be remembered that the bore and rifling are also vitally important. Inexpensive rimfire barrels produced by factories are not noted for being mirror smooth. In some cases, they can be lapped (see Chapters 2 and 4) to smooth the interior surfaces, but many of the barrels produced by custom barrel makers are the result of slow, painstaking work. The bores and rifling are already very smooth and held to tighter tolerances than on factory barrels. Some are even hand lapped. That is why it is not uncommon to spend more for a high-grade replacement barrel than the original cost of a complete Ruger 10/22.

In later chapters, a great deal of data will be presented to show the accuracy that we obtained from a large number of custom rifles. Keep in mind that not all barrels function equally well with all types of ammunition. It is not uncommon to find that barrel A functions better than barrel B with one type of ammunition while the reverse is true with a different type of ammunition. This is natural, and it shows that the shooter should experiment with several types of ammunition to evaluate accuracy regardless of the barrel being used. However, as will be shown later, four or five types of ammunition gave outstanding accuracy with almost all of the aftermarket barrels.

Types of Aftermarket Barrels

The number of sellers of aftermarket barrels is large and as a result, the number of types of barrels offered is enormous. This is an area where it is possible for the shooter to swap the factory barrel for one of almost any configuration. Perhaps the most common type of barrel installed on Ruger 10/22s is the so-called target barrel, which usually has a 0.920-inch diameter. Such barrels are available in a range of prices that reaches from less than $100 to well over $300. Moreover, target barrels are available in both blue and stainless steel, with or without flutes. Almost all of the major suppliers of barrels for the Ruger 10/22 offer one or more models of this general type. Heavy barrels from

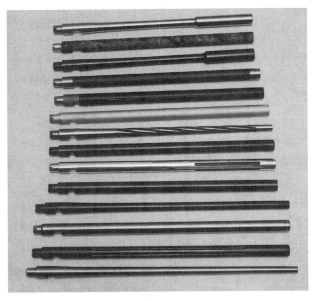

Aftermarket barrels for the Ruger 10/22 come in all types, sizes, and colors.

Adams & Bennett, Butler Creek, and Green Mountain are among the more economical models, but if you refer to the test results presented in Chapter 11, you will see that they give excellent accuracy. Toward the upper end of the price range are the fine barrels produced by Jarvis, Kidd Innovative Design, Lilja, and Shilen. We have used several of these superbly accurate barrels with complete satisfaction.

Installing a target barrel on your 10/22 will require a stock with a barrel channel to accommodate the barrel of larger diameter. This means that you must either modify the factory stock or get one with the large barrel channel. If you choose to modify the factory stock, the barrel band will not fit over the target barrel. To modify the barrel channel, you will need to take a short section of a dowel rod of appropriate diameter and wrap it with sandpaper. With this sanding device, you can now (laboriously) work on the barrel channel by removing wood until it will accept the target barrel. The other alternative (which is probably more often exercised and more satisfactory) is to buy a new stock having a 0.920-inch barrel channel from one of the aftermarket sources. We have discussed stocks in detail in Chapter 7.

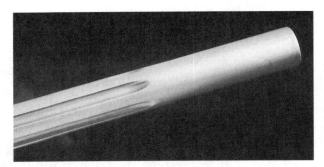

This Butler Creek barrel is a heavy model with straight flutes.

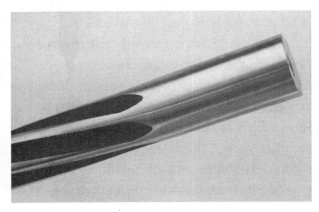

A slender barrel with helical flutes is very attractive. This E. R. Shaw barrel not only looks good, it delivers excellent accuracy.

Typical of the elegant barrels for the Ruger 10/22 is this highly polished stainless steel model from Kidd Innovative Design.

Aftermarket barrels are also produced which have the same (or very nearly the same) profile as the factory barrel. These so-called standard weight barrels can be used with the factory stock or with another that has a barrel channel of the same width. As is the case with target barrels, standard weight barrels are available in both blue and stainless steel. Several versions are available with flutes that are either straight or that spiral around the barrel. It might be assumed that the heavy target barrels would be much more accurate than those of standard weight, but this is not always the case. You may achieve as much improvement in accuracy as you desire with a lighter weight barrel. We have worked with these lighter weight barrels from Green Mountain, Jarvis, and Lilja. Studying the data shown in the tables in Chapter 11 will show just how accurate these barrels are.

Although many aftermarket stocks are available with barrel channels that fit barrels of factory dimensions, some owners of a Ruger 10/22 may want to utilize the factory stock. That limits the choice of barrels to those that have the standard contour. However, another popular type of barrel that fits the factory stock is the muzzle weighted or running boar model. This barrel has a diameter that matches that of the factory barrel except for the last four or five inches where the diameter

The Aluma-Lite barrel from Majestic Arms has an aluminum sleeve over the steel barrel.

increases to 0.920 inch. The heavy section near the muzzle adds weight forward of the hands which aids in steady holding. It also makes it easier to have a smooth swing when aiming at a moving target. We have used three outstanding barrels of this type, a Green Mountain blue version in .22 WMR, a Ranch Products blue .22 LR barrel, and a stainless Volquartsen in .22 LR.

Another type of barrel that appeals to many shooters is what might be called a "compound" barrel. This type of barrel consists of an inner rifled tube made of steel having a small outside diameter that is surrounded by an outer sleeve made of some material of lighter weight. The most common outer sleeves are made of aluminum or a carbon fiber composite material. Barrels of this type generally have a 0.920-inch diameter and are used with a stock having a barrel channel of that width. An outstanding barrel of the aluminum sleeved type that is available in all four rimfire calibers is the Majestic Arms Aluma-Lite barrel which has an inner barrel made by Lothar Walther. Although light in weight, they perform like true heavyweights.

Muzzle weighted barrels like this one from Volquartsen have some advantages of both standard and heavy versions.

This sleeved barrel from Magnum Research has a carbon fiber sleeve throughout most of its length.

An example of a barrel having a carbon fiber sleeve is the MagnumLite® barrel from Magnum Research which weighs only 12.8 ounces. These barrels are available in .22 LR, .22 WMR, .17 Mach 2, and .17 HMR calibers. Another fine carbon-sleeved barrel is the Ultra-Lite® marketed by Butler Creek which is produced with open sights. The Featherweight version from Butler Creek is furnished without sights. Both have Bentz type match chambers.

An unusual barrel of the sleeved type is available in .22 LR from Whistle Pig.

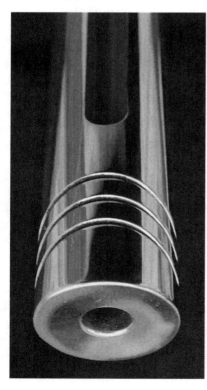

This barrel features a highly polished outer sleeve made of

With the cuts near the muzzle and colored flutes, this aluminum-sleeved barrel from Whistle Pig is both beautiful and accurate.

Tactical Solutions produces sleeved barrels with several external finishes including camo.

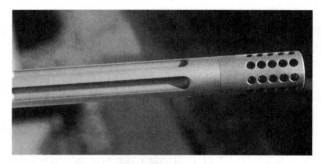

This fluted Tactical Solutions has a threaded muzzle for attaching a compensator.

aluminum that is fluted. Barrels are available with the insides of the flutes finished with enamel in a choice of colors. This provides a barrel that is light in weight (about 18 ounces), has a striking appearance, and gives excellent accuracy. Another producer of unusual sleeved barrels is Tactical Solutions. These barrels weigh a pound or less and are available in red, purple, green, blue, black, gray, and camo colors. These barrels are also available with or without flutes in .22 LR and .22 WMR calibers.

A tensioned barrel also consists of an inner sleeve that is held in an outer tube. In this case, the sleeve is constructed so that it is long enough to push forward on the muzzle end of the barrel while pushing backward on the breech end. This puts a tension on the barrel, which is supposed

The Green Mountain Aero has a slotted aluminum sleeve that does not touch the fluted steel barrel except near the breech.

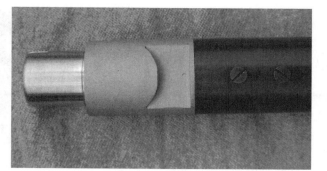

Two screws and two O-rings inside the sleeve hold the sleeve and barrel together on the Aero barrel.

The muzzle is about 7/8-inch behind the end of the aluminum sleeve of the Aero barrel.

to help control the vibrations that occur during firing. Tensioned barrels are available from Volquartsen among others.

Recently, Green Mountain introduced a remarkable type of barrel in .22 LR and .22 WMR for the Ruger 10/22. Those barrels, known as the Aero Series, have a slender stainless steel barrel measuring just 16 inches in length, which is surrounded by a metal sleeve. The 0.920-inch diameter metal sleeve extends about 7/8-inch beyond the end of the barrel, and it has oval slots throughout its length. The overall length of the sleeved barrel is 17 inches, and sleeves are available in black, green, blue, yellow, red, and polished aluminum colors. A Competition model in .22 LR has

a barrel weight that is contained within the shroud.

The stainless steel inner barrel of the Aero Series has shallow flutes, a Bentz-type chamber, and a rifling twist of one turn in 15 inches. It also has an 11-degree muzzle crown and is treated to relieve stress. Two O-rings around the chamber area are used to separate the shroud from the barrel. Additionally, the sleeves are intended to be free floating, and to give the proper clearance, they are supplied with a shim that can be placed under the lug where the barrel attaches. This lifts the barrel very slightly at the rear to make the assembly free floating. Weighing only 21.6 ounces, the Green Mountain Aero barrel is well suited for building ultra light rifles based on the Ruger 10/22 action.

It is not unusual for a given manufacturer to produce barrels in blue and stainless steel in different weights and lengths as well as sleeved barrels. Given that a manufacturer may produce as many as eight or ten types of barrels, the number of available options must run in the hundreds. Although we did not approach this number of barrels used in the tests, the number was still substantial. The accompanying table shows data for the barrels that were used in experiments as part of the data collection for this book.

Characteristics of Barrels Evaluated

Barrel Manufacturer and Type	Weight (oz.)	Length (in.)
.22 LR Standard Weight		
E. R. Shaw - stainless, spiral fluted	24.2	18.0
Factory Carbine - blue	28.9	18.5
Factory Compact Rifle	—	16.5
Factory Rifle	—	20.0
Factory Wal-Mart - stainless	32.0	22.0
Green Mountain - blue fluted	26.0	16.5
Green Mountain - blue fluted	30.0	20.0
Jarvis - blue	31.5	20.0
Jarvis - stainless	31.3	20.0
Lilja - stainless	30.8	21.0
Ranch Products - blue muzzle-weighted	36.2	16.5
Volquartsen - stainless muzzle-weighted	34.1	16.5
.22 LR 0.920" Diameter		
Factory Target	—	20.0
Adams & Bennett - blue	49.6	18.0
Butler Creek - blue	55.0	20.0
Butler Creek - blue fluted	48.7	20.0
Butler Creek - stainless	53.9	20.0
Butler Creek - stainless fluted	48.2	20.0
Green Mountain Aero (w/shroud)	21.6	17.0
Green Mountain - blue	55.1	20.0
Jarvis - blue	55.1	20.0
Kidd - stainless	54.4	20.0
Magnum Research - graphite	12.8	16.88
Majestic Arms Aluma-Lite	24.2	17.75
Shilen - blue	49.9	18.0
Shilen - stainless	49.0	18.0
Tactical Solutions - Realtree® camo	17.4	16.5
Tactical Solutions - green fluted	14.7	16.5
Whistle Pig - fluted (silver/red)	18.1	18.0
.17 Mach 2 0.920" Diameter		
Magnum Research - graphite	14.0	16.88
Majestic Arms Aluma-Lite	25.1	17.75
.22 WMR Standard Weight		
Factory - blue	28.5	18.5
Green Mountain Running Boar - stainless	40.7	22.0
Jarvis - blue	31.9	20.0
.22 WMR 0.920" Diameter		
Majestic Arms Aluma-lite	24.1	17.75
.17 HMR 0.920" Diameter		
Butler Creek - blue	56.4	20.0

As can be seen from the table of specifications, barrels generally fall into two categories based on barrel dimensions depending on whether they have the contour of the factory barrel or a 0.920-inch diameter. Although several of the barrels have a diameter of 0.920 inches, they are ultra light models. When selecting a barrel, keep in mind that the barrels fall into three general categories that can be considered as ultra light (under 25 ounces), standard weight (25 to 35 ounces), and heavy weight (over 48 ounces). Depending on the intended use for your custom Ruger 10/22, you may be more concerned with the weight than with diameter. Be assured that highly accurate barrels are available in all of the classifications either by weight or by diameter. When it comes to barrels, there is something for everyone who customizes the Ruger 10/22.

Chapter 9

FIRE CONTROL PARTS

If there is one area in which the factories err on the side of caution, it is with the triggers supplied as standard equipment. Several older firearms in our gun safe have crisp trigger let off with a pull of approximately 3 pounds. One almost never finds a trigger with this type of pull on a factory firearm today. Litigation has made it imperative for the factories to send firearms out that cannot be discharged with a slight or inadvertent contact with the trigger. As a result, it is not uncommon to find factory firearms that require a pull of over six pounds to fire the piece. One rifle used in the testing conducted for producing this book had a pull of over 11 pounds! A large part of the aftermarket industry associated with the Ruger 10/22 is concerned with replacing parts in the trigger assembly or simply replacing the entire trigger package to remedy the situation. In this chapter, we will address the trigger group of the Ruger 10/22 and some of the products that are available to improve it. Installation of these items requires the trigger group to be disassembled, and

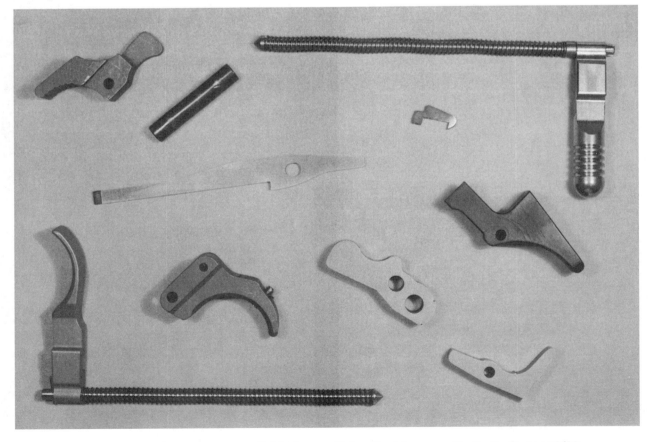

A wide variety of aftermarket parts are available for modifying the trigger and bolt of a Ruger 10/22.

instructions for doing this are presented in Chapter 5 where the complete disassembly of the trigger unit is described.

Bolt Stop

The design of the Ruger 10/22 is such that when a shot is fired the bolt is driven to the rear. To prevent the bolt from simply slamming into the back of the receiver (made of aluminum in the 10/22 but made of steel in the 10/22M), a steel pin is placed transversely through the receiver to stop the travel of the bolt. Appropriately known as the bolt stop pin, this steel pin passes through the receiver and is held in place by friction. When the action is held in place inside the stock, the stock covers the sides of the action so that the bolt stop is not visible. After the barrel and action are removed from the stock, it is a simple

Pushing with a punch of suitable size can move the bolt stop.

matter to drive the pin out of the receiver from either side and insert a replacement. In some rifles, the bolt stop fits loosely enough in the holes that very little pressure is required to drift it out of the receiver. In fact, it falls freely from the receiver of our 10/22 Magnum, and we lost it at the range while changing stocks. Fortunately, it was

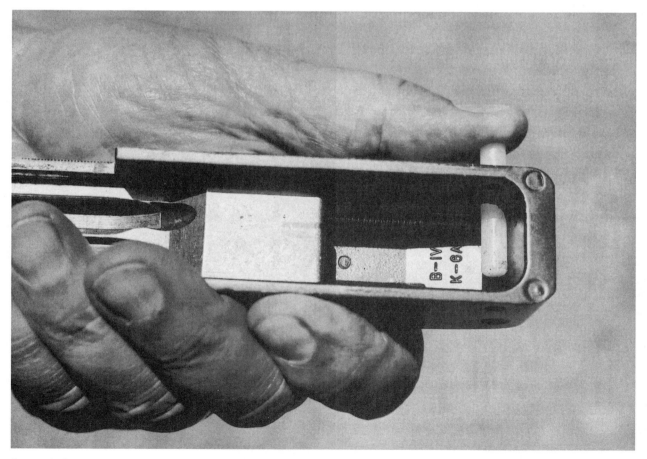

A new bolt stop can be inserted from either side of the receiver.

found on the next visit. Once the action of a 10/22 is placed in the stock, the vertical walls of the stock prevent sideward motion of the bolt stop and the pins that hold the trigger assembly to the receiver.

When the bolt strikes the bolt stop, there is a metal-on-metal contact, and a "clunk" sound and jolt result. One motivation for replacing the bolt stop is to provide a cushion so that stopping the rearward travel of the bolt occurs in a less violent manner. Aftermarket bolt stops are available in several types with the most common probably being either a solid stiff plastic or a steel pin encased in plastic. A bolt stop of either type adds an element of smoothness to the action. Because the metal bolt is not striking a metal bolt stop, the plastic replacement parts are sometimes called bolt buffers. Both noise and vibration are somewhat reduced. Considering that replacing the bolt stop is an operation that costs very little and that is easily carried out in a couple of minutes, it is a recommended modification.

Replacement Trigger Assemblies

The Ruger 10/22 owner who installs a custom trigger assembly or any components in the trigger assembly must understand that the factory warranty is voided. Furthermore, replacing or modifying the parts of an aftermarket trigger assembly will not endear you to the producer of the unit. If you have questions about an aftermarket trigger assembly, contact the producer before you make any alterations!

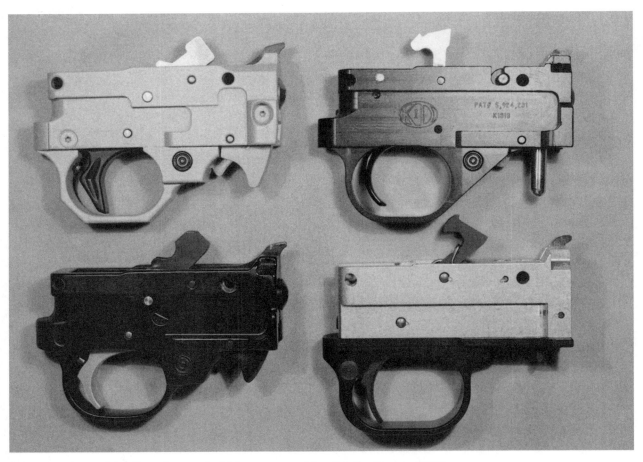

These are four of the fine aftermarket trigger assembles for the Ruger 10/22.

What constitutes a reasonable pull on the trigger to fire a rifle is open to some conjecture. A shooter who is competing in a benchrest competition may want a trigger pull of no more than one-half pound. On the other hand, a hunter walking in the woods with a 10/22 looking for squirrels may want a trigger pull of three or three and one-half pounds with a crisp let off. In fact, it is not safe to hunt with a rifle that has a very light trigger because of the possibility of touching it accidentally causing the rifle to fire. When the rifle is resting on a bench pointing down range between shots, there is little likelihood of firing the rifle inadvertently.

During the testing of Ruger 10/22s configured in many different ways for this project, we have worked with rifles that had unaltered trigger units as well as some with complete replacement trigger units from aftermarket sources. Trigger pulls on the factory rifles that we tested range from about 4.5 pounds for the 10/22 Target to about 6.3 pounds for a 10/22 Carbine except for one 10/22M that had a trigger pull of about 11 pounds. Two of the aftermarket triggers, those from Jard and Kidd, broke at just about two pounds. The triggers from Hornet Products and Volquartsen had slightly heavier pulls, but had crisp let off. In order to evaluate the trigger assemblies, they were requested with different pull weights.

In interest of correct reporting of things, our testing showed that replacing the barrel and stock had a much greater effect on accuracy than did the trigger used. One gets accustomed to the trigger action of a rifle after shooting it for some time. Replacing the trigger may make it easier to fire a particular rifle, but it does not increase the inherent accuracy that the barrel and shooting platform can deliver. If a rifle has a heavy trigger pull, it may be necessary to pay particular attention to the way the hand is placed and how the trigger finger increases pressure on the trigger. These are things that can be learned as the shooter becomes more familiar with the rifle. In that connection, it should be mentioned that some five-shot groups measuring about three-quarters of an inch were fired with the 10/22M that had the horrible 11-pound trigger pull. Of course, this is not a desirable type of trigger, and no one would want to have to pull that hard while trying to hold the sights aligned on a squirrel or prairie dog. A stationary bench and sandbags are much more forgiving when shooting a rifle with a heavy trigger pull. However, a trigger pull of 5-6 pounds is not too bad if the let off is crisp. If you shoot a rifle a lot, you adjust to the trigger action of that particular rifle.

All of this is to say that if you take a Ruger 10/22 and replace the trigger you should not expect to suddenly see the average group size cut in half. If you replace a factory barrel with a high-grade match barrel, you may very well get a considerable reduction in group size from this change alone. However, improving the trigger is certainly a worthwhile proposition because if there is one group of rimfire rifles that generally have less than perfect trigger action, it is the rimfire autoloaders. The Ruger 10/22 is by no means alone in this group of rifles. In fact, the Ruger 10/22 has a good reputation among inexpensive autoloaders with regard to trigger behavior. A bad trigger can still be used effectively when the rifle is fired from a bench, but a good trigger makes shooting offhand easier.

The easiest and quickest way to get good trigger action on a Ruger 10/22 is to replace the entire assembly with one of the fine aftermarket units. Although trigger assemblies are available from other sources, we worked extensively with trigger assemblies marketed by Hornet Products, Jard, Kidd, and Volquartsen. Each of these triggers is available from the manufacturer in a range of pull weights. In addition to having a better pull, other enhancements are generally included. For example, each of the trigger units we tested was furnished with an extended magazine release. Also as part of the design, the hammer and sear are greatly different from their factory counterparts, which can reduce lock time. When you install a complete aftermarket trigger unit, the other items are included, which makes replacing the entire trigger unit an attractive alternative for several reasons. Even in terms of cost, replacing the entire trigger assembly makes sense because purchasing several of the components separately can cost almost as much. Also, when you replace the entire trigger assembly you get a unit that has been configured professionally with all matching parts and tested for reliability.

Another nice aspect of replacing the trigger assembly is that it is so easy to do. The first step is to remove the barreled action from the stock. Next, remove the two pins that hold the trigger housing to the receiver. These fit so loosely in some rifles that they literally fall out when the barreled action is held on its side. Insert the new trigger assembly and replace the two pins. Understandably, many users of Ruger 10/22s would not think of taking apart the components that are contained within the trigger housing. For those persons, replacing the entire trigger assembly is an attractive alternative. Moreover, the trigger assembly can be ordered with the trigger pull you want and with some selection of magazine release, firing pin, and extractor. Some trigger assemblies also have the bolt lock modified so that the bolt remains open after the last shot is fired. Complete trigger assemblies for the Ruger 10/22 span a price range of about $100-300 depending on the manufacturer.

As mentioned earlier, the pins holding the trigger assembly to the receiver fit so loosely that they frequently fall out when the barreled action is turned on its side. Kidd Innovative Design markets a kit that allows the owner of a Ruger 10/22 to replace those somewhat troublesome pins. Each of the pins from Kidd has a small torx headed screw in each end of the pin.

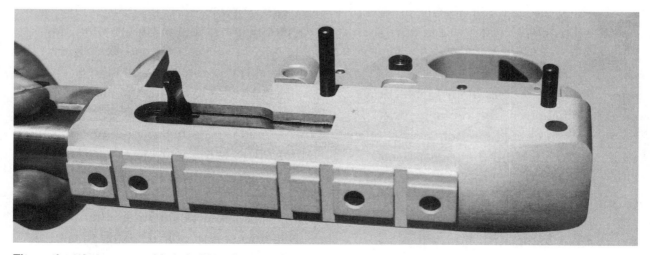

The entire trigger assembly is held to the receiver by two pins.

The easiest and quickest way to improve the trigger on a Ruger 10/22 is to replace the complete unit.

The heads of these end screws are slightly larger in diameter than the pins themselves and are beveled inward. When the screws are in place the pin cannot fall out or move laterally. One small inconvenience is that the ends of the pins must fit flush with the sides of the trigger housing. As a result, beveled surfaces must be made in the sides of the trigger housing to accommodate the screws. The pin kit from Kidd is supplied with a countersink that can be used to

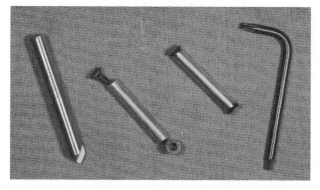

Kidd Innovative Designs produces a set of trigger unit pins that are locked in place by screws in the ends.

provide the correct surface to match the screws. The countersinking operation should allow the head of each retaining screw to be very slightly (0.003-0.010 inch below the surface of the trigger housing. Installing the Kidd pin kit eliminates the problem of pins falling out of the receiver.

All of the aftermarket trigger assemblies we tested fit perfectly in the receivers. No filing, fitting, or finagling was required. In all cases, the trigger units gave a crisp let off. The pull weights of the units tested were as follows: Hornet, 2.8 lbs; Jard, 2.0 lbs; Kidd, 2.4 lbs; and Volquartsen, 4.0 lbs. Keep in mind that we had specifically requested trigger units from the manufacturers having different pull weights so it is not as if one producer gives a unit having a lighter trigger pull. With most suppliers of complete trigger units, the consumer has the option of ordering a trigger with a pull weight within a certain range. Therefore, the trigger units were not intended to have the same weight of trigger pull. All of the units were within a couple of tenths of a pound of the weights requested.

All of the trigger assemblies were used without any modification. We made no attempt to disassemble or adjust them or to replace any of the parts. As a result, it is not possible to describe exactly how some of the parts differ from those of the factory trigger, but some observations will be presented. None of the trigger units had a provision to hold the bolt open after the last shot is fired, but all were equipped with an automatic bolt release. Pulling back on the bolt and releasing it allows it to go forward.

The trigger assembly from Hornet Products bears considerable resemblance to the factory unit and at approximately $85 was the least expensive of the units tested. The housing and all of the parts are finished in black except for the trigger, sear, and disconnector. The hammer has essentially the same configuration as the factory part, and it is moved by a coil spring and strut assembly. A spring-loaded plunger located behind the trigger keeps the trigger in the forward position. The bolt lock spring is a coil spring that is located

around the hammer pivot pin as it is in the factory trigger. The major difference is in the trigger, sear, and disconnector assembly, which are configured much differently from the factory parts. A large magazine release protrudes from the bottom of the unit in front of the trigger guard. The Hornet trigger assembly worked extremely well.

Known as the Ruger 10/22 Trigger System, the trigger assembly from Jard is radically different from the factory trigger in many ways. On the Jard trigger, the safety is located *behind* the trigger rather than in front as it is on a factory trigger unit. When you look at the Jard trigger unit, it is remarkable how little you can see without taking the unit apart. The housing is made in two parts, one of which is like a base plate while the other is a more or less vertical box that sits on the base plate. The base plate is actually called the Bottom Housing Plate while the box is known as the Housing. There are four transverse pins through the housing, but they bear little resemblance to those of the factory trigger either in location or function. Small dents have been made in the housing very close to the ends of the four pins on both sides of

This trigger assembly is produced by Hornet Products.

The Jard trigger was preset to a pull weight of about two pounds.

the trigger housing. These dents move metal slightly so that the pins are locked in place.

On the Jard trigger, the bolt lock is a spring-loaded bar that slides vertically at the front end of the right hand side of the trigger housing. A small portion of the bar protrudes from the bottom of the housing, and pushing it upward moves the bolt lock upward so that it engages the bolt to hold it open. The hammer is driven by a coil spring that is wound around the hammer pivot pin on both sides of the hammer. One unique feature of the spring is that the ends are inserted into holes in the housing, and the straight middle section passes behind the hammer. When the hammer is drawn back, it causes both of the coils to be wound. The magazine release is a lever pivoted in the middle that has a spring pushing it forward at the top. The lever has a hole in it near the top, which fits over the protruding pin at the rear of the magazine. The trigger is adjustable for over travel, but the hammer must be removed to gain access to the adjustment screw. Sear engagement is adjustable as is the disconnector. An instruction sheet is supplied with the Jard trigger that describes how to make these adjustments. We did not alter the trigger in any way neither did we feel any need to because it performed extremely well. The Jard trigger assembly sells for around $200.

A straight portion of the spring running behind the hammer connects the two coils.

The Jard trigger assembly utilizes a coil spring to move the hammer. The coils are located on both sides of the hammer.

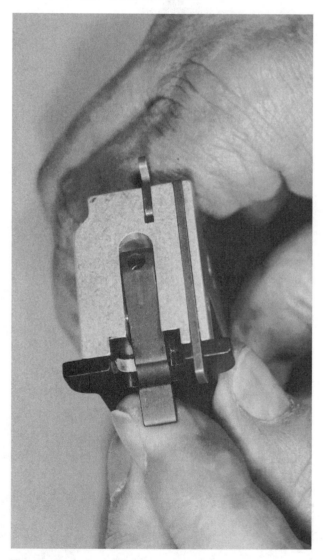

The Jard trigger utilizes a pivoted lever with a hole in it to secure the pivot pin in the magazine. The vertical bar along the edge of the housing is the bolt lock.

Kidd Innovative Design (KID) furnishes an instruction manual with their Ruger 10/22 Match Trigger. One of the cautions is that the trigger assembly must be used with barrels that have a barrel tenon that measures 0.750 inch in length. Since the bolt stops with the bolt face against the

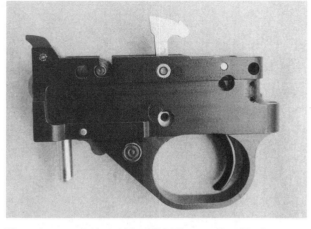

The trigger produced by Kidd Innovative Designs has many innovative features.

rear end of the barrel, the length of the barrel tenon determines how far forward the bolt goes. This in turn determines the relationship between the location of the hammer with respect to the bolt so the length of the barrel tenon is critical to the correct operation of the trigger unit.

A pull of only 2.4 pounds on the bright red trigger of the KID trigger assembly was required to release the sear. The KID trigger has so many unique features that it is difficult to describe it adequately. First, the magazine release on the KID trigger assembly is unique. It consists of a highly polished metal rod with a rounded end that projects downward for about three-quarters of an inch from the bottom the action. The magazine release or latch is tensioned by means of a coil spring located around the pivot pin. The latch would not make it easy

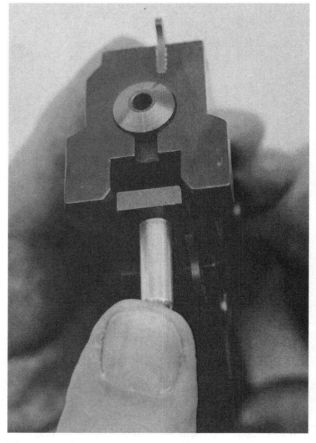

The magazine release on the Kidd trigger is a polished rod.

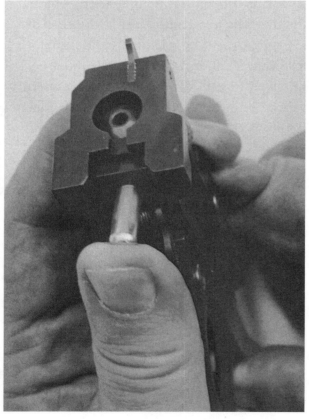

Pushing forward on the magazine release moves the magazine latch plunger back into the housing, which releases the magazine.

to carry the rifle with a hand placed directly in front of the trigger guard, but operates very easily and works well. Second, the ejector is not pivoted as it is in the factory trigger. The short ejector is permanently mounted by means of a roll pin.

A third unusual aspect of the KID trigger assembly is the hammer. Instead of being driven forward by a coiled spring behind the hammer, the KID trigger has a coil spring located in front of the hammer. The strut surrounding the spring pushes backward on a surface below the pivot point so the upper portion of the hammer is pushed forward. The strut is held in place by a large pin that runs transversely through the trigger housing, and the ends of the pin are held in place by notches in the top edge of the trigger housing. The pin has a recess that accepts the end of the strut and the hammer spring.

Finally, the two-stage KID trigger is totally unlike that of the factory unit or any of the other aftermarket triggers that we used. The sear is located behind the hammer and makes contact with the locking notch located on the back edge of the upper part of the hammer

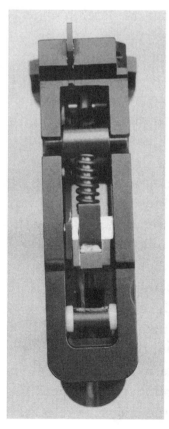

On the Kidd trigger, the hammer spring is located in front of the hammer. It pushes backward on the lower end below the pivot point, which moves the upper end forward.

The hammer spring is locked in place by the retaining rod that locks in notches on the sides of the trigger housing.

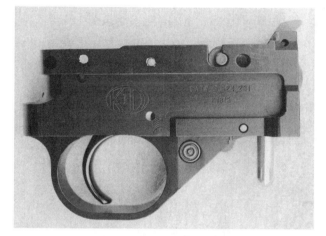

At the top of the trigger housing the hammer retainer can be seen with its ends resting in notches.

when it is cocked. A complex mechanism is employed to release the sear. Let off, overtravel, and trigger position with respect to the safety, and free travel are all adjustable. The detailed instruction manual gives directions for making these adjustments, but in our opinion a specialist should do any adjustment of this trigger. It comes with a factory set pull that can be as light as 6 oz. This is a unique, high quality trigger unit that sells for around $280.

The Volquartsen trigger assembly has a number of unique features. First, the hammer is not moved by the usual coil spring and strut assembly as it is in a factory trigger. The hammer spring is a

The unusually shaped hammer in the Kidd trigger has the notch that engages the sear at the upper rear position in this photo.

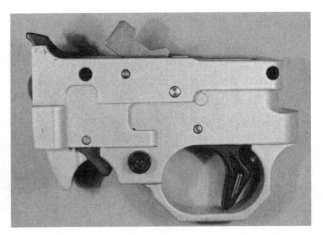

Only outwardly does this Volquartsen trigger resembles the factory trigger.

coil spring that is located around the hammer pivot pin on the left hand side of the hammer. The coil spring on the right hand side of the hammer is the bolt lock spring, just as it is in the factory trigger

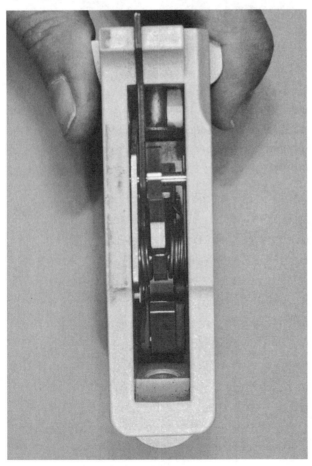

The coil spring to the left of the hammer is the hammer spring while that on the right is the bolt lock spring.

unit. With a coil spring on both sides, the hammer must be made much thinner than the factory hammer. Second, the spring-loaded plunger that is located behind the factory trigger is absent in the Volquartsen trigger unit. Its function is accomplished by a coil spring that is located around the trigger pivot pin. Third, the hammer, trigger, sear, and disconnector are highly polished steel parts. Fourth, the magazine latch plunger is made of metal rather than plastic, as is the factory part. The result of all these features is a trigger that is radically different from the factory unit, but one that gives outstanding trigger action. Retail price of the Volquartsen trigger unit is around $225.

As a result of firing a few thousand rounds through our Ruger 10/22 rifles with aftermarket trigger assemblies, it became clear that any of the units tested would be a welcome addition when customizing a Ruger 10/22. They performed in a splendid manner with each of the rifles on which they were installed. The only consideration was that the magazine releases on these aftermarket triggers protrude from the bottom of the action. The actual shape of the magazine releases on the trigger units were quite different. In most cases, an extended magazine release does not present a problem, but when the rifle is supported on certain types of rests an extended magazine release can make contact with the rest. Also, depending on the mode of carry, an extended magazine release can interfere with gripping the rifle, and can cause the magazine to be released inadvertently. These are minor concerns and in no way detract from the outstanding performance of the four aftermarket trigger assemblies we tested. Units from other suppliers would probably perform in an equally acceptable manner.

Hammer and Sear

There are some intrepid shooters who want to do it their way. For those individuals, we progress to individual components of the trigger assembly starting with the hammer and sear. Keep in mind that any work of this type voids the factory warranty! Any modification of a firearm by the owner is done completely at the owner's own risk and responsibility. The marketers of parts are certainly willing to give information and advice, but functioning and operation of the firearm are the responsibility of the owner! Although the modifications that we performed resulted in no change in the functioning of our rifles, the results with other rifles may be different. Manufacturing tolerances exist so the parts may not perform exactly the same in other rifles.

To install any of the fire control components in a Ruger 10/22, it is necessary to first remove the trigger assembly. Installing an extractor and/or firing pin requires the bolt to be removed from the receiver. These disassembly processes have been described in detail

in Chapter 5. Before setting out to replace components within the trigger assembly or the bolt assembly, review the disassembly procedures.

When the bolt of a Ruger 10/22 is drawn back, the recoil spring is compressed and the hammer is moved backward against the spring that moves it forward in firing. When the hammer reaches a certain point in its backward travel, the spring-loaded sear engages a notch in the hammer, which holds it back in the cocked position. Releasing the bolt allows it to fly forward and if a loaded magazine is inserted, the bolt picks up a cartridge and moves it into battery. As the bolt is moved backward during a firing cycle, all of this happens automatically. Pulling on the trigger until the sear releases the hammer, which then strikes the firing pin and fires the cartridge, can then fire the round. The basic problem in improving the firing mechanism of the Ruger 10/22 is to make the sear release the hammer in a way that requires a reasonable pulling force on the trigger without excessive travel.

As we have mentioned, much of the action of a trigger is related to the interaction of the hammer and sear. In the trigger assembly of the Ruger 10/22, the sear is attached to the trigger with a pin. The trigger moves backward against a spring-loaded plunger, which returns the trigger to its forward position after the pressure supplied by the trigger finger is released. When the sear releases the hammer, a strong compressed coil spring that surrounds a strut pushes the hammer forward so it strikes the firing pin. It is desirable for the minimum amount of time (known as the lock time, see Chapter 2) to elapse between these events so that motion of the rifle does not cause errant shots.

One motivation for replacing the hammer is to install one that has a lighter weight. This causes the hammer to be accelerated more rapidly by the hammer spring, which in turn reduces the lock time. A lighter hammer can be produced by making it out of a metal (such as titanium) that is less dense than steel. Making the hammer of smaller size also makes it lighter.

Because of the critical contact between the hammer and sear, no attempt should be made by an amateur to alter the bearing surfaces in an effort to obtain a lighter trigger pull. Leave this work to a qualified gunsmith!

As part of our customizing a Ruger 10/22, we installed a hammer, sear/disconnector spring, sear, trigger, and trigger pivot pin that were obtained from Power Custom. In addition to these parts, the Power Custom shims that fit along the sides of the sear were installed as were hammer shims that fit on the inside of the hammer bushings. The highly polished shims prevent the sides of the sear and hammer from

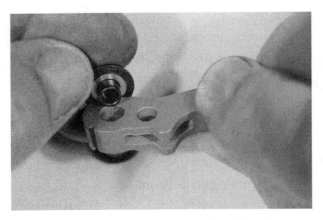

The hammer is separated from the bushings by shims to reduce friction.

rubbing on the trigger housing so that friction is reduced. When the trigger unit was reassembled and installed in the rifle, the trigger pull was measured using a Lyman Trigger Pull gauge, and the pull measured a crisp 3.6 pounds. Before the hammer and sear were installed, the trigger pull of this rifle measured 5.6 pounds. After installing the trigger kit, trigger action was markedly improved.

It is not necessary to install a complete set of aftermarket parts to see some improvement in trigger action. Installing

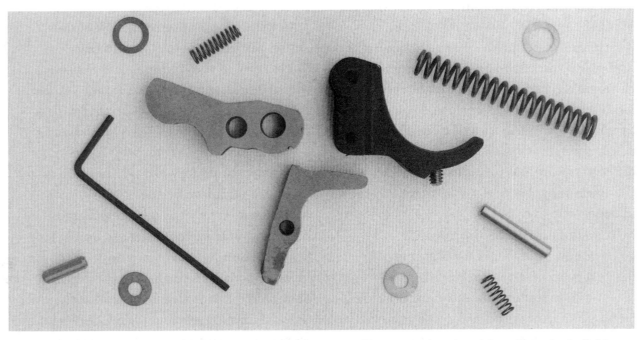

The factory trigger on a Ruger 10/22 can be improved by installing several parts such as those included in this kit from Power Custom.

only a high quality hammer and sear will improve trigger action to some extent.

The Power Custom trigger kit is furnished with a short "dummy" pin that is used to hold the trigger, sear, disconnector, and the disconnector/sear spring together temporarily as a unit before it is installed in the trigger housing. When this unit is placed inside the trigger housing, the actual trigger pivot pin can be pushed into place, which pushes the dummy pin out the other side of the housing. If you are working with a trigger kit that does not come with a temporary pin that is used to hold the parts together temporarily, you can easily make such a pin. A section of a matchstick that has been reduced in diameter so that it fits snugly in the hole through the trigger works well. Without the trigger, sear, and disconnector being held together, it is very difficult to get the parts lined up inside the trigger housing so that the trigger pin can be inserted properly.

On a Ruger 10/22, the safety is a sliding bolt located in front of the trigger. As the trigger is pulled to fire the rifle, the pivoted sear moves downward at the front. The safety functions by having a raised portion that slides under the sear when the safety is on. This prevents the front portion of the sear from moving downward when the trigger is pulled thus preventing the rifle from firing. THE SHAPE OF THE SEAR WHERE IT ENGAGES THE SAFETY IS CRITICAL!

Our sear from Power Custom was large enough in the forward area that the safety could not be put in the "on" position. The instructions that came with the trigger kit explained clearly the reason for supplying the sear in a slightly oversize form. If other parts were undersize because of manufacturing tolerances, the safety could move from side to side without the necessary friction to hold it in place. To make the sear engage the safety properly, it was necessary to remove a SMALL amount of the forward surface.

If you are replacing the hammer and sear as described here, look carefully at the factory sear when it is removed. Note the shape of the leading edge (which engages the safety). Now examine the aftermarket sear and you will see why some modification may be required as it was on our rifle. Follow the instructions that came with the aftermarket parts exactly when making the necessary changes to achieve correct contact between the sear and safety! REMOVE METAL FROM THE SEAR

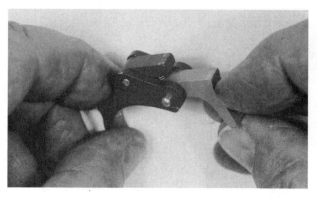

As shown here, the sear (on the right) is held to the trigger by means of a short pin that will be pushed out after the assembly is placed in the trigger housing.

The sear needed a small amount of polishing to enable the safety to slide over it.

ONLY WHERE THE INSTRUCTIONS TELL YOU TO, AND IF YOU ARE NOT SURE, CONTACT THE MANUFACTURER!

The only way to determine the correct amount of contact between the sear and the safety is to install the trigger with the disconnector and sear attached (using the short temporary pin) and try moving the safety. This requires the hammer assembly to be in place so it can be cocked, but it is not necessary for the magazine release and bolt lock to be in place. Therefore, replace the trigger and hammer assemblies, cock the hammer, and see if the safety can be slid to the "on" position. As you move the safety, look inside the trigger housing from the top and watch the safety as it moves under the sear. It is easy to see if the raised portion of the safety slides under the sear. The object is to shape the forward portion of the sear so that the safety can slide under it as it is pushed "on", but with enough friction to make the safety have be pushed rather hard to be placed in the "off" position. In some cases, it may look as if the safety is "on" but when the trigger is pulled the gun will fire. This is a somewhat delicate balance, and it must be achieved by trial and error in several stages by following the instructions supplied with your aftermarket parts. DO NOT REMOVE ENOUGH METAL FROM THE SEAR SO THAT THE SAFETY SLIDES "OFF" EASILY! After reassembly, check the safety to make sure it is functioning properly.

Magazine Release

The rotary magazine used in the Ruger rimfire rifles has an enviable reputation for reliable cartridge feeding as well as durability. However, before the magazine is loaded it must be removed from the rifle. The magazine release on the factory 10/22 is a flat piece of metal that is located on the bottom of the action at the rear end of the magazine. Because the flush-fitting magazine release forms part of the base plate of the action, there are no protruding parts. Pushing upward on the front edge of this small pivoted plate pushes a lever backward against spring pressure. That lever is connected to a plunger that has a recess in the front end that fits over a pin that is located at the rear of the magazine in its center. At the front edge of the magazine is a small recess that accommodates a fingertip. The correct procedure for removing the magazine involves pushing upward on the release with the thumb while sliding the tip of the forefinger in the recess. Although the magazine should fall into your hand, a slight downward pull on the forward end may be necessary.

Many shooters do not find the magazine release on the Ruger 10/22 to be convenient to operate. As a result, magazine releases are available in a profusion of styles from many manufacturers, and most cost only a few dollars. Almost all of these have some sort of tab that projects downward behind the magazine. Pushing forward on the tab forces the lever backward releasing the magazine. Many shooters find a release of

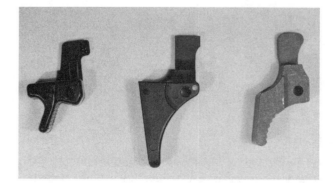

Aftermarket magazine releases are available in several styles.

this type more convenient to operate than pressing upward on the flush release on a factory rifle. However, when shooting from a bench using a support, care must be taken to prevent placing the rifle on the rest so that magazine release makes contact with the support. Also, with a protruding magazine release in place, carrying the rifle with one hand under or around its midsection is less convenient. Because of this, many shooters prefer a magazine that fits flush with the bottom of the action. Replacing the magazine release with an aftermarket model is a simple process.

After the barreled action is removed from the stock, the trigger assembly can be removed from the receiver. There are four pins that pass through the trigger housing which hold the parts in place. The pin that must be removed is the lower one that is located near the front of the trigger housing. It is on this pin that the magazine release pivots. As you press the pin out (on either side of the trigger housing), hold a finger on the spring-loaded plunger that locks the magazine in place. When the pin is removed, push the plunger backward into the trigger housing to remove tension on the magazine release. Pull the magazine release downward out of

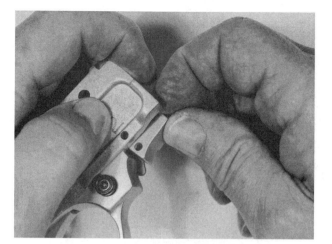

While holding the latch plunger in place with your finger, withdraw the magazine release.

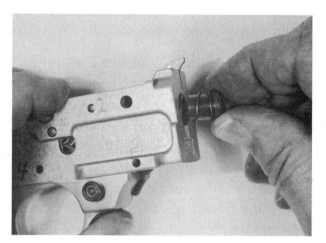

The magazine latch plunger and spring are removed from the front of the trigger housing.

To install a magazine release, first push out Pin 2.

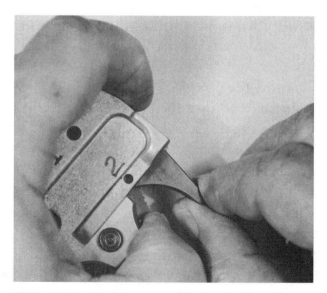

While holding the plunger and spring in place, insert the new magazine release and replace pin 2.

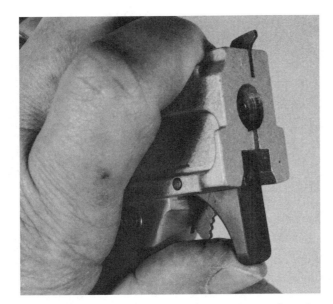

Pushing forward on the magazine release moves the magazine latch plunger backward.

the trigger housing and allow the plunger to move forward out of the trigger housing along with the spring that keeps tension on it. Note how the magazine release has a vertical bar that locks along the side of the shaft of the plunger. To install a different magazine release, replace the plunger and spring and push them fully into the trigger housing. Insert the magazine release in the trigger housing from the bottom so that the vertical bar rests along side the plunger shaft. While holding these parts in place, insert the pin. Details of the replacement of a magazine release will be found in Chapter 5 along with photographs to illustrate the process.

Manufacturers of the fine aftermarket trigger assemblies include a magazine release as part of the package. These magazine releases are produced in several forms, but the essential feature is that a lever of some sort is pushed forward rather than the flat release on the factory part being pushed upward. All of the aftermarket magazine releases operated satisfactorily. Keep in mind that if you replace the magazine release on a factory

trigger assembly that release will probably not be usable if you later install an aftermarket trigger assembly.

While making modifications to the trigger assembly, many shooters will choose to replace the factory bolt lock with an aftermarket one. One of the motivations for doing this is that most aftermarket bolt locks have the cut out section that fits over Pin 1 shaped so that when the tension is taken off the bolt (by pulling it backward slightly) it will automatically let the bolt close when it is released. It is not necessary to press upward on the tab located in front of the trigger guard. The bolt lock is easily inserted after the hammer is cocked by sliding the bolt lock in place in front of the hammer. Rotate the bolt lock spring so that the straight end projects upward so that when the bolt lock is inserted the curved end of the spring will be above the tab on the bolt latch. When it is in place, slide Pin 2 in place to hold it in approximately the correct position to permit Pin 1 to be inserted from the left hand side of the trigger housing. Insert Pin 1 through the housing wall and through the hole in the

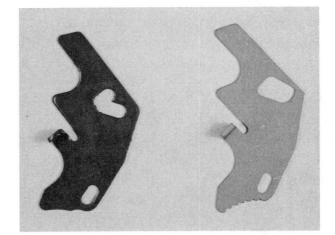

The factory bolt lock is shown on the left and the Power Custom lock is shown on the right. Note the difference in the shapes of the larger holes. The bolt lock on the right will allow the bolt to move forward after pulling it back and releasing it.

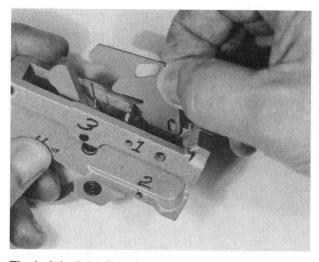

The bolt lock is placed in the trigger housing with the hammer in the rear (cocked) position and is secured by inserting Pins 1 and 2.

bolt lock. While having Pin 1 projecting through the bolt lock about ¼ inch, put the extractor in place with the hole over Pin 1. The curved end of the bolt lock spring should now be resting in the notch in the top edge of the projection of the bolt lock. Now push downward on the straight end of the bolt lock spring (which fits under Pin 1) with a punch and press Pin 1 in place over the end of the spring. With Pin 1 in place, remove Pin 2 and install the magazine release as described earlier.

Firing Pin

Although many shooters will have no occasion to replace the firing pin in a Ruger 10/22, others will leave no stone unturned to obtain even a small increment in performance. It is for the latter group that aftermarket firing pins are produced. Probably the most common type of replacement firing pin is one made of titanium. Being approximately 40 percent lighter than one made of steel, a titanium firing pin reduces the overall weight of the firing linkage, which results in some reduction in lock time. However, if the firing pin weighs too little, it may

have insufficient momentum to dent the cartridge head properly and misfires can occur. Power Custom produces both steel and titanium firing pins for the Ruger 10/22. Also from Power Custom are several other titanium parts (firing pin, extended bolt handle, trigger with adjustment for overtravel, magazine release) as well as the necessary springs and shims. Kidd Innovations offers a high quality bolt assembly for those who want to replace the factory bolt and related parts.

As illustrated in Chapter 5, replacing the factory firing pin in the Ruger 10/22 with the Power Custom titanium part requires the bolt to be removed. The first step is to separate the barreled action from the stock and then remove the trigger assembly from the receiver. Two pins hold the trigger assembly to the receiver, and they are easily pressed out from either side of the receiver. In fact, they sometimes fall out when the receiver is on its side. In order to remove the bolt, the bolt stop pin (or bolt buffer) must be removed by pushing it out of the receiver to either side. With the trigger assembly and bolt stop removed, the bolt can be removed by turning the receiver so the bottom is pointing up. Pulling the bolt fully to the rear inside the

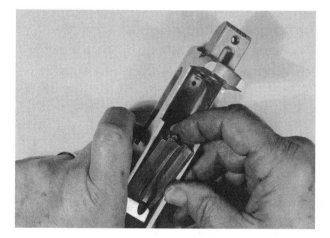

Replacing the firing pin begins with removal of the bolt.

receiver and lifting upward on the front end of the bolt allows it to be drawn upward past the retaining rail along the edge of the receiver and lifted out of the receiver. The bolt handle engages the top of the bolt by means of a section of the handle that fits in a square notch running across the top of the bolt. When the front end of the bolt is pulled upward, the bolt handle is freed from the notch in the bolt. The bolt handle, bolt guide (a rod), and recoil spring are lifted out as a unit.

With the bolt removed from the receiver, the firing pin can be removed by driving out the pin that holds it in the slot where it resides. The firing pin retaining pin is a hollow roll pin that fits tightly in a hole in the bolt. On our rifle, considerable force was required to move the pin. Using a 5/32-inch brass punch and tapping it with a gunsmith's hammer accomplished this. The bolt was laid on its side across a heavy metal support with a hole in it so that the pin would not strike the support as it is removed. A barbell plate works well as the support. With the retaining pin removed, the firing pin can be lifted out of the bolt. The firing pin is held in the rearward position by a rebound spring that fits inside the bolt below the firing pin where it pushes backward on a notch in the firing pin. Take care not to lose this tiny firing pin rebound spring as the firing pin is removed. Installing an aftermarket

The firing pin retaining pin must be driven out with a punch of suitable diameter.

firing pin requires the rebound spring to be inserted behind the lateral pin that holds it in place, and the firing pin inserted so that the front edge of the notch on its bottom rests against the rear end of the spring. Note that the firing pin must be inserted from the rear of the bolt because the groove near the front is constricted at the top by two "V" notches that force a partial closure of the groove.

The firing pin has an oval hole through which the retaining pin is driven. This oval hole allows the firing pin to move forward and rearward slightly but still be held within the bolt. With the firing pin rebound spring in place and the hole in the firing pin lined up with the hole in the bolt, the firing pin retaining pin (the hollow roll pin) is

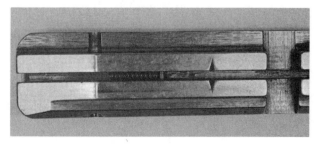

With the firing pin removed, the rebound spring is visible in the slot in the bolt.

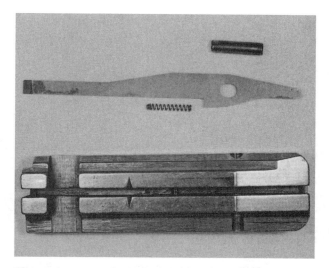

Shown here are the bolt, firing pin, firing pin retaining pin, and the rebound spring. Note how the rebound spring fits between the notch in the firing pin and the cross pin in the bolt.

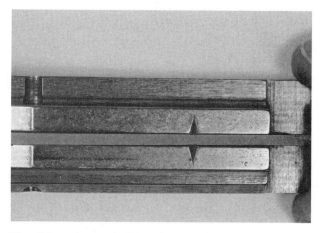

The firing pin must slide under the constriction made by the notches in the bolt.

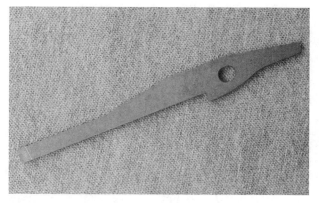

Note the oval hole in the firing pin through which the retaining pin passes. This allows the firing pin to move forward and backward while still being locked inside the bolt.

driven back through the bolt. On our rifle, this required rather heavy tapping while the bolt was securely supported on its side.

After the new firing pin has been installed, look carefully at the front edge of the bolt face. The firing pin should not protrude beyond the recess in the bolt where the cartridge head is supported. If it does, the forward motion of the closing bolt will cause the firing pin to strike the cartridge, which could cause it to fire. Check the movement of the firing pin by pushing it forward by applying pressure on the rear end (as the hammer does during firing). The firing pin should now protrude into the recess in the bolt face so that it will impact on the cartridge head as firing occurs.

With the new firing pin installed, the bolt is replaced in the receiver by first inserting the bolt handle assembly so that the rear end of the guide rod fits in the recess where it is held. Next push the handle backward slightly to compress the recoil spring and use a finger to compress the recoil spring fully. Place the bolt in the receiver so that it fits under the retaining rail as the bolt handle engages the groove in the bolt. Allow the bolt to be moved forward by the recoil spring and insert the bolt stop pin.

After a firing pin is installed, make sure that it does not protrude into the bolt face until it is pushed forward.

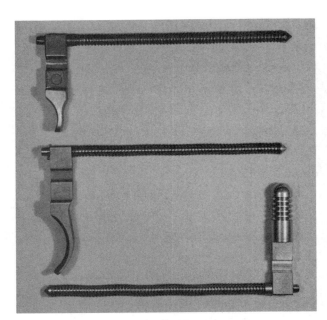

Shown here are bolt handle assemblies having different shapes.

Cycle the bolt to make sure that everything is working properly.

Extractor

Although case extraction is not often a problem with the Ruger 10/22, some shooters want a different extractor in their rifles. Replacing the extractor is not particularly difficult, but it is somewhat tricky. With the bolt removed as described earlier, lay the bolt on its side with the extractor side facing up. Note the spring-loaded plunger that pushes on the extractor to force the claw inward over the bolt face. That plunger must be forced backward past the hole in the bolt to allow the extractor to be wiggled out of the recess. If you are doing this alone, it is a great help to have the bolt held in a vice so that the plunger can be moved back with one hand while removing the extractor with the other.

The plunger can be moved backward using almost any suitable object that will fit in the extractor groove. We used a pair of heavy forceps, but an Allen wrench or

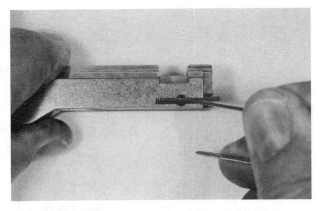

To remove the extractor, the plunger behind it must be pushed to the rear.

even a large bent paper clip will work. Move the plunger toward the rear of the bolt far enough the clear the hole in which the rear end of the extractor is held. With the plunger pushed backward, grasp the front part of the extractor and pull it toward you. This will free the hooked rear portion that is held inside the hole in the bolt. A pair of tweezers or forceps make it easier to grasp the small extractor. Take care not to let the device holding the plunger slip off! If you do, the extractor plunger and the extractor spring will be propelled to parts unknown. Unless you are replacing either the extractor plunger or extractor spring, you do not need to remove them completely from the bolt. Simply release the pressure slowly. The spring and plunger will remain in the recess in the side of the bolt.

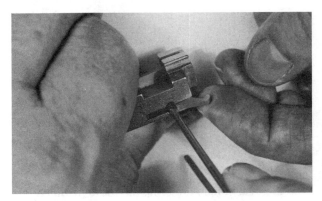

With the plunger pushed to the rear, the extractor can be pulled outward and unhooked from the hole in which it pivots.

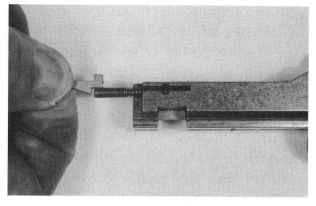

Note how the plunger fits against the notch in the extractor to push it forward.

Before you begin the installation of a new extractor, take a moment to see how the extractor fits in the bolt without the extractor plunger and extractor spring in place. Note how the rear portion enters the hole in the bolt and then hooks inside it. That movement is what is required to place the extractor in the bolt but with the plunger and spring in place and moved to the rear.

Begin the installation of the new extractor with the spring and plunger placed in the recess in the side of the bolt. With a suitable device, move the plunger backward to compress the spring sufficiently for the hole to be accessible. Use care in doing this because it is very easy to let the object used to move the plunger slide off. With no extractor in place to keep the spring and plunger in the recess, they will be expelled (and perhaps hard to find!). Now hold the extractor so that the hook points almost forward in line with the bolt and insert the rear, hooked end into the exposed hole in the side of the bolt. Move the hooked end of the extractor so that it resides in front of the bolt face. With the extractor completely inserted, slowly release the tension on the plunger so that it makes contact with the rear face of the notch in the side of the extractor. Test the movement of the

extractor by pushing the hook outward as if it were sliding over the rim of a cartridge.

After the extractor has been replaced, the bolt can be installed in the receiver. In some cases, a unit consisting of an aftermarket bolt handle, bolt guide, and recoil spring may replace the factory parts. This has been described in Chapter 5 and earlier in this chapter. After all the parts are in place, cycle the bolt manually to make sure that everything is working properly.

High Capacity Magazines

For some shooters, not only is rate of fire important but also the total capacity of the magazine. For many years, high capacity magazines were available for the Ruger 10/22, and these magazines manufactured before the ban went into effect continued to be available for a short time after the so-called assault rifle ban went into effect

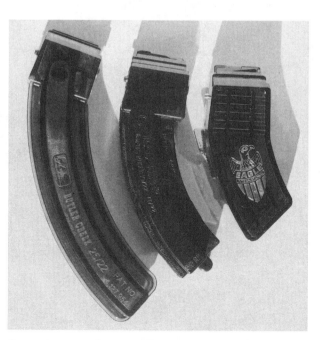

Several types of magazines are available for the shooter who wants to increase the capacity of a Ruger 10/22.

in 1994. That law was allowed to expire in 2004, so high capacity magazines are once again available.

One of the most common types of high capacity magazines for the 10/22 is the long, curved model that holds 25 or 30 rounds. Because of the curvature of these magazines, they are sometimes called "banana clips" since they loosely resemble the shape of that fruit. The top part of the magazine is configured like an ordinary 10-round Ruger magazine so that it fits in the recess in the stock and is held in place by the retaining pin. The magazine release continues to function in the same way as with a regular magazine. A long, curved magazine protruding from the bottom of the rifle does not enhance its looks or portability.

Although this magazine holds more cartridges than the 10-round factory version, it does not improve the appearance of the rifle.

Butler Creek produces a clear 25-round magazine for the 10/22 that sells for approximately $35.00. A similar model from Eagle International holds 30 rounds and sells for about $25.00. There is even a 50-round magazine produced by MWG. This unique magazine hold the cartridges inside the edge of a tear drop shaped container. Ram Line produces 25-, 30-, and 50-round magazines of different color plastics. One unique type of magazine is the Butler Creek Star Clip version that holds a total of 30 rounds and is shaped like a three-pointed starfish. In reality it is three Hot Lips magazines joined at the bottoms with the three "tails" each having a top section that is shaped like a Ruger magazine. When one "tail" is empty, the magazine is removed and another "head" is inserted. Because all Ruger rimfire rifles (10/22 autoloaders, 77/22 bolt actions, and 96/22 lever actions) can utilize the same magazines, the high capacity types can be used in any of these types of rifles. All of these products are available from many suppliers (see Chapter 13).

NOTE that even though the federal ban on larger capacity magazines expired in 2004, they may still be illegal in some jurisdictions. Many of the suppliers have statements to the effect "We do not ship these magazines to California, New York City, New Jersey, Washington, DC, Maryland, or Massachusetts." Not only may you not be able to order high capacity magazines in these areas, it may even be illegal to possess them. Before you decide to make your 10-shot Ruger into a 25-, 30-, or 50-shot model, check the restrictions that apply to your area! As mentioned in Chapter 7, other items such as folding stocks or those with pistol grips are also prohibited in some areas.

Chapter 10

SIGHTS FOR THE RUGER 10/22

In order to hit a target when shooting a rifle, it is necessary to have some means of aligning the barrel so that the bullet will go where it should. Because sighting is so important in rifle shooting, this entire chapter is devoted to sighting equipment for the Ruger 10/22.

It is possible to hit a target at a distance of a few feet simply by looking down the barrel, but this is hardly possible for targets farther away. Since the early days of rifle shooting, two objects placed on the barrel have been used to align the piece on the target. The most common form of open sights consists of some sort of bead near the front end of the barrel and a blade with a notch near the rear end of the barrel. Aligning the sights so that the bead is located in the notch of the rear sight while it is also aligned with the target gives the shooter a sight picture that is reproducible. Then, if the sights are properly regulated, the shots will strike where the sights are aligned.

Although the Ruger 10/22 Rifle comes with good open sights, other sighting equipment will lead to more accurate shooting.

All versions of the Ruger 10/22 except the target model come with sights on the barrel. The open sights used by Ruger are very good, but the limitation in accuracy is that imposed by how well two rather coarse objects at different distances are aligned. As we discuss sights in the remainder of this chapter, it is not in any way to point out deficiencies in the open sights that are furnished on Ruger rifles. The point is that no open sight is as good as some of the other types when highest accuracy is desired.

Another type of sighting arrangement retains the front sight but replaces the rear sight with an aperture that is placed so that it will be located near the eye of the shooter (usually on the receiver). With this type of sight, the shooter looks through the aperture at the front sight while placing the front sight correctly on the target. The human eye naturally seeks the brightest place to look through the aperture so the sights can be aligned accurately and reproducibly on the target.

Long ago someone reasoned that if the target could be magnified it would be possible to see more clearly where the sights were aligned. What was needed was some type of marker within the sight to place on the target so a reticule was installed. Thus was born the telescopic sight (scope). Since that time, scopes have been refined and a wide variety of types of reticules have been devised. We will have a lot to say about scopes later since they provide the highest degree of accuracy when shooting a rifle. Two other types of optical sights are the red dot and laser sights that have become popular in recent years. Although these types of sights are more commonly used on handguns, there is no reason they cannot be used on rifles.

Open Sights

The .22s that one of the authors used as a youngster consisted of a Stevens Model 15 single shot bolt action and a Winchester Model 90 pump chambered for the .22 Short. Both of these rifles had the typical bead front sight and a rear sight that consisted of a blade with a notch. Such sights were typical of the time. Neither rifle had any provision for attaching a peep sight or a scope.

Open sights are still found on many .22s, but a sizeable and increasing fraction of the models available have no sights when they leave the factory. In a way, it makes no sense to have open sights on a super accurate rifle. The human eye cannot focus sharply on the rear sight, front sight, and the target at the same time. As a result, open sights are the least accurate sights available. Much more accurate shooting can be done with a good peep sight and even better accuracy is possible when a scope is used. With open sights, the vision of the shooter is more likely to limit the accuracy obtainable with the rifle.

However, being traditionalists, we prefer open sights on rifles that are going to be used with a scope for several reasons. First, they are rugged, reliable, and weigh almost nothing. They do not change the configuration and balance of the rifle the way a scope and mount do. Second, it is possible for a scope or mount to be damaged if it suffers a blow. Scopes are rugged, and we are not talking about a blow that completely flattens the scope. All it takes is a blow sufficient to move the scope so that it is no longer sighted in, which is an entirely different proposition. It makes more sense to have iron sights that are correctly aligned on a rifle than a scope that is sighted in for somewhere unknown in relation to the target. Third, on any rifle that may be used in an "out there" or survival type of situation, iron sights should always be in place if for no other reason than to provide a sighting option to be a back up system to a scope.

In 1996, Ruger introduced the 10/22 Target, which has a heavy 20-inch barrel with no sights. In this case, it makes sense not to provide irons sights. This version is a target rifle, and with a target style stock the rifle weighs about 7.5 pounds. It is intended for target shooting and for most shooters this means a scope will be attached so iron sights are superfluous. To the credit of Sturm Ruger, all other variants of the 10/22 (Carbine, Sporter, International, and Rifle) have been produced complete with open sights. What percent of these rifles later have a scope attached is unknown, but there is no question that an enormous number of them have been used only with open sights.

For many years, the open sights furnished with Ruger 10/22s were of the same basic type. They consist of a front sight that has of a bead on a post and a folding rear sight. However, there have been numerous variations in the configurations of the sights. The length of the rail along the top of the front sight (that forms the bead when viewed from the rear)

The front sight on the 10/22 Carbine is of the bead type.

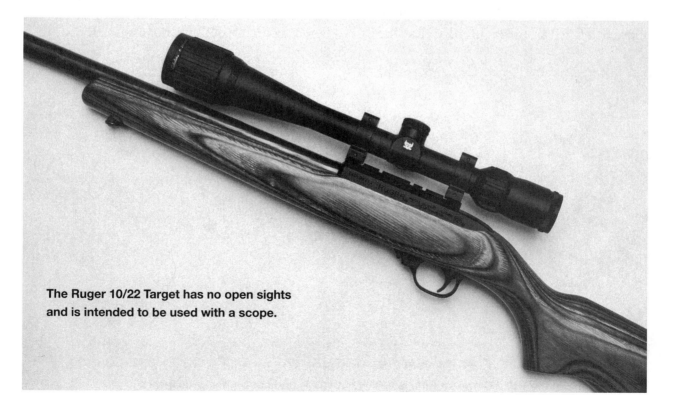

The Ruger 10/22 Target has no open sights and is intended to be used with a scope.

This rear sight on the 10/22 Rifle has a square notch that matches the square topped post front sight.

A fiber optic insert rests on top of the front sight used on the 10/22 Compact Rifle.

has varied. Rear sights have also been of more than one type because Ruger has not always contracted with the same supplier for the open sights used on 10/22s.

Beginning in 2005, Ruger began to produce 10/22s having the much in vogue fiber optic sights. The front sight consists of a post along the top of which is mounted a fiber optic insert. The rear sight has a blade with a notch with fiber optic inserts on either side. Proponents of fiber optic sights point out that they provide rapid acquisition of the target picture. Except in

combat situations or in dim light this is not usually a problem. One advantage of fiber optic sights is that the inserts on the front and rear sights form three bright spots that can be aligned horizontally very quickly. However, the front sight must still be placed in the proper position on the target. Some shooters prefer a bead or square topped post front sight and a rear sight with a notch of matching shape. Our Ruger 10/22 Rifle has the square post and square notch, and it provides a sight picture as good as any 10/22 we have tested.

The rear sight on the 10/22 Compact Rifle is easily adjustable and has a fiber optic insert.

A square topped post was used on this early 10/22 Rifle.

Virtually every aftermarket barrel for the Ruger 10/22 is produced without open sights. Mounting open sights on such barrels requires the services of a gunsmith. In contrast to this, we should mention a new barrel that is available from Butler Creek. This barrel is essentially unique in that it comes with open sights. These sights are the HIVIZ® version which have a folding, adjustable rear sight with fiber optic inserts on either side of the notch and a fiber optic front sight. Although the discussion here is not concerned with barrels, the Butler Creek barrel has a carbon fiber sleeve over a steel core. Unfortunately, we did not have this barrel for testing so it is not discussed in Chapter 11.

It is generally agreed that no one can properly sight in a rifle for someone else. To some extent this is true because two shooters may not align the sights on the target in exactly the same way. For example, one shooter may place the bead of the front sight lower in the rear sight notch than another. Also, one shooter may place the bead on the target in a slightly different way from another. Because of these variables, it is true that the rifle may not be sighted in correctly for all shooters.

When sighting in a rifle with open sights, it is almost always the case that the rear sight is the one moved. With the Ruger 10/22 factory sights the folding rear sight has a movable blade held in position by two screws. Loosening these screws allows the blade to be moved up or down to correct for elevation. There are reference marks for roughly determining how much the sight blade has been moved. Remember to move the rear sight in the direction you want the point of impact to move on the target. If the rifle is shooting low, raise the rear sight, etc. Correcting windage requires the entire sight to be moved laterally in the dovetail retaining slot. This is done by carefully tapping a brass punch with a small hammer with the amount being determined by trial and error. The 10/22 Compact Rifle has an entirely different type of rear sight that contains fiber optic elements, and as was discussed in Chapter 4, it is adjusted by means of two screws.

The alignment of the sights with each other and with the target constitutes what is known as the sight picture. Achieving skill with a rifle requires the sight picture to be the same for each shot. One of the best sight pictures is that achieved when using a square topped post and a rectangular notch in the rear sight. The technique in this case is to place the front sight blade in the rear notch with the top of the blade being at the same height as the top of the rear sight blade. To center the front sight in the rear notch, a small sliver of light should be visible on either side of the front sight blade. With that accomplished, the rifle is pointed in such a way that the target appears to be on top of the front sight. Because the bottom of a circular clock face is where the numeral 6 resides, the sight picture

Figure 10-1. The sights are adjusted so that the top of the post is positioned at the bottom of the bull. This is referred to as a "six o'clock" hold.

Figure 10-2. The sights are adjusted so that the top of the post is aligned with the center of the bull.

is known as a 6 o'clock hold. This works well for circular targets that are at a fixed distance from the shooter.

A more practical sight picture for field shooting is to regulate the rear sight so that when the front sight appears in the proper position in the rear sight notch the top of the post is positioned so that it represents the point of impact. With this arrangement, the shooter aligns the front sight in the rear sight then places the top of the post on the target where he or she wants the bullet to strike. This sight picture works well when the targets are of irregular shape and the targets are not always at the same distance, as is the case in hunting and pest shooting. Both the 6 o'clock hold and the top of the post method can be used with either a bead or square topped post, but the rounded top of a bead is often difficult to see clearly.

Fiber Optic Sights

Although recent developments in sighting equipment have been predominantly concerned with scopes, refinement of open

sights has also taken place. One way in which open sights have been updated is by the use of fiber optic inserts. A fiber optic rod allows light to enter from the sides, which causes the rod to appear to glow when viewed from the end. The small, circular end of the fiber optic element appears as a bright dot. A popular configuration for open sights using fiber optic inserts consists of one rod along the top of the front sight and elements on either side of the rear notch. In this way, three dots appear to the shooter. These dots can be aligned rapidly, and they are visible in dim light.

Although Ruger now markets some rimfire rifles with fiber optic sights, the Williams Gun Sight Company produces an aftermarket sight combination known as Fire Sights®. Sights of this type have been available for muzzle loading rifles and for shotguns for many years. The Ruger 10/22 Compact Rifle is furnished with this type of sights. In addition to Williams, fiber optic sights are also produced by HiViz® Sight Systems and Truglo® Inc. If the shooter of

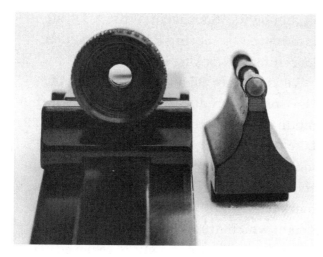

Williams produces this combination of a peep sight and fiber optic front sight for the Ruger 10/22.

a Ruger 10/22 needs a set of open sights for use in dim light, the fiber optic sights provide a useful alternative.

Peep Sights

A type of sight that is often overlooked is the aperture or peep sight. With a peep sight, much greater accuracy is possible than with open sights. The eye looks through the aperture at its bright point (the center) so that the front sight can be aligned on the target to establish the sight picture. Because the shooter does not have to try to focus on the rear sight, there are only two objects (the front sight and the target) to consider. The eye looks through the aperture, not at it.

Mounted on the receiver, the aperture is quite close to the shooter's eye. With the front sight being between two and three feet from the shooter's eye, it is relatively easy to place the front sight correctly on the target. As a result, fine accuracy is possible when using a peep sight correctly. Of course, formal target competition is conducted with rifles wearing peep sights. If the shooter has good eyesight, the accuracy attainable can rival that obtained when using a scope.

One of the advantages of the peep sight is that most types can be accurately adjusted. Some of the better models have click adjustments that are highly reproducible and permit adjustments in one-quarter minute clicks. Other models are adjusted by moving the aperture after loosening a locking screw then tightening it after making the adjustment.

Another advantage of the peep sight is that it adds very little weight and bulk to the rifle. Handling characteristics and weight distribution are essentially unchanged. When a scope and mount are added to a rifle, weight is added in a position that is between the hands of the shooter when holding the rifle in a normal way. This does not necessarily contribute to steady holding of the rifle. A scope sticking up on top of a rifle makes it harder to grasp and carry conveniently. The scope is also somewhat prone to catching on objects. Because it weighs so little and adds so little bulk, a rifle equipped with a peep sight handles almost exactly the same as it does with only open sights.

A receiver sight is placed close to the eye so it can be very fast to use if the aperture is not too small. Many years ago, most rifles came with holes in the receiver for attaching receiver sights. Today, because

This adjustable peep sight from Williams attaches to the two rear holes in the receiver.

of the emphasis on scope sights, few rifles come so constructed. However, the receiver of the Ruger 10/22 has four holes for attaching a scope base, and the two rear holes can be used to attach a peep sight to the receiver. Such a peep sight made specifically for the Ruger 10/22 is known as the XS Ghost Ring made by XS Sight Systems of Fort Worth, TX. The peep sight mounts on the receiver by making use of the two rear holes where the factory scope rail attaches. The front sight is attached by removing the front sight from its dovetail notch and forcing the XS post in place. Because the receiver sight is located so that it is above the action, it is higher than the usual rear sight. Therefore, a higher front sight is required so that the rifle can be sighted in. As a result, the Ghost Ring peep sight is marketed with a front sight of suitable height. The rear face of the XS post has a white line running along the sloping face, which makes it more visible

in dim light. Adjustment of the XS system is achieved by moving the aperture after loosening the locking screws.

Williams Gun Sight Company, Inc. of Davison, MI produces a fine peep sight that mounts on the receiver of the Ruger 10/22. Like the XS sight, it also attaches by making use of the two rear holes where the scope rail attaches. The Williams sight is marketed with a front sight of appropriate height which attaches to the dovetail groove after the front sight is removed. The aperture is mounted on an inclined ramp and held in place by means of a locking screw. When the screw is loosened, the aperture can be slid up or down the ramp to adjust elevation. Loosening a different

The XS Sight Systems peep sight is available with a front sight that has a white insert that is clearly visible.

Because this XS Sight Systems peep sight is close to the eye, it is very fast to use.

Apertures of different size can be used in the peep sight from XS Sight Systems.

Although it is very compact, this peep sight is easily adjusted for both windage and elevation.

screw allows the aperture to be moved laterally to provide windage adjustment.

It is not only possible to align a peep sight and front sight more accurately on the target than it is open sights but also peep sights allow for more accurate adjustment. The aperture may be moved an infinitesimal amount to make small changes in the point of impact. For the shooter who does not want the added bulk of a scope, a peep sight will permit more accurate shooting than is possible with open sights but retain the profile and handling characteristics of the rifle.

The Zephyr Sights

Although there is no shortage of aftermarket sights available for the Ruger

10/22, one of the most unusual options is known as the Zephyr system available from Eagle International of Hazen, ND. This sight combination consists of a front sight that fits in the dovetail that is cut into the front sight band. However, it is not simply another post, but rather a post that is encircled by a short hood or band. The rear sight is an unusual peep sight that is located between large protective ears that are rather like turned up edges on the base and which form the support structure for the aperture. The base has two holes that match the spacing of the two rear holes in the receiver where the scope rail normally attaches. The two screws that attach the rear sight to the receiver have Allen heads for ease of tightening without marring the screws.

The screw that passes through the front of the two holes in the rear sight base can be inserted easily. However, the rear screw is almost directly under the aperture and its mounting base. Therefore, the aperture itself must be removed before the rear screw can be attached. The aperture slides in a groove in its support and is held in place by friction that results from tightening small screws on either side of the movable aperture. With the screws

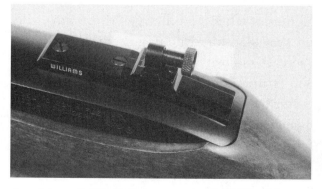

Apertures of different sizes are available for this Williams model that is produced specifically for the Ruger 10/22.

An unusual type of peep sight is this model from Eagle International.

loosened, the aperture can be removed by sliding it upward out of the base. With the aperture removed, the rear screw can be placed in the rear hole in the base and tightened in the receiver.

So far, the rear sight may sound like just another peep sight, but this is not so. The aperture is mounted on a screw that passes through the protective ears in such as way that turning the screw moves the aperture laterally. This is how windage adjustments are made. On one side, the hex head of the screw has a socket where an Allen wrench can be inserted to turn the screw. A pivoting lock can be turned so that it rests against one of the flat sides of the hex head so that the screw will not be inadvertently turned.

The aperture can be moved up or down within the boss in which it is mounted between the protective ears. Two screws with Allen heads lock it in place in the groove where it is held. Loosening the two screws allows the aperture itself to be moved vertically to adjust elevation. How much to move the aperture is something of a trial and error proposition.

The Zephyr sight system gives the owner of a Ruger 10/22 a peep sight option that is not unlike that found on the legendary

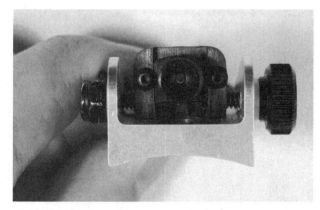

The Zephyr peep sight is fully adjustable since the aperture is held to a blade that can be moved after loosening two screws.

M1 Carbine. The encircled front post and rear sight with larger protective ears that support and protect the aperture have a military appearance. However, this is a functional sight combination that gives the shooter better capability than the factory open sights but without the additional bulk and weight that accompany the addition of a scope. We have enjoyed using this sight combination, which is available from several suppliers at a cost of approximately $33.

Scope Characteristics

The first .22 rimfire used many years ago by one of the authors, a Stevens Model 15 single shot, came with a bead front sight and an open rear sight that could be adjusted by means of a stepped ramp. There were no grooves along the top of the receiver for attaching a scope and no screw holes on the side for attaching a peep sight. In fact, there was absolutely no provision for adding any optional sighting device. This was typical of many rimfire rifles produced in the first half of the 1900s. Later, the ubiquitous grooves along the tops of receivers became commonplace on rimfire rifles. Along with this came an increase in the number of low priced scopes that were available. In the last decade or so, a large fraction of the rimfire rifles produced have no iron sights attached and many of these have no provision for attaching them. However, the vast majority of rimfire rifles come with one or more options for attaching scopes either by drilled and tapped holes for scope bases or grooves of one form or another. We have seen a change from iron sights only to scopes only in terms of sighting equipment even on rimfires.

The use of scope sights is now almost universal. In fact, the use of a scope is

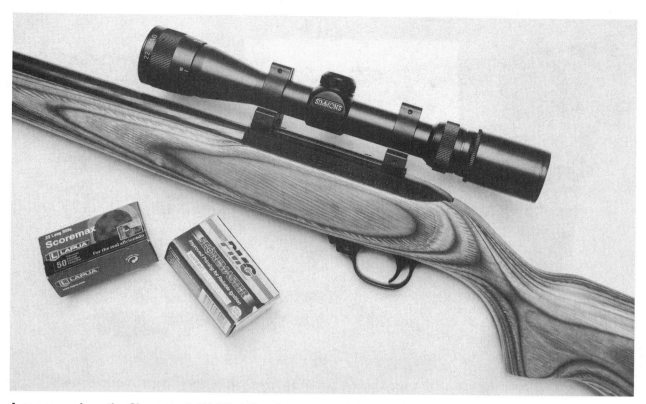

A scope such as the Simmons 3-9X AO makes it easy to shoot accurately.

assumed. For example, Ruger offers many versions of their very successful bolt-action rimfire, the Model 77, in its various calibers and forms. The 2005 catalog lists none of these as being furnished with open sights. This assessment is equally applicable to the centerfire bolt actions from Ruger for which 12 variants are offered with only one having iron sights. The Magnum rifle (in calibers .375 H&H Magnum, .416 Rigby, and .458 Lott) do have iron sights because they are intended for use at short range on large animals. In the 2005 Ruger catalog, the only rimfire rifles (in both standard and magnum calibers) that are shown with sights are the Model 96 lever action and 10/22 models. This is not meant as a critique of Ruger because the rifles offered by other manufacturers are similarly represented in terms of sights.

What does all this mean? It is a reflection of three things. First, fine accuracy almost always (we will omit the most sophisticated target-type receiver sights for the moment) requires the use of a scope. It is a simple matter to line up a crosshair reticule (there are several types) on a target and squeeze the trigger. A well-designed scope places the reticule on the target with both being in the same optical plane. Therefore, the

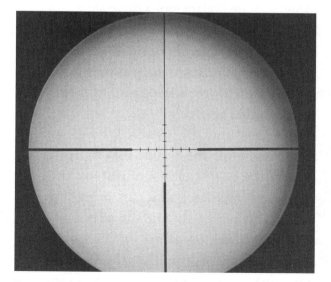

This scope reticule has tic marks that make it easier to estimate where the point of impact will be at different distances.

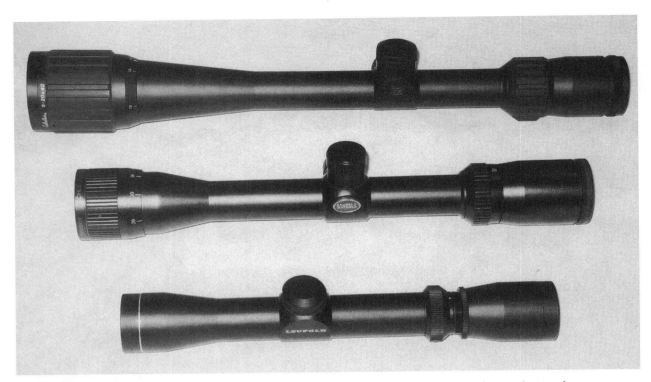

Scopes that are suitable for use on rimfires are available in all sizes. Shown here (top to bottom) are Cabela's Outfitter 6-20X, Scheels Rimfire Premier 4-12X, and Leupold 2-7X models.

problem of trying to align two sights with the target when all three are at different distances from the eye is eliminated. Second, scopes are rugged, dependable instruments that can be counted on to function well in a wide variety of situations. Third, scopes are available in an enormous range of types, sizes, and magnification. There is literally a scope available for almost any type of shooting. Although the price range for rimfire scopes is very large, it is possible to get a dependable scope for a reasonable price.

There are some irrefutable laws of optics. Scopes magnify the target. However, the greater the degree of magnification, the shorter the distance that can be in sharp focus. This is exactly like the situation with a telephoto lens on a camera. The longer the focal length of the lens, the shorter the depth of field (the region of apparently sharp focus) when the aperture is of fixed size. The depth of field depends on the

lens opening (aperture) with the region of sharp focus being greatest at the smallest aperture. Long telephoto lenses used "wide open" have very shallow depth of field. For example, if the object being photographed is 100 yards away, the region from 90-110 yards may be in sharp focus, but an object at 50 yards will certainly not be. If the lens is stopped down (size of the aperture decreased), the depth of field might increase to include objects 75-125 yards away. There is no escaping the fact that the longer the focal length of the lens (greater the magnification), the smaller the depth of field at a given aperture

While camera lenses have variable apertures that allow for some control of the depth of field, telescopic sights do not. The greater the magnification of the scope, the shorter the depth of field. Moreover, the shorter the distance at which the lens (scope) is focused, the shorter the depth of field. The higher the magnification of the

This Scheels variable power scope has a fast focus eyepiece.

scope, the smaller the field of view. These are simply the consequences of the laws of optics.

It is impossible to have a 10X scope focused in such a way that targets at 10 yards and 100 yards are simultaneously in sharp focus. The big game hunter who may encounter an animal at 100 yards or 200 yards will still find the target in acceptably sharp focus. He or she would certainly not find an animal at 10 yards in sharp focus! We well remember the story of a deer hunter who had a 3-9X scope set at 9X when a deer walked under his tree stand. With the deer at a distance of perhaps 20 feet, all the hunter could see was a patch of hide with no way to tell which end of the deer he was looking at. He did not manage to get off a shot. In such cases, open sights or at most a 2.5X scope would have been a much better choice than a 9X scope. Of course the 3-9X scope could have been set on 3X, but it is sometimes difficult to remember such things when the target animal is almost on top of you. Incidentally, this points out one factor related to scopes of variable power. They are usually set on one power (the lowest or highest available) and left there. It is essential that the power of the scope suite the type of shooting.

Because rimfire rifles are normally used at ranges from 25 yards to perhaps 75

or 100 yards, the scope chosen should normally be of modest magnification so that the depth of field is great. A good quality 4X scope offers enough depth of field to permit shooting at such distances. Variable scopes are quite popular, and a 2-7X range is a good choice for use on a rimfire rifle. A scope of higher magnification can be used on a rimfire if targets at one distance are being shot because the scope can be focused at that distance. Also, since most rimfire rifles, and certainly the Ruger 10/22, are rather compact, a scope of small dimensions is appropriate.

Another solution to some of the problems of optical design is to make a scope that can readily be focused at different distances. The most common way of doing this is by making the front lens movable by rotating its housing. This type of scope, known as an adjustable objective or AO model, allows the shooter to focus at different distances to bring the target into sharp focus. In this way, a scope of high magnification (even 16-24X) can be used. However, the drawback to this approach is that the scope will need to be refocused when targets are encountered at different

The Scheels Compact Elite can be focused at different distances.

distances, which is probably not going to happen when a hunter sights the game. Of course, the user of an AO scope can focus the scope at some intermediate distance so that objects within the most useful range are acceptably sharp. The principle regarding depth of field applies to AO scopes - the higher the magnification, the shorter the depth of field.

Some of the adjustable scopes of recent design make use of a dial (located on the side or top of the scope) to focus the scope at different distances. Other than the means of focusing, these scopes have the same general characteristics as those with rotating front lens mounts.

Hold your arm extended and point your finger at a distant object with one eye closed. While keeping your hand in the same place, view the object with the other eye. Note how the object appears to have moved in relation to your finger. This phenomenon is known as parallax. It refers to the apparent motion of an object when the viewing position is changed. In scope sights, the reticule and the target normally appear in the same plane. If moving your head slightly while the crosshair is aligned on the target causes the crosshair to appear to move, the scope is not correctly adjusted to remove parallax. Most scopes that are intended for use on centerfire rifles are adjusted to have no parallax at 100 yards. Scopes that are designed for use on rimfire rifles are usually adjusted so that there is no parallax at a distance of 50 yards. As a result, sighting errors that result from slight differences in eye position are eliminated. One notable exception is the outstanding Leupold 2-7X rimfire scope, which is parallax free at 60 yards, which is just the right distance for most field shooting with a rimfire.

One of the characteristics of AO scopes is that when the scope is focused at some distance, the scope is free of parallax at that distance. This is a very desirable feature for a rimfire scope because the shooter can not only focus the scope at any desired distance, but also correct for parallax at that distance. However, we recently examined an inexpensive AO scope that did not correct for parallax at the distance for which it was focused.

There may be a temptation to buy a scope of high magnification for general use on a rimfire rifle, but the magnification produces the limitations of shallow depth of field and narrow field of view. You want to be able to find the target quickly and have it in sharp focus throughout the useful range of the rifle. Therefore, a scope of modest power works well under most conditions in which a rimfire rifle is used, especially when hunting.

Scopes for Rimfires

In the previous section, we presented some of the basic principles that the shooter should consider when selecting a scope for a rimfire such as the Ruger 10/22. Ultimately, the scope chosen will be one that is compatible with the intended use of the rifle. If the rifle is to be used hunting squirrels, a 4X scope will be satisfactory. On the other hand, if the rifle is to be used in benchrest competition, a scope of higher magnification will be helpful. Keep in mind that some forms of benchrest competition have rules that limit the magnification of the scopes used (for example, 6X in some instances). For general use, a good scope of variable power, typically 2.5-7X or 3-9X, will meet the needs of the rimfire shooter.

The optics sections of catalogs from

suppliers of shooting accessories show that the selection of scopes is huge. The spectrum ranges from simple 2.5X and 4X models on one end to high magnification fixed power and variables on the other with prices ranging from less than $30 to over $500. Keep in mind that a book (*The Gun Digest Book of Sporting Optics*, Krause Publications, 2002) has been written on the subject of optics, and a great deal of it focuses (no pun intended) on scopes. In this chapter, we will review some of the scopes with which we have had first hand experience. This brief survey is in no way meant to be a complete review of scopes for rimfire rifles but rather is intended to give information on some representative models. When selecting a scope, one should always study the catalogs that are available from the manufacturers or visit their web sites on the Internet to narrow the selection. It would then be advisable to actually examine your preliminary selections by visiting some retail dealers. After examining several scopes, you may find that a particular model is exactly what you want (or may find that the one you thought you wanted isn't appropriate after all).

In this very abbreviated scope review, we will describe some very inexpensive models, but the very high priced models will be omitted. Part of the reason for this is that we have no very high priced scopes to report on. The price range of the scopes tested ranges from about $40 to about $250. Keep in mind that the so-called "list" price or the manufacturer's suggested retail price (MSRP) is an almost meaningless number. Scopes are heavily discounted and some of the suppliers listed in the last chapter of this book specialize in scopes. Shop hard before you buy. Also keep in mind that to some extent the old saying

"you get what you pay for" also applies to scopes. Do not expect a scope that sells for $50 to be equivalent to one selling for five times that amount. As is discussed later in this chapter, we have found that some inexpensive scopes perform extremely well and would meet most needs of the rimfire shooter.

Scope Mounts and Rings

Recoil of high-powered rifles cause a great deal of stress as the rifle goes to the rear and the scope is dragged with it. However, rimfire rifles generate almost no recoil. As a result, the stresses placed on the scope mounting system on a rimfire rifle are much less than they are when a scoped high power rifle is fired. As a result, many types of scope rings for use on rimfires are made of aluminum rather than steel. Although the scope mount used on a rimfire rifle may not be abused by recoil, it should not be a flimsy, puny affair. If it is, the scope may not stay sighted in or the mount may be bent when it is tightened.

Mounting a scope on a Ruger 10/22 is a trivial job. Each version of the rifle (except the 10/22M) is supplied with a scope rail that attaches to the receiver by means of

Ruger includes a scope rail with each version of the 10/22.

screws that fit in four holes on top of the receiver. Removing the fill screws allows the scope rail to be attached. When attaching the scope rail, do not attempt to tighten the screws excessively. The holes are small and if you have the hand strength of one of the authors, you can strip the threads. Although we have never had a problem with the base screws on a Ruger 10/22, if the screws work loose, try coating them with one of the various thread locking compounds before tightening them.

Because the receiver of the 10/22 is made of aluminum and has a broad, rounded top, it is not feasible to cut the grooves separated by 3/8 inch like those that are present on most rimfire rifles. Ruger's solution to the problem inherent in the receiver's design has always been to supply a separate scope base that is attached to the receiver by means of four screws. For many years, Ruger supplied a scope base that had grooves along the edges so that the ordinary clamp on scope mounts could be attached. That type of mount is one made popular many years ago by Weaver as the Tip-Off® mount although mounts of this design produced by other manufacturers are now called "tip-off" mounts. Strictly speaking, the Tip-

Off® trademark applies only to the original mount produced by Weaver. Beginning in 2004, Ruger supplied a scope base that not only has grooves along the edges but also transverse notches that allow the scope rings known as Weaver-type rings (but produced by many manufacturers) to be attached. As a result, it is no longer necessary to use the Tip-Off® mount, and a wide selection of rings can be used to mount a scope on a Ruger 10/22. The main advantage to Weaver-type rings is that a scope can be removed and replaced in the same position.

The situation is quite different with the 10/22M, which has a steel receiver. All Ruger firearms with steel receivers have raised sections with notches milled into the sides where rings with matching tabs can be clamped. The rings attach directly to the receiver with no separate base being required. In essence, the Ruger system is like a "tip-off" arrangement except that small notches on the receiver are utilized rather than long grooves. Each Ruger 10/22M is supplied with a set of Ruger rings. Initially, only Ruger produced the rings in this form, but several other producers such as Millet, Leupold, Burris, and other companies now market rings

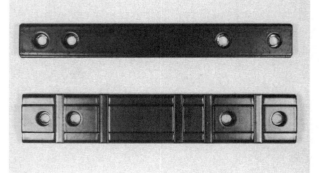

Until recently, the Ruger scope rails had grooves only along the edges for attaching scope mounts (top) but newer rails (bottom) also have notches for attaching Weaver-type rings.

These Weaver rings have bolts across the bottom that lock in the notches in the scope rail.

The Ruger 10/22M has a steel receiver with raised portions containing notches where the rings clamp.

Ruger rings clamp directly to the receiver of the Ruger 10/22M and have small tabs that lock into recesses to prevent backward and forward motion.

of similar design for mounting scopes on Ruger rifles with milled notches. Weigand Combat produces a one-piece base that clamps in the milled notches in the receiver of the 10/22M. The base has transverse notches so it can accept Weaver-type rings. The multiple grooves provide a great deal more flexibility in positioning the scope than do the two sets of notches in the receiver.

If your 10/22 is more than a couple of years old, it probably came with a scope base that accommodates only Tip-Off® style rings. Although this mounting technique is adequate, you can buy the

new style scope base directly from Ruger. Weaver also produces a one-piece scope base (the Models TO-9M and TO-9S which have matte and silver finish, respectively)

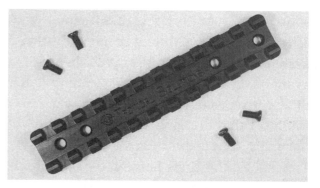

Scope rails like this Tactical Solutions model permit the scope rings to be placed in numerous locations.

When attaching Ruger rings to the 10/22M, make sure that the tabs on the locking bolts match the curved recesses in the receiver.

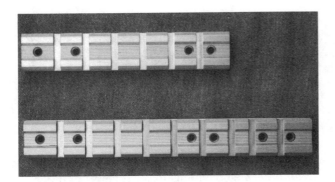

Long scope rails extend in front of the receiver making it possible to mount a sighting device far forward.

for the Ruger 10/22 and also the TO-11 base for the Model 96 lever action. Scope rails are also available from Power Custom, Tactical Solutions, Volquartsen, and other sources. Hornet Products of Sarasota, FL offers an extensive line of scope mounting systems for the Ruger 10/22. Rails are available in several styles to accommodate different types of rings. Rails are also available that are longer than those normally supplied for use on the 10/22. This allows the rings holding the scope to be placed farther apart to position the scope correctly in relationship to the eye.

Leopold produces a scope mount for the Ruger 10/22 that consists of a one-piece steel base that attaches to three of the four holes in the receiver (the front two holes

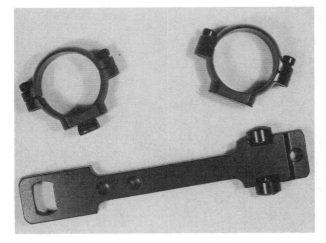

Leupold markets a high quality steel scope base and rings for the Ruger 10/22.

and rear hole are used). This base accepts rings that attach to the base by turning them so that by cam action they are wedged tightly in the base. Talley produces a base that attaches to the receiver of a Ruger 10/22 in the usual way but instead of having grooves along the edges, it has the notches that allow Ruger rings to be attached. Warne offers a two-piece base for the Ruger 10/22 (one piece attaches to the forward holes in the receiver and the other to the two holes at the rear). These bases accept Weaver-type rings. Cabela's offers a similar system in their Outfitter series. Tasco produces a two-piece base that clamps to a grooved receiver (or Ruger scope rail), and Weaver-type rings can be attached to the bases.

When it comes to selecting rings to attach the scope to the base, the selection is very large. We will comment primarily on some of the types that we have actually used to mount scopes on our rifles. A more complete list of manufacturers of scope mounts and rings will be found in Chapter 13. Scope rings are usually attached to the scope tube by pulling the two parts of the ring together by means of screws. The rings may have projections on the sides and be pulled together by screws that are vertical or they may have projections above the tube that are pulled together by screws running horizontally. In other words, the mount will have projections on the sides or on the top. An exception is the Weaver Tip-Off® mount that is discussed later.

The discussion of rings that follows is presented in alphabetical order by manufacturer and does not represent our assessment of suitability. Almost all of the rings have one stationary clamping edge and one whose movement is controlled by a large screw head. When the stationary

For scopes with large forward bells, high rings such as the Tasco World Class may be needed.

edge is placed in one groove, tightening the screw pulls the movable edge into the other groove and holds it securely. A top piece fits over the scope and is attached to the lower part by two (or sometimes four) screws that pass through flanges or ears on the outside edges. An exception to this, which will be discussed later, are rings consisting of two vertical halves held together by screws at the top and bottom which pass horizontally through the halves.

Burris produces two series of steel rings that clamp on grooved receivers or the grooved Ruger scope base. The first (and least expensive) type is constructed with the bands that fit across the top of the scope made of curved straps of uniform thickness. These rings come in different heights, and both silver and blue finish models are available. The Deluxe Burris rings are similar with regard to the mode of attachment, but the straps that fit over the top of the scope are nicely rounded and considerably heavier. Both types of Burris rimfire rings have screws with torx heads to reduce damage.

Leupold also produces rings for mounting scopes on rimfires. Known as the Rifleman series, the rings clamp over the scope with two screws that lie horizontally. Not only does the bottom screw pass through the two pieces of the mount to clamp it in the

grooves, but it also pulls the mount tight on the scope. As a result, only two screws are necessary for each ring. Although tightening the mount on the rifle and on the scope simultaneously can require some dexterity, this type of mount has been used with complete satisfaction.

Weaver is a name known to generations of shooters. The old steel tube Weaver scopes were produced in El Paso, TX, and many are still in regular use. Weaver pioneered the Tip-Off® mount which was probably named because when the two locking screws are loosened the scope can be tipped sideways to remove it. The Tip-Off® mounts are simple and durable. On each ring, the base has a single, large screw that passes through the movable curved blade that engages one of the grooves on the receiver. The other gripping surface is stationary. Clamping the rings to the scope is a separate process so it is possible to remove a scope that is sighted in and replace it on the rifle by tightening only two screws. The bands that pass over the scope are made of steel. Each band has a hook that engages one side of the base while the other end is attached by two screws.

A minor distraction is that the permanently curved heavy bands often

The Leupold Rifleman rings are made of aluminum and utilize screws with Allen heads.

The Weaver Tip-Off® mount has been popular for many years.

must be forced over the scope tube. This can scratch the tube unless care is taken to prevent this from happening. One way to prevent scratching the scope tube is to wrap a card like those that fall out of magazines around the tube before forcing the band over the tube. When the band is in place around the tube, the card can be slid out. With a hook on one end of the band, the screws that pull the band tight around the scope are located on the other side of the scope tube. When the screws are tightened to draw the band around the scope, there can be some slight rotating of the scope, which results in crosshairs that are not perfectly horizontal and vertical. Normally the screws are on the left hand side of the scope so when loosely placing the scope in position, leave the crosshairs

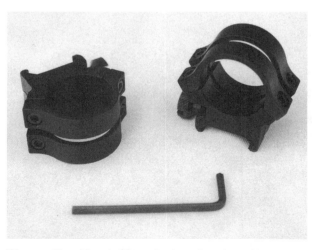

Weaver Quad Lock Rings feature two top straps which grip the scope securely.

tipped slightly to the right. In that way, tightening the screws causes the tube to turn slightly to the left, which brings the crosshairs into correct orientation.

A Closer Look at Some Rimfire Scopes

The prices of scopes for use on rimfires ranges from $25 or so up to several hundred dollars. We have more experience with scopes closer to the low end of the price range. To a certain extent, you get what you pay for in a scope. The higher priced models are better made, brighter, and generally more durable. Most people would not put a $25 scope on a $1000 rifle nor would they put a $500 scope on a $100 rifle. To some extent, it makes sense to match the scope to the rifle.

We would now like to describe a few of the rimfire scopes that have worked well for us. The first is the BSA .22 Special. This is a 4X scope that comes with a pair of rings that clamp in the grooves that are found on receivers of most .22s and on the Ruger scope rails. A relative has one of these scopes on his Remington 597 autoloader. For another project we tested that combination and found that it was possible to get 5-shot groups at 50 yards that averaged under an inch with appropriate ammunition. Although it is made in China (as are most inexpensive scopes), this budget scope will allow you shoot a .22 accurately.

Moving up in price to about $40 brings us to a 4X Simmons scope known as the .22 Mag. This scope is available in both blue and silver finish, and it also comes with a set of rings. We have had two of these scopes, and they worked well. On a .22 that gives good accuracy, a hunter is

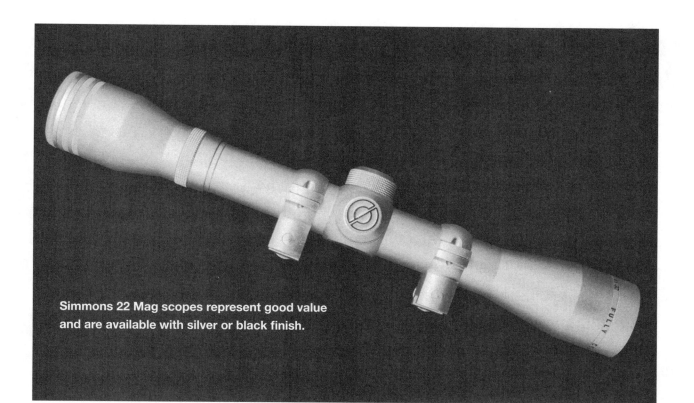

Simmons 22 Mag scopes represent good value and are available with silver or black finish.

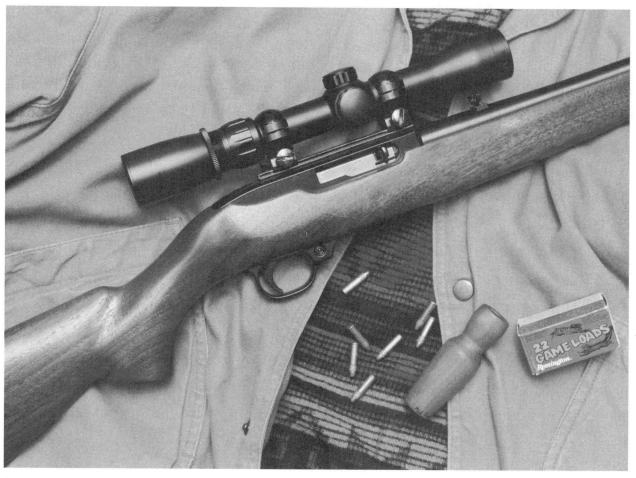

Cabela's Pine Ridge scopes for rimfires include this fine 3-9X model.

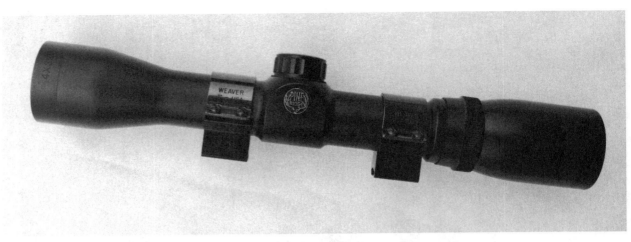

A compact Cabela's Pine Ridge 4X scope makes a good addition to a Ruger 10/22.

not handicapped much by having one of these inexpensive scopes instead of some higher priced model.

Retailing for $79.99 in Cabela's catalog is the Pine Ridge 3-9X variable rimfire scope. A 4X version is available for $49.99. We have used both of these scopes on rimfire rifles with complete satisfaction. The 4X is currently mounted on a Marlin Model 60 autoloader, and the 3-9X is the scope of choice on a Ruger lever action .22 Magnum. Either of these scopes will prove

satisfactory for the shooter who wants a dependable scope but does not want to spend a lot of money.

Scheels All Sports is a well-known chain of large sporting goods stores throughout the upper Midwest. This company markets scopes carrying their own label and made to their specifications. Our contact at Scheels has indicated that any of the stores will ship the scope to a buyer in a different location so you need not actually go to the store to get a scope. Introduced

This Compact Elite scope from Scheels All Sports is almost ideal for use on the Ruger 10/22 Compact Rifle.

This fine scope is a Simmons 1022T 3-9X AO model.

in late 2005 is the Scheels Compact Elite Model 432CE which is a 4x32 AO model. Although not specifically called a rimfire model, this scope is ideal for use on rimfire rifles because the AO feature means that parallax is corrected at the distance for which the scope is focused. The reticule is of the duplex type with coarse lines that become very fine at the crossing point. Eye relief is almost four inches, which allows for a lot of latitude in positioning the scope. The Compact Elite is truly a compact having a length of only 9.25 inches, which makes it an excellent choice for mounting on a rifle such as the Ruger 10/22. Optically, this scope is outstanding. Each click changes the point of impact ¼ inch at 100 yards, and the stops are sharp and precise. With a retail price of $79.99, this scope is a superb choice for any rimfire shooting where a 4X scope is sufficient (which it almost always would be).

One of our outstanding medium-priced rimfire scopes is the Simmons known as the Model 1022T. This is a 3-9X AO scope that is superb. It is one of the scopes that we have tested most thoroughly by performing a procedure known as shooting the square. This involves shooting a 5-shot group at 50 yards then adjusting the scope by changing the elevation by some number of clicks. Twenty-four clicks would be equivalent to six inches at 100

yards or three inches at 50 yards so this is the amount of adjustment we used. After changing the elevation (upward) 24 clicks, another 5-shot group was fired. Next, the windage was adjusted to the right 24 clicks and another group was fired. The elevation was lowered 24 clicks and another group was fired. Finally, changing the windage to the left 24 clicks should bring the shots back to the original point of

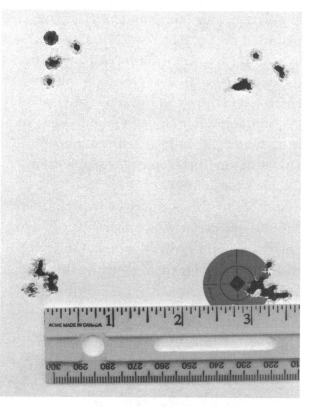

These groups were fired at 50 yards using a Simmons 1022T scope on a Ruger 10/22T by adjusting the scope 24 clicks between groups. The last group overlaps with the first.

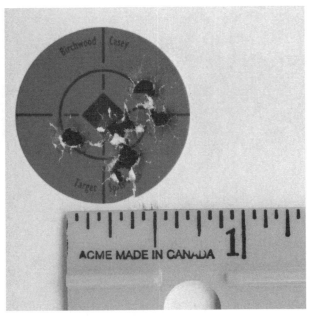

This group shows the result of firing one shot with a Simmons 3-9X scope set on each magnification. There is no change in point of impact as the magnification is changed.

impact if the adjustments are repeatable. The accompanying photo shows the results of this test with the Simmons 1022T mounted on a Ruger 10/22T using SK Jagd Standard Plus ammunition. It is clear from this 0.78-inch 10-shot group (five shots before any adjustment and five after all of the adjustments had been made) that there is no noticeable shift in point of impact. This outstanding scope is available from Cabela's for $119.99.

Another test that is routinely performed with scopes of variable magnification is to shoot a group in which one shot is fired with the scope on each power setting. The object of this test is to determine whether there is a shift in zero as the magnification is changed. The accompanying photo shows the seven-shot group when the Simmons 1022T was tested in this way on a Ruger 10/22 Target using SK Jagd Standard Plus ammunition.

Another of the fine scopes in the line from Scheels All Sports is a 4-12X AO rimfire model that sells for $149.99, and it is available from any of the over 20 Scheels stores. The rimfire scope is available in both blue and bright silver finishes to match your rifle. We have tested this scope on several rifles, and it has performed extremely well. Shooting the square showed that the adjustments are very accurate

Adjustments on the Scheels Compact Elite scope require no tools to turn the knobs.

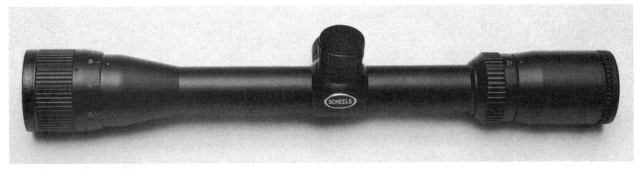

The Scheels Rimfire Premier is a 4-12X AO scope that will meet about any need on a rimfire rifle.

Some scopes, such as the Scheels Rimfire Premier, come with a sunshade.

This target shows the result of shooting the square with the Weaver 2.5-7X scope on a Ruger 10/22T.

and reproducible. Adjustment knobs can be turned by hand after removing the protective caps. This is an outstanding scope. The high magnification and focusing objective make fine accuracy possible. Additionally, the Scheels scope has a fast focus eyepiece that is very convenient to use because only the rear lens is rotated. On most scopes, the entire rear bell must be rotated and the locking ring tightened against it to change focus.

The Weaver name has appeared on scopes for many years, and it currently appears on two outstanding rimfire scopes.

The first is a 2.5-7X variable and the second is a 3-9X variable with AO. Both of these scopes have been extensively tested on several of our rimfire rifles, and they have performed flawlessly. They are bright and crisp optically, and the adjustments

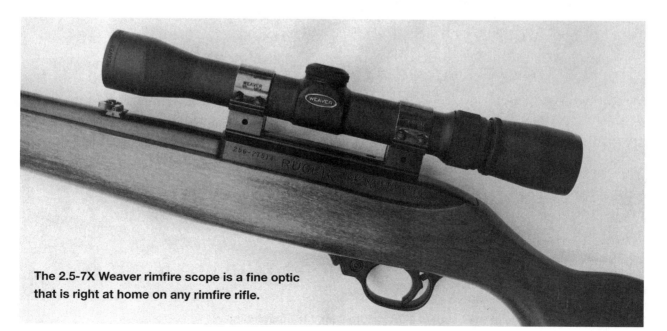

The 2.5-7X Weaver rimfire scope is a fine optic that is right at home on any rimfire rifle.

Adjustment knobs on the Weaver V-16 are finger adjustable and the dials can be rotated then locked in place.

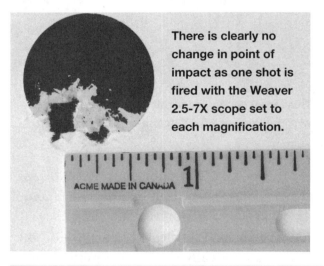

There is clearly no change in point of impact as one shot is fired with the Weaver 2.5-7X scope set to each magnification.

make shooting the square easy. The accompanying photo shows the results of performing these tests with the Weaver 2.5-7X scope on a Ruger 10/22 Target firing SK Jagd Standard Plus ammunition. The 2.5-7X sells for about $135-140 while the 3-9X AO model sells for about $210-220. Either of these scopes will prove adequate to bring out the best in almost any rimfire rifle.

Leupold produces the next rimfire scope in our stable. This scope is a 2-7X rimfire

The optical performance of the Leupold 2-7X rimfire scope is outstanding.

Unlike most other scopes that are adjustable by clicks, the Leupold scope uses adjustment screws that are held tightly by friction.

scope that is free of parallax at 60 yards, which is very practical for a scope intended to be used on a .22. The scope measures only 9.9 inches in length and weighs less than 10 ounces. Like other Leupold scopes, the adjustments are controlled by friction rather than the more common

click stops. This scope exudes the quality for which Leupold scopes are famous and it leaves little to be desired when used on any rimfire rifle. Optically, the scope is incredibly bright, and the reticle has a very fine crosshair at the intersection. We like it so much we are trying to figure out how to get another one to put on a different rifle. It is a spectacular scope that retails for approximately $200. We have tested no other rimfire optic of higher quality.

The last scope that we will describe is a recently introduced model from Sightron. It is known officially as the SII 3-9X with a 36mm AO objective. It has a retail price that is in the $250-300 range, but it is a superb scope. The reticle is a fine crosshair that permits outstanding aiming on small targets. On a low power setting this scope would be an excellent choice for the small game hunter and on a setting of 9X it would meet the needs of

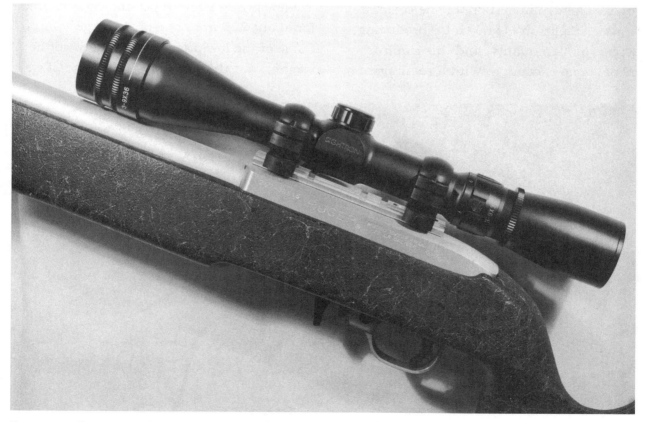

For a versatile scope to be used on rimfire rifles, it is hard to beat the Sightron 3-9X AO.

The focusing objective on the 3-9X Sightron scope rotates two full turns making fine focus possible.

the shooter who does sniping of small pests at extended rimfire ranges. We have used this scope in testing .22 WMR rifles, and it is a perfect companion. In fact, a 10/22M topped with the Sightron scope makes an excellent combination for the varmint hunter. Sightron is known for producing scopes of high quality, and this rimfire model is no exception. With a retail price of

about $250-300, it is a beautiful scope in every respect.

We know of some rimfire scopes that sell for upwards of $500, but you may rest assured that it is not necessary to spend anywhere near that amount to get a scope of very high quality. You may want a more expensive model, but in our opinion the Scheels, Cabela's, Simmons, Weaver, Leupold, and Sightron scopes have all the quality necessary to be at home on any rimfire. If we were limited to a scope selling for a price of $100-150, we would probably opt for the Simmons 1022T, the Weaver 2.5-7X or the Scheels rimfire scope without hesitation. Were we limited to a scope in the $50-100 range (as we certainly have been on many occasions!), we could be very happy with the Scheels Compact Elite or one of the Pine Ridge rimfire scopes from Cabela's. As mentioned earlier, we have done some good shooting even with one of the low priced BSA scopes that is available for about $25 from one of the large "marts." Some of the low priced scopes may not be elegant, but they do work. Of course, if we

Adjustment dials on the Sightron scope are clearly marked and easy to use.

were taking our fully tricked out 10/22s on a pest shoot a thousand miles from home, they would be equipped with better scopes. As with everything else, it essentially boils down to how much you want to spend, and to a great extent you get what you pay for.

Hopefully, this discussion will help you in selecting a scope for use on your rimfire rifle. The principles of optics dictate several factors that you should consider, and they are somewhat different for scopes used on different types of rifles.

Red Dot Sights

Another type of optical sight for use on firearms is the red dot sight. Although red dot sights are more often used on handguns, they are becoming more popular for use on rifles and shotguns. This type of sight utilizes a red dot produced by battery power that is projected onto a lens. There is no magnification, and the eye can be placed at any distance from the rear of the sight. A dial, which is actually a rheostat, controls the brightness of the dot. Windage and elevation adjustments are made in much the same way as on a scope. The construction of the sight is such that all the shooter has to do when aiming is to align the dot on the target. As a result, aiming can be very fast, and the sight is obviously easy to see in low light. Mounting a red dot sight on a rimfire rifle makes use of a mount that attaches to the dovetail grooves on the receiver or the transverse grooves that accommodate Weaver type rings. One advantage of red dot sights is that they are only 5-6 inches long and weigh only a few ounces.

Red dot sights have some disadvantages. The dot covers a large enough area on the target that precise aiming (as with a scope having a fine crosshair reticule) is not possible. A red dot sight is not the appropriate choice for highly accurate shooting. However, as one deer hunter who had taken four deer with a shotgun equipped with a red dot sight said, "All I have to do is put the dot on the deer and squeeze." He could do that because a target area of four or five inches at 75 yards is adequate for hunting deer. It would not be adequate for 50-yard benchrest competition.

Red dot sights like this Simmons model provide a useful alternative to scopes.

This dial on top of the Simmons red dot sight controls the brightness of the dot.

Elevation and windage adjustments on the Simmons red dot sight are made using dials that are much like those used on scopes.

In some cases, the dot covers as much as three minutes of angle (equal to three inches at 100 yards or one and one-half inches at 50 yards). The most sophisticated red dot sights have a control that allows the user to change the size of the dot.

Red dot sights have improved drastically in the last few years, and the models available today have only the red dot in common with early models. We have tested two sights of this type, a Simmons Model 800879 and a Sightron Model S33-4R. The Simmons sight comes with a mount that consists of two rails held together by two cross bolts. The mount can be attached in two different ways. When positioned one way, the cross bolts are used to fit in the slots in Weaver type bases. When the mount is taken off and flipped over, the edges of the side rails fit in the grooves found on the receivers of most rimfires or those on the scope base supplied with Ruger 10/22s. The Simmons red dot sight has eleven settings to vary the intensity of the dot that covers four minutes of angle (MOA) so it can be set so that it is visible in almost any light. Having a retail price of

Even though it provides no magnification the Sightron S33-4R red dot sight is a versatile sighting device.

approximately $35.00, the Simmons sight is representative of the lower end of the price spectrum, but it performs well for this type of sight.

The Sightron S33-4R is an elegant red dot sight. It is supplied with a two-piece ring mount that clamps to Weaver type bases. The tube diameter is 33 mm, which means that ordinary scope rings cannot be used. Extension tubes (sun shades) are supplied to attach to both ends of the sight tube. If that were not enough, a polarizing filter is furnished.

Being a high-end red dot sight that has a retail price of approximately $200, the Sightron would be expected to have some outstanding features and it does. First, by turning a dial, the user can select from four types of reticules. True, there is a red dot that subtends four inches at 100 yards, but one of the other selections is a red dot that is surrounded by a lighted circle. Another choice is a reticule that has a dot surrounded by a circle with projecting vertical and horizontal lines. Finally, there is a crosshair reticule. For different shooting situations, this sight offers a lot of versatility.

Second, the sight has a rheostat that allows the shooter to choose from 11 levels of brightness. In dim light, the reticules are clearly visible even on a setting of 1. When the power level is set to 11, the reticules glow brightly enough to be seen even in bright sunlight. Adjustments are precise and positive. Although the Sightron S33-4R sells for as much as a good scope, it is nonetheless an interesting and versatile sight.

Although we have described only two red dot sights, there are many models available since most producers of scopes also market red dot sights. They span the range from inexpensive models that sell for under $30 to the sophisticated versions that sell for about ten times as much. There is no doubt that sights of this type are becoming more popular. A compact red dot sight makes a good companion for the Ruger 10/22.

A choice of reticules can be made by turning a dial on the left hand side of the Sightron S33-4R sight.

A large knob on top of the Sightron S33-4R sight controls the brightness of the reticule.

The Sightron S33-4R is furnished with a set of rings, and it is easily adjustable for elevation and windage after removing the caps that protect the dials.

Chapter 11

TESTING SOME CUSTOM RIFLES

Shooters who modify Ruger 10/22s most often do so to enhance performance, and in the case of a rifle, performance means accuracy. Although the factory 10/22s perform well enough to satisfy many shooters, there is a large segment of owners who have a need (either real or perceived) for greater accuracy. It is for those shooters that this book is written. Before we describe the results we obtained with a wide variety of custom rifles, it is necessary to make an appraisal of the test procedures.

It must be emphasized that while a sizeable number of barrels was tested, they represent only a small fraction of the selection available. It is not uncommon for a particular manufacturer to produce a half dozen or more types of barrels to fit the 10/22 action. Therefore, the barrels tested are only representative of the products available, not the complete list. Testing *all* of the aftermarket barrels available would take so long that some of them would no longer be in production by the time testing was completed, and this book would appear several years later!

As you peruse the tables that show group sizes, keep in mind that *most* high velocity and inexpensive bulk pack ammunition does not deliver particularly outstanding accuracy even with a high quality barrel. We have included the results from some ammunition of these types for comparison purposes. When attempting to deduce the level of accuracy that barrels give, the results obtained with target or match ammunition go much farther toward revealing the accuracy potential of barrels.

Testing the accuracy of rimfire rifles requires good ammunition. These types performed well.

Testing Procedures and Goals

When a scientist performs an experiment, he or she usually designs the experiment in such a way that all variables can be controlled. We will illustrate with an example. When two solutions containing substances that react are mixed, there is a heat change, so the contents get hotter (heat liberated, temperature increases) or cooler (heat absorbed, temperature decreases). In order to carry out the experiment while controlling the variables, the solutions would be mixed in a container that insulates the mixture from the surroundings so that no heat is lost or gained from the outside (known as the surroundings). In a simple experiment, a covered foam cup can be used, but in an accurate experiment a very sophisticated piece of apparatus is used. The point is that in order to determine a very accurate piece of data, it is necessary to control all variables.

In order to approach the problem of determining the *ultimate* accuracy of a barrel, it is necessary to control variables to a point that they have no significant effect on the outcome. What are the variables that come into play when firing a rifle? First, there is the support, which must be so rigid that there is no motion of the rifle as it is fired. Second, aiming error

Although slender composite stocks work fine for plinking, they do not provide the stability needed for highest accuracy.

must be nonexistent. Third, there must be no external force on the bullet as it travels to the target, which means that there must be no air movement. Ideally, a barrel would be tested under optimal conditions with several lots of each type of ammunition because even when all other factors are controlled, there is some (and often considerable!) difference in how different lots of the same type of cartridge perform. A detailed, systematic study of a particular barrel could take days or weeks of testing.

These variables can be overcome to a great extent by firing the rifle from a special machine rest that is positioned exactly the same for each shot in the series. Aiming error is minimal when a scope of high magnification is used, but even at 8X or 10X there is some error. A special target that allows the crosshair to be seen more clearly than it can on a black circle also helps to reduce aiming error. In order to prevent air movement from exerting forces on the bullet, testing can be conducted in an closed tunnel. While these procedures can be used, they are not practical for most shooters. Our tests were conducted under "real world" conditions outdoors, from a variety of types of bench rests, with a variety of types of scopes, and with a wide range of types of ammunition.

The tests of custom rifles were performed not only to give information and data for barrels, but also on scopes, stocks, triggers, and ammunition. Consequently, we did not configure a particular rifle using a specific lock, stock, barrel, and scope combination and then grab 10 lots of one particular type of ammunition and head for the wind tunnel. Neither were we able to test everything at 70° F at sea level on a day when the atmospheric pressure was exactly one atmosphere. Some testing was conducted at 90° F at an elevation of 5,500 ft and some at 30° F at an elevation of 800 ft. The amount of testing performed precluded all of it being done under the same conditions.

As you look at the data we obtained, keep the above discussion of test conditions in mind. You should not infer that because a particular barrel gave smaller groups that it is necessarily capable of better accuracy. Also keep in mind that when two different barrels are tested, the first may give smaller groups than the second with three or four types of ammunition but the second may perform better than the first with three or four different types of ammunition. Also, it may be that for your particular needs, performance with one type of ammunition may be more important than the performance with other types. For example, if you are selecting a barrel to configure a rifle for varmint hunting, accuracy with a high-velocity hunting load such as CCI Velocitor or Winchester Power Point may be more important than is performance with several types of target loads.

You should also keep in mind that we tested only one barrel of each type. There must of necessity be some variation between individual specimens of any particular type of barrel. Even if manufacturing tolerances are small, variations still exist. It would be nice to see how half a dozen barrels of a certain type from a particular manufacturer shoot, but this is simply not practical. Your experience with a specific barrel may not be the same as ours. It could be better or worse, and it may be better with certain types (or lots) of ammunition and worse with others. Even the type of stock used can affect accuracy. The trim walnut stock that started out as a Carbine stock and was modified to give a sporter configuration (see Chapter 7) is much less stable on a rest than are most of the aftermarket stocks. Aftermarket stocks were used as received with no attempt to improve bedding, but some fit the barreled actions with correct pressures better than others.

The most common way of rating accuracy is in terms of group size. Generally, this is taken to be the distance between the centers of the two widest shots in the group. In order to minimize the effects of a stray shot, the experiment is replicated and several groups are shot so that the group sizes can be averaged. We have followed that practice and with each type of ammunition, five 5-shot groups were fired. The distance between the centers of the two widest shots was measured using a dial caliper that measures to the nearest 0.001 inch. However, with the uncertainty involved in locating the centers of the holes, the measurements were made only to the nearest 0.01 inch.

For exhaustive testing, it is preferable to fire groups of 10 shots rather than five. However, the group sizes when 10 shots are fired usually are slightly larger (as expected) than when five shots are fired, but the *trends* are usually (and should be) the same. It was simply a matter of the time available that led us to use the particular protocol that we followed.

Although it was discussed in Chapter 3, measuring the distance between the two widest holes overemphasizes the effect of one bad shot. Four bullets may pass through the same hole but if the fifth strikes one inch away, the result is a one-inch group. For example, when testing one of the rifles, four shots with Lapua Super Club gave a group that measured only 0.22

inch but the fifth shot enlarged the group to 0.50 inch. Clearly, too much weight is being placed on the one errant shot because four other groups measured from 0.24 inch to 0.35 inch. The overall average for five groups is 0.29 inch if the flyer is excluded and 0.34 inch if it is included. Therefore, the 0.50-inch group caused by one flyer must be considered suspect in light of the other data.

A better way to analyze groups is to determine the distance of each hole from the geometrical center of the group and then average these values. In that way, the effect of one shot that is rather far from the center of the group becomes only one value in an average rather than the shot that determines the group size. It should be apparent that one flyer that that increases the size of one group by half an inch would also increase the overall average group size significantly. When the mean dispersion measurement is used, one shot does not outweigh the other 24 that comprise the five 5-shot groups. Although groups should be measured in this way, few shooters have even heard of mean dispersion much less use the procedure.

The firearm, ammunition, and testing conditions constitute a system with an enormous number of variables. The best approach is probably to look at the data and see what the smallest group obtained is and to consider that as showing what the barrel can do under the best (but still not necessarily ideal) of circumstances. The results we present do not prove that barrel A is better than barrel B, and that was not the objective of the testing program. What you will see, however, is that virtually all of the customized rifles provide better accuracy than the factory rifles with the exception of the 10/22 Target.

Results of Accuracy Testing

Having so many wonderful aftermarket items to test, it was necessary to assemble rifles from the components and test them. It should be clear that if 10 stocks and 10 barrels that fit them are available, there will be 100 barrel/stock combinations that can be made up! It should also be clear that it would not be possible to test that many combinations without spending years at the work. When you also put four or five trigger assemblies in the mix, it becomes apparent that there would be literally hundreds of ways to configure the rifles. Now, just for fun, imagine that you are going to test 10 types of ammunition and want to use two or three lots of each type. The testing could become infinite. Therefore, we had to make some choices as to what combinations of aftermarket parts to test.

One rifle tested utilized the stock and barrel combination that is available from Midway USA. It consists of a Fajen thumbhole stock and a blue Adams & Bennett barrel having a diameter of 0.920 inch. In this case, the factory trigger had been replaced with the Jard trigger assembly, and a Weaver Classic V-16 scope mounted. The results obtained when this combination was tested with 15 types of ammunition are shown in the accompanying table.

Ruger 10/22 with an Adams & Bennett Blue 0.920" Barrel, Fajen Thumbhole Stock, Jard Trigger, and Weaver V-16 scope

Type of Ammunition	Smallest	Largest	Average
CCI Blazer	0.40	0.89	0.68
CCI Green Tag	0.77	0.89	0.82
CCI Standard Velocity	0.70	0.82	0.75
DN/RWS R50	0.43	0.57	0.51
Eley Match	0.47	0.61	0.51
Federal High Velocity HP	0.59	1.26	1.02
Lapua Super Club	0.32	0.73	0.57
Remington/Eley Club Xtra	0.51	0.82	0.71
Remington Game Loads	0.49	1.00	0.86
Remington Target	0.57	0.92	0.83
SK Jagd Standard Plus	0.31	0.68	0.51
Winchester Dynapoint	0.66	1.05	0.83
Winchester Power Point	0.85	1.22	1.01
Winchester Xpert	0.82	1.26	1.08
Wolf Match Extra	0.36	0.72	0.55
		Overall average	0.75

This accurate custom Ruger 10/22 that Jim is shooting has a Fajen thumbhole stock, an Adams & Bennett barrel, and a Jard trigger assembly.

The custom 10/22 with the Adams & Bennett barrel gave an overall group size of 0.75 inch, which is quite good when the external conditions are taken into account. Under the most favorable conditions, this value might be only 0.50 inch. Moreover, the largest groups were obtained with high velocity (Federal High Velocity and Winchester Power Point) and bulk pack (Winchester Xpert) loads. When the results obtained with these types of ammunition are omitted, the overall average group size shrinks to 0.68 inch. Five types of ammunition gave group sizes in the 0.5-0.6 inch range so this barrel is definitely capable of giving groups of less than 0.5 inch. It might take a little manipulating of the bedding, tension on the stock screw, and different lots of ammunition, but this barrel performs very well. If you study the data shown in the table, you will see that the six types of ammunition that performed best gave an average group size of only 0.56 inches. This is an indication of the capability of this fine barrel.

The combination of Fajen stock and Adams & Bennett barrel is available from Midway USA for $250 in blue barrel or $260 with a stainless steel barrel. However, this barrel combined with a CoreLite synthetic stock has a retail price of only $124.99 at Midway USA. As this is being written, the current sale price is only $84.99 for the combination! Although some of the barrels tested sell for approximately $300, the Adams & Bennett barrel does not give up much in terms of accuracy.

Butler Creek, a name that is well known to shooters, markets many items of interest. With regard to Ruger 10/22 users, Butler Creek sells stocks and

Aftermarket barrels and stocks are often sold as combinations. This is one of the combinations available from Butler Creek.

TRANSFORMS A 10/22® INTO A TACK-DRIVER!

BUTLER CREEK

TARGET
COMPETITOR Accurize Your Favorite Rifle!

RUGER
10/22®
TARGET
COMBO
PACK

CUSTOM TARGET STOCK &
BARREL GIVES ULTIMATE
ACCURACY TO YOUR 10/22
NO GUNSMITHING NEEDED!

STOCK:
● TARGET FOREARM
● SEMI-MONTE CARLO COMB
  FOR SCOPED SHOOTING
● RAISED, POSITIVE-GRIP
  CHECKERING
● ADULT TRIGGER PULL LENGTH
● DOUBLE PALM SWELLS
● SWIVEL STUDS INCLUDED
● ALL-WEATHER DURABILITY

BARREL:
● SHOOTS ALL .22 LR AMMO
● RECESSED TARGET CROWN
● BUTTON RIFLING
● NEW "EXCLUSIVE"
  SUPER MATCH CHAMBER
● INDUCTION HARDENED
  BREECH FACE
● FLUTED OR SMOOTH IN
  BLUED OR STAINLESS FINISH

New & Improved
STEEL PILLAR

DROPS RIGHT IN!
All it takes is a
screwdriver and
hex wrench!

20" .920 BARREL
☐ STAINLESS ☑ BLUED
☐ FLUTED ☑ SMOOTH
☐ TRI-PORT

barrels with some options being offered as combinations. Cabela's sells these combinations for $170-$190 depending on the barrel chosen. For this project, we tested rifles in which a Butler Creek composite stock was mated with a 0.920-inch blue barrel and a 0.920-inch blue fluted barrel attached to a Hogue OverMolded stock. In the first case, the trigger utilized was obtained from Hornet Products, and in the second the trigger unit from Kidd was installed. These combinations gave excellent rifles that can be obtained for a reasonable price. The accompanying table shows the results obtained from the accuracy testing.

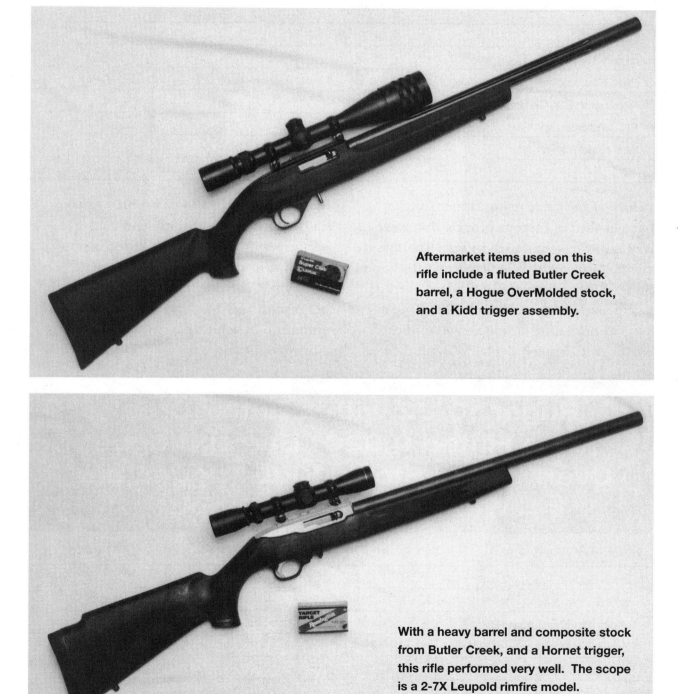

Aftermarket items used on this rifle include a fluted Butler Creek barrel, a Hogue OverMolded stock, and a Kidd trigger assembly.

With a heavy barrel and composite stock from Butler Creek, and a Hornet trigger, this rifle performed very well. The scope is a 2-7X Leupold rimfire model.

Ruger 10/22 with a Butler Creek Blue 0.920" Barrel, Butler Creek Stock, Hornet Trigger, and Leupold 2-7X Rimfire Scope

Type of Ammunition	Smallest	Largest	Average
CCI Green Tag	0.61	1.19	0.90
Lapua Super Club	0.46	0.84	0.65
PMC Scoremaster	0.53	0.80	0.65
Remington/Eley Target Rifle	0.32	0.85	0.55
SK Jagd Standard Plus	0.50	1.26	0.84
Wolf Match Target	0.49	0.77	0.62
		Overall average	0.70

Both of the rifles using Butler Creek barrels gave numerous groups that were well below one-half inch in size. The fluted barrel performed extremely well with Lapua Super Club, which resulted in an average group size of only 0.47 inch. CCI Green Tag did not perform well in the nonfluted barrel, but Remington/Eley Target did.

Remington Game Loads, an inexpensive high velocity hollow point cartridge, performed very well in the fluted barrel.

The most unusual result from the testing of the Butler Creek barrels was the performance of SK Jagd Standard Plus ammunition, which gave average group sizes of 0.84 and 0.87 inch. This load has

Ruger 10/22 with a Butler Creek Blue Fluted 0.920" Barrel, Hogue OverMolded Stock, Kidd Trigger, and Weaver V-16 AO Scope

Type of Ammunition	Smallest	Largest	Average
Lapua Super Club	0.33	0.62	0.47
PMC Scoremaster	0.28	0.69	0.56
Remington/Eley Target Rifle	0.62	0.86	0.71
Remington Game Loads	0.68	0.91	0.78
SK Jagd Standard Plus	0.65	1.08	0.87
Wolf Match Target	0.40	0.98	0.68
		Overall average	0.68

delivered outstanding accuracy in almost every barrel we have tested. The results obtained are not really bad, but for some reason, the Butler Creek barrels did not shoot as well with this load as they did with Lapua Super Club or PMC Scoremaster. The Standard Plus ammunition has given such consistently good accuracy in many .22s that it is among the first types tested, and in this case the results were not as good as those from other types.

Cabela's markets a stock and barrel combination that features a laminated thumbhole stock that carries their own label and a blue Green Mountain barrel that is 0.920 inch in diameter. Located in Conway, New Hampshire, Green Mountain Rifle Barrel Company is well known for producing high quality barrels for muzzle loading and rimfire rifles. This combination was tested with a Ruger 10/22 action that also had a Jard trigger assembly installed. The scope used in this case was a Weaver Classic V-16, and the results obtained are shown in the accompanying table.

Although tested by firing from a bench, this rifle consisting of a Cabela's thumbhole stock, a heavy Green Mountain barrel, and Jard trigger assembly is great for shooting offhand.

Ruger 10/22 with a Green Mountain Blue 0.920" Barrel, Cabela's Thumbhole Stock, Jard Trigger, and Weaver V-16 Scope

Type of Ammunition	Smallest	Largest	Average
CCI Green Tag	0.34	0.68	0.56
Eley Match	0.34	0.53	0.47
Federal Ultra Match	0.41	0.76	0.53
Lapua Super Club	0.39	0.55	0.47
Remington/Eley Target Rifle	0.46	0.59	0.51
SK Jagd Standard Plus	0.40	0.61	0.52
Wolf Match Target	0.45	0.68	0.57
		Overall average	0.52

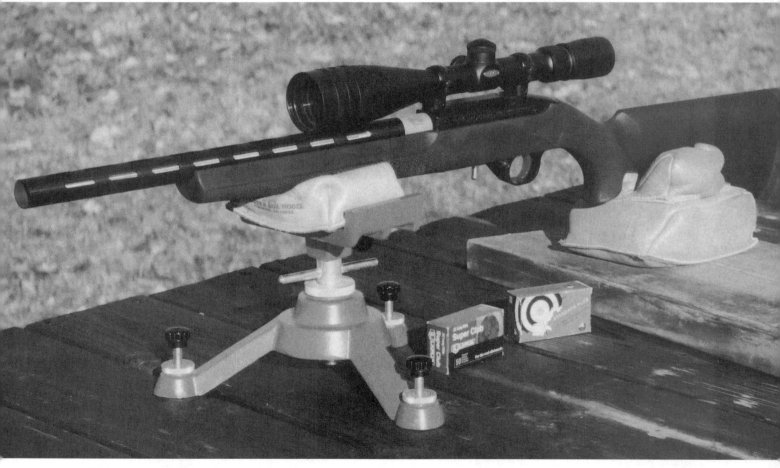

With its Green Mountain Aero barrel, Hogue OverMolded stock, and Kidd trigger assembly, this lightweight rifle carries well and shoots accurately.

Two facts are apparent from the data shown in the table. First, only target ammunition was tested in this combination. Second, the accuracy results obtained are truly excellent. Under the test conditions with absolutely no changes in bedding or tension on the stock screw, an average group size of 0.52 inch is outstanding. Two types of ammunition gave average group sizes of less than one-half inch. Perhaps more impressive is the fact that the largest average group size was only 0.57 inch. This barrel shoots extremely well with any of the types of target ammunition tested, and the excellent Jard trigger makes it possible. There is little doubt that with some tuning and perhaps trying different lots of ammunition, this combination of Green Mountain barrel and Cabela's thumbhole stock could easily give groups that average in the 0.3-0.4 inch range. This fine barrel/stock combination is available from Cabela's for $239.99 (with a blue barrel as tested) while the combination containing the stainless steel barrel sells for $259.99. Based on our observations with this particular barrel, the combination from Cabela's would be an easy way to trick out a Ruger 10/22 quickly and rather inexpensively.

Green Mountain Rifle Barrel Company produces a unique type of sleeved barrel assembly known as the Aero series. The actual barrel is a stainless steel tube of rather small diameter having a twist of one turn in 15 inches. That rifled tube is contained inside an aluminum sleeve that does not make contact with the barrel except for a short section near the breech. The aluminum sleeves come in several colors and have an outside diameter of 0.920 inch so they fit the channel of stocks designed for bull barrels.

Two screws located on the bottom of the barrel just ahead of where the sleeve joins the rear of the barrel and two O-rings hold the sleeve to the barrel. The presence of these screws, which protrude downward a slight amount, requires the barrel to be free floated. As an alternative, shims can be used on the bottom of the barrel-locking boss on the bottom of the action to raise the barrel in the channel slightly. In addition to the Aero barrel, our custom rifle also had a Hogue OverMolded stock and Kidd trigger unit. The results obtained with this rifle are summarized in the accompanying table.

Ruger 10/22 with a Green Mountain Aero 0.920" Barrel, Hogue OverMolded Stock, Kidd Trigger, and Weaver V-16 Scope

Type of Ammunition	Smallest	Largest	Average
Eley Match	0.56	0.72	0.67
Lapua Super Club	0.56	0.74	0.68
SK Jagd Standard Plus	0.66	0.84	0.77
Wolf Match Target	0.60	0.84	0.68
		Overall average	0.70

Before discussing the results obtained with the rifle using the Green Mountain Aero barrel, it should be mentioned that at the time of the tests the temperature was about 30° F and there was a slight swirling breeze. These are the hazards of a testing program that must be conducted outdoors and lasts for several months. Under these conditions, we deem that an overall average group size of 0.70 inch is very good. Although we fired target types of ammunition, the rifle did not show any great preference (or dislike) for any of the types. With the extremely light weight of the Aero barrel, it would be possible to customize a Ruger 10/22 to produce a compact rifle weighing only 4.5-5 pounds that would meet most uses for a rimfire. Moreover, the barrel could be in your favorite color.

Located in Hamilton, Montana, Jarvis has become one of the premier makers of rifle barrels, not only for the Ruger 10/22 but also for many other rimfire and centerfire rifles. Although we tested rifles using more than one Jarvis barrel, the rifle described here utilized the beautifully finished stainless steel model having a configuration of the standard weight barrel. To fit the slender barrel, we needed a stock with a standard barrel channel, and the one we chose was the Hogue OverMolded model. After installing a Volquartsen trigger assembly, the excellent Scheels 4-12X AO rimfire scope was mounted. Seven types of ammunition fired in this rifle gave the accuracy results shown in the accompanying table.

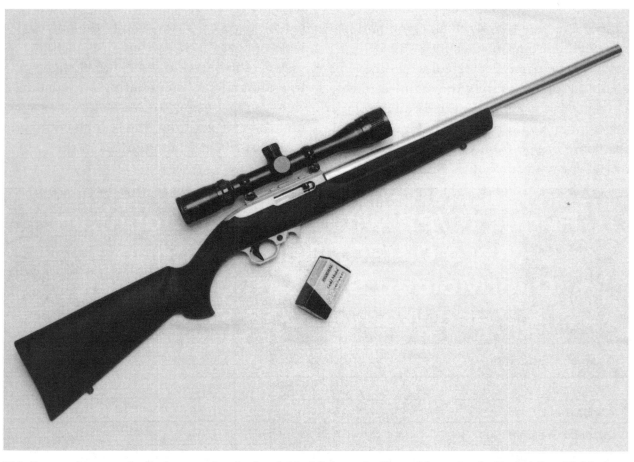

This fine custom sporter features a standard weight stainless steel barrel from Jarvis, Hogue OverMolded stock, Volquartsen trigger assembly, and a Scheels scope.

Ruger 10/22 with a Jarvis Standard-weight Stainless Barrel, Hogue Rubber OverMolded Stock, Volquartsen Trigger, and Scheels 4-12X AO Rimfire Scope

Type of Ammunition	Smallest	Largest	Average
CCI Green Tag	0.73	1.17	0.94
Eley Match	0.38	0.68	0.60
Federal Ultra Match	0.36	0.50	0.43
Lapua Super Club	0.52	0.77	0.68
Remington/Eley Target Rifle	0.41	0.68	0.55
SK Jagd Standard Plus	0.22	0.61	0.51
Wolf Match Target	0.27	0.67	0.49
		Overall average	0.60

Transforming a factory walnut stock into a sporter configuration resulted in this beautiful stock. Aftermarket parts include a standard weight blue barrel from Jarvis and a Kidd trigger assembly.

The results shown in the table make it apparent that the Jarvis barrel is capable of outstanding accuracy. Some of the smallest groups measured only about one fourth of an inch! It can also be seen that CCI Green Tag is not the most appropriate choice for this particular barrel. When that average group size of 0.94 inch is deleted, the other six types of ammunition give an overall group size of only 0.55 inch. Federal Ultra Match and Wolf Match Extra both gave average group sizes of under one-half inch. The accuracy shown by this rifle with Federal Ultra Match makes it apparent why we are glad to have a few boxes of this discontinued load hidden away. For a standard-weight barrel, the accuracy shown by this rifle with the Jarvis barrel is outstanding.

It is quite possible that with a stock that fits the barrel and action differently than the Hogue OverMolded and some adjusting of the tension of the stock screw, even better accuracy could be obtained. There is no doubt that the data show that this barrel has the potential to deliver outstanding accuracy, and that from a barrel of sporter weight. This barrel would be an excellent choice for someone who is configuring a 10/22 as a hunting rifle.

In addition to the Javis stainless steel barrel, we also tested a standard-weight barrel in blue finish. However, the rifle was configured much differently. Since the blue barrel is a standard-weight model, it fit perfectly in the walnut factory stock that had been modified (see Chapter 7). To complete the rifle, the outstanding Kidd trigger assembly was installed and a Weaver V-16 AO scope was mounted. The results obtained with this rifle are shown in the accompanying table.

When the first group was fired using Lapua Super Club, each shot simply enlarged the first hole. As the group grew slightly to 0.24 inch while firing five shots, it was apparent that this rifle was capable of outstanding accuracy. The average of five groups was only 0.34 inch with one of the groups consisting of a single ragged hole measuring 0.22 inch plus one "flyer" that enlarged the group to 0.50 inch. If that errant shot were omitted, the average group size with

Ruger 10/22 with a Jarvis Standard-weight Blue Barrel, Modified Factory Stock, Kidd Trigger, and Weaver V-16 AO Scope

Type of Ammunition	Smallest	Largest	Average
Eley Match	0.51	0.69	0.59
Lapua Super Club	0.24	0.50	0.34
PMC Scoremaster	0.56	0.70	0.63
SK Jagd Standard Plus	0.27	0.54	0.46
Wolf Match Target	0.59	0.78	0.70
		Overall average	0.54

Lapua Super Club would be 0.29 inch. Therefore, the overall average for five types of ammunition would be 0.53 inch. This is an impressive rifle. With the handsome walnut stock it is also beautiful. It is hard to imagine a rimfire semiautomatic sporter that would give better performance. Although Lapua Super Club gave the best accuracy, the other types of ammunition also performed well in this rifle. Both rifles that were configured with Jarvis standard-weight barrels performed extremely well, and the Volquartsen and Kidd triggers contributed to the fine performance.

With a gleaming, polished finish, the Kidd barrel is beautifully made. Being of the heavy 0.920-inch diameter pattern, a stock was selected to fit this barrel. The choice was the Revival Industries Yukon model, and the trigger assembly was the one produced by Hornet Products. Since we needed to test some of the fine rimfire scopes, we mounted the outstanding Leupold 2-7X rimfire scope on the rifle. The results of accuracy testing with this combination are shown in the accompanying table.

The accuracy delivered by the Kidd barrel is simply outstanding. For the seven types

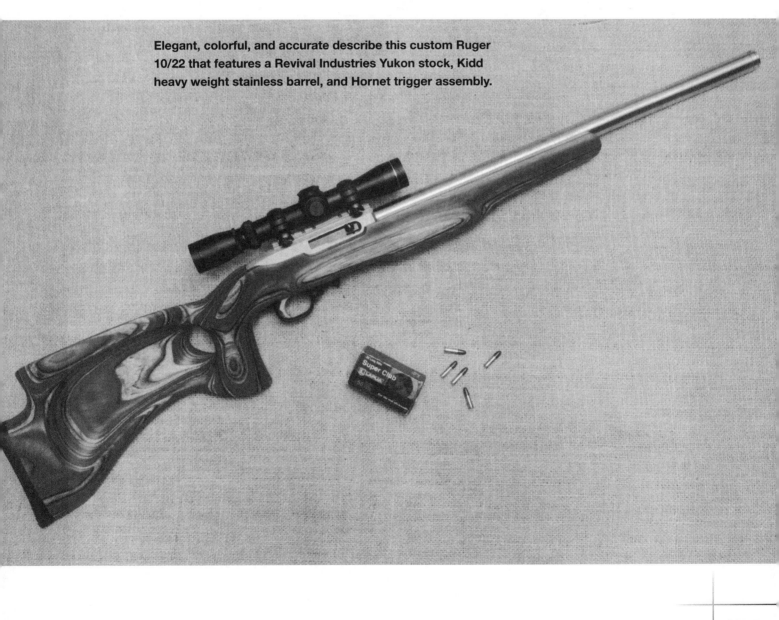

Elegant, colorful, and accurate describe this custom Ruger 10/22 that features a Revival Industries Yukon stock, Kidd heavy weight stainless barrel, and Hornet trigger assembly.

Ruger 10/22 with a Kidd Stainless 0.920" Barrel, Revival Industries Yukon Stock, Hornet Trigger, and Leupold 2-7X Rimfire Scope

Type of Ammunition	Smallest	Largest	Average
CCI Green Tag	0.53	1.00	0.74
Eley Match	0.32	0.77	0.53
Federal Ultra Match	0.23	0.88	0.54
Lapua Super Club	0.30	0.60	0.41
Remington/Eley Target Rifle	0.37	0.57	0.51
SK Jagd Standard Plus	0.37	0.56	0.46
Winchester T22	0.49	0.60	0.56
Wolf Match Target	0.28	0.58	0.40
		Overall average	0.52

This practical rifle was made by combining a standard weight Lilja barrel, a Hogue OverMolded stock, a Volquartsen trigger assembly, and a Scheels 4-12X scope.

of ammunition tested, the overall average is only 0.52 inch, and that includes a large number of groups that were in the 0.3-0.4 inch range. When the 0.74-inch average for CCI Green Tag is deleted, the overall average drops to only 0.49 inch. There is no doubt that even this value does not represent the true potential of this fine barrel. The scope, although an excellent one, is only a 7X model, and no attempt was made to alter bedding, screw tension, etc. When used on a highly tuned rifle, we believe that the Kidd barrel would easily deliver groups in the 0.2-0.3 inch range. A custom 10/22 configured using the components described is a precision shooting device.

Another fine barrel of standard weight configuration is that produced by Lilja of Plains, Montana. Available in both blue and stainless steel, these barrels reflect

the craftsmanship for which Lilja is justly famous. For this project on the Ruger 10/22, we chose to experiment with the standard-weight stainless steel barrel. The barrel, action and Volquartsen trigger unit were held in a Hogue OverMolded stock, and a Scheels 4-12X AO rimfire scope was mounted. The accuracy testing with this rifle yielded the results shown in the accompanying table.

The data show that for several types of ammunition the smallest groups produced by the Lilja barrel were in the 0.30-0.40 inch range. With Federal Ultra Match, the average group size was only 0.48 inch, and for all types of ammunition tested it was only 0.62 inch. This rifle with a standard-weight barrel has the potential to group consistently within 0.5 inch with appropriate ammunition. The outstanding Lilja barrel would be an excellent choice for

Ruger 10/22 with a Lilja Standard-weight Stainless Barrel, Hogue Rubber OverMolded Stock, Volquartsen Trigger, and Scheels 4-12X AO Rimfire Scope

Type of Ammunition	Smallest	Largest	Average
CCI Green Tag	0.68	0.82	0.74
Eley Match	0.37	0.66	0.52
Eley Tenex	0.30	0.73	0.53
Eley Tenex Semi-Auto	0.34	0.88	0.59
Federal High Velocity HP	0.58	0.93	0.78
Federal Ultra Match	0.33	0.60	0.48
Lapua Super Club	0.55	0.67	0.63
Remington Rifle	0.66	0.89	0.77
SK Jagd Standard Plus	0.36	0.71	0.51
Wolf Match Target	0.46	0.83	0.64
		Overall average	0.62

configuring an accurate 10/22 of medium weight for sporting uses.

Advances in technology have resulted in many new products for sportsmen and improvements in others. In fact, many items could not be produced without the use of materials known as advanced composites which are resins containing fibers of carbon, boron, or fiberglass. We have already described the use of such materials in the construction of stocks (see Chapter 7). Even barrels have been the subject of engineering to produce lightweight models that give outstanding accuracy. Magnum Research produces such a barrel for the Ruger 10/22. It has an inner barrel made of steel that is contained in a sleeve of carbon fiber material to give an outside diameter of 0.920 inch. As a result, the barrel has the configuration of a target model but weighs only 12.8 ounces! This barrel was tested on a rifle consisting of the Hornet trigger

with the rifle mounted on either the Bell & Carlson Anschutz style or the Butler Creek composite stock. The Leupold 2-7X rimfire scope was mounted to complete the arrangement. Testing the rifle with several types of ammunition gave the results shown in the accompanying table.

The data presented in the table show clearly just how far the technology of barrel making has advanced. Keep in mind that the overall average group size of 0.69 inch was produced with a barrel weighing only 12.8 ounces! Phenomenal is the word that comes closest to describing the results. With the Magnum Research barrel, a lightweight stock, and a compact rimfire scope, it is possible to make a rifle that weighs less than five pounds but delivers the accuracy required for serious rimfire shooting. We believe that building a rifle of this type is one of the best reasons to customize the Ruger 10/22. The results we obtained show that even with such an

When weight is a consideration, this rifle utilizing a Magnum Research carbon fiber sleeved barrel, a Hornet trigger, and a composite stock make an accurate, light rifle.

A fine rifle for sporting use has been configured using a Majestic Arms Aluma-Lite barrel and Hogue OverMolded stock.

Ruger 10/22 with a Magnum Research Barrel, Bell & Carlson Anschutz-style or Butler Creek Stock, Hornet Trigger, and Leupold 2-7X Scope

Type of Ammunition	Smallest	Largest	Average
Lapua Super Club	0.53	0.78	0.64
Remington/Eley Target Rifle	0.41	0.74	0.59
Remington Game Loads	0.57	0.91	0.72
SK Jagd Standard Plus	0.69	0.86	0.78
Wolf Match Target	0.51	0.91	0.70
		Overall average	0.69

ultra light rifle you do not sacrifice much in terms of accuracy.

During the testing of the rifle with the Magnum Research barrel, it was observed that the accuracy was affected by the tension on the stock screw. This is true of all the rifles we tested, but it seemed to be more sensitive when using this featherweight barrel.

In the case of the Aluma-Lite barrel from Majestic Arms of Staten Island, NY, we have a barrel that has the diameter of a target model but the weight of a standard barrel. The Aluma-Lite barrel weighs only 24.1 ounces. With a Lothar Walther steel insert encased in an aluminum sleeve, excellent accuracy can be expected. The Aluma-Lite barrel was installed on the action, and the barreled action was attached to a Hogue OverMolded stock. Because the Hogue OverMolded stock has rubber gripping surfaces and composite construction, it is an excellent choice for use on a rifle for hunting. Therefore, we configured one rifle in a sporter configuration using the Aluma-Lite barrel, Hogue OverMolded stock, and factory trigger unit.

We made up a second rifle in a target configuration using the Aluma-Lite barrel and the Jard trigger assembly held in an elegant Bell & Carlson Odyssey stock. This stock is fully adjustable for length of pull, height of the comb, and angle of cant of the butt plate. Both of the rifles using the Aluma-Lite barrel had a Weaver V-16 scope mounted. The results of accuracy testing with both of these rifles are shown in the accompanying table.

With an overall group size of only 0.60 inch obtained with the first rifle, the Aluma-Lite barrel lives up to its expectations. This barrel can be used to configure a light, handy 10/22 that is a pleasure to carry in woods or field, but one that will give excellent accuracy. Part of the theory behind the construction of the Aluma-Lite barrel is that the aluminum sleeve increases rigidity of the insert but equally important is the dampening effect on barrel vibrations. Note how all of the types of ammunition tested gave average group sizes that do not vary much. Such consistency may be due in part to the dampening effect of the aluminum sleeve.

An outstanding rifle was made using a Majestic
Arms Aluma-Lite barrel, a Bell & Carlson
Odyssey stock, and a Jard trigger assembly.

Ruger 10/22 with a Majestic Arms Alumi-Lite 0.920" Barrel and Weaver V-16 Scope

With a Hogue Rubber OverMolded Stock and Factory Trigger

Type of Ammunition	Smallest	Largest	Average
CCI Green Tag	0.25	0.83	0.57
Eley Target	0.49	0.85	0.68
Federal High Velocity HP	0.47	0.81	0.64
Lapua Super Club	0.54	0.69	0.49
Remington Game Loads	0.41	0.64	0.55
Wolf Match Target	0.45	0.84	0.67
		Overall average	0.60

With a Bell & Carlson Odyssey Stock and Jard Trigger

Type of Ammunition	Smallest	Largest	Average
CCI Green Tag	0.48	1.03	0.83
Eley Target	0.29	0.71	0.51
Lapua Super Club	0.42	0.64	0.49
Remington Game Loads	0.35	1.03	0.66
SK Jagd Standard Plus	0.38	0.72	0.54
		Overall average	0.61

Whatever the reason, the Aluma-Lite barrel performs very well.

In order to determine if the Hogue OverMolded stock might allow some slight movement of the barrel and action, the Bell & Carlson Odyssey stock was used as a replacement. Lapua Super Club gave the smallest group average when the Hogue stock was used, so it was fired in the rifle after the Odyssey stock was substituted. The average group size was identical (0.49 inch) in both cases. Whether this experiment could be repeated with another specimen of barrel and stock we cannot say. Our advice is simply not to worry about the any difference produced by the stock unless you are trying to shave 0.1 inch off your group size or unless there is

an obvious misfit. In field use any slight difference is not likely to be noted. The data reveal that the Aluma-Lite barrel gives outstanding accuracy with either stock. However, please note that except for Lapua Super Club, several different types of ammunition were used when the stocks were changed. There is certainly no measurable difference in accuracy depending on which of the two stocks was used. However, note that in the tests with the Bell & Carlson Odyssey stock, CCI Blazer (a very inexpensive load) and Remington Target (which has not given very good accuracy in any of our rifles) were included. When the results for those types are deleted, the overall group size shrinks to 0.51 inch.

Ruger 10/22 with a Ranch Products Blue Muzzle-Weighted Barrel, Factory Carbine Stock, Hornet Trigger, and Leupold 2-7X Scope

Type of Ammunition	Smallest	Largest	Average
CCI Green Tag	0.53	0.99	0.74
Eley Match	0.47	0.96	0.61
Lapua Super Club	0.56	0.84	0.69
Remington/Eley Target Rifle	0.56	0.91	0.65
Remington Game Loads	0.55	0.95	0.73
SK Jagd Standard Plus	0.46	0.64	0.52
Wolf Match Target	0.39	0.73	0.60
		Overall average	0.65

Ranch Products of Milinta, Ohio produces numerous items for shooters who use many types of firearms. Among the products are magazine releases, clips for holding rimless cartridges in revolvers, loading tools, and scope mounts for several rifles. The item of interest here is the target barrel for the Ruger 10/22. The barrel tested is the blued muzzle weighted version that fits the factory barrel channel. Muzzle weighted barrels are deservedly popular because they can be used with the factory stock, but they produce the weight forward feeling that is an aid to steady holding. We tested the Ranch Products barrel in a rifle consisting of the factory carbine stock and Hornet trigger assembly with the Leupold 2-7X rimfire scope attached.

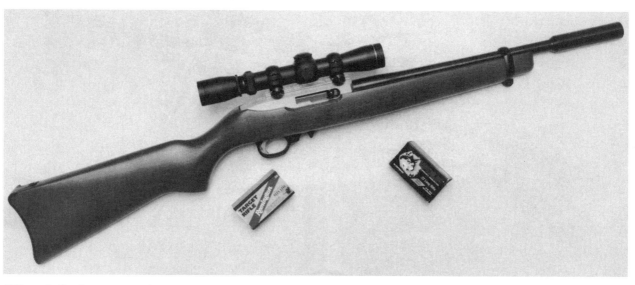

Although the factory stock was retained, this rifle features a muzzle-weighted barrel from Ranch Products and a Hornet trigger assembly.

The accompanying table shows the results obtained during accuracy testing.

The muzzle-weighted barrel from Ranch Products gave accuracy that would meet most expectations of a rimfire shooter. As we have often found, SK Jagd Standard Plus ammunition gave the best accuracy with groups that ranged from 0.46 to 0.64 inch and an average group size of only 0.52 inch. Noteworthy is the fact that of the 35 groups each consisting of 5 shots each not one group measured over one inch. This is an accurate, consistent rifle. If you want a customized Ruger 10/22 with a muzzle-weighted barrel, you should consider the barrel from Ranch Products.

E. R. Shaw of Bridgeville, Pennsylvania is well known as a producer of fine rifle barrels. It is not uncommon to find Shaw barrels on both fine custom sporting rifles and target models. The barrel chosen for testing on this customized Ruger 10/22 is the helical fluted stainless steel model of standard weight. Measuring 18 inches in length, this is a beautifully finished barrel that fits the barrel channel of the factory stock. For testing, the rifle was constructed using the Shaw barrel and a Kidd trigger assembly held in a modified factory stock with a Weaver V-16 scope. The results obtained are summarized in the accompanying table.

The data shown in the table indicate that the Shaw barrel delivers excellent accuracy. However, some explanation is in order. The stock used in these tests was originally a factory Carbine stock that was highly modified to produce a sporter stock (see Chapter 7). The result is that this stock has a very slick finish that does not give good purchase on the rest, especially on cold, dry days. Consequently, it was not possible to hold the rifle as securely as is necessary for firing very small groups. While this is not a problem when using the rifle in the field, it does point out the importance of choosing the correct stock for firing a rifle from a bench. We believe that the Shaw barrel is capable of even better accuracy than the data in the table indicates.

Having previously tested a couple of types of ammunition in the rifle, the

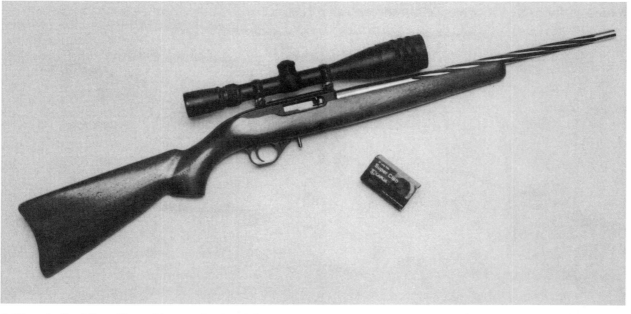

A Shaw helical fluted barrel in standard weight, a Kidd trigger assembly, and a Weaver V-16 scope were combined with a modified factory stock to produce this unusual sporter.

Ruger 10/22 with a Shaw Helical Fluted Standard-weight Barrel, Modified Factory Stock, Kidd Trigger, and Weaver V-16 AO Scope

Type of Ammunition	Smallest	Largest	Average
CCI Green Tag	0.77	1.66	1.23*
Lapua Super Club	0.40	0.69	0.56
Remington/Eley Target Rifle	0.37	0.88	0.73
Remington Game Loads	0.62	0.69	0.66
SK Jagd Standard Plus	0.57	0.87	0.78
Wolf Match Target	0.52	0.78	0.63
		Overall average	0.67

*Not included in calculating the overall average.

groups obtained using CCI Green Tag came as something of a shock. It was as if something had happened to the rifle, and it was necessary to check all screws before continuing. Nothing amiss was found, but the rifle configured with the Shaw barrel does not like CCI Green Tag. The data were included in the table only to underscore the fact that any barrel (even a very fine one) may not perform well with some particular type of ammunition. We have had excellent results with CCI Green Tag in some barrels, but not the Shaw barrel and some others.

The data presented in the table show that it is possible for a custom Ruger 10/22 with a standard weight barrel to give accuracy that rivals that of one with a target barrel. Because of the configuration, the Shaw barrel can be used to produce a customized 10/22 that is small and light in weight but still able to deliver outstanding performance. It provides a very attractive barrel option for customizing a Ruger 10/22.

Shilen Rifles, Inc. is a name that is recognized for producing barrels that often win in competition. For customizing the Ruger 10/22, Shilen barrels are available in a range of styles that should meet any requirement. The testing of custom rifles for this project included both stainless steel and blue versions in 0.920-inch diameter. The stainless barrel was mated with a Bell & Carlson composite stock made in what is known as the Anschutz style, a Kidd trigger, and a Scheels 4-12 AO rimfire scope. The blue barrel was used with the same stock, but a Cabela's Pine Ridge 3-9X rimfire scope and Hornet trigger were employed. Accuracy testing with these rifles gave the data shown in the accompanying tables.

The data shown in the tables make it clear that both rifles with Shilen barrels deliver excellent accuracy. However, the data certainly do not reveal that one barrel is superior to the other. First, not all types of ammunition were the same for both barrels. Second, the testing was conducted on different days under different ambient conditions. Third, a 12X scope was used in

A Bell & Carlson composite stock and Shilen stainless steel barrel have been combined with a Hornet trigger and Scheels 4-12X scope to produce a fine custom Ruger 10/22.

The custom Ruger 10/22 that Jim is shooting here has a heavy Shilen blue barrel, a Bell & Carlson Odyssey stock, and a Kidd trigger. The rifle is topped with a Cabela's Pine Ridge 3-9X rimfire scope.

one case while a 9X model was used in the other, and different triggers were installed. All that can be realistically concluded is that with several types of ammunition these barrels will deliver groups smaller than one-half inch with regularity. Note

Ruger 10/22 with a Shilen Blue 0.920" Barrel, Bell & Carlson Odyssey Stock, Kidd Trigger, and Cabela's Pine Ridge 3-9X Rimfire Scope

Type of Ammunition	Smallest	Largest	Average
CCI Green Tag	0.40	0.99	0.78
Eley Match	0.56	0.73	0.65
Federal Target 711B	0.54	1.09	0.80
Lapua Super Club	0.46	0.60	0.55
Remington/Eley Target Rifle	0.49	0.76	0.65
Remington Game Loads	0.40	0.75	0.54
SK Jagd Standard Plus	0.34	0.78	0.59
Winchester Power Point	0.42	0.87	0.64
Wolf Match Target	0.38	0.65	0.48
		Overall average	0.63

Ruger 10/22 with a Shilen Stainless 0.920" Barrel, Bell & Carlson Anschutz-style Stock, Hornet Trigger, and Scheels 4-12X AO Rimfire Scope

Type of Ammunition	Smallest	Largest	Average
CCI Green Tag	0.54	1.00	0.76
Eley Match	0.26	0.75	0.57
Federal Ultra Match	0.38	0.67	0.49
Lapua Super Club	0.33	0.52	0.43
Remington/Eley Target Rifle	0.29	0.69	0.53
SK Jagd Standard Plus	0.28	0.56	0.45
Winchester Supreme Match	0.62	0.85	0.74
Wolf Match Target	0.35	0.58	0.48
		Overall average	0.56

from the data that the smallest groups with several types of ammunition were frequently less than 0.4 inch. Under the testing conditions described earlier in this chapter, the performance of both of the rifles is outstanding. For additional information on the outstanding rimfire scopes used in testing the Shilen barrels, see Chapter 10.

Tactical Solutions offers barrels that are truly ultra lightweight models. We assembled rifles using two of these barrels, a green, fluted version that is threaded at the muzzle to accept a suppressor and a

This compact rifle features a fluted green barrel from Tactical Solutions, a Butler Creek stock, a Hornet trigger assembly, and a Leupold 2-7X rimfire scope.

Composed of a McMillan composite sporter stock, a camo sleeved barrel from Tactical Solutions, Leupold 2-7X scope, and a Hornet trigger assembly, this little rifle is a true lightweight.

camo barrel, both of which have 0.920" diameter. These barrels have weights of 14.7 ounces and 17.4 ounces, respectively. Barrels such as these make it possible to produce rifles that perform well while being eminently portable. Both of our rifles utilized the Hornet trigger assembly and the superb Leupold 2-7X rimfire scope. The results obtained with these rifles are shown in the accompanying tables.

As has been mentioned previously, much of the testing with the customized rifles was carried out under less than ideal conditions. This was certainly the case at the time these rifles were tested, but both of the ultra lightweight barrels from Tactical Solutions gave average group sizes of less than one inch with all types of ammunition. The camo barrel gave an overall average group size of 0.75 inch. If the average for the Federal High Velocity load is deleted from the results obtained with the green barrel having flutes, the overall average given by the rifle is 0.79 inch. There is

Ruger 10/22 with a Tactical Solutions Camo 0.920" Barrel, McMillan Stock, Hornet Trigger, and Leupold 2-7X Rimfire Scope

Type of Ammunition	Smallest	Largest	Average
Eley Target	0.59	0.93	0.81
Lapua Super Club	0.70	0.93	0.77
PMC Scoremaster	0.57	0.89	0.70
SK Jagd Standard Plus	0.46	0.65	0.59
Wolf Match Target	0.76	0.99	0.88
		Overall average	0.75

Ruger 10/22 with a Tactical Solutions Green Fluted 0.920" Barrel, Butler Creek Stock, Hornet Trigger, and Leupold 2-7X Rimfire Scope

Type of Ammunition	Smallest	Largest	Average
Eley Target	0.56	1.17	0.83
Federal High Velocity HP	0.73	1.25	0.95
SK Jagd Standard Plus	0.58	0.81	0.70
Wolf Match Target	0.70	0.93	0.83
		Overall average	0.83

little doubt that under more favorable test conditions and with additional types of ammunition, these barrels would perform even better. A barrel that weighs one pound and consistently gives groups that average around three-quarters of an inch is very interesting. That is exactly the case with the ultra lightweight Tactical Solutions barrels. With one of these barrels, a lightweight stock, and a compact scope it is possible to assemble a rifle that weighs less than five pounds. Such a rifle might not win in benchrest competition, but it is a very pleasant walk about rifle for hunting and pest control.

Keep in mind that any rifle with a barrel that has a threaded muzzle is illegal in some jurisdictions. Before you decide to use one of these fine barrels to build your ultra lightweight custom Ruger 10/22, check regulations in your area.

Volquartsen Custom Ltd. of Carroll, Iowa is a producer of many outstanding products for the shooter who uses small caliber rifles. Although the products have

always involved barrels and complete rifles in rimfire calibers, a centerfire autoloader in .223 Remington has recently been added to the product line. Stocks, barrels, and complete trigger assemblies are available for the 10/22 in both magnum and standard calibers. For the person modifying a 10/22 who does not want to replace the entire trigger assembly, Volquartsen offers triggers, hammers, sears, etc. for the do-it-yourself shooter to modify a trigger assembly. For this project, we used a trigger assembly and a muzzle-weighted stainless barrel to make a custom rifle. The barrel has the profile of the standard-weight barrel until a point approximately four inches from the muzzle where the barrel increases to 0.920-inch diameter. This provides a built-in muzzle weight, and a barrel of this configuration is sometimes known as a running boar model. Beautifully designed and finished, the muzzle-weighted barrel is also practical. The "weight forward" design enables the rifle to be held steady when

This modified Ruger 10/22 boasts a Volquartsen muzzle weighted barrel, a Hogue OverMolded stock, Volquartsen trigger assembly, and a 4-12X scope from Scheels.

shooting in the standing position.

For configuring a rifle for testing, we mated the Ruger 10/22 action with the Volquartsen muzzle-weighted barrel, attached to a Hogue OverMolded stock, and mounted a Scheels 4-12X AO rimfire scope. The results obtained when this rifle was tested with a wide variety of types of ammunition are shown in the accompanying table.

The types of ammunition tested in the Volquartsen barrel covered the spectrum from the very low priced CCI Blazer to rather sophisticated target loads like Eley Match. There are several significant aspects to the data shown in the table. First, only

one type of ammunition, Remington Target, gave an average group size of over one inch. Second, even the economical CCI Blazer gave an average group size of only 0.66 inch! This goes to show that it is often the quality of the barrel rather than the price of the ammunition that determines accuracy. Third, the results were uniformly excellent with almost all types of ammunition. Even some of the high velocity hollow point types like Winchester Power Point, Remington Game Loads, and Federal High Velocity gave some extremely small groups. With that in mind, the obvious conclusion is that this rifle would be an excellent choice for use as a varmint rifle. Although some might

Ruger 10/22 with a Volquartsen Muzzle-Weighted Stainless Barrel, Hogue OverMolded Stock, Volquartsen Trigger, and Scheels 4-12X AO Rimfire Scope

Type of Ammunition	Smallest	Largest	Average
CCI Blazer	0.39	0.91	0.66
CCI Green Tag	0.37	0.80	0.60
CCI Standard Velocity	0.60	0.79	0.68
Eley Match	0.40	0.67	0.56
Eley Tenex Semi-Auto	0.34	0.68	0.52
Federal High Velocity HP	0.27	0.93	0.70
Lapua Super Club	0.45	0.67	0.55
Remington/Eley Club Xtra	0.64	0.84	0.73
Remington Game Loads	0.36	1.00	0.69
Remington Target	0.77	1.53	1.09
SK Jagd Standard Plus	0.35	0.76	0.54
Winchester Dynapoint	0.61	1.10	0.79
Winchester Power Point	0.74	0.88	0.81
Winchester Xpert	0.56	1.29	0.89
Wolf Match Target	0.44	0.86	0.79
		Overall average	0.71

balk at using a stainless steel barrel in the woods, squirrels would be unsafe from a hunter using this rifle. This barrel and trigger represent the quality with which the Volquartsen name is routinely associated.

If there is one barrel that brings out the "Oh wow!" when it is shown, it surely must be the Whistle Pig Stainless Fluted barrel. This barrel is constructed with an inner rifled tube that is surrounded by an outer sleeve made of aluminum. Not only is the barrel fluted, but also it has an extremely bright polished surface. The insides of the flutes are coated with an enamel of contrasting color. We chose the bright red color, which makes a dramatic looking barrel. With the Whistle Pig barrel mated to

the Revival Industries Yukon stock (which is red and gray in color), the result was easily the most glamorous looking rifle we put together. In order to have a sight on the rifle, we mounted the outstanding Leupold 2-7X rimfire model. Although not particularly high in magnification, this scope is extremely bright and crisp, and the fine crosshair reticule permits accurate aiming in spite of the limited magnification. Data on the performance of the rifle made of these parts are shown in the accompanying table.

With its dual metal construction, the Whistle Pig barrel weighs only 18.1 ounces in spite of its outside diameter being 0.920 inch. Although it weighs approximately 10

A most unusual custom 10/22 is this rifle that is built from a Whistle Pig fluted barrel with enameled flutes, a Revival Industries Yukon stock, and a Hornet trigger assembly.

Ruger 10/22 with a Whistle Pig Stainless Fluted Barrel, Revival Industries Yukon Stock, Hornet Trigger, and Leupold 2-7X Rimfire Scope

Type of Ammunition	Smallest	Largest	Average
Eley Match	0.60	0.85	0.66
Lapua Super Club	0.56	0.91	0.74
Remington/Eley Target	0.50	0.84	0.66
SK Jagd Standard Plus	0.42	0.70	0.57
Winchester T22	0.32	0.85	0.60
Wolf Match Target	0.24	0.87	0.63
		Overall average	0.64

ounces less than the factory barrel for the Carbine, the Whistle Pig gives outstanding accuracy. For the six types of ammunition tested, the overall average was only 0.64 inch, and the range of values was from 0.57 to 0.74 inch. This is outstanding consistency. Once again, the marvelous accuracy of SK Jagd Standard Plus is shown. As you look at the tables, you will see how in many cases this outstanding cartridge gives the smallest groups of all of the types tested. In situations where it does not give the smallest group average, it is often virtually tied with the best performing load. As if that were not impressive enough, Standard Plus seems to give outstanding accuracy in *all* barrels. The rifle configured as described would be acceptable at all types of shooting parties.

Performance Summary

In this chapter, we have presented several tables that show the results of firing customized rifles composed of various parts. In most cases, many types of ammunition were used with each rifle. Due to circumstances beyond our control, such as weather and time constraints, some combinations were tested with only five or six types of ammunition. However, we found that most rifles performed better with a small number (usually three or four) of types of ammunition than with the other types tested. In order to give an overview of the results obtained with custom rifles made up of various aftermarket parts, we have prepared a summary table. In that table, the major components used to configure the rifle are listed (barrel, stock, trigger, and scope), but we have omitted small changes such as installing a different type of recoil buffer, etc.

Before you look at the table and conclude that barrel X is better than barrel Y, you must also remember that the enormous amount of testing done was carried out over a period of several months. Some tests were conducted at an elevation of 8,200 ft, others at 5,500 ft, and many others at 600 ft. The temperature ranged from around

30° F with the ground covered with snow to almost 90° F, and the wind was always a factor. At some ranges, the benches were massive concrete affairs. At others, we used a folding rest, and at another range the benches were made of wood. In some cases the scopes mounted on the rifles were models specifically intended for use on rimfire rifles, but in others they were not. Magnification of the scopes ranged from 7X to 20X.

In the table, we show the average size of five 5-shot groups obtained with the three types of ammunition that performed best with that combination of components. In the last column, we show the average group size obtained for five 5-shot groups with the ammunition that performed best in a rifle configured from those particular components. Incidentally, the best performing ammunition was most often SK Jagd Standard Plus, Eley Match, Remington/Eley Target, Lapua Super Club, Wolf Match Target, or Federal Ultra Match. This should come as absolutely no surprise. Target grade ammunition will almost always give better accuracy than other types. You should also keep in mind that not all of these types were used with every rifle. It may be that any of the rifles described would give better accuracy with some other type of ammunition that was not tested.

It would have been desirable to conduct all of the tests under identical conditions using identical types of ammunition, identical rests, and identical scopes, but this simply was not possible. Even if it were, the rifles would never be used under identical conditions after they were built.

The idea behind this table is simply to show that the components always allowed us to produce a custom rifle that performed very well. The table also includes the results obtained from firing the factory versions of the Ruger 10/22 for comparison. Therefore, the essence of this table is to show representative results for a large number of customized Ruger 10/22 rifles. The data presented in the table should be studied with that interpretation as a goal.

The data shown in the table indicate that all of the rifles we configured are capable of outstanding accuracy. The majority of the customized rifles produced groups that averaged less than one-half inch with at least one type of ammunition. Several combinations gave groups that averaged that small with at least three types of ammunition. Is better accuracy possible? Absolutely, if the wind is favorable, a rock solid bench is used, the most accurate ammunition is used, and a scope of high magnification is mounted on the rifle. The tests we conducted do not establish the absolute level of accuracy that any of the customized rifles can produce. In fact, we believe that with the limitations imposed by eyesight and weather, an average group size of approximately 0.40 inch is about as good as we can do.

One thing that is clear is that all of the customized rifles gave better accuracy than all of the factory versions except the 10/22 Target. The Ruger 10/22 Target is capable of performing as well as many of the customized rifles, but this should not be surprising. It has a heavy hammer forged barrel, target style stock, and better trigger than the other versions of the 10/22. Moreover, after the tests were conducted with our 10/22 Target, we found that the screw holding the front swivel had penetrated the forearm and cracked the stock. As a result, the barrel was riding on a hump of splintered wood rather than

Summary of Accuracy Testing of the Customized Rifles

Barrel	Trigger	Stock	Scope	Group Size, In. Best 3*	Best 1**
Adams & Bennett Blue 0.92"	Jard	Fajen T.H.	Weaver V-16	0.51	0.51
Butler Creek Blue Fluted 0.92"	Kidd	Hogue OM	Weaver V-16	0.57	0.47
Butler Creek Blue 0.92"	Hornet	Butler Cr. Comp.	Leupold RF	0.61	0.55
Green Mountain Aero 0.92"	Kidd	Hogue OM	Weaver V-16	0.68	0.67
Green Mountain Blue 0.92"	Jard	Cabela's T.H.	Weaver V-16	0.48	0.47
Jarvis Blue Std Wt.	Kidd	Mod. Factory	Weaver V-16	0.46	0.34
Jarvis S.S. Std. Wt.	Volquartsen	Hogue OM	Scheels Pr. RF	0.48	0.43
Kidd S.S. 0.92"	Hornet	Rev. Ind. Yukon	Leupold RF	0.42	0.40
Lilja S.S. Std. Wt.	Volquartsen	Hogue OM	Scheels Pr. RF	0.51	0.48
Magnum Research Carbon 0.92"	Hornet	B & C Anschutz	Leupold RF	0.64	0.59
Majestic Arms Aluma-Lite 0.92"	Factory	Hogue OM	Weaver V-16	0.54	0.49
Majestic Arms Aluma-Lite 0.92"	Jard	B & C Odyssey	Weaver V-16	0.51	0.49
Ranch Products S.S. Muz. Wt.	Hornet	Factory Carbine	Leupold RF	0.58	0.52
Shaw S.S. Fluted Std. Wt.	Kidd	Mod. Factory	Weaver V-16	0.62	0.56
Shilen Blue 0.92"	Jard	B & C Odyssey	Cabela's RF	0.52	0.48
Shilen S.S. 0.92"	Volquartsen	B & C Anschutz	Scheels Pr. RF	0.45	0.43
Tactical Solutions Camo 0.92"	Hornet	McMillan	Leupold RF	0.69	0.59
Tactical Solutions Green 0.92"	Hornet	Butler Cr. Comp.	Leupold RF	0.79	0.70
Volquartsen S.S. Muz. Wt.	Volquartsen	Hogue OM	Scheels Pr. RF	0.54	0.52
Whistle Pig Fluted 0.92"	Hornet	Rev. Ind. Yukon	Leupold RF	0.60	0.57
Factory Carbine	Factory	Factory	BSA Air Rifle	0.87	0.78
Factory Rifle	Factory	Factory	Simmons RF	0.73	0.68
Factory Compact	Factory	Factory	Cabela's RF	0.82	0.81
Factory Lipsey's	Factory	Factory	Scheels Pr. RF	0.98	0.87
Factory Target	Factory	Factory	Cabela's Otfttr.	0.56	0.45

*Average size of five 5-shot groups with the three best performing types of ammunition.

**Average size of five 5-shot groups with the best performing type of ammunition.

Abbreviations: S.S.=Stainless Steel; Muz. Wt.=Muzzle Weighted; OM=OverMolded; T.H.=Thumbhole; RF=Rimfire; Pr.=Premier; B&C=Bell & Carlson; Comp. = Composite; Mod.= Modified.

Scopes used were the BSA 3-12X AO Air Rifle; Cabela's 3-9X Rimfire; Cabela's Outfitter 6-20X AO; Leupold 2-7X Rimfire; Scheels Premier 4-12X Rimfire; Simmons 22 Mag 3-9X AO; and Weaver V-16 4-16X AO.

on the barrel channel. Not only is the 10/22 Target a good performer, the other factory rifles gave good accuracy as long as the ammunition was chosen carefully. Of course, the factory versions do not give accuracy equal to customized rifles, but the factory rifles do perform quite well. The Ruger 10/22 has always had a good reputation for accuracy, and the data show that few rifles in the same price range will perform better.

As intended, the data show that if you select good aftermarket components, mount a good scope, and experiment with several types of ammunition, you should end up with a customized Ruger 10/22 that is superbly accurate. The data also show that a very accurate rifle can result even though you may not select the most expensive aftermarket items available for building your rifle. As you study the data shown in the table, keep in mind that our tests were conducted over a period of several months, in all types of weather, at different elevations, and with numerous types of ammunition (not always the same lots) used which were not always the same types for all of the rifles. Consequently, results that you might obtain with a rifle made up of the same components would probably be somewhat different. We were impressed with the fact there were no bad combinations.

Custom .17 Mach 2 Rifles

Announced in 2004, the .17 Mach 2 cartridge is derived from the CCI .22 Stinger case by necking it down to hold a .172 caliber bullet. As a result, an enormous number of factory rifles and handguns chambered for the .17 Mach

2 cartridge are available. The reason is simply because most firearms chambered for the .22 LR are easily adapted to fire the .17 Mach 2 cartridge simply by installing a barrel chambered for that cartridge. The situation is not quite that simple when autoloading rifles are concerned because the chamber pressure remains higher for a longer period of time than it does when a .22 LR cartridge is fired (see Chapter 3). This is not a problem for locked-breech rimfires.

Although some autoloading rifles chambered for the .17 Mach 2 are available, Ruger has not marketed a version of the 10/22 to fire this cartridge. Quick to offer products for shooters, the producers of aftermarket products began to offer barrels chambered for the .17 Mach 2 that would fit the 10/22. However, it became apparent that because of the differences in pressure and cycling, other changes would be required. To make a heavier bolt assembly that would cycle slower, a heavier bolt handle and stronger recoil spring are used as an alternative to completely redesigning the bolt assembly. Currently, most aftermarket sources offer a combination of a .17 Mach 2 barrel and

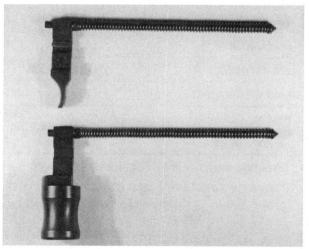

When converting a Ruger 10/22 to fire .17 Mach 2 cartridges, a special bolt handle is required.

a special bolt handle to make the Ruger 10/22 function safely and reliably with the .17 Mach 2 cartridge.

Realizing that many shooters are making the conversion of Ruger 10/22 rifles to .17 Mach 2, we configured our rifle in order to conduct some testing. We chose to utilize the bolt handle produced by Magnum Research combined with the factory trigger that had been altered by installing the trigger kit from Power Custom (see Chapter 9). Barrels in .17 Mach 2 caliber from Majestic Arms and Magnum Research were tested. The Majestic Arms barrel has an aluminum sleeve over a steel insert while the Magnum Research barrel has a carbon fiber sleeve over a steel insert. Although both barrels have an outside diameter of 0.920 inch, they are very light in weight and can be made up to give very light rifles.

Literature accompanying the Majestic Arms barrel indicates that it must be free floating. One outstanding stock that allows a 0.920 inch barrel to be free floating is that from McMillan. Initially, the barrel and action were attached to that stock, but it was found that the large bolt handle would

Because it has a different shape in the cut out area where the bolt moves, this Bell & Carlson stock could be used with the larger bolt handle.

not clear the cut out area around the bolt handle. The McMillan stock is configured for use with a standard size bolt handle. As a result, both of our custom .17 Mach 2 rifles were assembled with a Bell & Carlson stock of the Anschutz target style. A Sightron 3-9X AO scope was used for testing accuracy.

Currently, most .17 Mach 2 is produced either by CCI in the U.S. or by Eley in England. We chose to test our rifles with Hornady 17 grain V-Max and Eley 17 grain V-Max loads. The results obtained are

When the Magnum Research bolt handle was installed, it would not clear the step in the McMillan stock, which is shaped to follow the opening in the receiver.

This custom .17 Mach 2 was configured using a Majestic Arms Aluma-Lite barrel, a Bell & Carlson stock, and a factory trigger that had a Power Custom kit installed. The scope is a 3-9X AO from Sightron.

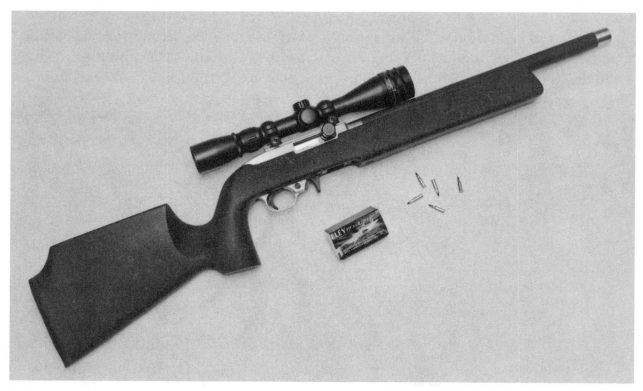

A distinctive rifle in .17 Mach 2 was prepared using a Bell & Carlson target stock, a Magnum Research carbon fiber sleeved barrel, a trigger enhanced with a Power Custom kit, and a 3-9X AO Sightron scope.

Ruger 10/22 Converted to .17 Mach 2 with a Majestic Arms Barrel, Bell & Carlson Stock, Factory Trigger with Power Custom Kit, and 3-9X AO Sightron Scope

Type of Ammunition	Smallest	Largest	Average
Eley	0.33	0.86	0.66
Hornady	0.49	0.77	0.67

shown in the accompanying tables.

Although the group sizes shown in the tables are respectable, they do not give a true representation of the accuracy that the Majestic Arms and Magnum Research barrels can give. With the time that could be allocated for testing growing short, it was necessary to test the .17 Mach 2 rifles when the temperature was hovering in the mid-30s on a somewhat breezy day. Undoubtedly, on a day when conditions were better, these rifles would give groups that average less than one-half inch. Functioning was reliable, and no problems were experienced. The barrels were essentially new with very little firing before the tests were begun. Accuracy shown by these barrels would probably improve with additional shooting. Also, the barrels were not free floating as is recommended by Majestic Arms. In spite of these factors, the results of our tests show that it is possible to customize a Ruger 10/22 to produce a rifle chambered for the .17 Mach 2 that is accurate enough to be effective on small pests at distances to at least 100 yards. The .17 Mach 2 is simply too short on power to use on larger species of varmints or at longer ranges. DO NOT ALTER A RUGER 10/22 TO FIRE .17 MACH 2 CARTRIDGES BY SIMPLY CHANGING BARRELS! DAMAGE TO THE RIFLE WILL OCCUR.

Ruger 10/22 Converted to .17 Mach 2 with Magnum Research Barrel, Bell & Carlson Stock, Factory Trigger with Power Custom Kit, and 3-9X AO Sightron Scope

Type of Ammunition	Smallest	Largest	Average
Eley	0.40	0.67	0.58
Hornady	0.49	0.76	0.64

Chapter 12

THE RUGER 10/22 MAGNUM

After the Ruger 10/22 semiautomatic was introduced in 1964, it became immensely popular. The Marlin Model 60, which was introduced in 1960, was a major competitor, and these two models captured a large share of the rimfire market. Total production of these two models totals nearly 10 million. For some reason, semiautomatic rifles in .22 LR are by far the most popular types. If you do not think so, just look at the catalogs or web sites of firearm manufacturers. The number of rimfire autoloaders sold far exceeds the number of bolt action and lever action rifles.

It was inevitable that autoloaders would be produced in .22 WMR caliber. Over the years, companies like Marlin, H&K, Brno, Volquartsen, and others have made models, but none has sold in large numbers. Part of the problem is cost. An autoloading rifle in .22 WMR must be constructed somewhat differently from one in .22 LR and that translates into higher cost. Another factor is that many shooters who use a rifle chambered for the magnum caliber are interested in eliminating varmints. Accuracy is far more important than rate of fire so the slower bolt action is not a handicap for such work. A similar situation exists for big game hunting for which bolt-action rifles are far more popular today than are other action types.

Ruger introduced the 10/22M chambered for the .22 WMR cartridge in 1999. In 2002, the .17 HMR cartridge was introduced, and both the 2004 and 2005 Ruger catalogs list a Model 10/17 chambered for the .17 HMR round. To the present time (January 2006) none have made it to dealers' shelves. In fact, as this book was being prepared, the 2006 Ruger catalog appeared, and it no longer shows the Model 10/17. The .17 HMR and .22 WMR cartridges are somewhat different and both are drastically different from the .22 LR. Therefore, it is appropriate to explain some of the problems associated with semiautomatic rifles in rimfire magnum calibers.

Design and Cycling

Firing any rimfire rifle involves pulling on the trigger to cause the sear to release the hammer (internal or external). There is no major problem associated with designing a mechanism to carry out this procedure. Subsequently, the hammer strikes the firing pin causing it to impact the cartridge to explode the priming mixture, which ignites the powder. There are no insurmountable problems associated with this part of the firing cycle. When the cartridge fires, pressure builds up rapidly, and an impulse is transmitted to the bolt. It is this part of the firing process that

The Ruger 10/22M looks much like the
.22 LR version, but has many differences.

causes design problems, especially for the magnum rimfire cartridges. The trick is to balance the forces so that the bolt opens as it should but not while the pressure in the chamber is high enough to spray gas and burning powder out of the chamber.

In most autoloading rifles chambered for centerfire cartridges, the bolt is locked by strong locking lugs at the time of firing. After the cartridge is fired but before the bullet leaves the muzzle, a small amount of the gas generated is allowed to escape from a port in the barrel. The gas enters a cylinder where it forces a piston backward. The piston is connected to a rod that pushes on a device that moves the bolt to unlock it. As the bolt moves backward, it withdraws the empty cartridge case, and as it moves forward it picks up a fresh cartridge from the magazine. Although there are other types of semiautomatic rifles, the so-called gas operated mechanism described here is the most common.

Rimfire cartridges are far less powerful than are almost all centerfire rounds. Moreover, rimfire cartridges operate at lower pressure, and the cases are small. As a result, the forces generated are much smaller than those produced when centerfire rifles are fired. For the .22 LR cartridge, the action of the semiautomatic can be of the simple blow back type, which means that the bolt is not locked in place at the time of firing. The bolt simply rests in its forward position where it is held in place against the end of the barrel by the recoil spring. Because of the relatively low power of the .22 LR cartridge, the bolt does not have to be very massive or the recoil spring very strong to prevent the bolt from being forced backward too rapidly which could cause damage to the firearm.

Firing a .22 WMR cartridge is an entirely different matter. The case head is not much different in size from that of a .22 LR, and the maximum pressures of the two cartridges are similar (about 22,000-25,000 lb/in^2). What differs greatly for the two cartridges are the pressure curves. The .22 LR utilizes a very small charge of fast burning powder, which causes the maximum pressure to be reached quickly. As the small powder charge is consumed, the pressure also drops quickly. The result is a backward force on the bolt that is high only for a very short period of time. The bolt is driven backward quickly by the impulse, but the recoil spring dampens the movement easily.

Because the .22 WMR uses a much larger charge of slower burning powder, the pressure may rise to the about same maximum value as it does for a .22 LR, but the pressure remains higher much longer. This results in the bolt being acted on by a higher back thrust for a longer period of time, which causes it to move backward with much more force. This must be balanced so that the bolt does not slam backward damaging the firearm but with enough force to cycle the action. It is a rather delicate balancing act.

There are two ways to compensate for the higher back thrust produced by the .22 WMR. First, the bolt can be made heavier than one used in a .22 LR rifle. As a result, it absorbs more of the back thrust energy simply because it takes more energy to move a heavy object. Second, the recoil spring can be made much stiffer than those used in .22 LR rifles. This makes it harder to pull the bolt back manually when preparing to fire the first shot. Both techniques are employed in the design of the Ruger 10/22M. Of course, Ruger could

Ammunition in .22 WMR caliber is available with several bullet styles and weights.

have designed a locked-bolt, gas-operated action, but the rifle would have to sell for a much higher price. For example, the Model 99/44 autoloader in .44 Magnum caliber is such a rifle, and it has a list price of $702.

The problem is how to make a heavier bolt without changing its dimensions greatly. After all, one does not want the receiver to be three inches thick or a foot long. Ruger solved the problem of the heavier but not much larger bolt by making use of new alloys that are referred to as heavy metal alloys (HMA). With the strength of steel but much higher density, a bolt made of this alloy has the required weight but small size necessary to function in the Ruger 10/22M.

Because of the considerably greater stresses produced when firing the .22 WMR, the receiver which houses all the moving parts must be much stronger than is required for a rifle firing .22 LR cartridges. Consequently, the receiver of the Ruger 10/22M is made of steel rather than cast aluminum as it is in the 10/22. This results in the magnum rifle weighing about a pound more than the .22 LR Carbine version, and it also drives the cost up (list prices are $536 and $258 for the .22 WMR and .22 LR rifles, respectively). The receiver of the magnum rifle has raised sections with milled notches for attaching Ruger scope rings. No scope base

is required as is the case for the .22 LR rifles. The higher cost of the magnum rifles is partially offset by the fact that they are shipped with a set of Ruger rings (that have a retail price of $63.55).

For some years, the Ruger 10/22M was produced with a single extractor located on the right hand side of the bolt as it is in the .22 LR caliber 10/22. Recently manufactured Ruger 10/22M rifles have dual extractors, one on either side of the bolt. Producers of aftermarket barrels are aware of this change and now offer their barrels with two extractor cuts to accommodate the new extractor configuration. If you have a new 10/22M with the two extractors and an older barrel that has one extractor cut, you can solve the problem by either of two ways. First, you can remove the extractor on the left hand side of the bolt. Second, you can have a second extractor cut made in the barrel tenon.

To this point, the discussion has been concerned with the differences between the .22 LR and .22 WMR versions of the Ruger

These cartridges are (left to right) the .22 LR, .17 HMR, and .22 WMR.

Note the difference in the holes in the .17 caliber barrel (left) and one in .22 caliber (right).

autoloader. What we have in the case of the .17 HMR version that was first announced in 2004 is somewhat different. First, we have no factory rifles available at the time of this writing, and the 2006 Ruger catalog does not show the model 10/17. Second, the design problems are somewhat different from those that either the .22 LR or .22 WMR cartridges present. The .17 HMR is a necked cartridge (sometimes referred to as a bottle necked case) because the diameter of the bullet is smaller than the diameter of the case. As the powder burns, there is a smaller orifice than in the .22 WMR case (about 41% smaller!) from which the gas can escape so the pressure stays high even longer than it does when a .22 WMR cartridge is fired. As a result, the weight of the bolt and stiffness of the recoil spring that adequately solve the problem of back thrust for the .22 WMR may not be correct for the .17 HMR. The tiny bores (.17 calibers) present different problems than the small bores (.22 calibers). Design parameters that will allow a .22 WMR autoloader to function safely and reliably may not be immediately adaptable to the same rifle chambered for the .17 HMR cartridge.

Sturm, Ruger & Company are not naïve. They are aware that aftermarket barrels are available that allow shooters to convert .22 LR rifles to .17 Mach 2 (or .17 Aguila) and to change .22 WMR rifles to .17 HMR. Therefore, whatever design is adopted in the factory .17 HMR rifles (if and when they appear) must present no problems if another barrel in the same caliber is installed. The difficulty arises when one of the .22 WMR rifles has a .17 HMR barrel installed but no other changes are made. As a result, Ruger must "get it right" before beginning to market a .17 HMR version of their 10/22M in .22 WMR which may later be converted to a .17 HMR. Undoubtedly, some of the .17 HMR rifles will eventually be converted to .22 WMR by barrel swapping, and Ruger wants to create a 10/17 so that the change would not present any problem. Of course, there is no problem associated with the caliber changes with closed breech rifles (bolt and lever actions) because nothing moves until being forced to manually by the shooter. Converting a .22 WMR to a .17 HMR and a .22 LR to a .17 Mach 2 is a common occurrence with rifles having bolt actions because the locked breech in such rifles means that no other changes are required.

Given the uncertainty that exists at the time of this writing with regard to a factory Ruger 10/17, we will refrain from discussing what might possibly be done with that rifle. Further, we do NOT recommend simply adding a barrel in .17 HMR to a receiver from a .22 WMR caliber 10/22M rifle as a way to change calibers *for continued use*. Such barrels are available, but since Ruger did not issued a 10/17 that is simply the 10/22M with a different barrel, we believe that is not advisable to put a .17 HMR barrel on existing 10/22M rifles for long term use. There may be durability issues that require more than just a barrel change to address. If a qualified gunsmith who makes the other necessary alterations performs the conversion, the situation is somewhat different.

Stocks for the 10/22M

Although it is hard to imagine almost any aftermarket industry equaling that associated with the Ruger 10/22, many products are also available for the 10/22M (and the 10/17M if it ever becomes available). Actually, the selection of stocks for the 10/22M is quite extensive. Boyds' Gunstock Industries of Mitchell, SD offers two fine stocks for the magnum rifle. One is the Dakota Will model that is a conventionally shaped stock. This stock is available only as the Virtual Inlet Part (VIP) item that is fully inletted, but it requires the external surface to be finished. The Dakota Will is available only with a barrel channel that accommodates

a barrel having the contour of the factory barrel. This laminated stock is available in two colors, nutmeg (brown) and pepper (dark gray). We worked with this model in nutmeg color on our 10/22M, and it is shown in the photos. Absolutely no work was necessary to fit the barreled action to the stock. However, the barrel channel needed to be widened slightly to allow the barrel to contact both sides equally. Only preparation of the external surface and application of finish (Birchwood Casey Tru-Oil® in this case) were required. This was done as described in Chapter 7.

Boyds' other stock for the 10/22M is a thumbhole (or silhouette) type known as the Blaster. This stock is available only with a barrel channel to fit 0.920-inch diameter barrels, but it is produced in both nutmeg and pepper shades. Finished and VIP stocks of this style are available with the completely finished version costing about $30 more.

The custom .22 WMR shown here features the Dakota Will stock from Boyds' Gunstock Industries, a Jarvis barrel, and a 3-9X Sightron scope.

Several aftermarket stocks are available for the Ruger 10/22M including this composite model from Butler Creek.

Butler Creek produces a molded composite stock that replaces the 10/22M factory item, but it is available only with a 0.920-inch barrel channel. It is a conventional sporter configuration that has checkering in the gripping and forearm areas, and it has a steel bedding post. This stock is available as a combination with a blue 0.920 inch barrel chambered for .17 HMR.

One of the inexpensive options for the person who wishes to replace the stock on a 10/22M is the Hogue OverMolded stock that has been described in detail in Chapter 7. With its rubber OverMolded sections, this stock affords an outstanding

The Butler Creek stock has very attractive and functional checkering in the grip area.

grip without weighing a great deal. We have used this stock on our 10/22M with aftermarket barrels having a diameter of 0.920-inch. These outstanding stocks retail for approximately $80 for 10/22 magnum rifles.

Examining the catalogs and web sites for other stock makers will show that numerous other stock options are available for customizing the Ruger 10/22M. The survey above includes details only for the models we had available.

Barrels for the 10/22M

The owner of a Ruger 10/22M who wants to replace the factory barrel has a rather wide range of options. Some barrels for the 10/22M are produced with a contour that matches (or very nearly matches) that of the factory barrel. With such barrels, the factory stock can be used if desired. However, there are many high quality barrels for the 10/22M of the target type that have a diameter of 0.920 inch. If this type of barrel is selected, the shooter must either buy an aftermarket stock with a barrel channel to fit the heavy barrel or do a lot of work to widen the barrel channel of the factory stock. If the later option is chosen, the barrel band will not fit over the heavy barrel so the stock has to be used without the band. This is not a severe handicap because on the Ruger 10/22 it is often more accurate if the barrel band does not make contact with the barrel.

Performance of our factory Ruger 10/22M was described in Chapter 4. While we did not make as many alterations to the rifle as we did our 10/22s, some experimentation was carried out. This work included changing barrels and stocks to produce rifles having several configurations. When contemplating a barrel change on the 10/22M, one must decide whether the barrel to be installed will have a standard contour or be one of the 0.920-inch diameter target models. When using barrels of 0.920-inch diameter, we always changed to an aftermarket stock for that type of barrel. We wanted to leave the factory stock unchanged so the rifle could be changed back to the factory configuration if desired. There are numerous barrels of 0.920-inch diameter available from most of the same manufacturers that produce barrels for the 10/22.

As described in Chapter 4, our 10/22M performed quite well in its factory configuration. However, in keeping with the spirit of this project, we reconfigured the 10/22M by using different barrel and stock combinations. In all cases, the factory trigger as enhanced by Herman Tom of Hornet Products was used without further alteration. Fine aftermarket .22 WMR barrels are available in both standard and heavy configurations from manufacturers such as Jarvis, Green Mountain, Volquartsen, and others.

In addition to the standard weight barrel, a different type of barrel will fit the barrel channel of the factory stock. It is the muzzle weighted or "running boar" model that has the contour of the factory barrel throughout most of its length. About four or five inches from the muzzle, the diameter of the barrel increases to 0.920 inch to provide a built in muzzle weight. This "weight forward" design enables the shooter to hold the rifle steadier in the

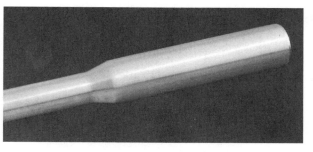

Note the heavy barrel section on this Green Mountain Running Boar barrel.

standing position and to swing smoothly to follow moving targets. We worked with an outstanding barrel of this type that was produced by Green Mountain Rifle Barrel Company of Conway, New Hampshire. Although the running boar barrels are produced in both blue and stainless steel, we tested the stainless version.

Another barrel that we tested was the Aluma-Lite that is produced by Dino Longueira of Majestic Arms in Staten Island, New York. This outstanding barrel in .22 LR caliber has been described in Chapters 8 and 11. It consists of an inner steel barrel made by famed barrel maker Lothar Walther and an outer sleeve made of aluminum. Although the diameter is 0.920 inch, the barrel is very light in weight, and it gives excellent accuracy.

Since it is possible install a barrel chambered for the .17 HMR cartridge on the Ruger 10/22M action, we configured a rifle in this way. The barrel was a heavy (and with only a .17 inch bore it is really heavy!) model from Butler Creek with an outside diameter of 0.920 inch. This barrel has a deep blue finish and a target crown.

Triggers

The owner of a Ruger 10/22M chambered for the .22 WMR has not been left out when it comes to aftermarket triggers. Complete trigger units are available from

Jard, Hornet Products, Volquartsen, and other suppliers. These high quality units are similar to their counterparts that are produced for the 10/22 in .22 LR caliber and are priced similarly.

For the person who does not want to replace the entire trigger assembly, the array of parts available is similar if less extensive than that for the 10/22. It is possible to obtain hammer, sear, springs, and firing pin to modify the factory trigger. Given some of the modified factory triggers that we have examined, this is a satisfactory process that is much less expensive than replacing the entire trigger.

Finally, if one does not want to run the risk of having parts left over (or missing) after disassembling the trigger unit, many gunsmiths will rework the factory trigger. Mr. Herman Tom of Hornet Products, Sarasota, Florida, modified the trigger on our 10/22M. Although the factory trigger required a pull of approximately 12 pounds, the modified trigger has a crisp let off at four pounds. The fee for this work is approximately $55 to $60, which is comparable to the fee we have been quoted

Shooters who favor the .22 WMR have many choices in ammunition.

by other shops. As modified by Herman Tom, our trigger unit was returned with an extended magazine release and a bolt lock that released automatically when the bolt was drawn back and released. For the rather limited modification of a magnum 10/22, the reworked trigger performed extremely well.

Testing Custom Ruger 10/22 Magnum Rifles

The first Custom Ruger 10/22 magnum made use of the Green Mountain Running Boar barrel. This stainless steel barrel has essentially the same configuration

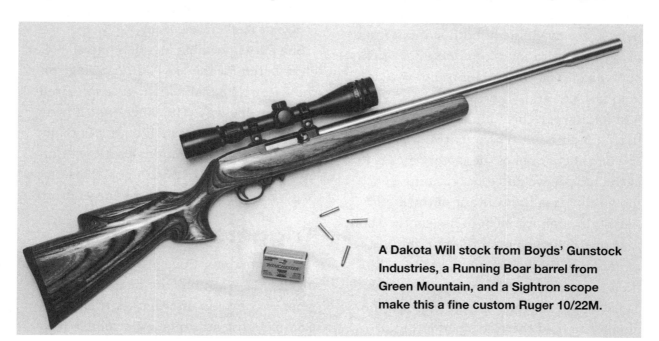

A Dakota Will stock from Boyds' Gunstock Industries, a Running Boar barrel from Green Mountain, and a Sightron scope make this a fine custom Ruger 10/22M.

Ruger 10/22M with a .22 WMR Green Mountain Running Boar Barrel, Hogue OverMolded Stock, Modified Trigger by Hornet Products, and Sightron 3-9X AO Rimfire Scope

Type of Ammunition	Smallest	Largest	Average
Remington Premier 33 gr V-Max	0.56	0.98	0.74
Remington PSP 40 gr	0.63	1.25	0.94
Winchester JHP 40 gr	0.40	0.85	0.60
Winchester Supreme 34 gr HP	0.55	1.04	0.82
		Overall average	0.78

as the factory barrel throughout most of its length, but it increases in diameter to 0.920 inch for the last four inches of its length.

Although the Green Mountain Running Boar barrel is described as a standard weight model, it has a slightly different taper and will not fit the factory barrel channel or those of most aftermarket stocks that we have with barrel channels intended for standard weight barrels. Having several barrels to test, we did not want to modify a factory stock specifically to fit the Green Mountain barrel because it would then not properly fit some other barrels. If one were permanently replacing the factory barrel with the Green Mountain Running Boar barrel, there should be no hesitancy about modifying the barrel channel, but our rifle was not being permanently configured. Consequently, the rifle with the Green Mountain Running Boar barrel utilized a Hogue OverMolded stock that has a 0.920-inch barrel channel. In that way, the barrel was free floating except for about two inches in front of the

receiver. However, we found that accuracy obtained when using the barrel in this way was not indicative of the capability of this fine barrel. To remedy the situation, we placed a shim near the end of the forearm inside the barrel channel after which accuracy improved markedly. The results of accuracy testing with this rifle after installing a shim under the barrel are shown in the accompanying table.

The Green Mountain Running Boar barrel is a beautifully constructed barrel. Because of not wanting to modify a stock to specifically fit this barrel with other testing to be carried out, it was tested in a rather makeshift arrangement. Given the accuracy that was obtained, we believe that this barrel will give groups of one-half inch or less when we properly fit it to a suitable stock.

In Chapter 11, we showed the results of testing a Majestic Arms Aluma-Lite barrel in .22 LR caliber. This barrel has a slender Lothar Walther rifled tube made of steel that is encased in an aluminum sleeve that measures 0.920 inch in diameter. Majestic

Ruger 10/22M with a .22 WMR Majestic Arms 0.920" Aluma-Lite Barrel, Hogue OverMolded Stock, Modified Trigger by Hornet Products, and Sightron 3-9X AO Rimfire Scope

Type of Ammunition	Smallest	Largest	Average
CCI Maxi Mag HP 40 gr	0.33	0.84	0.61
Remington Premier 33 gr V-Max	0.34	0.84	0.58
Remington PSP 40 gr	0.20	1.11	0.71
Winchester JHP 40 gr	0.59	0.88	0.69
Winchester Supreme 34 gr HP	0.64	1.04	0.83
		Overall average	0.68

Arms also produces a barrel of this type in .22 WMR caliber so we obtained one for customizing the Ruger 10/22M. This barrel was mounted on the 10/22M action, and the assembly was attached to a Hogue OverMolded stock. The result is a rifle that is light in weight and very comfortable to use either in the field or at the bench. We tested the rifle using several types of ammunition to obtain the data shown in the table.

Accuracy exhibited by the Majestic Arms barrel is quite good considering the conditions under which the testing was

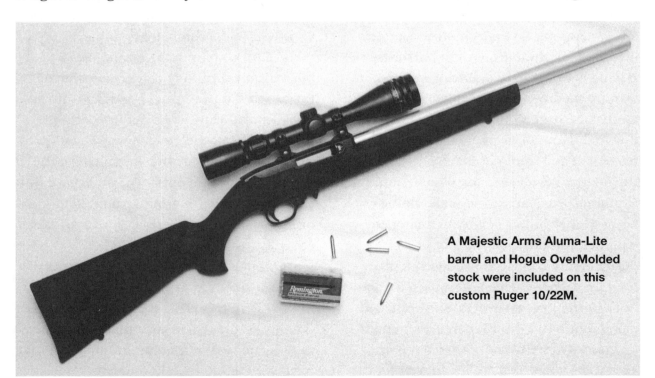

A Majestic Arms Aluma-Lite barrel and Hogue OverMolded stock were included on this custom Ruger 10/22M.

conducted. The temperature was around 30° F and a slight breeze was blowing so the data presented do not represent the true capability of this barrel. In spite of the less than ideal conditions, most types of ammunition gave groups that average 0.5-0.7 inch. This barrel performed best with the Remington Premier load that utilizes a 33-grain V-Max bullet. With most .22 WMR rifles, we have found that the ammunition loaded with 40-grain bullets seems to give most consistent accuracy. Some of our .22 WMR rifles do not give the best accuracy with either the light 30-34 grain bullets or the heavy 50-grain loads.

Although the data are not shown in the table, a few groups were fired using the Federal Classic 50-grain hollow point load. That load has performed very well in some .22 WMR rifles that we have tested, but it literally sprayed from this barrel. Groups over three inches were not uncommon. We have been told that generally Lothar Walther barrels tend to have minimum bore dimensions. If a .22 WMR bullet passes through such a barrel, the bullet must be swaged down because .22 WMR bullets measure .224 inch while the nominal diameter for .22 LR bullets is about 0.223 inch. Also, bullets used in .22 WMR cartridges are jacketed or at least have a heavy copper plating. While the swaging process does not seem to affect the accuracy when bullets weighing 30-40 grains are used, there is an adverse affect with the longer, heavier 50-grain projectiles.

Most .22 WMR barrels have a 1:16 twist which works better for bullets weighing about 40 grains. However, there were no visible signs that the 50-grain bullets had tipped in flight because the holes were round. Certainly not all .22 WMR barrels will handle heavy bullets, and this was probably one factor that led CCI to discontinue the 50-grain load that was produced for a few years. Since everything that needs to be accomplished with a .22 WMR can be done with a 40-grain bullet, this is not a serious limitation.

The Majestic Arms Aluma-Lite barrel is a worthwhile addition when customizing a 10/22M. As is the case with any barrel, it is necessary to experiment to find the type of ammunition that gives the best accuracy. There is currently only one 50-grain load available so if the Aluma-Lite barrel does not handle that bullet very well it is not much of a handicap. Our Aluma-Lite barrel certainly gave good accuracy with ammunition using other bullet weights.

Testing A 10/22M Converted To .17 HMR

Doubtless there are many owners of Ruger 10/22M rifles who want to convert them to fire .17 HMR ammunition, especially since Ruger has not marketed a factory 10/17 rifle and one does not appear in the 2006 Ruger catalog. Aftermarket barrels in .17 HMR are available from numerous makers, and one of the first companies to meet the demand was Butler Creek. The barrel we tested was a heavy, stainless version that weighs 56.4 ounces! This is the heaviest aftermarket barrel that we tested. This is not surprising since it is 20 inches in length and not much metal is removed to make the tiny hole. The rifle we constructed utilized the Butler Creek barrel, a Hogue OverMolded Stock, and a factory trigger that was reworked by Herman Tom of Hornet Products. Although .17 HMR ammunition is marketed with

Ruger 10/22M with a .17 HMR Butler Creek Stainless 0.920" Aluma-Lite Barrel, Hogue OverMolded Stock, Factory Trigger Modeified by Hornet Products, and Sightron 3-9X AO Rimfire Scope

Type of Ammunition	Smallest	Largest	Average
CCI TNT 17 gr HP	0.38	0.59	0.49
Federal Premier 17 gr	0.30	0.52	0.40
Hornady XTP 20 gr HP	0.54	0.62	0.59

CCI, Hornady, Remington, Winchester, and Federal labels, it is apparently all produced by CCI. Therefore, for testing we selected the Federal load that utilizes a 17-grain polymer-tipped bullet, the CCI TNT that has a 17-grain hollow-point bullet, and the 20-grain hollow-point Hornady XTP load. The results obtained from the accuracy tests are shown in the accompanying table.

The rifle built around the Butler Creek .17 HMR barrel produced groups that were tiny clusters. By any reasonable standard, this barrel gives excellent accuracy with the three types of ammunition that were used in it. Moreover, it does not seem to exhibit any strong preference for any one of the three types of bullets currently available in .17 HMR ammunition. The 20-grain hollow point loads performed just about as well as the 17-grain polymer-tipped or hollow point ammunition. Adding a Butler Creek .17 HMR heavy barrel to a Ruger 10/22M

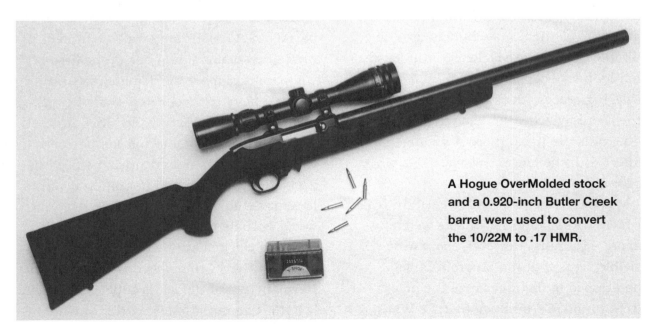

A Hogue OverMolded stock and a 0.920-inch Butler Creek barrel were used to convert the 10/22M to .17 HMR.

results in a rifle that would perform admirably on small varmints. Our only objection is that the rifle is very weighty as a result of the steel receiver and the very heavy barrel.

A Custom .17 HMR Autoloader

As mentioned earlier in this chapter, it does not appear that Ruger is anxious to release a 10/17 prematurely. Custom gun makers are, however, in business to produce something that is not offered by the large factories. Consequently, a number of Ruger 10/22M rifles have been converted to .17 HMR caliber. We have had some experience with one of these rifles so we believe that it is appropriate to describe it here.

The rifle described belongs to a friend and fellow shooter, Mr. Gene Adam. Clark Custom Guns in Princeton, LA, built his rifle. Long known for outstanding gunsmith work, Clark not only does custom work but also markets components for modifying 10/22s and other firearms. The .17 HMR described here started out as a Ruger 10/22M, but the receiver and stock are about the only factory parts that remain. First, a new standard-weight barrel chambered for the .17 HMR cartridge was installed. Next, the trigger was reworked and replaced, and the replacement bolt is clearly marked "Clark Custom." The rifle, which has no open sights, is equipped with a 3-9X Burris scope. Although the barrel band is in place on this rifle, it does not make contact with the barrel.

This custom .17 HMR was built by Clark Custom.

We tested this Clark conversion rifle on two windy days at the rifle range near Buffalo, Wyoming by firing some groups at both 50 and 100 yards. Federal 17-grain V-Shok and Hornady 20-grain Game Shok loads were chosen for the tests. The first group fired at 50 yards with the Federal V-Shok measured 0.58 inch, which is very reasonable considering the windy conditions at the time. Firing at the targets 100 yards away showed that the reported sensitivity of the tiny .17 HMR bullets to wind is correct. In spite of this, five 5-shot groups with the Hornady Game Shok load gave an average group size of 0.97 inch with the smallest measuring 0.87 inch. Remember, these are groups at 100 yards on a decidedly windy day. We have no doubt that this rifle is a real tack driver on a still day. We are indebted to Gene Adam for allowing us to test this fine rifle.

During the firing, no malfunctions were experienced. The quality of workmanship produced by Clark Custom was clearly evident. At the present time, if you want a .17 HMR autoloader, you would be well advised to contact Clark Custom, Volquartsen Custom, or some of the other fine shops listed in the Chapter 13. Some of them perform work on the customer's gun while others supply complete rifles. Making a .17 HMR out of a Ruger 10/22M may not quite as simple as changing barrels so make sure that all of the alterations needed are performed properly and that your rifle is functioning safely.

Jim tested the Clark Custom .17 HMR at the range near Buffalo, Wyoming on a windy day.

SOURCES FOR THE 10/22 SHOPPER

One of the things that impressed us as we worked on this book was just how vast the aftermarket industry surrounding the Ruger 10/22 is. Instead of three or four producers of barrels for the 10/22, there are perhaps 10 times that many. When it comes to stocks for the 10/22, there about as many as there are producers of barrels. Triggers, butt plates, magazines, sights, barrel bands, and magazine releases are produced in profusion. Parts that are contained in the trigger assembly including hammers, sears, and springs are available in a wide variety. Some of the parts are stainless steel and some are made of titanium. Firing pins and bolt stop pins (buffers) are available from many sources. While many custom barrel and stock makers may not offer items for the Ruger 10/22 on a regular basis, virtually any of them can make these items for almost any rifle, including the 10/22, on a special order basis.

As we began to see the enormous diversity of aftermarket items that are available for the Ruger 10/22, it became clear that a buyer's guide that listed sources of the various products could save the person who modifies a 10/22 a lot of time and energy. Consequently, we present here such a guide, but regrettably it cannot include all sources. We have expended a great deal of effort to try to make it complete, but there are probably some shops that escaped detection. This is totally inadvertent and not meant to indicate any preference for one supplier or manufacturer over another. There is only so much time available for any aspect of producing a book such as this, and at some point it must be declared complete. In spite of any omissions, we hope that this guide enables you to locate sources of the aftermarket items that you need to customize your Ruger 10/22. As you examine this guide, you should keep in mind that many of the manufacturers and suppliers do not sell directly to consumers. They can, however, direct you to a source for their products and answer any questions that you might have.

Adirondack Optics
P. O. Box 303
1512 Front Street
Keeseville, NY 12944
(518) 834-7093
www.adkoptics.com
Manufacturer of scopes and other optics.

Advanced Technology
102 Fieldview Drive
Versailles, KY 40383
(800) 925-2522
www.atigunstocks.com
Manufacturer of Fiberforce stocks for the 10/22.

Aearo Company
5457 West 79th Street
Indianapolis, IN 46268
(800) 327-3431
www.aearo.com
Manufacturer of Peltor hearing protectors and protective eye wear.

Aguila Ammunition
Centurion Ordnance, Inc.
11614 Rainbow Ridge
Helotes, TX 78023
(210) 695-4602
www.aguilaammo.com
Manufacturer of many types of ammunition including a wide range of rimfire cartridges.

Aimtech Mount Systems
P. O. Box 223
Thomasville, GA 31799
(229) 226-4313
www.aimtech-mounts.com
Manufacturer of a Weaver-style scope rail for the Ruger 10/22.

Alpen Optics
10329 Dorset Street
Rancho Cucamonga, CA 91730
(877) 987-8370
www.alpenoutdoor.com
Manufacturer of scopes and other optics.

American Gunsmithing Institute
(800) 797-0867
www.americangunsmith.com
Offers video courses on gun repair and modification of many models including the Ruger 10/22.

Andean, Inc.
875 Blakey Road
Heber Springs, AR 72543
(877) 926-3326
www.andean-inc.com
Catalog and on-line retailer of barrels, stocks, and other accessories for the Ruger 10/22, 10/22 Magnum, 17 HMR, and 17 Mach 2.

Bald Eagle Precision Machine Company
101 Allison Street
Lock Haven, PA 17745
(570) 748-6772
www.baldeaglemachine.com
Manufacturer of a .22 LR rim thickness gauge.

Barnes Custom Gunsmithing & Products
3050 U. S. Highway 50 West
Albany, Ohio 45710
(740) 707-1300
www.bcgunsmithing.com
Retailer of trigger kits and factory parts for the Ruger 10/22.

Barska Optics
1721 Wright Ave.
La Verne, CA 91750
(888) 666-6769
www.barska.com
Manufacturer of scopes and other optics.

Battenfeld Technologies
5885 W. Van Horn Tavern Road
Columbia, MO 65203
(877) 509-9160
www.fajen.com
Marketer for many products for the Ruger 10/22 including Fajen and CoreLite gunstocks and Adams & Bennett barrels.

Bell & Carlson
101 Allen Road
Dodge City, KS 67801
(620) 225-6688
www.bellandcarlson.com
Manufacturer of stocks including some models for the Ruger 10/22.

Big Shooter Products
P. O. Box 32382
Minneapolis, MN 55432-0382
(612) 386-5771
www.thebigshooter.com
Manufacturer of portable shooting benches.

Birchwood Laboratories, Inc.
7900 Fuller Road
Eden Prairie, MN 55344
(800) 328-6156
www.birchwoodcasey.com
Manufacturer of an extensive line of gun care and refinishing supplies.

Boyds' Gunstock Industries
25376 403rd Avenue
Mitchell, SD 57301
(605) 996-5011
www.boydsgunstocks.com
Manufacturer of many types of laminated and walnut stocks including both finished and unfinished models for the Ruger 10/22.

Break-Free
13386 International Parkway
Jacksonville, FL 32218
(800) 428-0588
www.break-free.com
Manufacturer of a line of gun care products.

Briley Custom
1230 Lumpkin
Houston, TX 77043
(800) 331-5718
www.briley.com
Gunsmith service offering rifles built on the Ruger 10/22 Magnum action.

Brownell's
200 South Front Street
Montezuma, IA 50171
(800) 741-0015
www.brownells.com
One of the major suppliers of tools and parts for all types of firearms including the Ruger 10/22.

Brown Precision, Inc.
P. O. Box 270 W
7786 Molinos Avenue
Los Molinos, CA 96055
(530) 384-2506
www.brownprecision.com
Manufacturer of fiberglass stocks for the Ruger 10/22.

BSA Optics, Inc.
3911 SW 47 Avenue, Suite 914
Ft. Lauderdale, FL 33314
(954) 581-2144
www.bsaoptics.com
Marketer of an extensive line of scopes and other optical sights.

B-Square
8909 Forum Way
Ft. Worth, TX 76140
(800) 433-2909
www.b-square.com
Manufacturer of scope bases and rings.

Buffer Technologies
P. O. Box 105047
Jefferson City, MO 65110
(877) 628-3337
www.buffertech.com
Manufacturer of recoil buffer for several rifles including the Ruger 10/22.

Burris Company
331 East 8th Street
Greeley, CO 80631
(970) 356-1670
www.burrisoptics.com
Manufacturer of a comprehensive line of high quality scopes and other optics.

BullpupGunStocks.com
300 Dry Gulch Road
Wytheville, VA 24382
(540) 551-4867
www.bullpupgunstocks.com
On-line retailer of the Bullpup stocks for the Ruger 10/22.

Bushnell Corporation
9200 Cody
Overland Park, KS 66214
(800) 423-3537
www.bushnell.com
Manufacturer of a broad range of scopes and optical equipment for the shooter.

Butler Creek
Division of Bushnell Outdoor Products
9200 Cody
Overland Park, KS 66214
(800) 845-2444
www.hoppes.com
Manufacturer of stocks, magazines, and barrels (carbon fiber, blue, and stainless steel) for the Ruger 10/22, 10/22 Magnum, and 10/17 HMR, and many other general firearm accessories.

Cabela's
One Cabela Drive
Sidney, NE 69160
(800) 237-4444
www.cabelas.com
Retailer of outdoor products including many for the Ruger 10/22. Products include stock and barrel combinations that carry the Cabela's name.

Carl Zeiss, Inc.
13005 North Kingston Avenue
Chester, VA 23836
(800) 338-2984
www.zeiss.com
Manufacturer of elegant scopes and other high quality optics.

Carpenter Innovations
403 5th Street
Walhalla, ND 58282
(701) 549-3202
Manufacturer of portable shooting benches.

CCI/Speer
2299 Snake River Avenue
Lewiston, ID 83501
(800) 322-2342 (Customer service)
(866) 286-7436 (Technical service)
www.cci-ammunition.com
One of the largest manufacturers of many ammunition including many types of rimfire cartridges.

Champion Traps & Targets
N5549 County Trunk 2
Onalaska, WI 54650
(800) 635-7656
www.championtarget.com
Manufacturer of targets and a .22 LR bullet trap.

CheapGunParts.com
5362 Raines Dr.
Mobile AL 36609
(251) 454-5128
www.CheapGunParts.com
On-line retailer of Ruger 10/22 and 10/22 Magnum accessories.

Cheaper Than Dirt Outdoor Adventures
2522 NE Loop 820
Fort Worth, TX 76106
(800) 421-8047 (orders)
(800) 559-0943 (customer service)
(817) 625-7171 (retail store)
www.cheaperthandirt.com
A large retailer of product for shooters including many for the Ruger 10/22.

Choate Machine & Tool, Inc.
P. O. Box 218
116 Lovers Lane
Bald Knob, AR 72010
(800) 972-6390
www.riflestock.com
Manufacturer of several types of fiberglass stocks for the Ruger 10/22.

Clark Custom Guns, Inc.
336 Shootout Lane
Princeton, LA 71067
(888) 458-4126
www.clarkcustomguns.com
Gunsmith service offering rifles built on the Ruger 10/22 and 10/22 Magnum actions. Also manufacturer of 10/22 barrels and offers a video on assembly/disassembly of the 10/22.

Clerke International Arms
101 Bacon Street
Raton, NM 87740
(505) 445-0100
www.clerkebarrels.com
Manufacturer of barrels for the Ruger 10/22 in both .22 LR and .17 Mach 2 calibers.

Competition Electronics
3469 Precision Drive
Rockford, IL 61109
(815) 874-8001
www.competitionelectronics.com
Manufacturer of chronographs.

Competitive Edge Dynamics USA
P. O. Box 486
Orefield, PA 18069-0486
(888) 628-3233
www.cedhk.com
Manufacturer of chronographs, shot timers, electronic scales, and shooting bags.

Connecticut Precision Chambering, L. L. C
1548 Saybrook Road
Middletown, CT 06457
(860) 343-0552
www.ct-precision.com
Manufacturer of custom barrels for the Ruger 10/22.

Coyote Jakes, Inc.
1305 Elm Street
Hays, KS 67601
(866) 650-0760
www.coyotejakes.com
Manufacturer of portable shooting benches.

Custom Shooting Technologies, Inc.
8794 Elmburg Rd.
Bagdad, KY 40003
(502) 797-3380
www.cstmtech.com
Manufacturer of many accessories for the Ruger 10/22.

Dixie Consolidated
(843) 423-2204
www.dixieconsolidated.com
Manufacturer of metal bullpup stocks for the Ruger 10/22.

Dog-Gone-Good
575 Collins Crest Court
Gladstone, OR 97027
(503) 657-5902
www.dog-gone-good.com
Manufacturer of shooting bags.

Doskocil Manufacturing Company, Inc.
P. O. Box 1246
Arlington, TX 76004-1246
(888) 707-7678
www.doskosport.com
Manufacturer of Gun Guard ® gun cases.

Doug Koenig Shooting Sports
www.dougkoenig.com
Manufacturers a stainless steel replacement barrel attachment block for the Ruger 10/22.

Dynamit Nobel - RWS, Inc.
81 Ruckman Road
Closter, NJ 07624
(201) 767-7971
www.dnrws.com
Manufacturer of many types of ammunition including many types of rimfire loads.

E. Arthur Brown Company
4353 Highway 27E
Alexandria, MN 56308
(800) 950-9088
www.eabco.com
Catalog and on-line retailer of barrels, stocks, and other accessories for the Ruger 10/22 and 10/22 Magnum including items for .17 HMR, and .17 Mach 2 calibers.

Eagle International, Inc.
MB Products, Inc.
P. O. Box 3003
1000 Highway Drive
Hazen, ND 58545-3003
(888) 932-4536
Manufacturer of many products for the Ruger 10/22 including the Zepher sight system.

Electronic Shooters Protection
15290 Gadsden Court
Brighton, CO 80603
(800) 767-7791
www.ESPAmerica.com
Manufacturer of hearing protectors.

Eley Limited
P. O. Box 705.Witton
Birmingham. B6 7UT.
England
www.eley.co.uk
A producer of an extensive line of rimfire ammunition including high quality target ammunition.

Elk Ridge Gunstocks
1031 NW Morgan
Grants Pass, OR 97526
(541) 471-9161
www.reamerrentals.com/elk_ridge.htm
Manufacturer of unfinished (95% inletted) stocks for the Ruger 10/22.

E. R. Shaw, Inc.
5312 Thoms Run Road
Bridgeville, PA 15017
(412) 221-3636
www.ershawbarrels.com
Manufacturer of barrels for the Ruger 10/22 and 10/22 Magnum including models in .17 HMR, .17 Mach 2, and .17 PMC calibers.

Federal Cartridge Company
900 Ehlen Drive
Anoka, MN 55303
(800) 322-2342
www.federalpremium.com
One of the largest producers of ammunition including rimfire ammunition of many types.

Fiocchi Ammunition
6930 Fremont Road
Ozark, MO 65721
(417) 725-4118
www.fiocchiusa.com
Manufacturer of many types of rimfire ammunition.

Firearms International, Inc.
High Standard Mfg. Co.
5200 Mitchelldale, No. E17
Houston, TX 77092-7222
(800) 272-7816
www.highstandard.com
Manufacturer of replacement barrels for the Ruger 10/22 action in .17 High Standard caliber.

Florida Gun Works
8306 Mills Drive, Box 571
Miami, FL 33183
www.floridagunworks.com
Retailer of Ruger 10/22 barrels, stocks, and other accessories.

Forster Precision Products
310 E. Lanark Avenue
Lanark, IL 61046
(815) 493-6360
www.forsterproducts.com
Manufacturer of a .22 LR headspace gauge and gunsmithing tools.

G. A. S., Inc.
15207 N. E. 19th Avenue
Vancouver, WA 98686
(360) 906-0854
www.gungoodies.com
On-line retailer of stocks, barrels, and other accessories for the Ruger 10/22 and 10/22 Magnum.

Gold City Gun & Cartridge Co., LLC
2112 Hwy. 19th North
Dahlonega, GA 30533
(706) 864-1205
www.22ammo.com
Retailer of many types of rimfire ammunition.

Graf & Sons, Inc.
4050 S. Clark Street
Mexico, MO 65265
(800) 531-2666
www.grafs.com
Retailer of ammunition, gunsmithing tools, gun care products, scopes, and stocks, magazines, barrels, and many other products for the Ruger 10/22 and 10/22 Magnum.

Great American Gunstock Company
3420 Industrial Drive
Yuba City, CA 95993
(800) 784-4867
www.gunstocks.com
Manufacturer of inletted, unfinished walnut stocks for the Ruger 10/22.

Green Mountain Rifle Barrels
P. O. Box 2670
153 W. Main Street
Conway, NH 03818
(603) 447-1095
www.gmriflebarrel.com
A large manufacturer of barrels for both cartridge and muzzle loading firearms. Barrels for the Ruger 10/22 and 10/22 Magnum include many models and styles in .22 LR, .22 WMR, .17 HMR and .17 Mach 2 calibers.

Gunslick
P. O. Box 39
Onalaska, WI 54650
(800) 635-7656
www.gunslick.com
Manufacturer of a line of gun care products.

Gunsmither Tools
www.gunsmithertools.com
On-line retailer and manufacturer of special tools to assemble/disassemble Ruger 10/22 bolt assemblies.

Harris Bipods
999 Broadway
Barlow, KY 42024
(270) 334-3633
www.harrisbipods.com
Manufacturer of bipods including models that attach to the front swivel studs.

Hawkeye Precision Borescopes
Gradient Lens Corporation
207 Tremont Street
Rochester, NY 14608
(800) 536-0790
www.hawkeyeshooting.com
Manufacturer of the borescope optical device for inspecting barrels.

Hawk Tech Arms
P. O. Box 734
Meridian, ID 83680-0734
(208) 941-9410
www.hawktecharms.com
On-line retailer of stocks, barrels, and other products for the Ruger 10/22 and 10/22 Magnum.

Hogue
P. O. Box 1138
550 Linne Road
Paso Robles, CA 93447-1138
(800) 438-4747
www.getgrip.com
Manufacturer of several types of stocks including the popular OverMolded type for the Ruger 10/22 and 10/22 Magnum.

Hoppe's
Division of Bushnell Outdoor Products
9200 Cody
Overland Park, KS 66214
(800) 845-2444
www.hoppes.com
Manufacturer of gun care products, targets, and shooting bags along with other gun accessories

Hornady Mfg. Co.
P. O. Box 1848
Grand Island, NE 68802-1848
(800) 338-3220
www.hornady.com
Designer of the .17 HMR and .17 Mach 2 rimfire cartridges. Markets these cartridges under the Hornady label.

Hornet Products
P. O. Box 1664
Sarasota, FL 34230-1664
(941) 359-1319
www.hornetproducts.com
Hornet bills themselves as "The Ruger 10/22 Super Store." Retailer of stocks, barrels, triggers, sights, and many other items for the 10/22. Also does custom work including modification of factory triggers.

Horus Vision
659 Huntington Avenue
San Bruno, CA 94066
www.horusvision.com
Manufacturer of scopes and other optics.

Hughes Products
P. O. Box 606
Wallburg, NC 27373
(336) 769-3788
www.hughesproductsco.com
Manufacturer of shooting bags.

Inventive Technology
554 South 100 East
American Fork, UT 84003
(801) 756-6017
www.inventivetechnology.com
A producer of portable shooting rests.

Ironsighter Company
P. O. Box 85070
Westland, MI 48185
(734) 326-8731
www.ironsighter.com
Manufacturer of see-through scope mounts for the Ruger 10/22.

Ironwood Designs
872 Ironwood Drive
San Jose, CA 95125
(408) 269-7102
www.ironwooddesigns.com
Producer of tactical-style stocks made of walnut (!) and other woods for the Ruger 10/22.

Jard, Inc.
2737 Nettle Avenue
Sheldon, IA 51201
(712) 324-7409
www.jardinc.com
Manufacturer of drop-in triggers with a pull of 1-3 pounds for the Ruger 10/22 and 10/22 Magnum.

Jarvis, Inc.
1123 Cherry Orchard Loop
Hamilton, MT 59840
(406) 961-4392
www.jarvis-custom.com
Manufacturer of barrels for the Ruger 10/22 and 10/22 Magnum in .22 LR, .22 WMR, and .17 HMR calibers.

J. Dewey Mfg. Co., Inc.
P. O. Box 2014
Southbury, CT 06488
(203) 264-3064
www.deweyrods.com
Producer of cleaning rods and a Delrin rod guide for the Ruger 10/22.

John Masen
1305 Jelmak Street
Grand Prairie, TX 75050
(972) 790-0521
www.johnmasen.com
A manufacturer of several types of accessories for the Ruger 10/22.

Kahles
2 Slater Road
Cranston, RI 02920
(866) 606-8779
www.kahlesoptik.com
A manufacturer of a line of high quality scopes and other optics.

Kidd Innovative Design
#8 Conisburgh Court
Columbus, GA 31907
(706) 568-1022
www.coolguyguns.com
A producer of barrels and two-stage match triggers for the Ruger 10/22. Triggers available with Super match (7-14 oz.), Match (14-28 oz.), and Sportsman (1.25-2.5 lbs.) pull weights.

Klean-Bore, Inc.
16 Industrial Parkway
Easthampton, MA 01027
(413) 527-0300
www.klean-bore.com
A marketer of an extensive line of gun care products.

Kowa Optimed, Inc.
20001 S. Vermont Avenue
Torrance, CA 90502
(800) 966-5692
www.kowascope.com
Manufacturer of scopes and other optics.

Kwik-Site
5555 Treadwell
Wayne, MI 48184
(734) 326-1500
www.kwiksitecorp.com
Manufacturer of See-Thru® scope mounts for the Ruger 10/22 and 10/22 Magnum.

Leckie Professional Gunsmithing
546 Quarry Road
Ottsville, PA 18942
(215) 847-8594
Manufacturer of trigger group pins for the Ruger 10/22 that fit tighter than the factory parts.

Leica Camera, Inc.
156 Ludlow Avenue
Northvale, NJ 07647
(201) 767-7500
www.leica-camera.com
Legendary producer of cameras and scopes of the highest quality.

Leopold & Stevens, Inc.
P. O. Box 688
14400 NW Greenbrier Parkway
Beaverton, OR 97075-0688
(503) 526-1400
www.leupold.com
One of the largest manufacturer of scopes of all types and other optics. Models available include those for any type of shooting.

Lilja Precision Rifle Barrels, Inc.
P. O. Box 372
81 Lower Lynch Creek Road
Plains, MT 59859
(406) 826-3084
www.riflebarrels.com
Manufacturer of high quality rifle barrels including many types for the Ruger 10/22 and 10/22 Magnum in .22 LR, .22 WMR, and .17 HMR calibers.

Lightforce USA, Inc.
1040 Hazen Lane
Orofino, ID 83544
(208) 476-9814
www.NightforceOptics.com
Producer of scopes and other optical equipment for shooters.

Lock, Stock, and Barrel Shooting Supply, Inc.
P. O. Box B
Valentine, NE 69021
(800) 228-7925
www.lockstock.com
Catalog and on-line retailer of a wide range of shooting supplies.

Lothar Walther Precision Tools, Inc.
3425 Hutchinson Road
Cumming, GA 30040
(770) 889-9998
www.lothar-walther.com
Producer of match grade rimfire and airgun barrels.

Lyman Products Corporation
475 Smith Street
Middletown, CT 06457
(800) 225-9626
www.lymanproducts.com
Marketer of a digital trigger pull gauge and many gunsmithing tools and supplies.

Magnum Research, Inc.
7110 University Avenue NE
Minneapolis, MN 55432
(800) 772-6168
www.magnumresearch.com
Manufacturer of graphite-sleeved barrels for the Ruger 10/22 and 10/22 Magnum in .22 LR, .22 WMR, .17 HMR, and .17 Mach 2 calibers.

Majestic Arms, Ltd.
101-A Ellis Street
Staten Island, NY 10307
(718) 356-6765
www.majesticarms.com
Producer of the Aluma-Lite barrels for the Ruger 10/22 and 10/22 Magnum in .22 LR, .22 WMR, .17 HMR, and .17 Mach 2 calibers. These barrels feature a Lothar Walther inner barrel bonded to an aluminum sleeve of .920" diameter.

McMillan Fiberglass Stocks, Inc.
1638 W. Knudsen Drive, Suite 101
Phoenix, AZ 85027
(623) 582-9635
www.mcmfamily.com
Manufacturer of high quality fiberglass stocks for many models of rifles including the Ruger 10/22.

Mectron LLC
8174 Middletown Road
Spring Lake, MN 55432
(612) 386-5771
www.thebigshooter.com
Manufacturer of portable shooting benches.

Midsouth Shooters Supply
770 Economy Drive
Clarksville, TN 37043
(800) 272-3000
www.midsouthshooterssupply.com
Retailer of many gun accessories including barrels, stocks, sights, etc. for the Ruger 10/22. Their website has an extensive list of vendor links.

Midway USA
5875 W. Van Horn Tavern Road
Columbia, MO 65203
(800) 243-3220
www.midwayusa.com
Catalog retailer of a enormous range of products related to the shooting sports. The items available for the Ruger 10/22 is extensive and includes some products carrying the Battenfield Technologies label.

Millcreek Arms
www.millcreekarms.com
On-line retailer of many products for the Ruger 10/22.

Millett Sights
16131 Gothard Street
Huntington Beach, CA 92647
(800) MILLETT
www.millettsights.com
Marketer of a well-known line of scopes, mounts, and other items for many firearms.

MOA Corporation
285 Government Valley Road
Sundance, WY 82729
(307) 283-3030
www.moaguns.com
Manufacturer of a stainless steel receiver that accepts many items produced for the Ruger 10/22. The receiver is considered to be a firearm and an FFL is required for purchase.

Montana X-Treme Gun Care Products
Western Powders, Inc.
P. O. Box 158
Miles City, MT 59301
(800) 278-4129
Marketer of a line of gun care products.

MTM Molded Products Co.
P. O. Box 13117
3370 Obco Court
Dayton, OH 45413
(937) 890-7461
www.mtmcase-gard.com
Manufacturer of shooting benches, shooting rests, gun vises, target stands and dry boxes.

Mobile Rest
P. O. Box 1009
Gilmer, TX 75644
(800) 329-0200
www.mobilehunter.com
Producer of portable rifle rests.

MPI Stocks
P. O. Box 83266
Portland, OR 97283
(503) 226-1215
A producer of fiberglass stocks for the Ruger 10/22.

MWG Company
P. O. Box 97-1643
Miami, FL 33197
(866) 307-1466
www.mwgco.com
Manufacturer of the Muzzelite Bullpup® stock for the Ruger 10/22.

Millett Sights

Nammo Lapua Oy
Lapua Site
P. O. Box 5
FIN-62101 Lapua, Finland
+358 6 431 0111
www.lapua.com
The European manufacturer of many types of rimfire ammunition including brands such as Lapua and SK Jagd.

Natchez Shooters Supplies, Inc.
P. O. Box 18212
Chattanooga, TN 37422
(800) 251-7839
www.natchezss.com
Catalog and on-line retailer of barrels, stocks, and other accessories for the Ruger 10/22 and 10/22 Magnum. Products offered cover all phases of the shooting sports.

National Rifle Association
11250 Waples Mill Road
Fairfax, VA 22030-9400
(800) 642-3888
www.nra.org
The largest organization fighting for your right to possess a Ruger 10/22.

Neco
108 Ardmore Way
Benicia, CA 94510
(800) 451-3550
www.neconos.com
Producer of a kit for pressure (fire) lapping .22 rimfire barrels.

Neilson Brothers Arms, Inc.
3006 Glenwood Drive
Rapid City, SD 57702
(605) 342-3421
www.neilsonbrothersarms.com
Manufacturer of a 22 LR concentricity gauge.

Neilsen-Kellerman
21 Creek Circle
Boothwyn, PA 19061
(610) 447-1555
www.nkhome.com
Markets the Kestral line of instruments for measuring wind velocity.

New Century Science & Technology, Inc. (NcStar)
10302 Olney Street
El Monte, CA 91731
(866) NCSTAR-8
www.ncstar.com
Manufacturer of optics and a scope base for the Ruger 10/22.

New England Custom Gun Service
438 Willow Brook Road
Plainfield, NH 03781
(603) 469-3450
www.newenglandcustom.com
Produces a peep sight that attaches directly to grooved receivers.

Nikon
1300 Walt Whitman Road
Melville, NY 11747-3064
(800) NIKON-US
www.nikonsportoptics.com
A well-known manufacturer of cameras, scopes and other optical devices.

North Pass
1941 Heath Parkway
Suite #1
Fort Collins, CO 80524
(800) 589-4315
www.hivizsights.com
Manufacturer of HiViz open sights for the Ruger 10/22.

Numrich Gun Parts Corp.
226 Williams Lane
West Hurley, NY 12491
(866) 686-7424
www.e-gunparts.com
A larger supplier of factory parts for many firearms including the Ruger 10/22.

Oehler Research, Inc.
P. O. Box 9135
Austin, TX 78766
(800) 531-5125
www.oehler-research.com
One of the premier manufacturers of chronographs.

On Target Shooting Benches
P. O. Box 57463
Murray, Utah 84157
(801) 352-0996
www.Gunbenches.com
Producer of portable shooting benches.

Outers
Route 2
P. O. Box 39
Onalaska, WI 54650
(800) 635-7656
www.outers-guncare.com
Marketer of an extensive line of gun care products.

Pac-Nor Barreling
P. O. Box 6188
99299 Overlook Road
Brookings, OR 97415
(541) 469-7730
www.pac-nor.com
A manufacturer of barrels for the Ruger 10/22.

Pentax U. S. A., Inc.
600 12th Street, Suite 300
Golden, CO 80401
(800) 877-0155
www.pentaxlightseeker.com
A company well-known for high quality scopes and other optics.

PMC Ammunition
Boulder City, NV 89005
(702) 294-0025
www.pmcammo.com
A manufacturer of an extensive line of ammunition including the rimfire calibers.

Power Custom
29739 Hwy. J
Gravois Mills, MO 65037
(573) 372-5684
www.powercustom.com
One of the manufacturers of parts for customizing the Ruger 10/22. Items offered include an adjustable trigger and sear, titanium firing pins, extended bolt handles, scope rails and many other accessories.

Pride Fowler Industries, Inc.
P. O. Box 4301
San Dimas, CA 91773
(909) 599-0928
www.rapidreticle.com
A manufacturer of scopes and other optical equipment.

Pro Ears
101 Ridgeline Drive
Westcliffe, CO 81252
www.proears.com
Manufacturer of hearing protectors.

Pro-Shot Products
P. O. Box 763
Taylorville, IL 62568
(217) 824-9133
www.proshotproducts.com
Marketer of an extensive line of gun care products.

Protektor Model
1-11 Bridge Street
Galeton, PA 16922
(814) 435-2442
www.protektormodel.com
Manufacturer of leather shooting bags.

Radians, Inc.
268 Appling Center Cove
Memphis, TN 38133
(877) 723-4267
www.radiansinc.com
Producer of hearing protectors.

Ram-Line/Onalaska Operations
P. O. Box 39
Onalaska, WI 54650
(800) 635-7656
www.ram-line.com
Manufacturer of stocks including black and Realtree® camo versions for the Ruger 10/22.

Ramshot Optics
Western Powders, Inc.
P. O. Box 158
Miles City, MT 59301
(800) 497-1007
www.ramshot.com
A supplier of scopes and other optics.

Ranch Products
P. O. Box 145
Malinta, OH 43535
(313) 277-3118
www.ranchproducts.com
Maker of a scope mount, extended magazine release, and barrels for the Ruger 10/22.

RB Precision
P. O. Box 96
Preemption, IL 61276
(309) 534-8175
www.rbprecision.com
Manufacturer of the Evolution stock for the Ruger 10/22.

RCBS
605 Oro Dam Boulevard
Oroville, CA 95965
(800)533-5000
www.rcbs.com
Manufacturer of reloading equipment, a trigger pull gauge, and gunsmithing tools.

Redfield USA
201 Plantation Oak Drive
Thomasville, GA 31792
(800) 285-4486
www.redfieldoptics.com
Manufacturer of one of the oldest and best known brands of scopes and other optics.

Remington Arms Co.
P. O. Box 700
870 Remington Drive
Madison, NC 27025
www.remington.com
One of the oldest and most respected firearms companies. Markets many types of rimfire ammunition.

Revival Industries
P. O. Box 587
420 German Street
Herkimer, NY 13350
(315) 866-8140
www.revivalindustries.com
Manufacturer of distinctive laminated stocks for the Ruger 10/22 and 10/22 Magnum.

Rhineland Arms, Inc.
PMB #484
1301 West FM 407, Suite 201
Lewisville, TX 75077
(972) 342-2105
www.rhinelandarms.com
A producer of tactical-style stocks for the 10/22.

Richard's Microfit Gunstocks, Inc.
P. O. Box 1066
8331 North San Fernando Road
Sun Valley, CA 91352
(818) 767-6097
www.rifle-stocks.com
Manufacturer of ready-to-finish laminated stocks for the Ruger 10/22 and 10/22 Magnum.

Rimfire Benchrest Association
5609 Lantana Avenue
Charlotte, NC 28212
(704) 536-8210
www.rba.benchrest.net
An organization devoted to benchrest competition.

Rimfire Sports & Custom
20280 Rosedale Court
Ashburn, VA 20147-3317
(703) 729-5446
www.rimfiresports.com
On-line retailer of barrels, stocks, and other accessories for the Ruger 10/22 and 10/22 Magnum.

Royal Arms Gunstocks
919 8th Avenue, NW
Great Falls, MT 59404
(406) 453-1149
www.imt.net/~royalarms
A producer of custom stocks for the Ruger 10/22.

Sack-Ups
1611 Jamestown Road
Morganton, NC 28655
(800) 873-7225
www.sackups.com
Producer of a type of gun sleeve for storage and transporting firearms.

Scheels All Sports
2101 W. 41st Street
Sioux Falls, SD 57105-6140
(605) 334-7767
www.scheelssports.com
A chain of retail stores that markets an extensive line of items for shooting. Also markets scopes, including rimfire models, made to Scheels specifications and carrying the Scheels label.

Schmidt & Bender, Inc.
P. O. Box 134
438 Willow Brook Road
Meriden, NH 03770
(800) 468-3450
www.schmidtbender.com
Manufacturer of high quality scopes and other optics.

Sellier & Bellot, U. S. A.
P. O. Box 7307
Shawnee Mission, KS 66207
(800) 960-2422
www.sb-usa.com
A manufacturer of many types of ammunition including the rimfire calibers.

Sharp Shoot-R Precision Products
Box 171
Paola, KS 66071
(785) 883-4444
www.sharpshootr.com
Marketer of a line of gun care products.

Shepherd Enterprises, Inc.
P. O. Box 189
Waterloo, NE 68089
(402) 779-2424
www.sheperdscopes.com
Manufacturer of scopes and other optics.

Shilen, Inc.
P. O. Box 1300
205 Metro Park Boulevard
Ennis, TX 75120
(972) 875-5318
www.shilen.com
One of the most respected names in aftermarket barrels. The Shilen name frequently appears in the list of winners in competitive events.

Shooter's Ridge
Onalaska Operations
N5546 County Trunk Z
Onalaska, WI 54650
(800) 635-7656
www.shootersridge.com
Manufacturer of shooting rests, bipods, monopods, and other shooting accessories.

Shooter's Choice
15050 Berkshire Industrial Parkway
Middlefield, OH 44062
(440) 834-8888
www.shooters-choice.com
Producer of a line of gun care products.

Shooting Chrony, Inc.
3840 E. Robinson Road
PMB 298
Amherst, NY 14228
(800) 385-3161
www.shootingchrony.com
A manufacturer of chronographs.

Sightron, Inc.
100 Jeffrey Way, Suite A
Youngsville, NC 27596
(800) 867-7512
www.sightron.com
Marketer of an extensive line of scopes, red dot sights, and other optical equipment.

Silencio
58 Coney Island Drive
Sparks, NV 89431
(800) 648-1812
www.silencio.com
Manufacturer of hearing protectors.

Simmons Outdoors Corporation
201 Plantation Oak Drive
Thomasville, GA 31792
(800) 285-0689
www.simmonsoptics.com
A larger marketer of scopes and other optical equipment whose products include many items.

Sims Vibration Laboratory
301 W. Business Park Loop
Shelton, WA 98584-8094
(360) 427-6031
www.limbsaver.com
Manufacturer of a rubber vibration damper that slides on the barrel.

Sinclair International
2330 Wayne Haven Street
Fort Wayne, IN 46803
(800) 717-8211
www.sinclairintl.com
A catalog retailer of an enormous range of products for shooters including rim thickness gauges.

Six Enterprises
320-D Turtle Creek Court
San Jose, CA 95125
(408) 999-0201
Manufacturer of stocks for the Ruger 10/22.

Small Caliber News
Technology Media Ventures
11220 Hilltop Road SW
Baltic, OH 43804
(330) 897-0614
www.smallcaliber.com
A quarterly publication devoted to small caliber firearms. Articled deal with many aspects of shooting sports including rimfires.

Stafford Sales
P. O. Box 4433
Baton Rouge, LA 70821
(225) 229-7338
www.staffordsales.com
On-line retailer of stocks, barrels, and many other items for the Ruger 10/22.

Steiner Germany
Pioneer Research
97 Foster Road
Moorestown, NJ 08057
(800) 257-7742
www.steiner-binoculars.com
Manufacturer of scopes and other optics.

Stoney Point Products, Inc.
Division of Bushnell Outdoor Products
9200 Cody
Overland Park, KS 66214
(800) 845-2444
www.bushnell.com
Manufacturer of monopods, bipods, rim thickness gauge, target stands, and other general shooting products.

Stukey's Sturdy Shooting Benches
P. O. Box 136
Kaycee, WY 82639
(307) 738-2245
www.shootingbenches.com
Manufacturer of portable shooting benches.

Sturm, Ruger, & Co., Inc.
Lacey Place
Southport, CT 06890
(603) 865-2442
www.ruger.com
The largest firearm manufacturer in the U.S. and producer of the legendary Ruger 10/22 and 10/22 Magnum.

Superior Products
355 Mandela Parkway
Oakland, CA
(707) 585-8329
www.slip2000.com
Marketer of a line of gun care products.

Superior Shooting Systems, Inc.
800 N. Second Street
Canadian, TX 79014
(806) 323-9488
www.DavidTubb.com
Manufacturer of the Final Finish .22 Rimfire fire lapping kit.

Superior Tactical Solutions
P. O. Box 573
Henderson, KY 42419
(800) 787-6939
www.superiortactical.com
On-line retailer of Ruger 10/22 trigger kits.

Swarovski Optik North America, Ltd.
2 Slater Road
Cranston, RI 02920
(800) 426-3089
www.swarovskioptik.com
Manufacturer of high quality scopes and other optics.

Swift Optics
1190 North 4th Street
San Jose, CA 95112
(800) 523-4544
www.swiftoptics.com
Marketer of scopes and other optics.

Tactical Precision Systems, Inc.
585 N. Front Street, Suite 162
Woodburn, OR 97071
(503) 463-9322
www.tacticalprecision.com
Producer of a type of scope base for the Ruger 10/22.

Tactical Solutions
P. O. Box 170126
800 E. Citation Court, Suite C
Boise, ID 83717
(866) 333-9901
www.tacticalsol.com
Manufacturer of several types barrels and a compensators for the Ruger 10/22.

Talley Mfg., Inc.
P. O. Box 821
Glenrock, WY 82637
(307) 436-8724
Swivels, studs, and Ruger 10/22 scope bases with integrated rings.

Tasco
9200 Cody
Overland Park, KS 66214
(800) 423-3537
www.tasco.com
A well-known manufacturer of scopes and other optics.

Tetra Products
FTI, Inc.
8 Vreeland Road
Florham Park, NJ 07932
(973) 443-0004
www.tetraproducts.com
Marketer of a line of gun care products.

The Stock Market
920 E. Truxton Avenue
Bakersfield, CA 93305
(800) 221-9015
Producer of a thumbhole-style stock for the Ruger 10/22.

Tomahawk Stocks
www.thegunstock.com
On-line retailer of the Apache stock (available finished or unfinished) for the Ruger 10/22.

Trijicon, Inc.
P. O. Box 930059
49385 Shafer Avenue
Wixom, MI 48393-0059
www.trijicon.com
Manufacturer of sights, scopes, and other optics.

Truglo, Inc.
710 Presidential Drive
Richardson, TX 75081
(888) 887-8456
www.truglo.com
Manufacturer of scopes and fiber optic replacement sights for many types of firearms including the Ruger 10/22.

Twisted Barrel, LLC
608 South 4th Street
Douglas, WY 82633
(307) 266-4463
www.twistedbarrel.com
Producer of a line of barrels for the Ruger 10/22 that have unique fluting patterns.

Uncle Bud's CCS
14122 Marsh Pike
Hagerstown, MD 21742
(301) 714-0008
www.unclebudscss.com
Manufacturer of shooting bags.

Uncle Mike's
Division of Bushnell Outdoor Products
9200 Cody
Overland Park, KS 66214
(800) 845-2444
www.bushnell.com
Marketer of a wide range of shooting accessories that includes sling swivels, studs, gun cases, slings, holsters, grips, and other accessories.

United States Rimfire Association
IR50/50
318 Wright Drive
Selma, AL 36701
(334) 875-1980
www.ir5050.com
Organization devoted to the rimfire shooting sports.

Valdada - IOR Optics
P. O. Box 270095
Littleton, CO 80127
(303) 979-4578
www.valdada.com
Manufacturer of scopes and other optics.

Varmint Masters LLC
P. O. Box 6724
Bend, OR 97708
(541) 318-7306
www.varmintmasters.net
A manufacturer of portable benchrests.

Volquartsen Custom
P. O. Box 397
24276 240th Street
Carroll, IA 51401
(712) 792-4238
www.volquartsen.com
One of the premier marketers of stocks, barrels, triggers, and many other accessories for the Ruger 10/22.

Walker's Game Ear, Inc.
P. O. Box 1069
Media, PA 19063
(800) 424-1069
www.WalkersGameEar.com
A manufacturer of hearing protectors.

Warne Manufacturing Company
9560 SW Herman Road
Tualatin, OR 97062
(800) 683-5590
www.warnescopemounts.com
Manufacturer of scope rings and Ruger 10/22 scope bases.

Warner Guns
(866) 296-5116
www.outdoorguides.com/outdoor/warnergn.htm
Retailer of accessories for the Ruger 10/22.

W. C. Wolff Company
P. O. Box 458, Dept. 100
Newtown Square, PA 19073-0458
(800) 545-0077
www.gunsprings.com
Offers replacement recoil springs and hammer springs for the Ruger 10/22 and 10/22 Magnum.

WeaponKraft Products
www.weaponkraft.itgo.com
On-line retailer of performance kits for the Ruger 10/22.

Weaver Mounts
P. O. Box 39
Onalaska, WI 54650
(800) 635-7656
www.weaver-mounts.com
Manufacturer of many types of scope rings and Ruger 10/22 bases.

Weaver
201 Plantation Oak Drive
Thomasville, GA 31792
(800) 285-0689
www.weaveroptics.com
One of the oldest names in rifle scopes. The Weaver line includes models for almost any type of shooting, and includes models specifically for rimfires.

Weigand Combat Handguns, Inc.
1057 South Main Road
Mountaintop, PA 18707
(570) 868-8358
www.jackweigand.com
Manufacturer of an integrated one-piece scope base and rings. Also manufactures a one-piece base to allow the Ruger 10/22 Magnum to utilize Weaver-style rings.

Whistle Pig Gun Barrel Co.
P.O. Box 418
Aurora, OR 97002
(971) 533-9670
www.wpgbc.com
Producer of unique barrels for the Ruger 10/22 that include fluted models with the groves painted with enamel of different colors.

Widener's Reloading & Shooting Supply, Inc.
P. O. Box 3009 CRS
Johnson City, TN 37602-3009
(800) 615-3006
www.wideners.com
Retailer of gunsmithing tools and a wide range of products related to the shooting sports.

Williams Gun Sight Company, Inc.
P.O. Box 329
7389 Lapeer Road
Davison, MI 48423
(800) 530-9028
www.williamsgunsight.com
Manufacturer of Williams Firesights and peep sights for the 10/22.

Winchester Ammunition
427 N. Shamrock Street
East Alton, IL 62024-1174
(618) 258-2000
www.winchester.com
Manufacturer of many types of rimfire ammunition.

Woodchuck Den, Inc.
11220 Hilltop Road SW
Baltic, OH 43804
(330) 897-0614
www.woodchuckden.com
Retailer of numerous products for the small-caliber shooter. Catalog available online or as published in issues of Small Caliber News.

Wolf Performance Ammunition
1225 N. Lance Lane
Anaheim, CA 92806
(888) 757-9653
www.wolfammo.com
Importer of the Wolf ammunition line that includes target types of rimfire ammunition.

XS Sight Systems
2401 Ludelle
Fort Worth, TX 76105
(888) 744-4880
www.xssights.com
Manufacturer of the Ghost Ring® sight system that includes a model for use on Ruger 10/22.